# RIGHTLY DIVIDED

*Readings in*
*Biblical Hermeneutics*

# Roy B. Zuck

GENERAL EDITOR

kregel
PUBLICATIONS

Grand Rapids, MI  49501

*Rightly Divided: Readings in Biblical Hermeneutics*

Copyright © 1996 by Roy B. Zuck

Published by Kregel Publications, a division of Kregel, Inc.,
P.O. Box 2607, Grand Rapids, MI 49501. Kregel Publications
provides trusted, biblical publications for Christian growth and
service. Your comments and suggestions are valued.

Cover design: Alan G. Hartman
Book design: Nicholas G. Richardson

**Library of Congress Cataloging-in-Publication Data**
Zuck, Roy B., gen. editor.
   Readings in biblical hermeneutics / Roy B. Zuck.
     p.    cm.
   Includes bibliographical references and index.
   1. Bible—Hermeneutics. I. Zuck, Roy B.
BS476.R54      1996     220.6'01—dc21     96-46208
                                        CIP

ISBN 0-8254-4099-8

Printed in the United States of America
1 2 3 4 5 / 00 99 98 97 96

# CONTENTS

# PREFACE

IMAGINE A SMALL BIBLE STUDY group meeting in the living room of a nice home every Thursday evening. The group has no designated leaders other than the host and hostess. Each week they study a passage in the book of Romans.

As they come to a difficult verse or group of verses, they each give their opinion on what it means. Their views differ and even conflict with each other. Having no way of determining which view is correct, they move on to another passage in the chapter, and again voice differing ideas. The so-called Bible study concludes with each having shared varied opinions but with no sense of whether the verses mean all those things shared, one of them, or none of them.

Why do informal Bible study groups face this problem? Basically, they lack some simple hermeneutical guidelines, helps on how to interpret the Bible.

Hermeneutics, the science and art of ascertaining the meaning of Scriptures, is a complex area of study, with numerous issues confronting both laypersons and scholars.

This compilation of twenty-two chapters introduces readers to a number of these issues. I hope this anthology will supplement standard introductory works on hermeneutics by gathering in one volume a variety of helps.

Obviously, a work of this kind is selective. But I have tried to include significant writings of many of the better-known evangelicals in this field of study. Also, chapters by writers of former generations, including Moses Stuart and Milton S. Terry, introduce readers to works not readily available.

May this volume provoke further thinking and provide important guidelines for everyone involved in interpreting or "rightly dividing" the Word of God.

ROY B. ZUCK

5

# ACKNOWLEDGMENTS

Chapter 1 taken from *Basic Bible Interpretation* by Roy B. Zuck, published by Victor Books. Copyright 1991 and used by permission of SP Publications, Inc., Wheaton, IL 60187.

Chapter 2 taken from *Playing by the Rules* by Robert H. Stein. Copyright 1994 and used by permission of Baker Book House Company.

Chapter 3 was originally entitled "Meanings from God's Message: Matters for Interpretation," by Walter C. Kaiser, Jr., *Christianity Today*, 5 October 1979. Used by permission of the publisher.

Chapter 4 taken from *Biblical Repository* 2:5 (January 1832).

Chapter 5 taken from *Theological Review* (February 1979): 2–8 and reprinted by permission of the Fountain Trust, 3a High Street, Esher, Surrey, UK KT10 9RP.

Chapter 6 taken from *An Introduction to Biblical Interpretation* by William W. Klein, Craig L. Blumberg, and Robert L. Hubbard Jr. Copyright 1993 and used by persmission of Word Publishing, Dallas, TX.

Chapter 7 taken from *An Introduction to Biblical Hermeneutics* by Walter C. Kaiser, Jr. and Moises Silva. Copyright 1994 by Walter C. Kaiser, Jr. and Moises Silva. Used by permission of Zondervan Publishing House.

Chapter 8 taken from *The Hermeneutical Spiral* by Grant Osborne. Copyright 1991 by Grant R. Osborne. Used by permission of InterVarsity Press, P.O. Box 1400, Downers Grove, IL 60515.

Chapter 9 taken from *The Language and Imagery in the Bible* by G. B. Caird. Copyright 1980 by G. B. Caird. Used by permission of Westminster/ John Knox Press.

Chapter 10 taken from *Biblical Hermeneutics,* Zondervan Publishing House, 1974.

Chapter 11 taken from *Grace Theological Journal* 5:2 (fall 1984): 229–45. Used by permission of Grace College and Seminary.

Chapter 12 taken from *Evangelical Roots: A Tribute to Wilbur Smith.* Ed. Kenneth S. Kantzer. Copyright 1978 and used by permission of Thomas Nelson, Inc., Nashville, TN.

Chapter 13 taken from *Bibliotheca Sacra* (July 1986): 218–27. Used by permission of Dallas Theological Seminary.

Chapter 14 taken from *Revelation and the Bible.* Ed. Carl Henry. Copyright 1958 and used by permission of Baker Book House Company.

Chapter 15 taken from *The NIV: The Making of a Contemporary Translation.* Copyright 1986 by The Zondervan Corporation. Used by permission of Zondervan Publishing House.

Chapter 16 taken from *Bibliotheca Sacra* (July 1985): 209–23. Used by permission of Dallas Theological Seminary.

Chapter 17 taken from *Bibliotheca Sacra* (October 1985): 306–19. Used by permission of Dallas Theological Seminary.

Chapter 18 taken from *Hermeneutic* by Henry A. Virkler. Copyright 1981 and used by permission of Baker Book House Company.

Chapter 19 taken from *JETS* (December 1978): 357–67. Used by permission.

Chapter 20 taken from *Understanding and Applying the Bible* by J. Robertson McQuilkin. Copyright 1992 and used by permission of Moody Press.

Chapter 21 taken from *Protestant Bible Interpretation* by Bernard Ramm. Copyright 1979 and used by permission of Baker Book House Company.

Chapter 22 taken from *Walvoord: A Tribute,* edited by Donald K. Campbell. Copyright 1982 and used by permission of Moody Press.

# CONTRIBUTORS

**Craig L. Blomberg**
    Associate Professor of New Testament, Denver Seminary, Denver, Colorado

**Darrell L. Bock**
    Research Professor of New Testament and Professor of Spiritual Development and Culture, Dallas Theological Seminary, Dallas, Texas

**G. B. Caird**
    Late Professor of Exegesis of Holy Scripture, Oxford University, Oxford, England

**Norman L. Geisler**
    Provost, Southern Evangelical Seminary, Charlotte, North Carolina

**Robert L. Hubbard, Jr.**
    Professor of Old Testament, Denver Seminary, Denver, Colorado

**Elliott E. Johnson**
    Professor of Bible Exposition, Dallas Theological Seminary, Dallas, Texas

**Walter C. Kaiser, Jr.**
    Colman M. Mockler Distinguished Professor of Old Testament, Gordon-Conwell Theological Seminary, South Hamilton, Massachusetts

**William W. Klein**
    Professor of New Testament, Denver Seminary, Denver, Colorado

**Charles H. Kraft**
    Professor of Anthropology and Intercultural Communication, Fuller Theological Seminary, Pasadena, California

**I. Howard Marshall**
Professor of New Testament Exegesis, University of Aberdeen,
Aberdeen, Scotland

**J. Robertson McQuilken**
President Emeritus, Columbia International University, Columbia, South Carolina

**Robert R. Nicole**
Visiting Professor of Theology, Reformed Theological Seminary,
Jackson, Mississippi

**Grant R. Osborne**
Professor of New Testament, Trinity Evangelical Divinity
School, Deerfield, Illinois

**Bernard Ramm**
Late Professor of Christian Theology, American Baptist Seminary of the West, Berkeley, California

**Moisés Silva**
Professor of New Testament, Westminster Theological Seminary,
Philadelphia, Pennsylvania

**Robert H. Stein**
Professor of New Testament, Bethel Theological Seminary, St.
Paul, Minnesota

**Moses Stuart**
Late Professor of Sacred Literature, Andover Theological
Seminary, Andover, Massachusetts

**Milton S. Terry**
Late Professor of Old Testament Exegesis, Garrett Biblical
Institute, Evanston, Illinois

**Henry A. Virkler**
Associate Professor of Counseling and Psychology, Liberty
University, Lynchburg, Virginia

**Ronald F. Youngblood**
Professor of Old Testament, Bethel Theological Seminary West,
San Diego, California

**Roy B. Zuck**
Senior Professor of Bible Exposition Emeritus, Dallas Theological Seminary, Dallas, Texas, and Editor, *Bibliotheca Sacra*

# ABBREVIATIONS

| | | | |
|---|---|---|---|
| Amplified | *The Amplified Bible* | JSOT | *Journal for the Study of the Old Testament* |
| AV | Authorized Version (=KJV) | KJV | King James Version (=AV) |
| BAGD | Walter Bauer, William F. Arndt, F. Wilbur Gingrich, and Frederick W. Danke, *A Greek-English Lexicon of the New Testament and Other Early Christian Literature* | LXX | Septuagint |
| | | NASB | *New American Standard Bible* |
| | | NCV | *New Century Version* |
| | | NEB | *New English Bible* |
| | | NICNT | *New International Commentary on the New Testament* |
| BDF | F. Blass, A. DeBrunner, and Robert W. Funk, *A Greek Grammar of the New Testament* | NIV | *New International Version* |
| | | NT | New Testament |
| Berkeley | *The Holy Bible: The New Berkeley Version in Modern English* | NTS | New Testament Studies |
| | | OT | Old Testament |
| | | *passim* | throughout |
| bis | twice | Phillips | *The New Testament in Modern English,* by J. B. Phillips |
| bk. | book | | |
| cf. | confer, compare | | |
| ch. | chapter | rev. | revised |
| *Claud.* | *Claudius,* by Suetonius | RSV | Revised Standard Version |
| ed. | edition; editor(s); edited by | SR | *Studies in Religion* |
| | | s.v. | *sub verbo,* under the relevant word |
| e.g. | *exempli gratia,* for example | TEV | *Today's English Version* |
| ICC | *International Critical Commentary* | TJ | *Trinity Journal* |
| | | TR | Textus Receptus |
| i.e. | *id est,* that is | viz. | *videlicet,* namely |
| JBL | *Journal of Biblical Literature* | vol., vols. | volume, volumes |
| | | WBC | *Word Biblical Commentary* |

# INTRODUCTORY ISSUES

# ONE

# THE WHAT AND WHY OF BIBLE INTERPRETATION

### Roy B. Zuck

A BUSINESSMAN WAS on a trip quite a distance from his hometown. A bachelor, he served as a top executive in a leading governmental agency. In fact he was the finance officer in charge of all the funds in that department.

Returning home from Palestine, he was on a desert road southwest of Jerusalem. Another person was driving, which gave him opportunity to read. As he was reading aloud, he looked up and saw a man who had come up beside him and had heard him reading. The man asked the businessman if he understood what was being read.

The reader was an Ethiopian, a court official of Candace, Queen of Ethiopia (Acts 8:27). On his way back to Ethiopia, he was joined by Philip, whom God told to meet the official (vv. 26–29). Philip struck up a conversation with the man by asking him a question—a question of Bible interpretation. "Do you understand what you are reading?" (v. 30). The finance officer responded, "How can I . . . unless someone explains it to me?" (v. 31). Inviting Philip to join him in the chariot, the African asked if the prophet Isaiah was speaking about himself or someone else (Isa. 53:7–8). His question revealed his need for help in interpreting the passage. Philip explained that the passage refers to Jesus. As a result of the conversation the African accepted the Lord as his Savior.

This desert dialogue points up two things. First, seeing the words on a page of the Bible does not necessarily mean that the reader catches their meaning. Observing what the Bible says is the first of several steps in Bible study. It is important to know what the text actually states. But this may sometimes lead to questions on the meaning of what is read. Many people, on reading portions of the Bible, come away confused about their meaning or come away with a false understanding.

Second, the evangelist-eunuch incident reveals that proper guidance can help others interpret what they read in the Bible. Philip's question, "Do you understand what you are reading?" implied that the reader probably did not understand but that it was possible to understand. In fact, the treasurer's request for someone to explain the passage to him was an admission on his part that he could not properly understand the passage by himself and that he felt the need for help in interpretation.

Several months after Nehemiah completed the rebuilding of the Jerusalem walls and the Israelites had settled in their towns, Ezra the scribe read to them from "the book of the Law of Moses" (the first five books of the Bible) as the people were assembled before the Water Gate at Jerusalem (Neh. 8:1). Ezra read from the Law from daybreak until noon (v. 3). The Levites also read aloud from the Law, "making it clear and giving the meaning so that people could understand what was being read" (vv. 7–8). As a result the people were joyful "because they now understood the words" (v. 12).

## WHY IS BIBLE INTERPRETATION IMPORTANT?

### It Is Essential for Understanding and Teaching the Bible Properly

We must know the meaning of the Bible before we can know its message for today. We must understand its sense for then before we can see its significance for now. Without hermeneutics (the science and art of interpreting the Bible) we are jumping over and missing out on an indispensable step in Bible study. The first step, observation, asks, What does it say? The second step, interpretation, asks the question, What does it mean? The third step, application, raises the question, How does it apply to me?

Interpretation is perhaps the most difficult and time-consuming of these three steps. And yet cutting Bible study short in this area can lead to serious errors and faulty results. Some people knowingly "distort the Word of God" (2 Cor. 4:2). Some even "distort" the Scriptures "to their own destruction" (2 Peter 3:16). Others unknowingly come away from the Bible with faulty interpretations. Why? Because of inadequate attention to the principles involved in understanding the Scriptures. In recent years we have seen a great surge of interest in informal Bible study. Many small groups meet weekly in homes or in churches to discuss the Bible—what it means and how it applies. Do people in those groups always come away with the same understanding of the passage studied? Not necessarily. Some may say, "To me this verse means this," and another person in the group may respond, "To me the verse doesn't mean that; it means this." Studying the Bible in this way, without proper hermeneutical guidelines, can lead to confusion and interpretations that are even in direct conflict. Did God intend for the Bible to be treated in this way? If it can be made to mean anything we want, how can it be a reliable guide? Conflicting interpretations of many passages abound. For example, one person reads John 10:28, "I give them eternal life, and they shall never perish; no one can snatch then out of My hand," and understands that verse to be teaching eternal security. Others read the same verse and explain that though no one can snatch a Christian out of God's hand, the believer may remove himself from God's hand by persistent sin. Some people suggest that Paul's statement in Colossians 1:15 that Christ is "the Firstborn over all creation" means He was created. Others understand the verse to be saying that like a firstborn son in a family He is the Heir. Some Christians practice so-called speaking in tongues, based on 1 Corinthians 12–14. Others read the same chapters and understand that this practice was only for the Apostolic Age and not for today. Some have read Nahum 2:4, "The chariots storm through the streets, rushing back and forth through the squares," and have concluded that this verse was prophesying heavy automobile traffic in our cities today. In the Parable of the Good Samaritan (Luke 10:25–37), some have sought to give a "spiritual" meaning to the passage by explaining that the inn to which the Samaritan took the injured man represents the church and that the two silver coins given to the innkeeper represent the two ordinances of the Lord's Supper and water baptism.

The Mormon leader Brigham Young justified his having more than thirty wives by pointing to the fact that Abraham had more than one wife, namely, Sarah and Hagar. The Mormon practice of being baptized for dead relatives and others is based, they argue, on 1 Corinthians 15:29. Some people handle poisonous snakes, based on their reading of Mark 16:18. Whether women should teach men is based on how one interprets 1 Corinthians 11:5; 14:34–35; and 1 Timothy 2:12. Some teach that Christ's present reign in heaven means He will not establish a thousand-year reign on the earth after His return. Others, however, say the Bible teaches that Christ, though reigning over the universe now, will manifest His kingdom in a physical way when He rules as the Messiah over the nation Israel on the earth in the Millennium.

All these—and many others—are matters of interpretation. Obviously these various conflicting views point up that not all readers are following the same principles for understanding the Bible.

The lack of proper hermeneutics has also led to the Bible being highly abused and maligned. Even some atheists seek to support their position by referring to Psalm 14:1, "There is no God." Obviously they are overlooking how those words are introduced: "The fool says in his heart, 'There is no God.'" "You can make the Bible say anything you want," some argue. And yet how many of the same people say, "You can make Shakespeare say anything you want"? Of course it is true that people can make the Bible say anything they wish so long as they disregard normal approaches for understanding written documents.

## Bible Interpretation Is Essential as a Step Beyond Observation

When many people approach the Bible, they jump from observation to application, skipping the essential step of interpretation. This is wrong because interpretation logically follows after observation. In observing what the Bible says, you probe; in interpretation, you mull. Observation is discovery; interpreting is digesting. Observation means depicting what is there, and interpretation is deciding what it means. The one is to explore, the other is to explain.

Observation is like a surgeon cutting into a problem area. He sees a growth, or perhaps loose blood, or discolored tissue, or a blockage. Then the question is, What does it mean? How is it to be explained? What kind of growth is it? What caused the diffused blood? Why the discolored tissue? Why is this blockage here?

Observing what we see in the biblical text, we then should correctly handle it (2 Tim. 2:15). The participle "correctly handling" (incorrectly translated in the King James Version "rightly dividing") translates the Greek word *orthotomounta*. This combines two words that mean "straight" (*ortho*) and "cut" (*tomeō*). One writer explains the meaning of this as follows:

> Because Paul is a tentmaker, he may have been using an expression that tied in with his trade. When Paul made tents, he used certain patterns. In those days tents were made from the skins of animals in a patchwork sort of design. Every piece would have to be cut and fit together properly. Paul was simply saying, "If one doesn't cut the pieces right, the whole won't fit together properly." It is the same thing with Scripture. If one doesn't interpret correctly the different parts, the whole message won't come through correctly. In Bible study and interpretation the Christian should cut it straight. He should be precise . . . and accurate.[1]

## Bible Interpretation Is Essential for Applying the Bible Properly

Interpretation should build on observation and then lead into application. It is a means to an end, not an end in itself. The goal of Bible study is not simply to determine what it says and what it means, but rather to apply it to one's life. If we fail to apply the Scriptures, we cut short the entire process and have not finished what God wants us to do. True, the Bible gives us many facts we need to know about God, ourselves, sin, salvation, and the future. We go to the Bible for information and insight, and this is proper. But the question is, What will we do with that information and insight? Interpretation is the step that moves us from reading and observing the text on to applying and living it out. Bible study is an intellectual pursuit in which we seek understanding of what God says. But Bible study must go beyond that to include spiritual discipline, in which we seek to put into practice what we read and understand.

Heart appropriation, not merely head apprehension, is the true goal of Bible study. Only in this way can believers grow spiritually. Spiritual maturity, in which we become more like Christ, comes not just from knowing more about the Bible. It comes from knowing more about the Bible and applying it to our spiritual needs. This was Paul's goal, that he might encourage and teach others so that they would become mature in Christ (Col. 1:28). And Peter wrote that we should "crave pure spiritual milk, so that by it [we] may grow up in [our] salvation" (1 Peter 2:2). Paul wrote that "knowledge puffs up" (1 Cor. 8:1). Jesus told the Jewish leaders of His day, "You diligently study the Scriptures" (John 5:39). But then He added that their study was of no value because they refused to come to Him to have life (v. 40).

One of the classic passages on the inspiration of the Scriptures is 2 Timothy 3:16. And yet most of that verse, along with the following verse, speaks of the *usefulness* of Scripture. It is to be used for "teaching, rebuking, correcting and training in righteousness, so that the man of God may be thoroughly equipped for every good work."

It is one thing to read 2 Timothy 1:9, noting that God has "called us to a holy life," and to understand that holiness is a life of purity and godliness, made possible by the sanctifying work of the Holy Spirit. But it is another thing to deal with sin in our lives so that we are in fact leading holy lives. It is one thing to study what the Scriptures say about the return of Christ in passages such as 1 Thessalonians 4:13–18 and 1 Corinthians 15:51–56. But it is another thing to build on and move beyond those facts to the point of loving His appearing (2 Tim. 4:8), that is, longing for and anticipating His coming, and continuing steadfast in serving the Lord (1 Cor. 15:58).

Bible interpretation, then, as the second step in Bible study is absolutely essential. Interpretation is foundational to application. If we do not interpret properly, we may end up applying the Bible wrongly.

How you interpret many passages has a direct effect on your conduct and the conduct of other people as well. For example, if a pastor interprets certain passages as saying that remarriage is acceptable after divorce, then that influences how he counsels divorcees about remarriage. If a pastor understands 1 Corinthians 11:3–15 to teach that women should wear hats in church, then his interpretation affects what he teaches his congregation.

Whether abortion is right or wrong, how to find God's will, how to lead a meaningful life, how to be an effective husband or wife or parent, how to react to suffering—all these depend on and relate to hermeneutics and how you interpret various passages. As one writer put it, "Interpreting the Bible is one of the most important issues facing Christians today. It lies behind what we believe, how we live, how we get on together, and what we have to offer to the world."[2]

## THE CHALLENGE OF BIBLE INTERPRETATION

We are responsible then to seek to know the truth as presented in God's Word. This is essential for our own spiritual lives and for effectiveness in ministering to others. In sharing the Word of God, whether in personal counseling, teaching a Sunday school class or Bible study group, or preaching, the knowledge we impart, based on our understanding of the Scriptures, will definitely affect others. Their lives are in our hands.

Without proper biblical interpretation, the theology of an individual or of an entire church may be misdirected or superficial and its ministry unbalanced.

Understanding the Bible is a lifelong process. As you study the Word, you will be asking yourself, What does this mean? Is this view correct? Why or why not? What about this interpretation? Is it valid? As you hear sermons and listen to teachers, you are continually confronted with the question, Is what he is saying about the Bible correct? As you discuss the Bible with others, you will be faced with the question of which of several possible views is more likely the meaning of the passage being considered. Seeking to determine what a passage really means is an intriguing intellectual and spiritual challenge. And as you share the Word of God, people will be asking you, "What does this verse mean?" "How are we to understand this passage?" Because of the extent of content in the Bible, and the diversity of the kinds of literature in the Bible, hermeneutics is an area of study with numerous problems and issues.

For example, how do we know if a passage was intended only for the people to whom it was initially addressed or if it is intended for ensuing generations? Can a passage have more than one meaning, and if so, how are they to be determined? Did some of the Bible authors write more than they understood? Is the Bible more than a human book? If it is also a divine book, how does this affect our interpretation of various passages? How are we to interpret various proverbs in the Bible? Are they universally applicable? If we believe in literal interpretation, how does that affect our understanding of figures of speech? If the Bible includes figures of speech, then is all the Bible to be interpreted in a "spiritual" or mystical sense? How do we understand prophecy? Since there are varying views on how to interpret Bible prophecy, how can we know which view is more likely the accurate one? Why does the New Testament quote the Old Testament in ways that seemingly alter the way the verses read in the Old Testament? How can we move from interpretation to application?

## PROBLEMS IN BIBLE INTERPRETATION

One of the major reasons the Bible is difficult to understand is that it is an ancient book. The first five Old Testament books were written by Moses around 1400 B.C. The last book of the Bible, Revelation, was written by the apostle John around A.D. 90. So some of the books were written about 3,400 years ago and the latest one was written about 1,900 years ago. This suggests that in hermeneutics we must seek to bridge several gaps posed by our having such an ancient book in our hands.

### A Time Gap (Chronological)

Because of the extensive time gap between ourselves and the writers and initial readers of the Bible, a huge chasm exists. Since we were not there, we cannot talk with the authors and with the initial hearers and readers to discover firsthand the meaning of what they wrote.

### A Space Gap (Geographical)

Most readers of the Bible today live thousands of miles from the countries where Bible events took place. The Middle East, Egypt, and the southern Mediterranean nations of present-day Europe were the places where Bible people lived and traveled. These extend from Babylon in present-day Iraq to Rome (and possibly Spain, if Paul traveled there). This geographical distance puts us at a disadvantage.

### The Customs Gap (Cultural)

Great differences exist between the way people in the Western world do things and think and the way people in Bible lands lived and thought. Therefore it is important to know the cultures and customs of peoples in Bible times. Often faulty interpretations stem from an ignorance of those customs.

## A Language Gap (Linguistic)

Besides gaps in time, space, and customs, there is also a chasm between our way of speaking and writing and the way people in Bible times spoke and wrote. The languages in which the Bible is written—Hebrew, Aramaic, and Greek—have peculiarities unknown in the English language. For example, the Hebrew and Aramaic of the original Old Testament manuscripts included only consonants. Vowels were understood and therefore not written (though they were filled in hundreds of years later, around A.D. 900, by the Masoretes). Also Hebrew and Aramaic are read from right to left rather than from left to right. In addition no spaces were inserted between words. The words in all three biblical languages ran together.

An example of this in English would be the following: DNRTCHTGNRB. Reading these words from right to left the Hebrew reader would automatically sense that it included four words, which in English would be as follows: BRNG TH CT RND. It is not too difficult to sense that the sentence is saying "Bring the cot around." On the other hand the two letters CT could be understood as cat or coat as well as cot. How then would a reader know which word was intended? Usually the context would give the reader a clue to the intended meaning. If earlier or later sentences referred to a cot, then it is most likely that this sentence would also refer to a cot. In some cases, however, the context may give no clue and therefore it becomes a problem in interpretation to know which word was actually intended.

Another reason the language gap is a problem is that the original Bible languages have unusual or obscure expressions, difficult to comprehend in English. Also some words occur only once in the entire Bible, thus making it impossible to compare them with how they are used in some other context to help us understand their meaning.

Another problem contributing to the linguistic gap is the transmission of the original manuscripts. As manuscripts were copied, scribal errors occasionally crept in. Sometimes one scribe read a manuscript to another scribe. The copyist wrote what sounded like the word pronounced by the reader. The words, "This is led" might be written, "This is lead." Sometimes a copier would mistake one letter for another letter that was very similar to it in shape. The Hebrew letters for *d* and *r* are similar (though not identical), as are the letters *w* and *y*. Sometimes a word was repeated and other times a word was skipped. If a manuscript included some of these accidental scribal mistakes, they might then be copied by the next copyist, thus transmitting the readings for probably several "generations" of manuscripts. Other times, however, a scribe would correct what he thought was an incorrect word or letter. The process of seeking to determine which readings are the original ones is called textual criticism. These variations, however, do not affect major doctrines of Scripture, nor do they affect the doctrine of the inerrancy of Scripture, which relates to the original manuscripts, not the copies.

## A Writing Gap (Literary)

Differences exist between the styles and forms of writing in Bible times and the styles and forms of writing in the Western world today. We seldom speak in proverbs or parables, and yet a good portion of the Bible is proverbial or parabolic. In addition the fact that there are approximately forty human authors of the Bible books sometimes poses problems for Bible interpreters. One Gospel writer stated, for example, that one angel was present at Jesus' empty tomb and another referred to two angels. Figurative language, frequently used, sometimes poses problems for our understanding. For instance Jesus said, "I am the door" and "I am the Shepherd." Obviously He did not mean He is literally made of wood with hinges or that He actually owns sheep which He cares for in a field. It is the business of the interpreter to seek to ascertain what Jesus did mean by those statements.

## A Spiritual Gap (Supernatural)

It is also important to note that a gap exists between God's way of doing things and our way. The fact that the Bible was written about God puts the Bible in a unique category. God, being infinite, is not fully comprehensible by the finite. The Bible speaks of God's performing miracles and making predictions about the future. The Bible also speaks of difficult-to-comprehend truths such as the Trinity, the two natures of Christ, God's sovereignty, and man's will. All these and others contribute to our difficulty in understanding fully all that is in the Bible.

Since God is the divine Author of the Book, it is unique. It is one of a kind. The Bible is not simply a book with man's thoughts about God, though it includes them. It is also God's thoughts about God and man. The Bible reports what God did and communicates what He is and what He desires. The Bible is also unique in that it was written by God and man. Human authors wrote as they were guided by the Holy Spirit (2 Peter 1:21). This fact of dual authorship poses problems. How could God use people of differing personalities to record the Scriptures and yet have the final product be the work of the Holy Spirit? How does this affect the individual authors' own personalities and writing styles?

These six gaps pose serious problems when a person seeks to understand the Bible. Even the Ethiopian in Acts 8 faced several of these gaps, including the chronological, geographical, linguistic, and supernatural. While much of the Bible is plain and easy to understand, admittedly other parts are more difficult. Even Peter wrote, "Our dear brother Paul also wrote . . . some things that are hard to understand" (2 Peter 3:15–16). Some Bible verses remain a mystery even to the most skilled interpreters.

## DEFINITIONS IN HERMENEUTICS

Exactly what is hermeneutics? And how does it differ from exegesis and exposition? The English word "hermeneutics" comes from the Greek verb *hermēneuō* and the noun *hermēneia*. These words point back to the wing-footed messenger-god Hermes in Grecian mythology. He was responsible for transmuting what is beyond human understanding into a form that human intelligence can grasp. He is said to have discovered language and writing and was the god of literature and eloquence, among other things. He was the messenger or interpreter of the gods, and particularly of his father Zeus. Thus the verb *hermēneuō* came to refer to bringing someone to an understanding of something in his language (thus explanation) or in another language (thus translation). The English word *interpret* is used at times to mean "explain" and at other times "translate." Of the nineteen times *hermēneuō* and *hermēneia* occur in the New Testament, they are more frequently used in the sense of translation. In Luke 24:27 the verb *diermēneuō* is used: "And beginning with Moses and all the prophets, He explained to them what was said in all the Scriptures concerning Himself." When Jesus spoke to Simon He said, "'You will be called 'Cephas' (which, when translated, is Peter)" (John 1:42). The word "translated" renders the Greek *hermēneuō*. In a sense a translation is an explanation, explaining in one language what is conveyed in another language. Thus interpretation involves making clear and intelligible something that was unclear or unknown.

Hermeneutics, as mentioned earlier, is the science and art of interpreting the Bible. Another way to define hermeneutics is this: It is the science (principles) and art (task) by which the meaning of the biblical text is determined. As Terry wrote:

> Hermeneutics, therefore, is both a science and an art. As a science, it enunciates principles, investigates the laws of thought and language, and classifies its facts and results. As an art, it teaches what application these principles should have, and establishes their soundness by showing their practical value in the elucidation of the more difficult Scriptures. The hermeneutical art thus cultivates and establishes a valid exegetical procedure.[3]

What then is exegesis and exposition? Exegesis may be defined as the determination of the meaning of the biblical text in its historical and literary contexts. Exposition is the communication of the meaning of the text along with its relevance to present-day hearers. Exegesis is the actual interpretation of the Bible, and hermeneutics consists of the principles by which the meaning is determined.

Homiletics is the science (principles) and art (task) by which the meaning and relevance of the biblical text are communicated in a preaching situation, and pedagogy is the science (principles) and art (task) by which the meaning and relevance of the biblical text are communicated in a teaching situation.

Exegesis is the study in private, and exposition is the presentation in public. Exegesis is done in the study; exposition is done in the pulpit or at the teacher's desk or podium. The primary concern in exegesis is an *understanding* of a biblical text, whereas the primary concern of exposition is the *communication* of the meaning of the text.

An effective expositor is first an effective exegete. Exegesis precedes exposition, just as baking a cake comes before serving it. The exegetical process takes place in the workshop, the warehouse. It is a process in private, a perspiring task in which the Bible student examines the

---

### Definitions of Hermeneutics and Related Terms

**HERMENEUTICS**
> The science (principles) and art (task) by which the meaning of the biblical text is determined.

**EXEGESIS**
> The determination of the meaning of the biblical text in its historical and literary contexts.

**EXPOSITION**
> The communication of the meaning of the text along with its relevance to present-day hearers.

**HOMILETICS**
> The science (principles) and art (task) by which the meaning and relevance of the biblical text are communicated in a preaching situation.

**PEDAGOGY**
> The science (principles) and art (task) by which the meaning and relevance of the biblical text are communicated in a teaching situation.

backgrounds, meanings, and forms of words; studies the structure and parts of sentences; seeks to ascertain the original textual reading (textual criticism); etc. But not all those details are shared when he preaches or teaches the Bible. An artist, in the process of creating his work, agonizes over the minutia of his painting, but in the end he wants others to see not the fine details but the whole and how the parts are related.

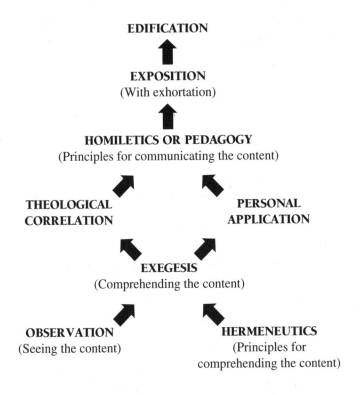

**EDIFICATION**

↑

**EXPOSITION**
(With exhortation)

↑

**HOMILETICS OR PEDAGOGY**
(Principles for communicating the content)

**THEOLOGICAL
CORRELATION**                    **PERSONAL
APPLICATION**

**EXEGESIS**
(Comprehending the content)

**OBSERVATION**                    **HERMENEUTICS**
(Seeing the content)              (Principles for
                                  comprehending the content)

Exegesis is thus a means to an end, a step toward exposition. Exegesis is more technical and is basic to exposition, which is more practical. In the privacy of his study the exegete seeks to comprehend the exact meaning of the Bible passage being studied. But in the pulpit or classroom the expositor, having built his material on an exegetical base, seeks to communicate that content. One is to the other as the foundation is to the building. "To be valid, exposition must be firmly based on exegesis: the meaning of the text for hearers today must be related to its meaning for the hearers to whom it was first addressed."[4]

Hermeneutics is like a cookbook. Exegesis is the preparing and baking of the cake, and exposition is serving the cake. The chart above illustrates the relationship of these and other elements, all of which lead to the final step of edification, that is, spiritual growth in the life of the interpreter/communicator and the hearers or readers.

In playing a game such as football or the table word game Boggle, rules are to be known and followed. If football players are on the field and have a football, but do not know the rules of the game, they can make no progress. If a person is playing Boggle, he may have all the parts but not know what to do with them. The rules enable the players to proceed. Similarly hermeneutics provides the rules or guidelines, the principles and theory governing a proper approach to understanding the Bible. Biblical interpretation, however, is not like a computer program. We cannot plug in certain principles and expect to receive automatically a printout with the proper interpretation.

## QUALIFICATIONS FOR INTERPRETING THE BIBLE

No one can fully comprehend the meaning of the Bible unless he is regenerate. The unsaved person is spiritually blind (2 Cor. 4:4) and dead (Eph. 2:2). Paul wrote, "The man without the Spirit does not accept the things that come from the Spirit of God, for they are foolishness to him, and he cannot understand them, because they are spiritually discerned" (1 Cor. 2:14). Does this mean an unsaved person cannot understand the words of Scripture? No. Instead it means he has no spiritual capacity for welcoming and appropriating spiritual truths. As Martin Luther once said, the unregenerate can understand the grammar of John 3:16, but they do not act on those facts. It is in this sense that they are unable to know the things of the Spirit of God.

The unsaved do not welcome the truth of the Scriptures because it strikes at the very core of their sinfulness. The Greek word rendered "accept" in 1 Corinthians 2:14 is the word *dechomai*, which means "to welcome." An unsaved person, devoid of the indwelling Holy Spirit, may understand mentally what the Bible is saying, but he rejects its message, refusing to appropriate it and act on it. By contrast people in Berea "received [*dechomai*] the Word with great eagerness" (Acts 17:11, NASB) and the Thessalonians "welcomed [*dechomai*] the message with the joy given by the Holy Spirit" (1 Thess. 1:6).

First Corinthians 2:14 also states that the unsaved do not "understand spiritual things." The Greek word *ginōskō* ("to understand") does not mean comprehend intellectually; it means know by experience. The unsaved obviously do not experience God's Word because they do not welcome it. Only the regenerate have the capacity to welcome and experience the Scriptures, by means of the Holy Spirit.[5]

More than regeneration is necessary. Also reverence for and interest in God and His Word are essential to interpreting the Bible properly. A lackadaisical or cavalier attitude toward the Bible does not contribute to proper understanding of God's truth. The Scriptures are called holy and should be treated as such (2 Tim. 3:15).

Other spiritual qualifications are a prayerful attitude and humility. An interpreter must recognize that other readers of the Bible over the centuries have struggled to determine the meaning of many of the same biblical passages, and as a result, they may have some insights into those portions of Scripture. No interpreter is infallible. Therefore he should acknowledge the possibility that his interpretation of a given passage may not be correct.

The Scriptures should also be approached with a willingness to obey them, a willingness to put into practice what has been learned in the Word. When one sees how the Lord has worked in the lives of people in the Bible who obeyed or disobeyed Him, and when he comprehends the precepts and instructions given in the Bible for one's life, he should willingly follow those examples and instructions. Absence of a reverence for the Word, lack of prayer, pride, or an unwillingness to obey the truths of the Scriptures will hinder one's skill in comprehending what the Bible says.

The interpreter must also depend on the Holy Spirit. As Moule wrote, "The blessed Spirit is not only the true Author of the written Word but also its supreme and true Expositor."[6] The role of the Holy Spirit in biblical interpretation suggests several things.

First, His role does not mean that one's interpretations are infallible. Inerrancy and infallibility are characteristics of the Bible's original manuscripts, but not of the Bible's interpreters. Individuals have the right to interpret the Bible but this right does not mean that all the results of private interpretation will be accurate.

Second, the work of the Spirit in interpretation does not mean that He gives some interpreters a "hidden" meaning divergent from the normal, literal meaning of the passage.

Third, as already suggested, a Christian who is living in sin is susceptible to making inaccurate Bible interpretations because his heart and mind are not in harmony with the Holy Spirit.

Fourth, the Holy Spirit guides into all truth (John 16:13). The word *guide* means "to lead the way or guide along the way or road." Jesus' promise to the disciples was that the Holy Spirit would clarify and amplify what Christ had given them. After Christ ascended, the Holy Spirit came on the Day of Pentecost to indwell believers, and the disciples then understood the significance of Jesus' words regarding Himself and His death and resurrection. Though verse 13 was addressed specifically to the Twelve (v. 12), all believers may be similarly guided into the truth about Christ. Believers, however, are not automatically led by the Spirit to comprehend the truth of Scripture because, as already stated, obedience is necessary. Guidance implies obedience to the Guide and a willingness to be led. Only by the Holy Spirit can believers apply, that is, personally appropriate the Scriptures.

Fifth, the place of the Holy Spirit in interpreting the Bible means that He does not normally give sudden intuitive flashes of insight into the meaning of Scripture. Many passages are readily understood, but the meaning of others may come to light only gradually as the result of careful study. The Spirit's part in hermeneutics does not suggest some mysterious work that is unexplainable and unverifiable.

Sixth, the Spirit's role in interpretation means that the Bible was given to be understood by all believers. Its interpretation is not in the hands of an elite few scholars.[7]

However, these spiritual qualifications do not automatically mean that an individual's interpretations of the Bible are all correct. These are prerequisites, not guarantees.

Besides these spiritual qualifications, other qualifications are helpful in approaching the Bible. A willingness to study is essential. This may include a knowledge of Bible backgrounds, Bible history, and theology. As Ramm has explained, "Matters of fact cannot be settled solely by spiritual means. One cannot pray to God for information about the authorship of Hebrews and expect a distinct reply. Nor is it proper to pray for information with reference to other matters of biblical introduction expecting *a revelation* about *the revelation*."[8]

The Bible student must also approach the Scriptures with sound judgment and reason, seeking to be as objective in his approach to the Bible as possible, without coming to the Scriptures with prejudice or preconceived notions.

Does all this mean that the average layperson cannot comprehend the Bible? Must a person be educated in a Bible college or seminary to be able to interpret the Bible properly? No, the meaning of the pages of Scripture is not limited to a few. Made in the image of God, man is a rational (as well as an emotional and volitional) being. He has the intellectual capacity to understand the Bible. As a revelation of God, the Bible, written in human languages, is capable of being understood.

On the other hand, this does not mean that human teachers are not needed and that a person can be instructed by the Bible alone without any attention to what others believe about it.[9] Some have been given the gift of teaching (Rom. 12:7; 1 Cor. 12:28; Eph. 4:11). The 3,000 disciples saved on the Day of Pentecost "devoted themselves to the apostles' teaching" (Acts 2:42). Peter and John "entered the temple courts . . . and began to teach the people" (5:21). They continued "teaching the people" (v. 25) and "day after day. . . they never stopped teaching" (v. 42). "Barnabas and Saul . . . taught great numbers of people" in Antioch (11:26). In Corinth Paul was "teaching them the Word of God" for a year and a half (18:11). In Ephesus, Paul "taught . . . publicly and from house to house" (20:20). He was accused of teaching all men everywhere (21:28). Even when he was in Rome under house arrest he "boldly. . . taught about the Lord Jesus Christ" (28:31). If each individual believer could comprehend fully the Scriptures by himself apart from anyone else, then why were the apostles involved in teaching believers, and why is the gift of teaching given to some in the church today? Receiving the teaching of others can be in person or through written instruction in commentaries. Being open to the Spirit's leading of others can help Bible students avoid some of the dangers discussed earlier. This leads to the question of whether the Bible possesses clarity.

## CAN THE BIBLE BE UNDERSTOOD?

Bible scholars sometimes refer to the perspicuity—or clarity—of the Scriptures. But if the Bible is clear, then why the need for rules or principles of interpretation? Why would any Christian coming to the Bible need the help of other teachers or written materials such as Bible commentaries, as just discussed?

Some people respond by saying it is impossible to understand the Bible. They read a Bible passage, determined that they will discover its meaning, but then find that the meaning eludes them. They conclude that if scholars who have studied the Bible for years cannot agree on how to interpret certain passages, how can they as laypersons do so? For them the Bible hardly seems to possess the quality of clarity.

If the Scriptures possess clarity, then why discuss interpretation at all?

Granted, some passages of the Bible, as already stated, are difficult to understand. And yet the basic message of the Bible is simple enough for any person to comprehend. The Scriptures are not obscure in themselves.[10] The teachings of the Bible are not inaccessible to the average person, as some have suggested. Nor is the Bible written as a puzzle, a book of secrets and riddles given in jumbled incommunicable form. The fact that the Bible is a book means that it is to be read and understood. As God's written revelation, the Bible *reveals* to us His character, plans, and standards. The human authors, whose writings were given by the inspiration of the Holy Spirit, wrote to be understood, not to confuse or bemuddle. As Martin Luther affirmed, the priesthood of all believers (1 Peter 2:5) means the Bible is accessible and understandable by all Christians. This opposed the alleged obscurity of the Bible, according to the Roman Catholic Church, which said that only the church could disclose its meaning.

Yet there are hindrances to communication. What was clear to the writer may not be immediately clear to the reader. This means that interpretation is necessary to help remove these obstacles to communication and to understanding. Exegesis and interpretation then are necessary to help expose the clarity that the Scriptures possess in themselves. As a divine Book in which God is communicating to man, the message is basically clear, and yet as God's Word it does include a profundity that can challenge the most diligent scholars.

# TWO

# WHO MAKES UP THE RULES?

### Robert H. Stein

THE TERM *HERMENEUTICS* frightens people. This is both unfortunate and unnecessary. The word comes from the Greek term *hermēneuein*, which means to explain or interpret. In the Bible it is used in John 1:42; 9:7; Hebrews 7:2; and Luke 24:27. In the Revised Standard Version the latter verse reads as follows: "And beginning with Moses and all the prophets, he [Jesus] *interpreted* to them in all the scriptures the things concerning himself." The New International Version reads, "And beginning with Moses and all the Prophets, he [Jesus] *explained* to them what was said in all the Scriptures concerning himself." The word translated "interpreted" and "explained" in these two versions of the Bible is the word [*di*]*hermēneuein.* A noun formed from this verb, *Hermes,* was the name given to the Greek god who was the spokesman or interpreter for the other gods. This is why in Acts 14:12 we read that after Paul healed a cripple at Lystra, the people thought that the gods had come to visit them. "Barnabas they called Zeus, and Paul they called *Hermes* because he was the chief speaker" (cf. also Acts 9:36; 1 Cor. 12:10, 30; 14:5, 13, 26–28; etc.). The term *hermeneutics,* which comes from these Greek words, simply describes the practice or discipline of interpretation. In interpreting the Bible, who determines the rules?

## THE GAME ITSELF: THE VARIOUS
## COMPONENTS INVOLVED IN HERMENEUTICS

In all communication three distinct components must be present. If any one is lacking, communication is impossible. These three components are the *Author,* the *Text,* and the *Reader,* or, as linguists tend to say, the *Encoder,* the *Code,* and the *Decoder.* Still another way of describing this is: the *Sender,* the *Message,* and the *Receiver.* (If we carry this over to the analogy of playing a game, we have the *Creator of the Game;* the *Game Parts* [pieces, cards, dice, board, etc.]; and the *Players.*) Unless all three elements are present, communication (the game) is impossible.

The main goal, or at least one of the main goals, of interpreting the Bible is to discover the "meaning" of the text being studied. We want to know what this text "means." Yet where does this meaning originate? Where does it come from? Some interpreters argue that it comes from one component, whereas others argue that it comes from another.

### The Text (i.e., the Game Parts) as the Determiner of Meaning

Some have suggested that meaning is a property of the text. It is the text that determines what a writing means. We have probably all heard or even said something like, "Our text tells us . . ." And who has not heard Billy Graham say, "The Bible says . . ."? Yet those who argue that meaning is a property of the text mean something very different than what Billy Graham means. This view argues that a literary text is "autonomous." As a text it possesses semantic autonomy in the sense that its meaning is completely independent of what its author meant when he or she wrote. What the biblical author was thinking about and sought to convey by the text is quite irrelevant with respect to the meaning of the text. This is because a text possesses autonomy and is totally independent of its author. As a result, reading a related work such as Galatians in order to help us understand what Paul meant when he wrote Romans makes little or no sense. We could just as well read Charles Dickens's *A Tale of Two Cities*. Furthermore, what Paul actually meant when he wrote Romans is no more valuable in determining the actual meaning of Romans than any other person's opinion. According to this view, the text is independent of and has no connection with its author. It possesses its own meaning(s).

For Billy Graham, as he preaches from Romans, "The Bible says" and "Paul means" are synonymous. For those who argue that the text possesses its own meaning, however, these two things are not in any way the same. Every text is an independent work of art that is to be interpreted independently of its author. According to this view, when a work becomes "literature" the normal rules of communication no longer apply; this piece of communication has been transformed into a work of "art." Because it is art, the original composer no longer possesses control of it; the art itself possesses its own meaning completely apart from its creator. If in some way Paul could appear before those who argue for the semantic autonomy of the text and say, "What I meant when I wrote this was . . ." the response would essentially be, "What you say, Paul, is interesting but quite irrelevant." Paul's willed meaning of his text, what he sought to communicate in his writing, is no more authoritative than any other person's interpretation. Thus, it is illegitimate to place any authorial control over the meaning of a text. This is a very popular approach among literary critics.

Perhaps the biggest problem with this view, that the text itself is the determiner of meaning, involves what a "text" is and what "meaning" is. A written text is simply a collection of letters or symbols. Those symbols can vary. They can be English or Greek letters, Japanese symbols, or Egyptian hieroglyphics. They may proceed right to left, left to right, up or down. They can be written on papyrus, animal skins, stone, or metal. Yet both the letters and the material upon which they are written are inanimate objects. Meaning, on the other hand, is a product of reasoning and thought. It is something only people can do. Whereas a text can convey meaning, it cannot produce meaning, because it cannot think! Only the authors and readers of texts can think. Thus, whereas a text can convey meaning, the production of meaning can only come from either the author or the reader.

## The Reader (i.e., the Player)
## as the Determiner of Meaning

Some interpreters claim that the meaning of a text is determined by the reader. (This "reader" is sometimes called the "implied reader," the "competent reader," the "intended reader," the "ideal reader," the "real reader.") The person who reads the text gives to it its meaning or "actualizes" it. This should not be confused with thinking that the reader learns-deciphers-discovers-ascertains the meaning the text possesses in and of itself (the view described above). Nor should it be confused with the view that the meaning is determined by what the author meant when he or she wrote the text (the view described below). On the contrary, this view maintains that the person who reads the text determines its meaning. Each individual as he or she reads the text creates the meaning!

According to this view (sometimes called "reception theory," "reception aesthetics," "reader-response criticism," etc.), if different readers come up with different meanings, this is simply due to the fact that a text permits the reader to discern multiple meanings. Thus, we can have Marxist, feminist, liberationist, egalitarian, evangelical, or Arminian "readings" or interpretations of a text. This view assumes that there are many legitimate meanings of a text, for each interpreter contributes his or her meaning to the text. The text functions somewhat like an inkblot into which the reader pours his or her own meaning. Sometimes, in popular usage, we hear an individual say something like, "What this biblical text means to me is . . ." or, "This passage may mean something different to you but for me it means . . ." As we shall see later, however, such statements are best understood as describing the many different applications (or implications) of the author's intended meaning.

## The Author (i.e., the Creator of the Game) as the Determiner of Meaning

The more traditional approach to the study of the Bible has been to see the meaning as being controlled by the author. According to this view, the meaning of a text is what the author consciously intended to say by his text. Thus, the meaning of Romans is what Paul intended to communicate to his readers when he wrote his letter. This view argues that if Paul were alive and told us what he meant to convey in writing Romans, this would settle the issue. The text means what Paul just told us he meant. (This is why in seeking to understand Romans it is more helpful to read Galatians, which Paul also wrote, than to read Ernest Hemingway's *The Old Man and the Sea* or Homer's *Iliad*.) Similarly, the meaning of the Gospel of Luke is what Luke purposely willed to convey to Theophilus when he wrote.

This view argues that the Bible and other great works of literature are not to be treated as unique works of "art" possessing distinct rules supposedly appropriate only to art. On the contrary, they are to be interpreted in the same way that we interpret other forms of verbal communication. This is essentially the commonsense approach to communication. All normal conversation assumes that the goal of interpretation is to understand what the speaker or writer means by the words he or she is using. We cannot even argue against this view without at the same time agreeing with it, for we must seek to understand what writers mean by their words in order to engage in discussion with them. For instance, in your attempt to understand this paragraph are you not seeking to understand what I wanted to communicate by it?

This issue has been a major one in the 1980s and 1990s with respect to constitutional law. The basic issue at stake in the Supreme Court nomination hearings of Robert Bork and Clarence Thomas involved whether the meaning of the Constitution is determined by what the original framers of the Constitution meant when they penned these words (the author) or what the present judges think that the words of the Constitution mean apart from the original intent of its framers (the text or the reader). On the one side a Supreme Court judge has stated that the desire to follow the original intent of the framers of the Constitution is "Arrogance cloaked as humility" and that "it is arrogant to pretend that from our vantage we can gauge accurately the intent of the framers . . . to specific, contemporary questions." On the other hand, James Madison argued long ago that if "the sense in which the Constitution was accepted and ratified by the nation be not the guide in expounding it, there can be no security . . . for a faithful exercise of its power."

It has been argued that "literature" is to be interpreted differently from all other forms of written communication. In other written works, as well as in general communication, we are to seek the author's intended meaning, but when a work becomes "'literature" it is no longer to be treated in this manner. Literature does not fall under the rules of written communication but of "art." As a result the author's willed intention, what he meant when he wrote, is to be rejected or ignored, and meaning is to be determined either by the text itself or by the interpreter.

But who determines what is "literature"? There is no rule, law, or consensus that can be used to determine what is literature and what is not. (If we say that a work of literature is one that has been acknowledged over a period of time, then there is no such thing as a twentieth-century work of literature. If we say, on the other hand, that a work becomes literature when it has gained great popularity, then Mickey Spillane is the greatest writer of literature in the world!) The very fact that the classification of a work as "literature" is quite arbitrary indicates that to interpret such a work differently from all other written forms of communication is based on a debatable classification from the start.

Second, no one has yet been able to prove that "literature" should be interpreted by a different set of rules than other writings. There is no convincing answer to the question "Why should this written work be interpreted differently from other written works?" Surely the burden of proof lies with those who would argue that a particular written work (arbitrarily called "literature") should be interpreted differently from the way all other works (nonliterature) should be interpreted. Yet such a proof has not been demonstrated.

To deny that the author determines the text's meaning also raises an ethical question. Such an approach appears to rob the author of his or her creation. To treat a text in complete isolation from its author's intended purpose is like stealing a patent from its inventor or a child from the parent who gave it birth. If we list a work under the name of its author, we are at least tacitly admitting that it "belongs" to its author. He or she "owns" this work. To take it and place upon it our own meaning is a kind of plagiarism. There is a sense in which we have stolen what belongs to someone else. A text is like a "will" the author leaves for his or her heirs. It is mischievous to interpret such a will and ignore the intention of its author. For a will's executor to ignore what the author intended by his or her will is criminal and violates everyone's sense of fairness. For an interpreter to do the same with an author's literary work likewise seems unethical and disrespectful of the willed legacy of the author.

## OBJECTIONS TO THE AUTHOR
## AS THE DETERMINER OF MEANING

Several objections have been raised against the view that the meaning of a text is determined by the author, and that in seeking the meaning of a text we are in essence trying to understand what an author like Paul consciously willed to communicate by his text. One of the most famous of these objections is called the "intentional fallacy." This objection, made famous by William K. Wimsatt, Jr., and Monroe Beardsley, argues that it is impossible to climb in to the mind of an author, such as Paul, and experience everything that was going through his mind as he wrote. A reader can never relive the experiences of the author. The innermost emotions, feelings, and motives Paul had as he wrote are simply not accessible to the reader, unless the author chose to reveal them in his text. As a result of such considerations, it is argued that the meaning Paul willed is inaccessible.

But when reading a Pauline text, the primary goal is not to experience or reduplicate Paul's mental and emotional experiences when he wrote. Rather the goal is to understand what Paul "meant," what he consciously sought to communicate to his readers by what he wrote. This objection confuses two different aspects of communication. The first involves the mental and emotional acts experienced by Paul; the second involves what Paul wanted to communicate. A careful distinction must be made between what Paul wished to convey in his text and the mental, emotional, and psychological experiences he went through while writing. What Paul sought to convey by his text is in the public realm, for he purposely made this available to the reader in the text itself. On the other hand, the inner mental and emotional experiences of Paul, or his "mental acts," are private and not accessible to the reader, unless Paul explicitly revealed them in his text. The goal of interpretation is not to relive Paul's emotional and mental state, but to understand what he meant by the written text he gave us. The intentional fallacy appears to confuse the meaning of a text with the experiences of the writer as he wrote. A text means what an author such as Paul wished to convey by his words. We have access to this because we have access to Paul's words. We do not have access to his mental acts.

The intentional fallacy has also argued that an author at times may intend to convey a particular meaning but be incapable of adequately expressing this. The author may be linguistically incompetent. All of us at some time or other have realized that we may not have expressed adequately what we wished to communicate. Even very capable communicators can at times fail to express correctly what they meant. It is therefore quite possible that an author could fail to express in an understandable way what he or she sought to communicate. Authors could even mislead the reader by a poor or wrong choice of words. This objection, however, tends to be more hypothetical than real. Most writers, such as Paul, possess sufficient literary competence to express their thoughts adequately. In fact, those who write articles outlining this problem and drawing it to their readers' attention usually think that they are sufficiently competent to express their thoughts quite adequately. If they did not, why would they write? Why then deny this competence to other writers?

For the Christian, an additional factor comes into play at this point. The belief that the Bible is inspired introduces a component of divine enabling into the situation. If in the writing of Scripture the authors were "moved by the Holy Spirit" (2 Peter 1:21), then it would appear that the authors of the Bible were given a divine competence in writing. This competence enabled them to express adequately the revelatory matters they wanted to communicate in their writing.

Another objection to the view that the reader should seek the authorial meaning of the text involves the psychological differences between the author and the reader. Since the psychological makeup of each individual is unique, it is argued that a reader cannot understand the thoughts, emotions, and feelings the author possessed when he or she wrote. The reader is simply too different psychologically. As a result, a reader can never understand what an author truly meant by his or her text.

A related objection is the view that a modern reader is not able to understand the meaning of an ancient author such as Paul. The radical difference between the present situation of the reader and that of the author does not permit this. How can the modern-day reader, familiar with computers and megabytes, jet airplanes and international travel, television, heart transplants, lunar landings, and nuclear power understand an ancient author writing thousands of years ago in a time of sandals, togas, and animal sacrifices? According to this view, the culture of the author and the culture of the reader are so radically different that it is impossible for a present-day reader to understand what an ancient writer meant. The author and reader live too many centuries, even millennia, apart.

These objections are well taken, and should not be minimized. The differences between the time and thought-world of an ancient author and the modern reader are very real. Far too often we tend to modernize ancient writers and assume that they thought exactly like twentieth-century Americans. Consequently we misunderstand them. On the other hand, we can also overemphasize these differences. After all, we are not trying to understand the thoughts of worms or toads! The common humanity we share with the authors of the past and the fact that we both have been created in the image of God facilitate bridging this gap of time. The basic needs for food, clothing, warmth, security, love, and forgiveness the ancients had are still the basic needs we have today. Thus, while difficult, understanding an ancient author is not impossible. In a similar fashion the common possession of the image of God assists in overcoming the psychological differences between the author and reader as well.

One final objection that can be raised with regard to the interpretation of the Bible involves those texts in which an author appeals to a faith experience. How can an atheist or unbeliever understand the meaning of the psalmist when he states, "Blessed is he whose transgressions are forgiven, whose sins are covered. Blessed is the man whose sin the LORD does not count against him and in whose spirit is no deceit. When I kept silent, my bones wasted away through my groaning all day long. For day and night your hand was heavy upon me" (Ps. 32:1–4a). Whereas a believer may be able to understand the experience of faith that the author is talking about, how can an atheist? We must, however, distinguish here between understanding what the author means by these words and understanding the subject matter he is discussing. An atheist can understand that the psalmist is talking about the joy of being forgiven by the Lord and the personal agony that preceded this. On the other hand, an atheist cannot understand the experience, the subject matter, of which the psalmist is speaking. He or she may in fact seek to explain that subject matter via Freudian psychology because of not being able to accept the divine element involved in it. Yet an atheist can understand what the psalmist means by his discussion of this issue. The psalmist is speaking of the agony of guilt and the joy of forgiveness. An atheist, however, can never understand the truth of the subject matter, the experience, of which the psalmist speaks. . . .

## THE ROLE OF THE AUTHOR

Texts do not simply appear in history. They do not evolve from trees or from papyrus plants or from animal skins. An ancient text did not come into existence because some animal lost its skin or some papyrus plant shed its bark and written symbols miraculously appeared on it. Someone, some time, somewhere wanted to write these texts. Someone, some time, somewhere willed to say something and have others read it. If this were not true, these texts would never have appeared. A thinking person consciously willed to write a text for the purpose of conveying something meaningful to the reader. Since this took place in past time, what the author willed to convey by the linguistic symbols used (whether the symbols were Hebrew, Aramaic, Greek, or Latin is immaterial) possesses a meaning that can never change. What a biblical author willed by his text is anchored in history. It was composed in the past, and being part of the past, what the author willed to communicate back then can never change. What a text meant when it was written, it will always mean. It can no more change than any other event of the past can change, because its meaning is forever anchored in past history.

Yet what an author such as Paul consciously willed to say in the past also has implications of which he was not necessarily aware. Those implications are also part of the meaning of the text. When, for instance, Paul wrote in Ephesians 5:18, "Do not get drunk on wine," he was consciously thinking that the Ephesian Christians should not become intoxicated with the mixture of water and wine (usually two to three parts water to one part wine) that they called "wine." This saying, however, has implications that go beyond what Paul was consciously thinking. Paul gave a principle or pattern of meaning that has implications about not becoming drunk with beer, whiskey, rum, vodka, or champagne. If asked, Paul would state that although he was not consciously thinking of these other alcoholic beverages, he meant for Christians not to become drunk by using them as well. Certainly no one in Ephesus would have thought, "Paul in his letter forbids our becoming drunk with wine, but I guess it would not be wrong to become drunk with beer." Paul's text has implications that go beyond his own particular conscious meaning at the time. These implications do not conflict with his original meaning. On the contrary, they are included in that pattern of meaning he wished to communicate. It is true that they go beyond his conscious thinking when he wrote, but they are included in the principle Paul wished to communicate in this verse. Thus, what an author of Scripture stated in the past frequently has implications with respect to things of which he was not aware or did not even exist at the time the text was written!

The purpose of biblical interpretation involves not just understanding the specific conscious meaning of the author but also the principle or pattern of meaning he sought to communicate. If Paul did in fact prohibit becoming drunk with whiskey and modern-day alcoholic beverages, does he also forbid in Ephesians 5:18 the unnecessary use and abuse of narcotics? That other statements of Scripture forbid the abuse of the human body in such a manner is clear. But does this specific passage forbid its use? If we understand Paul's command as a principle, then it would appear that this passage does indeed prohibit the use of narcotics. If the principle or pattern of meaning willed by Paul in this saying is something like "Do not take into your body substances like wine that cause you to lose control of your senses and natural inhibitions," then the use of narcotics is likewise prohibited by this verse. If we were able to ask Paul about this latter instance, would he not reply, "I was not consciously thinking of narcotics when I wrote, but that's exactly the kind of thing I meant"? The fact is that every text has implications or unconscious meanings its author was not aware of but which fit the meaning willed in the text. More often than not, the main concern of interpretation is to understand what the legitimate implications of an author's meaning are.

We might pause for a moment to consider whether Jesus was thinking along these lines when he said, "You have heard that it was said to the people long ago, 'Do not murder . . .' but I tell you . . ." or "You have heard that it was said, 'Do not commit adultery.' But I tell you . . ." (Matt. 5:21–48). It appears that Jesus here describes what is involved in the higher righteousness referred to in Matthew 5:20 by bringing out the implications of Moses' commandments. Whether Moses was consciously thinking of these implications when he wrote these commandments is immaterial. They are legitimate implications of the principles he wished to convey in them. At this point someone might raise the following objection: "But isn't God the author of Scripture?" This sounds devout enough, but Scripture does not claim God as its immediate author. Paul's letters do not begin, "God, the Father, Son, and Holy Spirit, to the church at Rome." No book of the Bible claims God as its immediate author! Christians, of course, believe that behind the books of the Bible stands the living God, who has inspired His servants in the writing of these works. But the Scriptures were written by men, not God. As a result, to understand the meaning of the biblical texts we must understand what their human authors consciously willed to convey by their texts. The divine meaning of the biblical texts is the conscious willed meaning of God's inspired prophets and apostles. To understand the divine meaning of Scripture, then, is to understand the conscious meaning of God's inspired servants who wrote them. It is in, not behind or beyond, the meaning the author wished to share that we find the meaning God wished to share in the Scriptures!

The term *conscious* has been used on numerous occasions with respect to the willed meaning of the author. Although this may seem awkward, it has been used intentionally. The reason for this is to avoid two errors. One involves those interpreters who argue that "myths" are present throughout the Bible. According to this view the miracle stories found in Scripture are to be understood not as historical accounts, but as fictional stories or myths. The meanings of these myths, they argue, are "subconscious" truths and Christian values that were at play in the subconscious thinking of the early church and the Christian writers. Thus the meanings of these "myths" are not found in what the authors of Scripture consciously sought to express in the pattern of meaning they wrote. The "meaning" of these myths were, on the contrary, totally unknown to them and are independent of any conscious pattern of meaning they wished to convey. The meaning lies in their subconsciousness, which gave rise to these myths. They were, however, completely unaware of this. Attributing the meaning of a text to the "conscious" willed meaning of the author avoids this error.

The term *subconsciousness* must not be confused with what is referred to as the "unconscious" meaning of the text. "Unconscious" meanings, or implications, are indeed unknown to the author, but they fall within his conscious, willed pattern of meaning. The "subconscious" meaning sought in this mythical approach, however, has nothing to do with what the author consciously wished to convey. In fact, it is usually quite opposed to the author's willed meaning, because the author believed in the facticity of the events he was reporting and wished to share the meaning of those events with his readers. . . .

On the opposite extreme are those who argue that the Bible must be interpreted literally at all times. This, too, is an error, for it loses sight of the fact that the biblical writers used various literary forms in their works such as proverbs, poetry, hyperbole, and parables. They never intended that their readers should interpret such passages literally. They intended for them to be interpreted according to the literary rules associated with such forms. Thus, the conscious willed meaning of Jesus when He said, "If anyone comes to me and does not hate his father and mother, his wife and children, his brothers and sisters—yes, even his own life—he cannot be my disciple" (Luke 14:26), is not that His disciples must literally hate their parents. It means rather that to be disciples of Jesus we must place Him before everything and everyone. The meaning of Luke 14:26 is therefore what Jesus and Luke consciously sought to communicate by these words and not the literal meaning of the words. Similarly, the parable of the rich man and Lazarus (Luke 16:19–31) is to be interpreted as a parable, and thus according to the rules governing the interpretation of parables. It is not to be interpreted as a historical account. (Luke reveals this by the introduction "A certain man . . ." which is used in the Gospel to introduce parables [cf. Luke 10:30; 14:16; 15:11; 16:1; 19:12]. This is clearer in the Greek text than in most translations, but it is fairly obvious in the NASB.)

## THE ROLE OF THE TEXT

A text consists of a collection of verbal symbols. These symbols can be various kinds of letters, punctuation marks, accents (Greek), or vowel pointing (Hebrew). A biblical author could have used any symbols he wanted to write his text. In fact, he could have invented a language that only he, and those whom he chose, knew. Special codes are created for this purpose. A secret code is a text that authors want to keep hidden from others; they will reveal the meaning only to those who know the "code." In times of war such codes are especially important. When others "break" that code, as U.S. naval intelligence did in World War II at the Battle of Midway, this may have disastrous consequences for those assuming that only their side understands the code.

However, if an author wishes to convey meaning to as many people as possible, as the biblical authors did, then he or she will choose a code, a collection of verbal symbols, which the readers will understand. This code will involve consonants, vowels, punctuation, words, idioms, and grammar that the author and readers share in common. In writing, an author therefore creates a text that possesses "shareability." Shareability is the common understanding of a text's words and grammar possessed by both author and reader. Apart from this a reader cannot understand what an author wills to say. As a result an author purposely submits himself or herself to the conventions and understanding of language possessed by the readers. Thus, if we understand how the author's intended audience would have understood the text, we, as readers today, can also understand the meaning of that same text. Because we can learn how a contemporary of Paul would have understood the Greek words (vocabulary), grammatical construction (syntax), and context of the text, we can also understand Paul's meaning, for the apostle purposely submitted himself to the norms of the language of his readers.

Because of the need for shareability, an author will abide by the "norms of language" and use words and grammar in a way familiar to his audience. If he uses a word in an unfamiliar way, a good author will explain this in some way to his reader. (Cf. how the author of Hebrews explains what he means in 5:14a by "mature" in 5:14b; how John explains what Jesus meant in 2:19–20 by "temple" in 2:21; and what he meant by 7:37–38 in 7:39.) Within the norms of language, however, words possess a range of possible meanings. We can find this range of meanings in a dictionary or lexicon. An author is aware, when he uses his words, that they must possess one of these meanings. But when he uses these words, the context he gives to them narrows down the possible meanings to just one—the specific meaning found in the statement itself.

For example, the word *love* can mean a number of things. It can mean such things as profoundly tender, passionate affection; warm personal attachment; sexual intercourse; strong predilection or liking; a score of zero in tennis; a salutation in a letter. In the sentence "He lost six-love," however, it can only mean a zero score in tennis. The sentence "Let us love one another," on the other hand, is quite ambiguous. It can mean one thing when found in the context of Jesus' teachings and quite another thing in the context of a pornographic magazine. Through the specific context an author provides his verbal symbols—the sentence in which these symbols occur, the paragraph in which they are found, the chapter in which he places them—he reveals the specific meaning of his words. Linguists sometimes use the French word *langua* to describe the range of possibilities that a word possesses in the norms of language and the French word *parole* to describe the specific meaning of the word as it is used within the sentence, that is, the norms of the utterance.

Because of the shareability of the verbal symbols the biblical author uses, a text can communicate his meaning. A text, however, can communicate a great deal more. A text can open up to the reader vast areas of information. By reading a text a reader may learn all sorts of historical, psychological, sociological, cultural, and geographical information. A text can be a storehouse of information, "subject matter," and a reader can investigate a text to acquire such information. We can read the Gospel of Mark, for instance, to learn about the history of Jesus, about the shape and form of the Jesus traditions before they were written down, about the Markan literary style. We can study the book of Joshua to learn about the geography of Palestine or second-millennium military strategy. We can study the Psalms to learn about ancient Hebraic poetry or Israelite worship. All this is both possible and frequently worthwhile, but when this is done, we should always be aware of the fact that this is not the study of the text's meaning. The meaning of those texts is what the authors of Mark, Joshua, and the Psalms willed to teach their readers by recounting this history, these traditions, this geography, this poetic form.

As a result, when investigating an account such as Jesus calming the storm (Mark 4:35–41), we must be careful to focus our attention on the meaning of the account rather than on its various subject matters. The purpose of this account is not to help the reader acquire information concerning the topography of the Sea of Galilee (a lake surrounded by a ring of high hills) and how this makes it prone to sudden, violent storms (4:37). Nor is it primarily about the lack of faith on the part of the disciples (4:40) or the shape and size of boats on the Sea of Galilee in the first century (4:37). On the contrary, Mark has revealed in the opening verse of his Gospel that this work is about "Jesus Christ, the Son of God." This account, therefore, should be interpreted in light of this. The meaning that Mark sought to convey is also clear from the account itself. The account reaches its culmination in the concluding statement, "Who is this? Even the wind and the waves obey him!" (4:41). The meaning of this account, what Mark sought to convey, is therefore that Jesus of Nazareth is the Christ, the Son of God. He is the Lord, and even nature itself is subject to His voice!

Perhaps the greatest need in reading the Bible is to distinguish the vast amount of information that we can learn from the biblical texts from the meaning the authors give to that information. . . .

### THE ROLE OF THE READER

Using the verbal symbols of the author, that is, the text, the reader seeks to understand what the author meant by these symbols. Knowing that the author intentionally used shareable symbols, the reader begins with the knowledge that the individual building blocks of the text, the words, fit within the norms of the language of the original readers. (This means that in reading the works of Shakespeare we must use a sixteenth- rather than a twentieth-century English dictionary!) Seeing how the words are used in phrases and sentences, and how the sentences are used within paragraphs, and how paragraphs are used in chapters, and how chapters are used in the work, the reader seeks to understand the author's intent in writing this work. This process is called the "hermeneutical circle." This expression refers to the fact that the whole text helps the leader understand each individual word or part of the text; at the same time the individual words and parts help us understand the meaning of the text as a whole. This sounds more confusing than it really is, for all this goes on simultaneously in the mind of the interpreter. The mind is able to switch back and forth from the part to the whole without great difficulty. It functions like a word processor in which the computer switches back and forth at great speed when copying from disk to disk. Similarly, the mind switches back and forth from the meaning of the individual words and the general understanding of the whole text until it comes to a successful resolution of the text's meaning.

Because the reader is interested in what a biblical author meant by his text, he or she is interested in his other writings as well, for these are especially helpful in providing clues to the meaning of the words and phrases in his text. Other works written by people of similar conviction and language are also helpful, especially if they were written at the same time. The writings of people who had different convictions but lived at the same time may also be helpful, but less so, in revealing the norms of language under which the author worked. As a result, to understand what Paul means in a particular verse in Romans the reader should look at the way he thinks and writes in the verses surrounding that text, in the neighboring chapters, in the rest of that book, then in Galatians (which is the Pauline writing most like Romans), then in 1 and 2 Corinthians, and then in the other Pauline writings. After having worked through the Pauline materials, the reader can also look elsewhere. Probably the order of importance after the Pauline materials would be: the rest of the New Testament; the Old Testament; the intertestamental literature; the rabbinic literature; the early church fathers; contemporary Greek literature. (This order would be determined by which of the others best reflects the way Paul thought.) In a similar way a verse in the Gospel of Luke is best interpreted by the verses surrounding it, the paragraphs and chapters surrounding that verse, the rest of the Gospel of Luke, and then the book of Acts. Acts would reveal better how Luke thought than Matthew, Mark, or John, but other Gospels would be better than Isaiah, which in turn would be better than Josephus, a Jewish historian of the first century.

It is also important for the reader to understand the particular literary form being used by the author, for different forms of literature are governed by different rules. If the author has expressed his willed meaning in the form of a proverb, we must then interpret that proverb by the rules governing this literary form. If he has used a parable, we must interpret the parable in light of the rules associated with parables. The careful argumentation of Paul in Romans must be interpreted differently from the poetic form in which the psalmist has expressed his meaning. What is common in the interpretation of every literary form, however, is that we are in each instance seeking to understand the meaning the author willed. Furthermore, we can assume that, since he sought to share that meaning with his readers, he was abiding by the common rules associated with the particular literary form he was using.

Once the reader knows the meaning of the author, he or she will need to seek out those implications of that meaning that are especially relevant. If the pattern of meaning Paul willed when he wrote Ephesians 5:18 is "Do not take into your body substances like alcohol that cause you to lose control of your senses and natural inhibitions," what implications arising out of this paradigm of meaning are most relevant for the reader? Because Paul's text has far-reaching implications that he was not aware of, the value of a text, its "significance," is multiple and varied. Although the meaning of a text never changes because it is locked in past history, its significance is always changing. This is why some people claim that the Scriptures have different "meanings." Yet a text does not have different "meanings," for an author like Paul willed a single specific pattern of meaning when he wrote. (The instances in which an author willed a "double meaning" pun are quite rare.) A text, however, has different "significances" for different readers. For example, the words of Jesus, "and you will be my witnesses in Jerusalem, and in all Judea and Samaria, and to the ends of the earth" (Acts 1:8), have a single meaning. Jesus wanted to see the message of the Gospel spread throughout the entire world. Yet the value of various implications, the significance of Jesus' words, will no doubt vary a great deal for each reader. For me it involves teaching in a theological seminary; for my daughter and son-in-law it involves going overseas to a foreign land to work among an unreached people; for my sons and their wives it involves working in their local churches. For others it may involve working in a rural church or in the inner city or witnessing about Christ at work. For a non-Christian it no doubt would involve a rejection of the meaning. There is one meaning to a text, that meaning consciously willed by the author, but the particular way that meaning affects the readers, its significance, will be quite different.

# THREE

# ISSUES IN CONTEMPORARY HERMENEUTICS

## Walter C. Kaiser, Jr.

THE DISCIPLINE OF HERMENEUTICS is emerging as the new dominant movement in both European and American theology. The number of articles and books appearing on this topic is matched only by the magnitude of the questions they are raising.

These questions are not the traditional hardy annuals: What is literal and what is figurative? What is descriptive reporting and what is normative teaching? Instead, our generation is being invited to ask the most fundamental question of all communication and interpretation. It is, surprisingly, in the area of general hermeneutics that the debate has aroused the sharpest disagreement. The implications of this debate for the evangelical and for the interpretation of Scripture are enormous. Our energetic entry into this discussion is thus no longer an optional luxury; it must be placed highest on our list of investigative priorities.

### THE NEW ORIENTATION

The basic crisis is this: hermeneutics is more a matter of the text interpreting itself and the interpreter, than it is our interpreting the text. It is not the former focus on "What does the text mean?" or "What did the author mean?" Rather, we now ask the text to interpret us, and to become itself a new event as we read or hear it.

This new orientation has sprung from the philosophical roots of Martin Heidegger, who concluded that understanding happens when the reality to which language points becomes present for the individual and merges in such a way as to coincide with his own present reality.

Currently, however, the most important theoretician of philosophical hermeneutics is Hans-Georg Gadamer. In *Wahrheit und Methode* (1960) he accepted and extended Heidegger's thought. Thus by 1964 James M. Robinson could speak of the school of "The New Hermeneutic."

At the heart of Gadamer's concern was the premise that the meaning of a text was not the same as the author's meaning. The author's meaning was, in any case, inaccessible to us. Instead, the meaning of a text was in its subject matter, which was at once independent of both the author and reader, and somehow also shared by both of them. Moreover, no one could ever say this is *the* meaning of a text, since the number of possible meanings was practically endless and constantly changing. And, argued Gadamer, what a text meant to an author could not be reproduced in the present. The past was alien to the present, for differences in time necessarily involved difference in being.

If Gadamer signaled a new modern consensus for what may be called the Heideggerian version of hermeneutics, Emilio Betti, an Italian historian of law, and E. D. Hirsch, Jr., an American professor of English, represented the minority opinion that was trying to reinstate the older form of hermeneutics. Both scholars insisted on two basic distinctions: "meaning" was that which was to be found in a text as indicated by its grammar, the author's use of his words, and his truth-intentions; and "significance" merely named a relationship between that discovered "meaning" and another person, time, situation, or idea. Thus meaning was unchanging and single, while significance did and must change since interests, questions, times, and concerns of interpreters also changed. Betti did acknowledge that in the interpretive process the interpreter involved his own subjectivity. But if the interpreter does not succeed in penetrating beyond that subjectivity, Betti cautioned, he most likely will achieve nothing more than projecting his own ideas and preferences onto the text he honestly believed he was interpreting.

Of course, Gadamer justifiably insists that every interpretation also involves an application to the present. This is precisely the situation in interpreting legal cases to locate precedents for the contemporary situation. But according to Betti and Hirsch the significance of the text is grounded in the text itself as judged by the *author's* use of grammar. Gadamer, however, is too preoccupied with the *interpreter's* assignment of meaning to an object, and with the easy equation of this subjective assignment to the text's meaning.

Both Betti and Hirsch insist that the price for ignoring this distinction and definition of meaning and significance is high. It will jeopardize the integrity of all that is objectively valid in the whole spectrum of the humanities, for there will be no method of validating and testing which meaning more adequately represents the correct one. All criteria for measurement are abandoned for purely subjective and personal replacements.

Understanding of the objective model argued here (and we definitely prefer Betti and Hirsch to Gadamer) is like grasping the inner logic and coherence of a mathematical proposition or the working parts of a machine (Otto Bollnow's illustrations). Nor can such understanding be "better than an author's," unless we mean "better" in the sense that we can complete what is unfinished in the subject, or that we can better clarify certain assumptions or guiding principles that the author's work uses without consciously reflecting on them or explicitly stating them as such.

When the New Hermeneutic or aspects of it are applied to the biblical text, the results are startling. Every text has a plethora of meanings that are said to exist without any norms for deciding between which are right and which are wrong. If and when norms are allowed, by some evangelical forms of this hermeneutical revolution, they still stand opposed to what the author intended to say through his use of these words. Rather, it is claimed that the text itself is autonomous and free from the author once he has written it; it is ready only to be shaped by our act of understanding it. This we cannot accept. Should this argument persist, this writer would recommend that beginning immediately, all explanations of the theory of understanding emanating from this Heideggerian fountainhead be interpreted on the basis of their own theory and not on the basis of the objective single meaning theory they are attacking. In fact, one of the best critiques of this position is deliberately to take the exact opposite point of view as the meaning we [that is, "what it means to me"] allegedly receive from their statements—which eventually makes communication impossible.

## THE NEW CONTEXTUALIZATION

The crisis over the general theory of understanding (= general hermeneutics) and its high price of an eventual loss of communication is not the only problem we face in biblical interpretation. Recently, Charles Taber has also raised the question of whether one's hermeneutical stance is not part and parcel of the cultural heritage each received (*Gospel in Context* I, 1978, pp. 8–9).

Taber's point is that possibly there are as many proper, yet differing, approaches to the text of Scripture as there are cultures and societies. In Taber's curious line of reasoning, the precedent and legitimization for so many hermeneutical approaches to the Scripture may be found in that same text. In his view, the New Testament writers practiced a form of rabbinic hermeneutics in that they appealed to Old Testament citations which said "X was the fulfillment of Y," when to Western moderns it seemed to be no more than "X reminds us of Y." Yet contemporary Western Christianity rejects this hermeneutic, presumably because of our cultural heritage.

If Taber is right in his analysis of the New Testament, his suggestion might follow. But his question ought not to be as troublesome as it appears. As we have argued and documented elsewhere ("Legitimate Hermeneutics," in *Inerrancy*, ed. N. Geisler, Zondervan, 1979), the general rules for interpreting oral or written speech are not learned, invented, or discovered by men; rather, they are part and parcel of our nature as individuals made in the image of God. This art has been in use since God gave the gift of communication and speech itself. Thus the person spoken to is always the interpreter; the speaker is always the author.

This is not to argue that everyone is automatically and completely successful in the *practice* of the art and science of hermeneutics just because each possesses this gift of communication as part of the image of God. Precisely at this point the distinctiveness of the cultural context of the reader/interpreter becomes most embarrassingly obvious. Certainly even when the speaker and listener/reader share the same culture and age there may still be some general subjects and vocabularies that may not be a part of the interpreter's experience and therefore his ability to interpret is frustrated. In this case, it will be necessary for the interpreter to engage first in some serious study before he can be a successful interpreter.

But when the interpreter is removed from the original author by many years, governments, societies, and even religious conditions, how can the general rules for interpreting be part and parcel of our natures as made in the image of God? Again, the answer is the same. This question merely confuses one type of learning—which is only preparatory and an antecedent study—with the task of interpretation which still must follow. Had birth and providence favored us so that they would have been present and would have participated in that culture from which the writing emanated, we could have dispensed with this search into backgrounds, culture, and even at times languages. But we would still have been obligated to engage in the task of interpreting the text. Thus we still contend that the principles of interpretation are as natural and universal as is speech itself. To argue the reverse (in human speech which assumes someone is listening with understanding) is either to involve oneself in downright duplicity or ultimately to be reduced to a solipsism where only I speak, and only I know what I am saying.

All men and women in all cultures are made in the image of God. And when this fact is joined with a biblical concept of truth as having an objective grounding and reference point in the nature of God and in the doctrine of creation, the possibility for *adequate* (even if no one knows *comprehensively* except God) transcultural communication has been fairly provided and secured.

Furthermore, few have argued in this generation more strenuously than this writer against inference that the New Testament writers were following *midrashic* or *pesher* types of exegesis when they cited passages from the Old Testament to establish doctrine. Taber's charge is an old one. But to quote only one source from 1885, Fredric Gardner in his book *The Old and New Testament in Their Mutual Relations* was right in asserting: "In all quotations, which are used argumentatively, or to establish any fact or doctrine, it is obviously necessary that the passage in question should be fairly cited according to its real intent and meaning, in order that the argument drawn from it may be valid."

He challenged the very charge currently made: "There has been much rash criticism of some of these passages, and the assertion has been unthinkingly made that the Apostles, and especially St. Paul, brought up in rabbinical schools of thought, quoted the Scriptures after a rabbinical and inconsequential fashion. A patient and careful examination of these passages themselves will remove such misapprehension" (pp. 317–18). This examination we have undertaken in a number of articles elsewhere and have found it entirely correct.

Nevertheless, none of the above arguments should be interpreted as a denial of the presence of cultural items in Scripture or that there are real problems in transcultural communication. We have merely contended that there is in principle the possibility of communicating with and understanding men and women in other cultures and times than our own.

Hermeneutics enters into this discussion when we encounter truth that comes in a cultural vehicle or context. It then becomes the interpreter's job to recognize the vehicle, illustration, or clothing for what it is without evaporating the revelation of God one whit. This task, we are learning, is easier said in theory than accomplished in practice. But never mind the difficulty; Peter's apostolic status and revelatory stance did not guarantee even to him any kind of automatic and trouble-free path to interpreting some of his fellow apostles' meanings. In 2 Peter 3:16 he frankly admitted that his "beloved brother Paul" had indeed written "some things hard to understand" that were liable to be twisted by the ignorant and unstable to their own undoing. And what was true for Paul, Peter allowed, was also possible in "the other Scriptures." The church must give more attention to this aspect of hermeneutics than it has in the past. (See this writer's seminal suggestions for some guidelines in the essay mentioned above, "Legitimate Hermeneutics.")

## THE NEW RULE OF FAITH

One more current crisis needs to be discussed here. This has its roots in Origen's misappropriation of the words from Romans 12:6, "according to the analogy of faith" (which in the context of spiritual gifts did not refer to a body of truth) and in the Reformers' proper rejection of the *Glossa ordinaria*, a commentary that preserved a uniformity in all matters relating to doctrine and discipline. The Reformers' objection to this *Regula fidei* (Rule of faith) set up by the church of Rome was that it was an authority *independent* of Scripture. By what means, then, could the Reformers determine which interpretations were valid and which were not true? They could not appeal to any *new* rule of faith, for they had by now trumpeted forth the principle of *sola scriptura*: doctrine and discipline must now be based on Scripture alone. The solution was to argue that the Bible was to be its own interpreter. In opposition to the principle that allowed tradition or the *Glossa ordinaria* to interpret Scripture, the Reformers championed the hermeneutical principle that "Scripture interprets Scripture," commonly called "the analogy or rule of faith."

Unfortunately, contemporary men and women pervert this dictum that "Scripture interprets Scripture" when they fail to realize that the Reformers used it only as a *relative* expression aimed especially at tradition: it was never intended to be understood as an absolute and positive principle that excluded learning, grammar, syntax, and the need of commentaries, or a trained ministry that would return to the original languages for a detailed and more precise understanding of the text. Otherwise, why did Calvin and Luther also write commentaries and preach God's Word to the church?

Some will then ask, "What has happened to the teaching about the 'perspicuity of the sacred writings'? Are not the Scriptures 'clear enough' so that the simplest person can understand all that is in them?" But here again, we respond that the Reformers never meant to declare that the Bible was *totally* perspicuous to all alike. Rather, perspicuity was again a relative expression and not an absolute one that claimed everything in the Bible to be equally clear and apparent to all readers at all times. Instead, it too was a word aimed at the objectionable application of tradition to the exposition of Scripture. As far as the Reformers were concerned, the Bible was sufficiently perspicuous without the need for the church's tradition or regulation of interpretation. The Bible is sufficiently clear in and of itself to bring its learned and unlearned readers into an understanding of the basic message of salvation and a walk with God.

Yet there was at least some room left for ambiguity, if not outright opposition between principles, when the Reformers went on to illustrate and define their further use of the "analogy of faith." Some passages of Scripture, the Reformers assured us, could only be understood by the analogy of faith. In some passages, Luther confessed, faith might force us to abandon the natural or grammatical sense of a passage!

The corrective for some of the past and present cries generated by an improper or premature use of the analogy of faith, is the recognition that there is indeed a theological aspect to interpreting Scripture. But this analogy, when used as a hermeneutical tool, must be carefully restricted to those passages that *preceded* in time the passage currently under study. It must be controlled diachronically and put into the sequence of the progress of revelation. And to minimize subjectivity, this should be done only when the passage being exegeted warrants it. Such clues in the passage under examination will be: (1) the use of terms that by now have taken on technical status, (2) the allusion to the same events, and (3) the quotation of or general reference to previous passages that are now part of the Holy Scriptures in the possession of that author and audience to which this new word is being delivered. Only such a procedure of limiting ourselves *for exegetical purposes* (doing systematic theology is another matter which ought to follow this step in any case) to the "informing theology" or that "rule of doctrine" in the existence when this new passage came in the progress of revelation will save us from allowing the analogy of faith to undercut the principle of *sola scriptura*. Otherwise, we will have quietly restored tradition to its previous place of authority alongside Scripture.

## CONCLUSION

These are not the only matters troubling the hermeneutical house, but these three crises are, in our estimation, each in and of themselves sufficient to bring the whole orthodox case for Scripture tumbling down. It would be the ultimate irony if our generation were to be noted as the generation that contested most earnestly for the sole authority and inerrancy of Scripture as its confessional stand, but which generation also effectively denied that stance by its own hermeneutical practice and method of interpretation. This in itself, given the contemporary pressures, is reason enough to call the evangelical community throughout Christendom to a whole new hermeneutical reformation. We trust that under God we may be so favored in our generation.

FOUR

# INTERPRETING THE BIBLE LIKE A BOOK

## Moses Stuart

ARE THE SAME PRINCIPLES of interpretation to be applied to the Scriptures as to other books? A question this of deeper interest to religion and sacred literature than most persons would be apt at first to suppose. In fact, the fundamental principles of scriptural theology are inseparably connected with the subject of this inquiry; for what is such theology, except the result of that which the Scriptures have taught? And how do we find what the Scriptures have taught, except by applying to them some rules or principles of interpretation? If these rules are well rounded, the results which flow from the application of them will be correct, provided they are skillfully and truly applied. But if the principles by which we interpret the Scriptures are destitute of any solid foundation, and are the product of imagination, of conjecture, or of caprice, then of course the results which will follow from the application of them will be unworthy of our confidence.

All this is too plain to need any confirmation. This also, from the nature of the case, renders it a matter of great importance to know whether the principles by which we interpret the sacred books are well grounded and will abide the test of a thorough scrutiny.

Nearly all the treatises on hermeneutics, which have been written since the days of Ernesti, have laid it down as a maxim which cannot be controverted, that the Bible is to be interpreted in the same manner, i.e., by the same principles as all other books. Writers are not wanting, previously to the period in which Ernesti lived, who have maintained the same thing. But we may also find some who have assailed the position before us, and labored to show that it is nothing less than a species of profaneness to treat the sacred books as we do the classic authors, with respect to their interpretation. Is this allegation well grounded? Is there any good reason to object to the principle of interpretation now in question?

In order to answer these inquiries, let us direct our attention, in the first place, to the nature and source of what are now called *principles or laws of interpretation*. Whence did they originate? Are they the artificial production of high-wrought skill, of labored research of profound and extensive learning? Did they spring from the subtilties of nice distinctions, from the philosophical and metaphysical efforts of the schools? Are they the product of exalted and dazzling genius, sparks of celestial fire which none but a favored few could emit? No; nothing of all this. The principles of interpretation, as to their substantial and essential elements, are no invention of man, no product of his effort and learned skill. No, they can scarcely be said with truth to have been discovered by him. They are coeval with our nature. They were known to the antediluvians. They were practiced upon in the garden of Eden by the progenitors of our race. Ever since man was created and endowed with the powers of speech, and made a *communicative*, social being, he has had occasion to practice upon the principles of interpretation and has actually done so. From the first moment that one human being addressed another by the use of language, down to the present hour, the essential laws of interpretation became, and have continued to be, a *practical* matter. The person addressed has always been an *interpreter* in every instance where he has heard and understood what was addressed to him.

All the human race, therefore, are, and ever have been, interpreters. It is a law of their rational, intelligent, communicative nature. Just as truly as one human being was formed so as to address another in language, just so truly that other was formed to interpret and to understand what is said.

I venture to advance a step farther, and to aver that all men are, and ever have been, in reality, good and true interpreters of each other's language. Has any part of our race, in full possession of the human faculties, ever failed to understand what others said to them, and to understand it truly? Or to make themselves understood by others when they have in their communications kept within the circle of their own knowledge? Surely none. Interpretation, then, in its basic or fundamental principles, is a *native* art, if I may so speak. It is coeval with the power of uttering words. It is of course a universal art; it is common to all nations, barbarous as well as civilized.

One cannot commit a more palpable error in relation to this subject, than to suppose that the art of interpretation is one which is like the art of chemistry, or of botany, or of astronomy, or any of the like things, viz., that it is in itself wholly dependent on *acquired* skill for the discovery and development of its principles. Acquired skill has indeed helped to all orderly exhibition and arrangement of its principles; but this is all. The materials were all in existence before skill attempted to develop them.

Possibly it may excite surprise in the minds of some to be told that, after all, hermeneutics is no science that depends on learning and skill, but is one with which all the race of man is practically more or less acquainted. Yet this is true. But so far is it from diminishing the real value of the science that it adds exceedingly to its weight and importance. That it is connate with us, shows that it is a part of our rational and communicative nature. That it is so, shows also that it is not, in its fundamental parts, a thing of uncertainty, of conjecture, of imagination, or of mere philosophical nicety. If it were a far-fetched science, dependent on high acquisitions and the skillful application of them, then it would be comparatively a useless science. In such a case, only a favored few of the human race would be competent to understand and acquire it, still fewer could be satisfactorily assured of its stable and certain nature.

An interpreter well skilled in his art will glory in it, that it is an art which has its foundation in the laws of our intellectual and rational nature, and is coeval and connate with this nature. He finds the best assurance of its certainty in this. It is only a quack (if I may so speak) in this business that will ever boast of anything in it which is secret or obscure or incomprehensible to common minds.

All which has ever led to any such conclusion, is, that very few men, and those only learned ones, become critics by profession. But the secret of this is merely that professed critics are, almost always, professed interpreters of books in foreign languages not in their own mother tongue. Then again, if they are interpreters of their own vernacular language, it is of such exhibitions of it as present recondite and unusual words. Now in order to interpret a foreign language, or in order to explain the unusual words of one's own vernacular tongue, a good degree of learning becomes requisite. This is not, however, because the rules of interpretation, then applied either to foreign languages, or to unusual words or phrases in one's own language, are different from the rules which all men every day apply to the common language employed by them in conversation. Learning is necessary to know the meaning of foreign words, or of strange vernacular words, on the same ground, and no other, as it was necessary for us to learn originally the meaning of the circle of words which we usually employ in speaking or writing. The same acquaintance with foreign words that we have with our everyday ones, would of course make them equally intelligible and equally supersede any *studied* art of hermeneutics in order to interpret them.

When a man takes up a book, which contains a regular system of hermeneutics all arranged and exhibited to the eye, and filled with references to choice and rare volumes, he is ready to conclude that it contains something almost as remote from the common capacity and apprehension of men as Newton's *Principia*. But this is a great mistake. The *form* of the treatise in question, it is true, may be altogether a matter of art. The quotations and references may imply a very widely extended circle of reading and knowledge. But after all, the principles themselves are obvious and natural ones; at least if they are not so, they are worth but little or nothing. The illustration and confirmation of them may indeed be drawn from a multitude of sources widely scattered and some of them very recondite, and a great display of learning may be made here. But still the same thing is true in this case as in many other departments of learning and taste. Nature first teaches rules; art arranges, illustrates, and records them. This is the simple truth as to hermeneutics. Systems have digested and exhibited what the rational nature of man has taught—of man who was made to speak and to interpret language.

I may illustrate and confirm this by a reference, for example, to epic or lyric poetry. Men did not first invent rules by the aid of *learned* art, and then construct epic and lyric poems by the aid of these rules. Nature prescribed these rules to a Homer, a Pindar, and to others. They followed nature, and therefore wrote with skill and power. That they have become models for all succeeding epic and lyric writers can be accounted for only from the fact that they followed the promptings of nature in their respective kinds of composition, and others cannot swerve essentially from their course without swerving from nature. Then of course they will offend against what we may truly call the common sense of mankind.

It is the same in hermeneutics. Many a man has, indeed, laid down rules in this science which were a departure from the principles taught us by our reasonable nature; and where he has had personal influence, he has obtained disciples and imitators. But his popularity has been short-lived, or at least he has sooner or later been taken to task for departing from nature, and has been refuted, in the view of sober and unprejudiced men, in regard to such principles as violate the common rules of interpretation which men daily practice.

There are only two ways in which men come to the knowledge of words: the one is by custom, education, the daily habit of hearing and speaking them; the other is, by studying them in books, and learning them in the way that philology teaches. Now the first method supersedes the second. But as the second is the only way left for all such as wish to understand the Greek and Hebrew Scriptures, so the thorough study of those books which are necessary to impart the knowledge in question, renders a good degree of learning a matter which of course is necessary. All this occupies time, and costs labor and effort. Few succeed, after all, to any great extent, in making the acquisition under consideration; hence the general apprehension of its difficulty. Hence too the idea that the art of interpretation is the result of learned skill rather than the dictate of common sense.

I do not aver, indeed, that a man destitute of learned skill can well interpret the Greek and Hebrew Scriptures. But this I would say, viz., that his *learning* applies more to the proper knowledge of Greek and Hebrew words in themselves considered than it does to the principles by which he is to interpret them. In the estimation of men in general, however, these two things are united together. It is in this way, that hermeneutics comes to be looked upon as one of the more recondite and difficult sciences.

I certainly do not wish to be understood as denying here that the *practice* of the hermeneutical art in a successful manner does require learning and skill. Surely this must be true when it is applied to the explanation of the original Greek and Hebrew Scriptures, because no one can well understand these languages without some good degree of learned skill. But I say once more that the learning necessary to understand the meaning of particular words in these languages, and that which is employed in the proper *interpretation* of them are not one and the same thing. When the words are once understood, the Hebrew and Greek Scriptures are interpreted by just the same rules that every man uses in order to interpret his neighbor's words. At least this is my position, and one which I expect to illustrate and confirm, by showing more fully still, that from the nature of the case it must be so, and moreover that it is altogether reasonable and proper.

I have urged at so much length and repeated in various forms the sentiments contained in the preceding paragraphs because I view them as of essential importance in respect to the subject before us. If God has implanted in our rational nature the fundamental principles of the hermeneutical art, then we may reasonably suppose that when He addresses a revelation to us, He intends and expects that we shall interpret it in accordance with the laws of that nature which He has given us. In showing that the science of interpretation is not a production of art and learned skill, but that it is merely developed and scientifically exhibited by such skill, I have shown that the business of interpreting the Bible need not necessarily be confined to a few, but may be practiced, in a greater or less degree (if we except the criticism of the original Scriptures), by all men who will attentively study it. It is true that all men cannot be critics upon the Greek and Hebrew Scriptures, for the greater part of them never can obtain the knowledge of the words necessary for this purpose. But still, there is scarcely any man of common understanding to whom a truly skillful critic may not state and explain the principles of interpretation, by which he is guided in the exegesis of any particular passage, in such a way that this man may pass his judgment on the principle and make it the subject of his approbation or disapprobation. This proves incontrovertibly that the principles of the science in question are in themselves the dictates of plain common sense and sound understanding. If this be true, then they are principles which may be employed in the interpretation of the word of God. For if there be any book on earth that is addressed to the reason and common sense of mankind, the Bible is preeminently that book.

What is the Bible? A revelation from God. A revelation! If truly so, then it is designed to be *understood*; for if it be not intelligible, it is surely no *revelation*. It is a revelation through the medium of human language—language such as men employ, such as was framed by them and is used for their purposes. It is a revelation *by men* (as instruments) and for men. It is made *more humano* because that on any other ground it might as well not be made at all. If the Bible is not a book which is intelligible in the same way as other books are, then it is difficult indeed to see how it is a *revelation*. There are only two ways in which the Bible or any other book can be understood: the one is by miraculous illumination in order that we may have a right view of contents which otherwise would not be intelligible; the other is, by the application of such hermeneutical principles as constitute a part of our rational and communicative nature.

If you say, now, that the first of these ways is the true and only one; then it follows that a renewed miracle is necessary in every instance where the Bible is read and understood. But, first, this contradicts the experience of men; secondly, I cannot see of what use the Scriptures are, provided a renewed revelation or illumination is necessary on the part of heaven in every instance where they are read and understood. It is not the method of God's wisdom and design thus to employ useless machinery. Nor does such an idea comport with the numberless declarations of the Scriptures themselves, that they are plain, explicit, intelligible, perfect, in a word, all that is requisite to guide the humble disciple or to enlighten the ignorant.

I must then relinquish the idea of a miraculous interposition in every instance where the Bible is read and understood. I trust that few enlightened Christians will be disposed to maintain this. And if this be not well grounded, then it follows that the Bible is addressed to our reason and understanding and moral feelings, and consequently that we are to interpret it in such a way as we do any other book that is addressed to these same faculties.

A denial of this throws us at once upon the ground of maintaining a miraculous interposition in all cases where the Bible is understood. An admission of it brings us to the position that the Bible is to be interpreted in the same way as other books are.

Why not? When the original Scriptures were first spoken or written (for very much of them, in the prophets for example, was *spoken* as well as written) were they designed to be *understood* by the men who were addressed? Certainly you will not deny this. But who were these men? Were they inspired? Truly not! They were good and bad, wise and foolish, learned and ignorant; in a word, men of all classes both as to character and knowledge.

If now the prophets in addressing such men expected to be understood, intended to be so (and clearly they did), then they expected these men to understand them in a way like to that in which they understood anyone else who addressed them, i.e., by means of applying the usual principles of interpretation to the language employed. Anything which denies this, of course, must cast us upon the ground of universal miraculous interposition.

Let us now, for a moment, imagine ourselves to stand in the place of those who were addressed by the prophets. Of course we must suppose ourselves to have the same understanding of the Hebrew language, to have been educated within the same circle of knowledge, and to be familiar with the same objects both in the natural and spiritual world. Should we need lexicons, grammars, and commentaries in order to understand Isaiah or any other prophet? The supposition is, upon the very face of it, almost an absurdity. Are our common people, who have the first rudiments even of education, unable to understand the popular preachers of the present day? If it is so, it is the egregious fault of the preacher and not of his hearers. It is because he chooses words not contained in the usual stores of language from which most persons draw, and which he need not choose and should not select, because he must know that such a choice will make him more or less unintelligible. But who will suppose the prophets to have acted thus unwisely? The inspiration by the aid of which they spoke and wrote surely enabled them to speak and write *intelligibly.* If so, then were we listeners to them, and in the condition of those whom they actually addressed, we could of course understood them, for just the same reasons and in the same way, that we now understand the popular preachers of our time. All our learned apparatus of folios and quartos, of ancient and modern lexicographers, grammarians, and critics would then be quietly dismissed, and laid aside as nearly or altogether useless. At the most, we should need them no more than we now need Johnson's or

Webster's Dictionaries in order to understand a modern sermon in the English language.

All this needs only to be stated in order to ensure a spontaneous assent to it. But what follows? The very thing, I answer, which I am laboring to illustrate and establish. If the persons addressed by the Hebrew prophets understood them, and easily and readily understood them, in what way was this done? Plainly by virtue of the usual principles of interpretation which they applied in all the common intercourse of life. They were not held in suspense about the meaning of a prophet until a second interposition on the part of heaven took place, i.e., a miraculous illumination of their minds in order that they might perceive the meaning of words new and strange to them. Such words were not employed. They were able, therefore, at once to perceive the meaning of the prophet who addressed them in all ordinary cases. This is true throughout, with exceptions merely of such a nature as still occur, in regard to most of our preaching. Now and then a word is employed which some part of a common audience does not fully comprehend. Now and then a sentiment is developed, or an argument is employed, which the minds of some are not sufficiently enlightened fully to comprehend. But in such cases, the difficulty arises more from the *subject* than it does from the language.

The prophets indeed complain, not infrequently, that the Jews did not understand them. But this complaint always has respect to a spiritual perception and relish of the truths which they delivered to them. They heard but understood not; they saw, but perceived not. The fault, however, was the want of spiritual taste and discernment, not because the language, in itself, was beyond human comprehension.

Admitting then that the prophets spoke intelligibly and that they were actually understood by their contemporaries, and this without any miraculous interposition, it follows, of course, that it was the usual laws of interpretation which enabled their hearers to understand them. They applied to their words, and spontaneously applied, the same principles of interpretation which they were wont to apply to the language of all who addressed them. By so doing, they rightly understood the prophets. At any rate, by so doing, they might have rightly understood them; if so, then such laws of interpretation are the right ones, for those laws must be right which conduct us to the true meaning of a speaker.

I can perceive no way of avoiding this conclusion unless we deny that the prophets were understood, or could be understood, by their contemporaries. But to deny this would be denying facts so plain, so incontrovertible, that it would argue a desperate attachment to system or something still more culpable.

In view of what has just been said, it is easy to see why so much study and learning are necessary, at the present time, in order to enable us correctly to understand the original Greek and Hebrew Scriptures. We are born neither in Greece nor Palestine; we have learned in our childhood to read and understand neither Greek nor Hebrew. Our condition and circumstances, our course of education and thought, as well as our language, are all different from those of a Jew in ancient times. Our government, our climate, our state of society and manners and habits, our civil, social, and religious condition are all different from those of Palestine. Neither heaven above nor earth beneath, is the same in various respects. A thousand productions of nature and art in the land of the Hebrews are unknown to our times and country. And multitudes of both are familiar to us, of which they never had any knowledge. How can we then put ourselves in their places, and listen to prophets and apostles speaking Hebrew and Greek without much learning and study? It is plainly impossible. And the call for all this learning and study is explained by what I have just said. All of it is designed to accomplish one simple object, and only one, viz., to place us, as nearly as possible, in the condition of those whom the sacred writers originally addressed. Had birth and education placed us there, all this study and effort might be dispensed with at once. For, as has been already stated, we could then understand the sacred writers in the same way and for the same reason that we now understand our own preachers. When we do this, we do it by spontaneously applying the laws of interpretation which we have practiced from our childhood; such would have been the case had we been native Hebrews, contemporary with the prophets and apostles.

When the art of interpretation, therefore, is imagined or asserted to be a difficult and recondite art, dependent on great learning and high intellectual acuteness, the obvious mistake is made of confounding with it another sort of learning. This learning is only preparatory and conditional, but does not constitute the principles themselves of hermeneutics.

It seems to my own mind that we have arrived at the conclusion which it was proposed to examine and confirm in a very plain, natural, and simple way. The substance of all is: The Bible was made to be understood. It was written by men and for men. It was addressed to all classes of people and was for the most part understood by them all, just as our present religious discourses are. And of course it was interpreted in such a way, or by the aid of such principles, as other books are understood and explained.

But there are objectors to this position. Some of them, too, speak very boldly, and with great zeal and confidence. Candor requires that we should listen to them, and examine their allegations.

## Objection 1

"How can the common laws of interpretation apply to the Scriptures, when confessedly the Bible is a book that contains revelations in respect to supernatural things, to the knowledge of which no human understanding is adequate to attain?"

The fact alleged I cheerfully concede. But the inference drawn from it, I do not feel to be at all a necessary one, nor in fact in any measure a just one. So far as the Scriptures are designed to make known a *revelation* to us, respecting things that are above the reach of our natural understanding, just so far they are designed to communicate that which is intelligible. If you deny this, then you must maintain that to be a revelation which is not intelligible; or, in other words, that to be a revelation, by which nothing is revealed.

If you say that a new interposition on the part of heaven is necessary in order that anyone may understand the Scriptures, then you make two miracles necessary to accomplish one end. The first, in giving a so-called revelation which after all is unintelligible; the second, in supernaturally influencing the mind to discern what is meant by this revelation. The reply to this has been already suggested above, viz., it contradicts experience, and it is contrary to the analogy of God's dealing with us in all other respects.

As far then as any *revelation* is actually made in the Scriptures, so far they are intelligible. But perhaps some one will here make another objection, viz.

## Objection 2

"Intelligible to whom? A man must be enlightened in a *spiritual* respect before he can understand the Scriptures. How then can the *usual* laws of interpretation enable him to understand and to explain them?"

The fact here alleged is rather overstated. I mean to say, the assertion is too general. That there are parts of the Scriptures which no unsanctified man can fully understand and appreciate is and must be true so long as the fact is admitted that there are parts which relate to *spiritual* experience. "The natural man receiveth not the things of the Spirit of God, for they are foolishness to him, neither can he know them because they are spiritually discerned." Most freely and fully do I concede what is here meant to be affirmed. How can any man fully understand what is said of religious experience and feelings who is not himself, and never has been, the subject of such experience and feelings?

After all, however, there is nothing new or singular in this, at least so far as the principle itself is concerned. The same *principle* holds true, in regard to other things and other books.

Before a man can understand them, he must be in a condition to do so. Who can read Newton's *Principia* or the *Mecanique Celeste* of La Place and understand them unless he comes to the study of them with due preparation? Who can read any book of mental or moral science and enter fully into the understanding of it unless he is himself in a state which enables him throughout to sympathize with the author, and to enter into all his feelings and views? Who, for example, can read and fully understand Milton and Homer, without the spirit and soul of poetry within him which will enable him to enter into their views and feelings? Who can read intelligently even a book of mathematics without sympathizing with the writer?

The answer to these questions is too plain to need being repeated. How then does the *principle* differ when I ask: "Who can read the Scriptures intelligently who does not enter into the moral and religious sympathies of the writers?" I agree fully to the answer which says, "No one." The thing is impossible. But it is equally impossible in all other cases to read intelligently without entering into the sympathies of the writers.

Those then who are solicitous for the honor of the Scriptures have in reality nothing to fear from this quarter in respect to the principle which I have been advocating. A demand for *religious feeling* in order fully to enter into the meaning of the sacred writers rests on the same principle as the demand for a poetic feeling in order to read Milton with success, or a mathematical feeling in order to study intelligibly Newton and La Place. How can any writer be well and thoroughly understood when there is not some good degree of community of feeling between him and his reader? This is so obvious a principle that it means only to be stated in order to be recognized.

But still, it would be incorrect to say that Newton or Milton is unintelligible. They have both employed language in its usual way. If not always so, yet they have furnished adequate explanations of what they do mean. The laws of exegesis are the very same in reading and explaining Milton as they are in reading and explaining Pope or Cowper. They are the same in respect to La Place as they are in respect to Day's mathematics. But in both these cases, higher acquisitions are demanded of the reader in the former instance than in the latter.

It is incorrect, therefore, to say that the Bible is unintelligible, or to say that the usual laws of interpretation are not to be applied to it, because an individual's feelings must be in unison with those of the writers in order fully to understand all which they say.

Let me add a word also by way of caution in regard to the subject now under consideration. There is a way of inculcating the truth that "the natural man receiveth and knoweth not the things of the Spirit," which is adapted to make a wrong impression on the minds of men. They are prone to deduce from certain representations of this subject which have sometimes been made the conclusion that natural men can understand no part of the Bible, and that they must be regenerated before they can have any right views of the Scriptures. But this is carrying the doctrine much beyond its just limits. A great part of the Bible is addressed to intelligent, rational, moral beings as such. All men belong to this class. Because this is so, they are capable of understanding the sacred writers, at least so far as they are designed originally to be understood by all, and so far as the great purposes of warning and instruction are concerned. It is the condemnation of men that "light has come into the world, and they love darkness rather than light, because their deeds are evil." Our Savior could not have said that if "he had not come and spoken to the Jews, they would not have had sin," except on the ground that the light which He communicated to them rendered them altogether inexcusable. Let the preachers of the divine word take good care, then, that they do not so represent the ignorance of sinners as to diminish their guilt. When this ignorance is represented as involuntary, or as a matter of dire necessity, then is the offense committed.

## Objection 3

"But is it not *God* who speaks in the Bible, and not man? How can we expect the words of God Himself to be scanned by the rules of human language?"

The answer is brief and like to that which has already been given. When God speaks to men, He speaks *more humano*—in human language—this, in condescension to our wants. Does He expect us to understand the language of angels? He does not. The Bible is filled with the most ample illustrations of this. Everywhere, *human* idioms and forms of speech common to the Jewish nation and to individuals are employed by the sacred writers. All the varieties of style and expression are observable in these writers which we see anywhere else. The same figures of speech are employed, the same modes of address and instruction. We have historic narration, genealogical catalogs, prose, poetry, proverbs, addresses, sermons, parables, allegories, enigmas even; and all this in a way similar to that found in the works of uninspired writers. It is the *matter* rather than the *manner* that characterizes the superiority of the Scriptures. The manner indeed is sublime, impressive, awful, delightful. But this is intimately connected with the elevated matter, the high and holy contents, of the Bible. After all due allowances for this, we may say that the manner is *the manner of men*; it is *by men and for men*.

We come then, after canvassing these principal objections against the position that has been advanced to the conclusion before stated, viz., that the rules of interpretation applied to other books are applicable to the Scriptures. If their contents are peculiar (as they are), still we apply the same laws to them as to other books that are peculiar. For example, we construe them in accordance with the matter which they contain. If there are peculiarities belonging to individual writers, as is the fact with respect to several of them, we still apply the same principles to the interpretation of them which we do to other peculiar writers. For example, we compare such writers with themselves and illustrate them in this way. In short, no case occurs to my mind in which the general principle above stated will not hold good, unless it be one which has been often proposed and strenuously asserted, and which still has deep hold on the minds of some in our religious community. I mean the position that some part of the Scriptures has a *double* sense, a temporal and spiritual meaning at one and the same time. If this be true, it is indeed an exception to all the rules of interpretation which we apply to other books. But whether it be well grounded, in my apprehension may be doubted, *salva fide et salva ecclesia*. The discussion of the question respecting this however would occupy too much room for the present. If Providence permit, it will be made the subject of examination at some future period.

# FIVE

# THE HOLY SPIRIT AND THE INTERPRETATION OF SCRIPTURE

## I. Howard Marshall

THE THEME OF THIS ARTICLE is not one I chose for myself because I felt that I knew something about it and wanted to share it with other Christians. It is rather the result of an editorial suggestion, and I accepted the invitation to take up this theme in order to make myself ponder the issue. I suspect that other people may share my ignorance in this area, for I would find it hard to know what to recommend as a reading list on the topic. The standard evangelical textbooks certainly refer to the importance of the Spirit's place in the interpretation of Scripture, making the familiar point that apart from the Spirit's illumination our minds are blind to spiritual truth and unable to believe God's message. But this is about as much as is said, and it seems that some further consideration of the matter is needed. The question may be put most sharply by considering the works of biblical scholarship which have been produced by Jews and other non-Christians who have sought to understand the biblical text in an honest and sympathetic fashion, and asking how their works differ from those written by believing Christian scholars. There is no doubt that many true and valid insights into the meaning of the Bible have been reached by scholars who are not Christians, and Christian scholars gratefully accept these insights. Is the Spirit at work in this situation? Does He work in a different way in Christian scholarship?

Our starting point is that the subject of the Spirit's work in interpreting the Scriptures is part and parcel of the general subject of the Spirit's work in the individual believer and in the church. That is to say, we meet the same basic problem of the relation between the natural and the supernatural in the task of interpreting the Scriptures as we do in other aspects of Christian living. We ascribe our good impulses and our noble deeds to the influence of the Spirit who indwells us—

> And every virtue we possess,
> And every conquest won,
> And every thought of holiness,
> Are his alone.

And yet we are well aware that we must work at our own salvation, and that the Scriptures command us to think and do certain things. We would repudiate the "Quietism" which claims that the Spirit will make us holy independent of our own efforts. We would say rather that the Holy Spirit works in and through our own efforts to serve God, inspiring our holy desires and giving us the strength to carry them out. We would also have to admit that the operation of the Spirit may produce imperfect results. Whether or not Christian perfection is possible for believers in this life (a problem which fortunately we do not need to solve here!), it is the case that very frequently our thoughts are less than holy and our wills are weak and wayward in living holy lives. Nevertheless, the basic principle holds that in our Christian living the guidance and power of God are brought to us by the Spirit, so the same thoughts can be ascribed both to the Spirit and to ourselves. The relationship between the Spirit and the human personality is something that we cannot describe. It is difficult enough for a psychologist to explain the working of the human personality on a natural level. The activity of the Spirit takes place on a different level of causation in ways that we cannot fathom. The classical example of this is the king of Assyria, as described in Isaiah 10, who thinks that he is acting on his own initiative and by his own strength in attacking Israel, while at the same time he is fulfilling a divine plan and can even be said to be like an ax in the hand of the woodsman.

The work of the Spirit in the reading and understanding of Scripture falls within this general framework. He is active in our understanding so that without Him our sinful minds cannot understand the Scripture, and yet it is we who carry out the task of understanding. And the relationship between these two actors—ourselves and the Spirit—is one that cannot be explained in human terms. We are, one might say, dealing with two incommensurable quantities, neither of which can be reduced to the terms of the other.

This means that we are not to understand the work of the Spirit in terms of a "God of the gaps" theory, in the sense that we explain as much as we can of a process in natural terms and then postulate God as the explanation of the remaining bits. Thus it used to be possible to explain many things in the natural world on a natural level and then to call in God as the explanation of the processes that we had so far been unable to explain in the ordinary way. The progress of science has eventually reduced the room left for God to play His part to such tiny proportions that, on this way of looking at things, He is in danger of being rendered quite unnecessary. It therefore makes better sense to think of God as being involved throughout the whole of the process. We are not to think of biblical interpretation as a human process, with the Spirit being called in to help simply at the difficult parts. When all this has been said, however, it remains true that we can identify areas in human history where God can be seen to be especially active, where there is a concentration of His power and presence. Sometimes this can be seen in specifically supernatural events, such as the Bible itself describes to us. Other cases are less obviously so. And yet we would want to say that the conversion of a sinner into a saint, the process that we call the new birth, is emphatically a special work of the Spirit. There are some people who would try to "demythologize" the concept of the Spirit's activity in the individual, but to do so is to take away something vital from Christian theology and to reduce conversion to some kind of purely human process. What is true of the beginning of the Christian life is true of its continuation. We believe that the Spirit continues to be effective in our lives in ways that transcend ordinary human causation.

It is against this background that we must consider the work of the Spirit in the interpretation of Scripture. There is, first of all, a very general way in which we can speak of the Spirit being active in this process. As a student, I used to make a practice of saying a prayer before I sat down to take an examination. I did so before school and university examinations in all kinds of subjects. When I began to study the Bible and theology, I continued the practice. The unspoken presupposition was no doubt that studying the Bible was like any other kind of study, and that it was proper to ask that God's will be done concerning my study in both cases.

But can we be more specific than this? Here I call to mind an impressive testimony by Dr. W. L. Lane in the preface to his commentary on the Gospel according to Mark: "Only gradually did I come to understand that my primary task as a commentator was to listen to the text and to the discussion it has prompted over the course of centuries as a child who needed to be made wise. The responsibility to discern truth from error has been onerous at times. When a critical or theological decision has been demanded by the text before I was prepared to commit myself, I have adopted the practice of the Puritan commentators in laying the material before the Lord and asking for His guidance. This has made the preparation of the commentary a spiritual as well as an intellectual pilgrimage through the text of the Gospel. In learning to be sensitive to all that the evangelist was pleased to share with me I have been immeasurably enriched by the discipline of responsible listening."[1]

What Dr. Lane is here suggesting is surely that the task of understanding Scripture is not simply an intellectual one, such that a person with the right academic gifts can come to the right conclusions by his own unaided efforts. There are some aspects of biblical study where this may be true. But for an understanding of the text as part of the Bible this would be a partial and inadequate understanding. The correct approach is going to be one which summons the aid of the One who inspired the authors of Scripture so that we have His authoritative guidance. There can be no doubt that this applies particularly at the level of the exposition and the application of Scripture. Once the sense of the text has been understood, there is the task of seeing what it has to say to a particular audience, be it the probable readers of a book or the congregation listening to a sermon. The sense of Scripture is something that can be determined with a measure of objectivity as something that is fixed; it is what the original writer intended his original readers to learn from what he wrote. The application of this to new sets of readers in new situations can be very varied. It is here that the expositor particularly feels his dependence upon the Spirit in the task of making Scripture speak again in the new situation. In a sense he is trying to repeat what the original authors had to do—to speak forth God's Word in a way that would grip their audiences; receiving Scripture as God's Word, he now has the task of speaking it forth so as to grip his audience. If the original authors were dependent upon the inspiration of the Spirit to do so, how much more is the modern expositor thrown back upon the guidance and illumination of the Spirit in his task?

The biblical basis for this view is to be found in such passages as 1 Thessalonians 1:5 and 2:13 which indicate that Paul's preaching was effective because the Spirit was active in and through the preaching of the Word to produce faith. The Spirit works through the Word to convert and upbuild, but clearly this process is not limited to the actual moment of delivery of a message, but must also include the preparation of the message so that the Spirit-intended words reach the hearers. What then happens is that the Spirit works through the Word to make the hearer conscious that the Word is addressed to him and to arouse in him the response of faith and joy. The paradigm case of this from the later history of the church is the conversion of John Wesley, a man who knew and understood the Gospel of justification by faith and not by works, and yet lacked the assurance that it was true for him. In a famous passage he has described his experience.

> In the evening I went very unwillingly to a society in Aldersgate Street, where one was reading Luther's preface to the Epistle to the Romans.

About a quarter before nine, while he was describing the change which
God works in the heart through faith in Christ. I felt my heart strangely
warmed. I felt I did trust in Christ, Christ alone, for salvation: and an
assurance was given me, that he had taken away my sins, even mine,
and saved me from the law of sin and death.[2]

There is no mention of the Spirit in this passage—we would not
expect one perhaps, since this is a description of Wesley's conscious
feelings at the time and not a theological explanation of what took
place, but it can certainly be argued that this is a description of the
subjective work of the Spirit in his heart. But must we not also say that
the text which led to Wesley's personal appreciation of the Gospel
was composed under the guidance of the Spirit?

It is this thought of application that perhaps holds the clue to our
problem. Consider the case of the Old Testament. It is a book that
points forward to the future, prophesying what God will do for His
people. Even after Jesus came, and died and rose again, it was still
possible for many of the Jews to fail to recognize that He was the
theme of the prophecies. Apart from Jesus, many of the prophecies
remain unfulfilled and even incomprehensible. But once it is assumed
that they are about Jesus, then they begin to make sense. Jesus is the
key that unlocks the door of Old Testament interpretation. But does
not the understanding that Jesus is the key spring from the illumination of the Spirit which reveals that He is the Messiah? It is the Spirit,
then, who supplies the key to the understanding of the Old Testament.

The key could, of course, be misapplied. Once it was seen that
Jesus was the key Old Testament interpretation, there were scholars
who proceeded to find references to Him everywhere and perverted
the plain meaning of the text. They forgot that Scripture had first of all
a message for its original readers, and attempted instead to find a
specific Christian message throughout. Where the text could not be
forced to yield such a meaning by straightforward means, they resorted
to allegorization and similar processes. Now it must be allowed that
some passages of Scripture had perhaps an exclusively future reference.
Peter writes: "The prophets who prophesied of the grace that was to be
yours searched and inquired about this salvation; they inquired what
person or time was indicated by the Spirit of Christ within them when
predicting the sufferings of Christ and the subsequent glory. It was
revealed to them that they were serving not themselves by you, in the
things which have now been announced to you by those who preached
the good news to you through the Holy Spirit sent from heaven, things
into which angels long to look" (1 Peter 1:10–12). But this quotation
is far from proving that *all* the Old Testament is prediction of the

sufferings of Christ and the subsequent glory; it is concerned simply
with those passages which do have this function, and we are still left
with the other passages which had other themes and a more direct
contemporary relevance for the first hearers and readers.

Such understanding of the Old Testament is sometimes called charismatic. The Spirit illumines the readers to see the significance of the
Scriptures in terms of some key which it points out to them.

Now it follows that we are the inheritors of the guidance given to
the first Christians. What the Spirit taught them as interpreters of the
Old Testament is something that we inherit. In a sense the Spirit does
not have to repeat the lesson individually for every Christian, but in a
more general way He illuminates us to accept the lessons given in
earlier days. This is another way of saying that the Spirit works in and
through the church. What He gives to specific individuals is a gift for
the church as a whole. The hermeneutical gift given to the first Christians was a gift for the benefit of the whole church, and therefore it
does not need to be repeated for every individual. Of course, in any
given generation the church may become blind to the wisdom of former
ages, and then it needs the special work of the Spirit to recall it to the
truth.

It is in this context that we can understand how non-Christian interpreters of the Bible may nevertheless be true interpreters of its message. Some three factors are at work. First, there is the operation of
what is sometimes called common grace, the activity of God's Spirit
which acts for the general good of mankind even when His presence is
not recognized or respected. To discuss this theme properly would
take us into some difficult territory; it is part of the general problem of
how unregenerate people can think and do things that are good and
loving apart from the regenerating work of the Spirit. There is no
doubt that there is such goodness in this world, and ultimately we
must attribute it to the gracious action of the Spirit of God. Included in
this gracious work is the general illumination of human minds to
understand something of the revelation of God.

Second, there is also the fact that non-Christians can read and benefit
from the writings of Christian scholars. They stand, as it were, on the
fringe of the church and hear what goes on in it, and they can profit
from what they hear and make good use of it. It would be wrong to
suggest that only Christians can possibly attain to true insights about
the meaning of Scripture. Those who stand on the fringe can sometimes
help those of us who are in the church to a better appreciation of the
truth in the Bible.

Third, a good deal of biblical interpretation involves the same kind
of technical skills and methods that are employed in the understanding

of any ancient text. The methods of textual criticism, for example, are the same for any text from the ancient world, and, for the most part, one does not need any special Christian insights to carry out the process. (There may of course be some cases where a sympathetic Christian understanding of the writer's intentions will greatly assist the scholar's judgment of what he is likely to have written or intended to convey to his readers.) Similarly, the study of the background to the Bible and a recognition of where this sheds light on the biblical story need not demand any special spiritual insight. In these areas the non-Christian scholar will have as much to contribute as the Christian, and a practicing Jew may shed as much light on the text as a Jewish Christian. We have learned to value the contributions of both an Alfred Edersheim and a David Daube. And indeed we also value the contributions of non-Christian scholars alongside those of liberal Christians and evangelical Christians. God alone knows whether some of the biblical scholars of the late nineteenth century were Christians in any recognizable sense of the term, but we can still turn to the writings of some of them with profit.

But we can quickly spot the dangers in this type of approach. We may observe, for example, how so much biblical study at the end of the last century and the beginning of this one degenerated into an arid study of literary sources and oral forms. Some critics appear to have thought that when they had divided up the Pentateuch or the Gospels into their sources they had done all that was necessary. Even Christian scholars were tempted to fall into the trap. Only in recent years has it been realized again that the Bible is a theological book with a theological message, and that the task of the biblical scholar and commentator is to spell out that theological message in all its rich variety. To see the Bible merely as a history book or as a quarry for source critics was to miss the whole point of it. N. Snaith, himself a "critical" scholar, wrote:

> Even the good order of J, E, D, and P may corrupt the scholarly world. We have been so very energetic in isolating each from other, and even within each, in separating stratum from stratum, that we have tended to forget that there might be method even in the madness which so thoroughly dovetailed them in together. Perhaps after all that madness was divine.[3]

The point is clear: the Bible must be understood and interpreted in line with its intended function, and that function is to lead people to God and a knowledge of His salvation. Put otherwise, we must recognize the intention of the author. If we believe that the author is God

Himself, inspiring human instruments by His Spirit, then this does make a difference to our understanding of the book. Surely the task of the Spirit is to lead us to recognize that the Bible is the Word of God and to interpret it accordingly. The task of the Spirit in biblical interpretation is thus to enable us to recognize the true character and purpose of the Bible and then to interpret the text in the light of this fact. The Author Himself comes to our side and helps us to understand what He has written. He gives us the eyes of faith and the mind of Christ so that we receive the message that God intends for us.

If so, we must read and study the Bible in a way which will allow the Spirit to guide and help us. Dr. Lane's example of praying to the Lord when confronted by difficult exegetical decisions applies to *all* of our reading of the Bible. As we open our minds to the Lord in prayer, so He will illumine them by the Spirit to understand the Word. Obviously this does not take away the need for our wrestling with the text, using all the tools of scholarship at our disposal. Nor does it mean that the Spirit-filled student will necessarily get higher marks in a biblical examination than one who scorns the Spirit's help. But it does mean that God will speak to us the message that He wants us to receive, and that He will use us to convey this message to other people.

Perhaps too it should be emphasized that a reliance on the Spirit will not necessarily save us from erroneous interpretations of Scripture. There are people who have claimed to be led by the Spirit who have promulgated shocking heresies. What went wrong? Did the Spirit mislead them? Is He not to be trusted? Or is it not rather the case that such people depended purely on what they conceived to be the Spirit's help and so landed themselves in a subjective approach? They failed to compare Scripture with Scripture and arrive at an understanding of particular passages which was consonant with the rest of Scripture, and they failed to listen to the voice of the Spirit as He spoke to other interpreters of Scripture within the fellowship of the Christian church over the centuries. In scriptural interpretation as in any other area, it is essential that we "test the spirits" (1 John 4:1). Spiritual guidance is not individualistic in character. If the gifts of the Spirit are given to individuals for the upbuilding of the church, so too the gifts given to different individuals must be exercised in conjunction with the gifts given to other believers. To sum up:

1. The Spirit acts in terms of God's "common grace" to enable men in general to have some understanding of the teaching of the Scriptures.
2. The work of the Spirit in enabling believers to understand the Scriptures is part of His general task of equipping them for God's

service, and the "psychology" of His action lies beyond our understanding.

3. The Spirit acts in believers in a general way when they use their minds to understand the Scripture, just as when they use their minds for any other purpose.

4. The Spirit operates especially in enabling us to apply the message of Scripture to our own lives and the lives of others. He enables us to reapply the Word which He originally gave to a particular group of recipients, and He enables us to believe and obey the Word in our situation.

5. The Spirit enables us to understand the Scripture by giving us the key to its interpretation, just as He gave the early church the insight that Jesus Christ is the key to the Old Testament. He shows us that the Bible contains a theological message and enables us to appreciate that message instead of seeing the Bible simply as a literary work or a history book.

6. The gift of interpretation is a gift to and for the church. The individual interpreter needs the insights which the Spirit has given to other Christians in order to interpret the Scriptures rightly.

7. The Spirit and the Word belong together. To rely solely on the Spirit and to fail to compare Scripture with Scripture leads to subjectivism and error in interpretation.

8. We cannot understand and apply the message of Scripture without the aid of the Spirit. "The man without the Spirit does not accept the things that come from the Spirit of God, for they are foolishness to him, and he cannot understand them, because they are spiritually discerned" (1 Cor. 2:14 NIV). "The god of this age has blinded the minds of unbelievers, so that they cannot see the light of the gospel of the glory of Christ, who is the image of God" (2 Cor. 4:4 NIV). We must, therefore, come to the study of the Scriptures praying the psalmist's prayer:

> Open my eyes, so that I may see
> the wonderful truths in your law (Ps. 119:18 TEV).

# SIX

# PREUNDERSTANDINGS
# AND THE INTERPRETER

William W. Klein, Craig L. Blomberg, and Robert L. Hubbard, Jr.

## A CHRISTIAN PREUNDERSTANDING

AS RESPONSIBLE INTERPRETERS we seek to employ whatever rational methods will enable us to understand the correct meaning of the biblical texts.[1] But when it comes to making judgments about the "theological" significance of those texts, we must go beyond our analytic methods. Though we share many of the critical methods of the secular historians, we do so with our own preunderstanding of the significance of the documents we are studying.

Secular historians may view the Bible only as a collection of ancient religious texts. To treat it as such—which often occurs in academia or among theologically liberal critics—cannot lead to valid conclusions about the religious value or significance of the Bible. The results are clearly "sterile." However, as authors we believe that the Bible is the divine word of God. Only from that stance can we use our historical and critical methods and arrive at theologically meaningful and pertinent results. Hirsch puts it forcefully: "An interpreter's notion of the type of meaning he confronts will powerfully influence his understanding of details."[2] We posit that our stance provides the best basis for a valid understanding of the biblical texts. Richardson makes this point succinctly,

> That perspective from which we see most clearly all the facts, without having to explain any of them away, will be a relatively true perspective. Christians believe that the perspective of biblical faith enables us to see very clearly and without distortion the biblical facts as they really are: they see the facts clearly because they see their true meaning.[3]

We are members of the evangelical community. We have committed ourselves to the faith understood by evangelicalism. This informs our preunderstanding and provides the boundaries for our reading of the Bible. Though we must always submit to the teachings of the Bible as our sole and final authority, our actual preunderstanding of the Bible as God's revelation guides our interpretation of its pages. We insist, as well, that our commitment to the authority of the Bible derives from our prior conviction of its truthfulness.

In a sense, our subsequent discussion of how to understand a text must be closely tied to this discussion of preunderstanding. A document consisting of words on a page remains an inert entity. What are ink and paper, after all? The significance we give to those words depends to a large extent upon us: what significance do we want to give to the words? The modern readers can do anything they please; no court of law restricts how texts can be used or abused. We must decide if we want to hear the words in terms of what they most likely meant at the time they were written, or whether we want to use, or handle, or employ them in other ways. The authors, editors, or communities that formulated the biblical texts obviously cannot contribute to the present process of interpretation. Nor can the first readers be consulted for their input. As ongoing debates in political circles about interpreting the U.S. Constitution illustrate, people today decide how they will use old documents.[4] The biblical texts or the creeds of the church may well claim inspiration for the Scriptures, but modern interpreters still decide how they will handle those claims. Are theology and Christian practice to be based upon what the biblical texts seem to communicate, upon the objectives, concerns, and agendas of the modern community that interpret those authors, or upon some combination of the two? Evangelicals may insist (correctly we believe) upon the primacy of the biblical affirmations; however, the history of interpretation clearly demonstrates the pervasive influence of the interpreter's agenda or preunderstanding.

Can we avoid being biased by our preunderstanding? Is there a way to critique and correct our preunderstanding when it so completely encompasses all that we are? If Christians are committed to being thoroughly biblical, then one solution is to subject our views to the scrutiny of Scripture. In other words, where beliefs and commitments derive from our culture and contradict or oppose biblical truth, we must identify them, and, somehow, specify and control their effects in the interpretive process.

What is the optimum Christian preunderstanding? We insist it should be one that derives from the set of presuppositions listed earlier in this chapter. Bernard Ramm agrees with our stance. He argues that the Bible has unique features that make one's interpretation of it different from the interpretation of other literature.[5] Christians must bring an understanding of these unique features to the process of constructing a hermeneutical system. These presuppositions form the basis of our preunderstanding of the task of interpreting the Bible. What are the unique features of the Bible that formulate our preunderstanding?[6]

1. First, we must recognize "*the spiritual factor*."[7] The full purpose of the Bible is realized only by the work of the Holy Spirit "who illuminates the mind and witnesses to the veracity of the divine verities."[8] Illumination does not provide data or information (the Holy Spirit does not provide further revelation to the interpreter) nor does illumination guarantee a correct understanding of the meaning of a passage. Ramm agrees that the ministry of the Spirit cannot replace careful analysis and sound exegesis, but it does assure that in conjunction with such diligence the believer can apprehend the significance and scope of God's revelation. The Scriptures themselves describe this scope: "All Scripture is given by God and is useful for teaching, for showing people what is wrong in their lives, for correcting faults, and for teaching how to live right. Using the Scriptures, the person who serves God will be capable, having all that is needed to do every good work" (2 Tim. 3:16–17 NCV).[9]

So the question is not whether a believer is biased, since all interpreters are biased, but, rather, does "the spiritual factor" irreparably bias the believer and thus prevent an objective and true understanding? Not necessarily. In fact, the opposite is true. Given the spiritual nature of the Bible, only a spiritual interpreter can accurately assimilate its contents. All others will simply miss the spiritual dimension— they may even ignore it altogether, whether consciously or unconsciously. Given the Christian presupposition of the Bible's inspiration, if the divine Spirit who inspired the Bible also enables believers to interpret it, then one could argue that they are *better* able to discern its true meaning![10] In fact, if the Bible informs correctly, God promised through the prophet Jeremiah that He would put His instruction in the minds and hearts of His covenant people (Jer. 31:33).

This "internal instruction" does not replace learning from the Bible, nor implementing the process of hermeneutics, but it does suggest that God's people occupy a unique position to grasp His message. Paul recognized that only a spiritual person possesses the capacity to apprehend spiritual truths (1 Cor. 2:15ff.). Commenting on this text Fee speaks of "the main concern of the entire passage, namely, that God's wisdom can be known only by God's people because they alone have the Spirit."[11] God's anointing has educative value (1 John 2:17). Concerning this latter verse, Smalley says: "So complete is the spiritual instruction which the true believer has received, John concludes that the need for temporal teaching is removed."[12] Of course, we must view this assertion in context. Smalley notes that in opposition to Gnostic teaching, John stresses that "the 'consecrated' Christian . . . has no need of (basic?) spiritual instruction. He is already 'set apart' for God's truth."[13] In other words, the believer occupies a privileged position to grasp and implement God's truth,

2. *The entire Bible*—the accepted canon—*is our inspired text* and object of study. As Ramm puts it, "The unity of Scripture and the harmony of Scripture is Jesus Christ and the redemption and revelation which centers in him."[14] That is, the church believes that both testaments constitute a Christian book, for the theme of salvation accomplished in Christ comprises its essential message.[15] The message of both testaments fits together. What the OT teaches finds fulfillment and completion in the NT. In no NT text do we discover any hint that Christians should jettison the OT.[16]

3. *God has revealed His message in the Bible progressively over time.* One cannot do justice to interpreting various sections of the Bible apart from recognizing and taking this factor into account. God meets people where He finds them and then, over time, develops and expands His purposes and program in the world and with His people. The Bible reflects this progression as the OT prepares for and, in some instances, gives way to the NT. Where the NT amends the significance or application of the OT in light of Jesus' coming, the NT takes precedence and becomes the glasses through which we view the OT.[17] In many instances the NT does not supplant or alter the OT, and in such places the pertinence of the OT remains. The book of Proverbs is a prime example of sage advice that transcends time and culture. Truth is truth, and we must carefully hear and understand *all* sections of the Bible—in *both* testaments. We must see how His purposes unfold over time and throughout His revelation in the Bible.

4. *The whole of Scripture* (its overriding message or teaching) *best interprets specific parts.* At the same time, we must derive our understanding of the whole from a careful study of the parts. Isolated texts cannot be construed to overturn well-established teaching. The parts and the whole comprise one piece. Ramm refers to "the self-interpretation of Scripture."[18] In other words, as the Reformers insisted in reaction to Roman Catholic teaching, Scripture—not the Catholic hierarchy—is its own best interpreter, particularly concerning its central teachings.

5. *Scripture's meaning is clear and plain.* The Bible is not a riddle or cryptogram whose meaning lies hidden and accessible only to a select few or the especially clever. This is not to imply that its meaning is simple or simplistic; indeed, it conveys the most profound ideas

and speaks to issues of ultimate significance and reality. Nor does it imply that all people will understand its message equally well or with identical comprehension. Yet God intends to convey His message to His people and, thus, has cast His words in forms that readily accomplish this purpose.

6. *The supernatural is affirmed in Scripture.*[19] In contrast to scientific naturalism that refuses to speak of the supernatural, we accept the potential reality of the supernatural. Though God does not "normally" contravene the natural laws of the universe, which He set up, He can, for His own sovereign purposes, act in ways that seem to us miraculous. Thus, when we encounter reports of the supernatural in the Bible, we accept them as credible and possible, provided they are true miracles. We reject the purely naturalistic explanation (or better, rejection) of the miraculous accounts in the Bible, which purports that they were written by gullible people in primitive times. If a supernatural God has acted in human history, we see no valid reason to reject the presence of the miraculous or the possibility that God's revelation would report such incidents.

7. *The Bible is a theological book.* Ramm puts it in terms of "theological exegesis."[20] He explains, "Theological exegesis extends grammatical exegesis in that theological exegesis is interested in the largest implications of the text."[21] The Christian interpreter does not simply want to explain the historical meaning of a text but also seeks to draw out its theological significance and implications for people today. . . .

## PREUNDERSTANDINGS CHANGE WITH UNDERSTANDING

Interpreters approach texts with questions, biases, and preunderstandings that emerge out of their personal situations. Inevitably, those preunderstandings influence the answers they obtain. However, the answers also then affect the interpreter: the text interprets the interpreter who becomes not only the subject interpreting but the object interpreted. Recall our African student with her preunderstanding about snow. Once she realized that snow fell from above, that it did not emerge out of the earth, she revised her understanding about this precipitation. In her adjusted understanding it fit in the same category as rain, rather than in the category of dew.

This scenario has led interpreters to speak of a hermeneutical circle, or better, a hermeneutical spiral.[22] Every interpreter begins with a preunderstanding. After an initial study of a biblical text, that text performs a work on the interpreter. His or her preunderstanding is no longer what it was. Then, as the newly interpreted interpreter proceeds to question the text further, out of this newly formed understanding further—perhaps, different—answers are obtained. A new understanding has emerged. It is not simply a repetitive circle; but, rather, a progressive spiral of development.

### HERMENEUTICAL SPIRAL

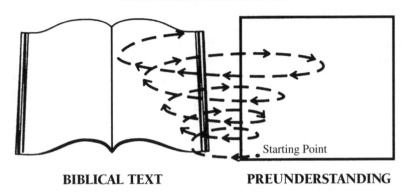

**BIBLICAL TEXT**                    **PREUNDERSTANDING**

Admittedly there is an inevitable circularity in interpretation. When we posit the requirement of faith to understand the Bible fully and then we go to the Bible in order to understand God's self-revelation in Christ in whom we have faith, the process has a definite circularity. But we argue simply that an appropriate level of preunderstanding is necessary for any kind of knowledge. This, as we have seen, is the nature of all inquiry. Thus, one must have some knowledge of God even to arrive at the preunderstanding of faith. Then that stance of faith enables the Christian to study the Bible to come to a deeper understanding of God and what the Scriptures say. As we learn more from our study of Scripture we alter and enlarge our preunderstanding in more or less fundamental ways. In essence, this process describes the nature of all learning: it is interactive, ongoing, and continuous. When believers study the Bible they interact with its texts (and with its Author), and, as a result, over time they enlarge their understanding.

### PREUNDERSTANDINGS AND
### OBJECTIVITY IN INTERPRETATION

Following such a discussion of preunderstanding, one may wonder if we are doomed to subjectivity in interpretation. Can we ever interpret the Bible in an objective fashion, or do we simply detect in its pages only what we want or are predisposed to see? Can we only say what is "true for me" and despair of finding truth that is universal or absolute? These questions hinge on the validity of our presupposition that the Bible communicates truth and constitutes God's revelation to us. If God has revealed truth in the Bible, then it seems reasonable also that He has made us capable of apprehending that truth, or at least some measure of it. Thus, though we inevitably bring preunderstandings to the texts we seek to interpret, this does not mean that we cannot apprehend the meaning they impart. Particularly if our goal is to discover the meaning the texts conveyed at the time they were written, we have some objective criteria to validate our interpretations.

Thus we refuse any charge that our view simply jettisons all inductive assessment of the facts or data of the text and its situation. Recognizing the role of our preunderstanding does not doom us to a closed circle—that we find in a text what we want to find in a text—though that looms as an ever-present danger. The honest, active interpreter remains open to change, even to a significant transformation of preunderstandings. This is the hermeneutical *spiral*. Since we accept the Bible's authority, we remain open to correction by its message. There are ways to verify interpretations or, at least, to validate some interpretive options as more likely than others. It is not a matter of simply throwing the dice. There is a wide variety of methods available to help us find what the original texts most likely meant to their initial readers. Every time we alter our preunderstanding as the result of our interaction with the text we demonstrate that the process has objective constraints, otherwise, no change would occur; we would remain forever entombed in our prior commitments.

W. Larkin makes the valid point that because God made people in His image they have the capacity to "transcend preunderstanding, evaluate it, and change it."[23] People are not so captive to their preconceptions that they cannot with conscious effort transcend them. One of the tactics, Larkin believes, that fosters the process of evaluating and transcending our preunderstanding as interpreters is to "seek out the definite and fixed meaning intended by the author of the text and to use Scripture as the final critical authority for judging extrabiblical thought-patterns."[24]

The hermeneutical spiral can be very positive as God through His Holy Spirit brings new and more adequate understanding of His truth and its application to believers' lives. If the Bible is true (and this takes us back to our presuppositions), then subscribing to its truth constitutes the most adequate starting point for interpreting its content. But alone that would be insufficient to comprehend the Bible. To understand the Bible's message adequately demands appropriate methodology and the willingness of interpreters to allow the Bible to alter or clarify their preunderstandings. The metaphor of a spiral suggests the most healthy approach to an adequate comprehension of the Bible. As Ferguson has said: ". . . all knowledge is elusive, and to grasp it demands a great deal of effort on our part, not the least of which is keeping a watchful eye on our own personal and societal forms of preunderstanding."[25]

# LANGAUGE AND MEANING

# SEVEN

# USING AND ABUSING LANGUAGE

### Moisés Silva

WE ALL LIKE TO THINK of ourselves as rational and astute human beings, especially if we are involved in an argument with somebody. Understandably, whenever we find ourselves losing ground in the dispute, we are ready to use our best weapon—indeed, the ultimate squelch—"You're being illogical!" Along with "That's just your interpretation" and other choice rejoinders, the complaint that our opponent is not logical can be simply a cheap shot.

That is not to deny that sometimes we may have good reason to suspect our opponent's powers of reasoning. It may well be, for example, that when we state, "That's just your interpretation," we have perceived that the other party is merely asserting an opinion and thus has confused the meaning of the text with one of the available interpretive options. It might be more productive (though we can hardly guarantee it!) to specify which other meanings seem reasonable and to point out that we should have persuasive grounds for choosing one over the others.

Similarly, there is greater likelihood of progress in a debate if, instead of throwing out a general allegation about an individual's logical lapse, we make an effort to identify the specific fallacy we have detected. Note the word *effort*. Most of us are lazy thinkers. We may be vaguely aware that an argument is weak, but we are not really prepared to say precisely how. Unfortunately, this problem is not restricted to personal arguments. The same questions arise when we read a biblical commentary, or even when we are pondering by ourselves what the point of a verse might be.

The goal of this chapter is to provide some help in the evaluation of arguments. We will not attempt to give a full treatment, since several excellent textbooks are available.[1] Moreover, our primary concerns do not correspond in every respect with those of the philosophical discipline we call logic but focus more narrowly on the use of language. The connections between logic and language are very close indeed, but we are less directly interested in the traditional concerns of philosophy than in the typical problems that arise when students of the Bible seek to figure out the meaning of the text and when they seek to defend their interpretation.

Since a large proportion of exegetical arguments are based on appeals to Greek and Hebrew, we shall need to pay special attention to the proper use of the biblical languages. We may begin by considering two opposite tendencies that often show up in the study of Scripture, namely, the minimizing and the overemphasizing of the original languages.

### DON'T MINIMIZE THE IMPORTANCE OF THE ORIGINAL LANGUAGES

For some Christians, hearing references to Greek or Hebrew can prove quite intimidating. The reason may be that they have received poor teaching, such as the view that the King James Version is inspired and is therefore all one needs. This is not a very "logical" position because it raises numerous unanswerable questions. How do we know that the KJV and not another translation is inspired? What did English speakers use before the KJV was produced in the seventeenth century? Does God inspire individual translations into each modern language? Besides, we can demonstrate that those who produced the KJV themselves had to translate from the original languages.

Other believers, realizing that no translation is infallible, have a more reasonable objection. It has to do with the biblical principle that we need no human intermediaries (whether priests or scholars) between ourselves and God. Jesus Christ is the only mediator (1 Tim. 2:5). If I have to depend on a specialist in languages to understand the Bible, don't I compromise this precious truth?

Part of the answer to this concern is to affirm without misgivings that the English translations available to us are indeed adequate. Even some of the versions that are not of the highest quality present quite clearly the basic message of the Gospel and the obedience God requires of us. We should never suggest that a person without a knowledge of Greek and Hebrew or without direct access to a scholar is in jeopardy of missing the essential truths of Scripture.

Let us never forget, however, that whenever we read an English translation, we are in fact recognizing, though indirectly, our dependence on scholarship. *Someone* had to learn the biblical languages and to make great efforts over a long period of time before English readers could make use of a translation they understand. Though the Scriptures affirm that we have direct access to God, the Scriptures also make clear that God has given teachers to His church (e.g., Eph. 4:11).

Surely there would be no point in having teachers if Christians never need guidance and instruction in their understanding of God's revelation. Scholars may not impose their views on the church, nor may they act as though they were the great depositories of truth, but the church must not forget how much it has benefited from their labors throughout the centuries.

In any case, it would be a great mistake to deny the importance of paying attention to the original languages. Some years ago, a minister was giving a midweek Bible study on Ephesians 4. Working from the KJV, he read verse 26, "Be angry and sin not." He then proceeded to affirm that this verse forbids anger in the life of a Christian.

It is understandable why this preacher felt compelled to interpret the verse in this way. After all, other passages in the Bible seem to condemn anger quite vigorously (e.g., Matt. 5:22), so he must have figured that the Ephesians passage could not mean something contrary to the rest of Scripture. His conclusion was that the word *not* applied to both verbs, *sin* and *be angry*. But this interpretation is not really possible. If there is any ambiguity for the modern reader, there is none in the original Greek, where the negative particle (which always affects the word that follows) comes after the verb for "be angry" and before the verb for "sin." Some further reflection on the biblical teaching about anger—including the fact that God Himself is sometimes portrayed as being angry (e.g., Rom. 1:18)—makes clear that this human emotion is not necessarily sinful in itself. What the apostle wants us to understand is that while there may be occasions when anger is appropriate, we cannot allow that anger to turn into an occasion for sin.

Midweek Bible teachers are not the only ones who occasionally misuse the Bible by failing to take into account the original languages. Scholars too can falter. One rather distinguished writer, who happens to be a proponent of so-called existentialist theology, has argued that the essence of being is a dynamic "letting-be." At a later point in his argument he remarks: "It is significant that the Bible does not begin by merely affirming God's existence but with his act of creation, which is the conferring of existence. His first utterance is: 'Let there be light!' and so begins the history of his letting-be."[2]

What the author of these words fails to tell the reader is that there is nothing in the Hebrew text of Genesis 1:3 that corresponds precisely to the English verb *let*. While Hebrew (as well as many other languages) has a specific verbal form for the third person imperative, English lacks such a form. English does have a second person imperative, such as "Come!" To express the imperative idea in the third person, however, we have to use other means, such as "John must come!" or "Let John come!" In the second example, the verb *let* does not have its usual meaning of "allow," nor does it have any supposed dynamic sense; rather, it functions merely as a helping verb to express the imperatival idea. In short, this theologian's appeal to the *English* rendering of Genesis 1:3 in support of his proposal has very little to commend it. Using the same line of argument, we could point to verse 11 ("let the land produce vegetation") and conclude that the Bible encourages us to speak about God's letting-produce.

More often than not (as these examples may suggest), some knowledge of the biblical languages proves its value in a negative way, that is, by helping us set aside invalid interpretations. This point becomes particularly significant when we realize that heretical views are often based on a misuse of the text. Some groups, especially the Jehovah's Witnesses, routinely appeal to the fact that in John 1:1c, "And the Word was God," the Greek term for God, *theos*, does not have the definite article, and so, they argue, it means either "a god" or "divine." Even a superficial knowledge of Greek, however, allows the student to note that in many passages that indisputably refer to the only God, the definite article is missing in Greek (even in John 1, see vv. 6 and 18). Students with a more advanced knowledge of the language will know that one of the ways Greek grammar distinguishes between the subject of the sentence (here "the Word," *ho logos*) and the predicate ("God," *theos*) is precisely by retaining the article with the former but omitting it with the latter.

But many features of the biblical languages also have a positive value for interpretation, particularly when the biblical author exploits one of those features for stylistic purposes. In Exodus 16:15, for instance, we are told that the Israelites, upon seeing the manna, asked what it was. Moses responded, "It is the bread the LORD has given you to eat." Now the last phrase may be translated literally, "for you for food." It is not a common expression, and an important Jewish scholar has suggested that it may be a subtle allusion to Genesis 1:29, where the same phrase is found.[3] If so, the writer of Exodus may want his readers to view the wilderness experience as a time of testing comparable to the testing of Adam and Eve. This interpretation could be supported contextually from Exodus 16:4 and Deuteronomy 8:2–3.

In the New Testament, no book uses allusions of this sort more frequently than the Gospel of John. One interesting possibility is 19:30, which describes Jesus' death with the expression "and gave up his spirit." It has been noted that the verb John uses here for "gave up" (*paredōken*, "handed over, delivered") is not the common word used in this type of context. Since the gospel has numerous references to Jesus' giving of the Holy Spirit to His disciples, some scholars have suggested that the expression here serves to recall that theme. It would be pressing things too much to suggest that the giving of the Spirit actually took place at that moment. More likely, John is reminding his readers that the dreadful event of the crucifixion is not a sign of failure. On the contrary, it is the "lifting up" of Jesus (3:14; 12:32), the time of His glorification, which makes possible the fulfillment of His promise (7:39).

This interpretation of the language of John would not be accepted by all. Indeed, the approach that looks too hard for subtle allusions of this sort often runs the danger of discovering things that are not there in the text. Later in this chapter we shall look at this hazard in more detail. Certainly, we should not place too much weight on such interpretations unless they can be confirmed by the context. Nevertheless, there are plenty of good examples where attention to these stylistic subtleties has helped interpreters shed new light on the text.

The conclusion to be drawn from this section is not that every Christian must attend seminary and become an expert in Greek and Hebrew. What we should keep in mind, however, is that the English versions *by themselves* cannot be the exclusive basis for formulating doctrine. In particular, we must be careful not to adopt *new* ideas if they have not been checked against the original text. Moreover, when there is a difference of opinion among students of the Bible, an attempt should be made to find out whether the Greek or the Hebrew sheds light on the debate. It is also worth pointing out, however, that ministers ought to gain some proficiency in the biblical languages if at all possible. Those who teach their congregations week after week and who must provide leadership in theological questions cannot afford to neglect such an important tool in their ministry.

## DON'T EXAGGERATE THE IMPORTANCE OF THE BIBLICAL LANGUAGES

In some respects, it is not possible to overemphasize the value of knowing Greek and Hebrew. Many students of the Bible, however, by shifting the focus of their attention, have indeed overstated the significance of these languages. As we suggested in the previous section, it would be most unfortunate to say that Christians who have access to the Bible only through their modern translations are unable to learn by themselves what God's message of salvation is. Seminary students have been known to give the impression that anyone unacquainted with the original languages must be a second-class Christian. And more than one scholar has seemed to argue, at least indirectly, that the church can say nothing that has not been cleared through the experts.

One common way of overemphasizing the biblical languages is by romanticizing them, by giving the impression that Greek and Hebrew have a unique (and almost divine?) status. For example, in the attempt to show the beauty of Hebrew, some writers look for peculiarities in the grammar that may support their contention. One very frequent illustration given is the fact that Hebrew has no neuter gender, a linguistic feature that is supposed to have some special significance.

While nouns in Greek may belong to one of three genders (masculine, feminine, and neuter), Hebrew nouns can be only masculine or feminine. Now abstract concepts are often expressed in Greek by means of the neuter gender, so some writers have inferred that the two facts are closely related. As one older textbook put it: "The Hebrew thought in pictures, and consequently his nouns are concrete and vivid. There is no such thing as neuter gender, for to the Semite everything is alive."[4]

A moment's reflection, however, should make clear that whether or not the Hebrews thought abstractly has little to do with the structure of their language. In English, for example, there is no gender distinction at all in nouns and adjectives (only in the personal pronouns). Does that fact say anything at all about an English speaker's ability or disposition to think abstractly? It is true that the special interests of a community are sometimes hinted at in its language, particularly the vocabulary. But if we want to know what a group of people really thinks or believes, we should look at the *statements* made, not at the grammatical structure of the language used.

Part of the problem here is that we tend to transfer the qualities of what people say to the medium they use to say it. That is especially true of Greek, a language that has received a great deal of attention. In fact, Greek has been romanticized to extremes. Charles Briggs, a very notable biblical scholar in the last century, put it this way: "The Greek language is the beautiful flower, the elegant jewel, the most finished masterpiece of Indo-Germanic thought." In describing classical Greek, Briggs uses such terms as *complex, artistic, beautiful, finished, strong*, and *vigorous*. He then adds: "Its syntax is organized on the most perfect system. . . . . [the Greek language] wrestles with the mind, it parries and thrusts, it conquers as an armed host." Later, when God chose Greek to convey the message of the Gospel, this language was "employed by the Spirit of God, and transformed and transfigured, yes, glorified, with a light and sacredness that the classic literature never possessed."[5]

We should keep in mind that this viewpoint was in part influenced by the opinion—very common in the nineteenth century—that the classical languages, Greek and Latin, were inherently superior to others. This opinion, in turn, was related to the emphasis that linguists in that century placed on the comparative and historical study of languages. During the twentieth century, however, scholars have made intensive studies of languages spoken in "primitive" cultures, such as the Indians of North and South America, African tribes, and other groups. The very grammatical features that used to be associated with the alleged superiority of the classical languages (e.g., a complex verbal system) turn out to be present to an even greater degree in the "primitive" ones.

The greatness of Greek civilization is not to be equated with the grammatical system of its language. It is what people did with the language rather than the language itself that deserves admiration. Interestingly, the form of Greek used by the New Testament writers is simpler than that used by the great writers of the earlier, classical period. For example, New Testament Greek contains fewer "irregular" forms, and the word order of the sentences is less involved. One of its most distinctive features, in fact, is that it approximates the language used commonly by the people in their daily conversation.

Such facts do not disprove the beauty of the biblical languages. To some extent, this is a matter of personal taste, and the authors of this textbook happen to believe that Hebrew and Greek are about as beautiful as they come! Nor do we need to deny that the powerful message of the Gospel had a significant impact on Greek, particularly its vocabulary.

In the end, however, we must not confuse the divine message itself with the human means God used to proclaim it. This issue has clear relevance to the topic of biblical interpretation. Some of the fallacies that we shall look at in the rest of this chapter have arisen because of the exaggerated importance attached to human linguistic systems (Hebrew and especially Greek). The biblical authors did not write in a mysterious or coded speech. Under inspiration, they used their daily language in a normal way.

## DON'T EQUATE THE MEANING OF
## A WORD WITH ITS HISTORY

Perhaps the most common error one comes across in discussions involving language (and particularly the biblical languages) is the tendency to misuse the study of *etymology*, that is, the origin and development of words. One important reason behind this problem is the inherent interest of the subject. No doubt about it, etymological information can prove to be simply fascinating. I vividly recall from my college days a sermon on the theme of sincerity. To help his audience understand the concept, the speaker appealed to the etymology of the English word *sincere*. It comes, he told us, from the two Latin words *sine cera*, "without wax." The terminology was used to describe statues that, one might say, could be trusted: wax had not been used to cover up defects.

It is important to note that, *as an illustration*, this piece of information was quite effective. The thought was almost captivating, and it helped us see the virtue of sincerity in a new light. The danger, however, lies in the possible inference that the Latin origin of the English word sincere actually corresponds to the meaning of the word today. The fact is that, when English speakers use this word, wax and statues are the furthest thing from their mind. For that matter, the meaning "pure" or "unadulterated" for this word is now archaic. When shakers use the word, the meaning they seek to convey is simply "true" or "honest."

But the problems run even deeper. The transference from the physical (literal wax) to the figurative may have been accidental or trivial. Such a shift in meaning would not necessarily prove that anyone understood the virtue of sincerity with reference to the selling of nondefective statues. And even if someone did, why should we adopt that person's understanding of sincerity? Moreover, the Bible was not written in Latin, and so the association with statues could not have been part of the meaning the New Testament authors had in mind.

As if all that were not enough, a brief check of etymological dictionaries of English quickly reveals that there is no certainty whatever that English *sincere* comes from Latin *sine cera!* And some scholars who believe there is such a connection suspect that the real setting was the description, not of statues, but of honey. Etymological reconstructions are often tentative and sometimes purely imaginary. Some thinkers have nevertheless been known to develop great conceptual edifices based on such reconstructions. Very influential, particularly among existentialist philosophers, has been the supposed etymology of the Greek word for "truth," *alētheia*. It is possible that this word was formed by combining the negative particle *a-* with the verb *lanthanō*, "hide," and that possibility is alleged to show that the real significance of truth is "unhiddenness."[6] But this etymology is debatable, and even if it were not, we could not prove that it reflects a philosophical view of truth—much less would it prove that such a view is correct!

One of the unfortunate results of appealing to etymology is that it lends to the argument a scientific tone and makes the speaker's position sound much more authoritative than it really is. Some writers, aware of the tentativeness of their etymological arguments, but unable to resist the temptation of using them anyway, include a "perhaps" or some other qualification, but most readers are unduly influenced by the arguments and end up accepting the conclusion, even though no real evidence has been presented.

The best way to illustrate this point is to make up a few outrageous examples:

I have mistrusted ranchers ever since I met a few who seemed mentally unbalanced. It is probably not a pure accident that English *ranch* (< rank < Old French *reng* < Indo-European *sker*) is etymologically related to *deranged*.

Christians should be optimists. We should keep in mind that the word *pessimist* comes from the Latin word for "foot," *pes*. Because we stumble with our feet, we find the related verb *peccare*, "sin," and the English cognate *pecadillo*. We may perhaps describe pessimists as people who are in the habit of committing little sins.

In our religious group we do not believe in having ministers. The word *clergy* (from Indo-European *kel* "to strike") is related to *calamity* (< Latin, "a severe blow"). Not surprisingly, clergy throughout the centuries have abused their power and hurt people.

Dancing is surely forbidden to Christians. Isn't it suggestive that the word *ballet* comes from Greek *ballō*, which is also the origin of *diabolos*, "devil"?[7]

The possibilities are endless! Apart from their outlandish content, the type of argument (i.e., the logic) exemplified in these four observations is exceedingly common. And precisely because this logic is most often used to make points that are not ludicrous and seem otherwise plausible, many people are persuaded by it, even though as a rule no substantive evidence accompanies it.

In biblical commentaries and other serious works, one also comes across etymological comments that usually shed no real light on the meaning of the text. It is common, for example, for writers to comment that the Hebrew word translated "glory," *kabōd*, basically means "weight, heaviness." (Incidentally, the words *basic* and *basically*, when applied to word meaning, are exceedingly ambiguous and are usually—and wrongly—taken to imply something like the "real" or "essential" meaning.) In this case, the connection cannot be doubted, and one can easily see how the notion of "weight" can be related to that of "importance" and thence to the more specific meaning when used in reference to God. While this historical development of the word is accurate and interesting, does it genuinely enhance our understanding of the word (or even the concept behind the word) in passages that speak of God's awesome manifestations? Most doubtful—unless we have good *contextual* reason to think that the biblical author himself was associating this word with the concept of weight.

This problem shows up even more frequently in New Testament studies, since many compound Greek words are relatively "transparent," that is, one can easily see which words have been combined into one. One of the most common examples is the verb *hypomenō* ("be patient"), which is made up of the preposition *hypo*, "under," and the verb *menō*, "remain." Preachers will frequently remark that the Greek word *really means* "to stay under" and then proceed to describe someone carrying a heavy burden for a prolonged period of time.

As an illustration, that imagery may prove useful, but it is highly questionable whether it brings us any closer to the meaning intended by the biblical author. We need to keep in mind that figurative language quickly loses its freshness, a process that results in many "dead metaphors." Consider the English word *understand*. Would it help a foreign student to be told that this word comes from *stand* and *under* (though most English speakers themselves are normally conscious of this fact) and that it was originally a figure of speech (though we cannot tell precisely how the new meaning developed)? The figurative etymology of the word is, in fact, quite irrelevant to modern speakers, *since what they mean can be made perfectly clear without a knowledge of the word's origins.*

Of course, one must always keep open the possibility that a biblical writer has deliberately exploited the history (or other associations) of a word. Such a literary technique is more frequently found in poetry than it is in prose. But the only way to determine whether the author has done so is to pay close attention to the context. We cannot presume that an author would necessarily have been aware of a word's etymology. And if he was, we cannot assume, without some evidence, that he intended his readers to grasp the connection. About the only evidence available to us, we must emphasize again, is the context, the thrust of a passage (or even the book) as a whole. With very few exceptions, we will find that the context supports the common usage of a word rather than unfamiliar senses.

### DON'T READ THE VARIOUS MEANINGS
### OF A WORD INTO A SPECIFIC USE

Students are often advised to check how a particular word is used throughout the Scriptures. Even Christians who have not learned the biblical languages can use certain concordances (as well as other tools) that are keyed to the Greek and Hebrew terms. In principle, the advice is sound, for such a method helps us to determine the "semantic range" of the word in question; that is, if we are aware of the possible uses of

a word, *we are in a better position to decide which specific use* occurs
in the passage or passages that we are studying.

The words italicized in the previous paragraph highlight the proper
aim of such a word study. In practice, however, students often ignore
that very aspect. What happens, instead, is that the whole complex of
meanings is injected into one passage. Usually, this takes place in a
subtle way. Even a responsible commentator, hoping to shed light on a
word, may inform the reader that the word in question is used in a
variety of ways in the New Testament. There will follow a list of those
uses, including quotations of various passages, with the implication
that all of them in some way contribute to the meaning of the word in
the verse being analyzed.

From time to time one comes across more glaring misuses of the
method. A successful preacher once speaking on Hebrews 12 focused
attention on one specific word in that chapter and told his congregation that the word had four meanings. On that basis he had produced a
four-point outline that led to four sermonettes with four different texts,
even though ostensibly he intended to expound on Hebrews 12.

If we reflect for a few moments on our own language, however, we
can appreciate how such an approach succeeds only in distorting meaning. Suppose that an Asian tourist comes across this sentence: "The
patient had an acute pain in her knee." This foreigner is not familiar
with the word *acute* and asks us what it means, so we respond:

> In geometry, the word is used of angles less than 90 degrees, while in
> music it may indicate a high-pitched sound. It also is used to describe
> an accent mark in some languages and scripts. In objects it indicates a
> sharp point. The word can be used as a synonym for "keen, discerning,
> shrewd." Things of great importance can be said to be *acute*. In medi-
> cine, it may describe a disease that is approaching a crisis. Finally, the
> word can mean "severe."

Such a disquisition may prove very interesting and informative, but
to understand the sentence in question, the foreigner needed merely
the last word. The only other meaning that might shed any light on the
subject is that of "sharp," since an acute pain is one that is often
likened to the sensation of being hurt with a pointed object. Most
words in any language have a variety of meanings, but as a rule the
context automatically and effectively suppresses all the meanings that
are not appropriate, so that the hearers and readers do not even think
of them.

The matter gets more complicated when we consider whether certain associations may be present in a particular sentence (cf. above the

examples from Exodus 16 and from John 19). It is not always easy to decide this question. If we read in a magazine that "the disagreement among the scholars was acute," we will quickly take the meaning to be "intense, severe," but are we influenced by the frequent combination *acute pain*, so that we deduce, consciously or unconsciously, that the scholars in question were undergoing a painful experience? Is it also possible that, since the people involved are scholars, the meaning "keen, discerning" affects us? Perhaps and perhaps not. It would surely be precarious, however, to come up with interpretations based on what is only a theoretical possibility (unless supported by strong contextual evidence).

While this section has focused on the vocabulary, we should note a related problem when appealing to grammatical facts. In a recent article dealing with the difficult passage on women in 1 Timothy 2, the author has this to say with regard to verse 12 ("I do not permit a woman to teach"):

> In order to gain insight into the meaning of this instruction we may find help in an examination of the verbs in our text. This is the third instance in chapter two of Timothy of a first-person singular verb. First Timothy 2:8 began with the first person, "I want the men in every place to pray." The same verb is implied in verse 9 where the author addresses the women—"(I want) women to make themselves attractive." Now in verse 12 we have first person verb—"I do not permit." In the Greek language there are nine different uses of the present tense. [Here, one of the standard grammars is footnoted.] According to P. B. Payne the first-person present of the verb can be used to indicate temporary restriction. With that sense of the verb a time restriction comes into play. Until women have learned what they need in order to get a full grasp of the true teaching, they are not to teach or have authority over men. There is no reason these women might not later be allowed to teach and have authority (like Phoebe, Prisca, and Junia) if they will learn the true teaching, submitting to Timothy for instruction.[8]

The first part of this paragraph is in fact irrelevant to the author's point. (If anything, it undermines that point, since the verb in verse 8 certainly has no temporal restriction.) From time to time one comes across discussions of biblical texts that appeal to the original languages perhaps only to make an impression; readers need to be discerning whether something substantive is in fact being argued. Our main concern, however, is with the second half of the paragraph, which does contain a substantive argument on the basis of Greek grammar. For our present purposes, we need not determine whether the verb in verse 12 has a temporal restriction; the question, rather, is whether the appeal to the Greek is cogent.

The logic of this author is simply to look for the various attested uses or meanings of the present tense, then choose one that fits that author's understanding of the passage. This approach is not exactly the one that we have already discussed; in the present case the interpreter has not read all of the meanings into one specific occurrence. The problem is similar, however, since the interpreter's decision (as far as we can tell) was merely based on a range of uses and was not controlled by the context. At the very least, we must say that the interpreter *did not offer a contextual reason* for choosing the temporally restricted function of the Greek present tense.

## DON'T OVEREMPHASIZE SUBTLE POINTS
## OF GRAMMAR AND VOCABULARY

The view that the biblical languages—Greek in particular—are uniquely rich or precise has led many students to rely heavily on distinctions of various sorts. Very common is the tendency to look for differences among synonyms as a key to the interpretation of passages. It cannot be doubted, for example, that the several Hebrew words used in reference to sin have distinctive meanings (comparable to the differences in such English words as *sin, wickedness, evil, transgression*, etc.). Any careful study of Old Testament texts that contain these words requires some attention to the distinctions, and a slipshod approach to word use is inexcusable.

We can never forget, however, that writers often use a diverse vocabulary for simple reasons of style, such as a desire to avoid repetition. In these cases, we may say that the differences among the words are "neutralized" by the context. Even when an author makes a lexical choice for semantic (rather than stylistic) reasons, it does not follow that our interpretation stands or falls on our ability to determine precisely why one word was chosen rather than another. After all, people normally communicate not by uttering isolated words but by speaking whole sentences.

Important as words are, what really matters, then, is how those words have been combined by the speaker. Since the focus of meaning is therefore the sentence (or even the paragraph), the specific force of any one word depends to a large extent on the broader context. That is not to deny that individual words have a stable range of meanings—after all, without such stability communication would be impossible. It is useful to think of the relationship between word and sentence as a reciprocal one. The word makes a contribution to the meaning of the whole sentence, but the sentence as a whole also contributes to the specific meaning of the word.

We could even say that languages have a built-in system of redundancy. This feature makes it possible for us to understand some sentences even if a sneeze or some other noise keeps us from hearing one or two words. (Similarly, we do not necessarily fail to grasp the total meaning of a sermon if our mind wanders for a couple of minutes.) Consider how your English vocabulary continues to grow whether or not you look up words in the dictionary. Consciously or unconsciously, you learn the meaning of new words simply by hearing them used in specific sentences, since the sentences as a whole supply that meaning for the hearer.

If that is the way language works, we should infer that subtle lexical distinctions play only a secondary role in interpretation. How many writers are likely to throw all their eggs into one basket and hope that the readers catch the one small distinction that determines the meaning of the whole sentence? One cannot deny, for example, that there are some distinctions between the two Greek verbs for love, *agapaō* and *phileō*. It is less clear, however, whether these distinctions are reflected, say, in the interchange between Jesus and Peter recorded in John 21:15–17. The NIV translators must have thought so, since they translated the former verb (found in Jesus' question) with the words "truly love," while the latter (used by Peter in his response) is translated simply "love." Such a distinction is highly debatable. To mention only one problem, the latter verb is used of the Father's love for the Son in 5:20. But even if the distinction could be sustained, is it reasonable to think that the proper understanding of the passage hangs on our ability to discover such a faint contrast? A solid interpretation should be built on much broader evidence than that.

We may say, generally speaking, that the greater the weight placed on distinctions among synonyms, the more likely it is that such distinctions are being overstated. For example, the Greek verbs *oida* and *ginōskō* can both be translated "know." The most frequently suggested distinction between these verbs is that the latter can more easily be used in contexts that deal with the acquisition of knowledge. Accordingly, *oida* is often found where such acquisition is not in view, but that leaves innumerable contexts where the verbs could be used interchangeably. In spite of that, some scholars proceed to argue that *ginōskō* refers specifically to experiential knowledge, that is, something acquired by experience as opposed to innate or intuitive knowledge. This claim, though plausible, is at best tentative and does not fully take into account the many passages where such a distinction is not present. Those who accept it, however, sometimes go further and suggest that *oida* indicates greater assurance, simply because it is found in some contexts (e.g., Rom. 8:28) that speak of assurance. Others even argue that it reflects divine knowledge.

If there is danger in overstating lexical distinctions, what shall we say about grammatical ones? Think of it this way: when was the last time that you felt you did not understand an English sentence because you could not decide why the speaker chose a simple present tense (e.g., "How do you feel?") rather than a progressive tense ("How are you feeling?")? With rare exceptions, those kinds of decisions are made not on the basis of careful deliberation but more or less automatically. And even when we deliberate about some grammatical choices, that is usually because we are concerned about "proper" English, not because the meaning will be substantially different (e.g., "After he left, the problems began" means the same as the more formal expression, "After he *had left*, the problems began").

When it comes to the Greek New Testament, however, students spend a great deal of effort trying to interpret grammatical subtleties. Consider Hebrews 1:2: "In these last days he has spoken to us by his Son." The last three words translate two Greek words, *en huiō*, literally, "in son." Now it turns out that the use of the definite article in Greek does not correspond exactly with that of English *the*. One of the differences has to do with the omission of the Greek article when we, because of our English habits, expect to see the article. In some instances, the omission may reflect the possibility that the writer's focus is less on the identity of the object than on its quality.

The distinction is barely perceptible (in some passages not at all) and cannot be reproduced in English. When people try to convey the idea, they end up exaggerating (e.g., with such a paraphrase as "in someone who is by nature a son"). One popular expositor waxes mystical: "Again we feel the poverty of English idiom, and must translate, 'His Son,' or 'a Son.' But if we say over and over to ourselves the very words, *God did speak unto us in Son*, our hearts will feel the meaning, though our words cannot translate."[9] In fact, the presence or absence of the article here does not alter the meaning of the clause. It was a stylistic choice that the original readers of the epistle (and perhaps even the writer!) possibly would not have been able to account for in a satisfactory way.

The most common misuse of grammatical subtlety has to do with the Greek tenses. Part of the reason is that the Greek verbal system includes a tense form that has been labeled *aorist*. Since the term is not used when describing English, it conveys a quasi-esoteric feeling and encourages overinterpretation. Another reason is the fact that Greek verbs expoit "aspectual" distinctions more frequently that English verbs do. The distinction between the English simple past tense ("I ate") and the imperfect ("I was eating") is an aspectual one and corresponds more or less to a similar distinction in Greek. In addition, however,

Greek maintains the distinction in the nonindicative moods, such as the imperative, and that fact creates problems for the English student.

The aorist tense (or better, aspect) was given its name by ancient Greek grammarians who recognized that there was something indefinite about it (the Greek word *aoristos* means "undefined"). Curiously, many New Testament interpreters view it as special in some sense and greatly exaggerate its significance. One of the commentary sets most frequently used by students of the Greek New Testament abounds in this tendency. For example, on Philippians 2:15, "so that you may become blameless," this commentator interprets the aorist verb to mean "may definitely and permanently be." And on Revelation 2:5, "Repent and do the things you did at first," he says that the "two imperatives are ringing, peremptory aorists: 'and repent (completely) and do (decisively) the first works!' as was done in the first love during the days gone by."[10]

In certain cases the choice of aspect (or some other grammatical detail) by a Greek author perhaps contributes somewhat to a meaning that is otherwise clearly expressed in the context. If so, the grammar is at best a secondary support to the interpretation of the passage. However, if a proposed meaning cannot be established apart from an appeal to a grammatical subtlety, chances are that the argument is worthless. The biblical writers were clear and explicit and did not expect their readers to have to decipher complicated linguistic riddles. In any case, lay students of Scripture should not be swayed too easily by an "expert" who tries to persuade them through technical argumentation of this sort.

## SUMMARY

Although the principles discussed in this chapter consist of "don'ts," it should be evident that all of them imply positive guidelines. We may summarize these guidelines by rephrasing them:

1. *Do recognize the significance of the biblical languages for proper interpretation.* Attempt to become familiar with Greek and Hebrew. If that is not possible, accustom yourself to the notion that there is a linguistic and cultural distance that separates us from the biblical text. While this distance should not be exaggerated, beware of reading into the Bible ideas that can be supported only from the English translation.

2. *Do keep in mind that English translations are reliable for most purposes.* While we should be grateful for specialists who can help us with details and ambiguities, it is important to remember that the teaching of Scripture as a whole is readily accessible to all believers.

3. *Do place priority on the attested and contemporary usage of*

*words*. While the origins and development of a word may be interesting, writers depend on the way language is actually used in their time. Normally, proposed meanings are valid only if they can be confirmed by references contemporaneous with the text.

4. *Do focus on specific uses in context*. Being aware of a word's broad range of meaning can be useful as a basis for making a choice, but we must remember that (aside from puns and other types of rare allusions) meanings other than the one specified by the context do not normally occur to the speaker and the audience.

5. *Do emphasize the context*. This is the fundamental principle. It is in fact the guideline that undergirds all of the others. For example, the reason we do not have to be slavishly dependent on scholars is that the broad context of Scripture can be understood without a knowledge of technical details. Before tackling a specific problem in one verse, we ought to read and reread the whole chapter—indeed, the whole book of which it is a part. Surely, constant reading of the Scriptures in their totality is the best prescription for handling the Word aright.

# EIGHT

# FIGURES OF SPEECH

## Grant R. Osborne

FIGURATIVE EXPRESSIONS traditionally have been discussed in a topical section labeled "special hermeneutics," which included such diverse topics as language (metaphor, simile), genre (prophecy, parable) and theology. I believe, however, that this is artificial and prefer to deal with these linguistic elements logically in accordance with the developing structure of hermeneutical criteria. Figures of speech contain both grammatical and semantic aspects (as we will see) and so are properly discussed as a specific section of syntactical analysis.

Figures of speech form the third level of the "multiple senses" of meaning, following the primary or most common meaning and the secondary or less common uses of the semantic range. Figurative expressions associate a concept with a pictorial or analogous representation of its meaning in order to add richness to the statement. Literal meaning comprises the first two levels and identifies the basic thrust of a term. A "roof," for instance, is the cover over a house or other structure. A figure of speech concerns an associative relation between senses, such as the "roof" of one's mouth.

The Bible constantly employs colorful imagery drawn from a multitude of experiences. Business terminology is used to depict discipleship ("steward," "servant," "husbandman"), and domestic affairs describe the relationship between God and His people ("groom-bride," "father-child").[1] In fact, a knowledge of customs and culture is necessary in order to understand many of the images adduced. For instance, the "scroll written on both sides, sealed with seven seals" (Rev. 5:1) is built upon either the Roman last will and testament (which was sealed with seven seals) containing the inheritance of the saints or the Roman doubly inscribed contract deed containing blessings and curses (my preference). Either will fit the word picture, but the modern reader could not possibly know the options without a knowledge of ancient customs. Yet the symbolism behind Revelation 5–6 is greatly enhanced by uncovering such background information.

Beekman and Callow describe two major groups of figurative or associative senses.[2] Contiguous relationships between words are built upon proximity or nearness of meaning. This group has three types: (1) In temporal associations, a time-note replaces an event, as in the technical "day of the Lord," which refers not just to the parousia itself but to all the events of the "last days." In another sense Jesus said, "Abraham rejoiced to see my day" (John 8:56), referring to the Incarnation. (2) Spatial relations utilize local ideas, as when "heaven" is used for God (Matt. 21:25, "was the baptism of John from heaven or men?"). In Ephesians (1:3, 20; 2:6; 3:10; 6:12) "the heavenlies" speaks of the spiritual realm where the cosmic conflict is fought.[3] (3) Logical or cause-effect relations substitute the cause for the effect or vice versa. For instance, the "hand of the Lord" (cause) refers to judgment and the "sword" to persecution and division (Matt. 10:34), to discipline (Rom. 13:4) or to conviction (Heb. 4:12).

There are also three types of part-whole associations: (1) In member-class relations, a specific member stands for the generic whole. One of the best-known examples is "Give us this day our daily bread" (Matt. 6:11), where the "bread" refers to all the believer's needs, physical and spiritual. The beatitude on those who "hunger and thirst after righteousness" (Matt. 5:45) represents the class of intense desires by the single metaphor of hunger-thirst. (2) In constituent-whole relations, a single part of a larger structure stands for the whole, such as "roof" for house (Matt. 8:8) or "three thousand souls" for people converted to Christianity (Acts 2:41). (3) Attribute-whole relations occur when the traits or purposes of a thing are used for the thing itself. An interesting example is "serpent," which is used negatively in "You serpents, you generation of vipers" (Matt. 23:33) but positively in "wise like serpents" (Matt. 10:16). Two different traits associated with snakes are obviously intended in the disparate passages.

The major difficulty in interpreting figures of speech is that languages develop their associative relations independently; therefore, metaphorical language in Hebrew or Greek often does not correspond at all to English expressions. Of course this is similar to differences between modern languages.[4] It is a problem in semantics and must be investigated at that level.

When the original language employs an idiom or figurative expression, it can be translated in three possible ways: (1) If the figure of speech is paralleled in the receptor language, we can translate directly. This situation occurs more frequently in Western languages due to the impact of Christianity upon our culture and thus upon the development of our languages (for example, the influence of Luther's translation of the Bible upon modern German). Expressions like "the Lord saves his anointed" (Ps. 20:6) or "they began to speak in other tongues" (Acts 2:4) are easily understood (though in many other languages this may not be true). (2) If the transfer of meaning is not automatic, but there is still a slight correspondence, the term itself may be retained but a clarification added to clear up any ambiguity. At times Scripture itself does this, such as "dead in their trespasses and sins" (Eph. 2:1; compare Rom. 6:11, "dead to sin"). However, we will often have to add the clarification ourselves, such as "the hour is at hand" (Matt. 26:45) = "the time when I must die is near." (3) If there is no correspondence at all between the original and the receptor language, the figure of speech will be replaced by a corresponding idiom. Beekman and Callow specifically mention euphemistic expressions for death, sex, God and the Gentiles here. An obvious example would be the frequent use of "he knew his wife," which must be translated "he had sexual relations with his wife." This idiom in Matthew 1:25 is translated "did not know her" in the New King James and "he had no union with his wife" in the New International Version.

The solution is to back transform the biblical figure of speech into the appropriate "kernel" and then to forward transform it into the proper equivalent in the receptor language, allowing the needs of the audience to decide which of the three is best in a given situation. Indeed, this is why there cannot be any final or universal translation of the Scriptures into English or any other language. Not only does the language change from year to year; it differs radically from locality to locality. In England or Germany a person's home can be pinpointed to the very village or town by the dialect spoken. Every hamlet favors its own set of idiomatic expressions. The preacher must be sensitive to translate the Word afresh for each audience.

There is enormous tensive power in figurative language to evoke fresh images in the mind of the learner. Ricoeur's discussion of metaphor (which includes all figures of speech) is helpful here.[5] He argues that figurative expressions operate not so much at the level of semantics but in the broader sphere of discourse or communication. A metaphor sets up a state of tension between the literal and figurative meanings of the word, which causes the former to "self-destruct" "in a significant contradiction."[6] Ricoeur means that a figurative expression is a deliberate choice on the part of an author who uses it to force the readers into a new awareness of the message. At first, the readers are jarred by the incongruity of the thought, for normal literal meanings do not fit. They are led to a new word picture of reality and forced to rethink the categories of the proposition stated.[7] A new world of discourse is fashioned, and the reader is drawn into it.

Of course, the value of this new vision of reality depends entirely upon a correspondence between the author's and the reader's worlds of experience. This could not be assumed even in biblical times. Paul was frequently misunderstood and himself made cultural gaffes (the Lycaonians in Acts 14:8–18). The problem becomes even greater with the passing of the centuries; if metaphors are as central to the process of speech communication as Ricoeur argues, the necessity of translating them properly for our audiences becomes even greater. This sense of the importance of our topic will guide our discussion in the ensuing pages.

While some have attempted a new linguistic organization of the various figures of speech (see Eugene Nida, et al., *Style and Discourse* [New York: Bible Society, 1983], 172–87), I feel that the traditional pattern (Bullinger, Mickelsen, Kaiser and others) still makes the best sense. There are six basic types—comparison, addition, incompleteness, contrast, personal figures and association or relation. It is helpful to note the specific type of figurative expression used in a context because that will provide important hermeneutical data for interpreting the statement more precisely. Many passages remain obscure until the figurative language is isolated and understood.

## FIGURES OF COMPARISON

Two figures, metaphor and simile, deal with direct comparisons between items. A simile establishes a formal comparison employing connective terms such as "like" or "as." Similes are used often in Proverbs; for instance, "When calamity overtakes you like a storm, when disaster sweeps over you like a whirlwind" (1:27) or "Free yourself, like a gazelle from the hand of a hunter, like a bird from the snares of the fowler" (6:5). Jesus also used similes constantly, and they function in much the same way as His parables, which have rightfully been called extended similes ("the Kingdom of God is like . . .") or metaphors. They add poignant meaning to His statements, as in "How often I wanted to gather together your children as a hen gathers under her wings her chicks, but you refused" (Matt. 23:27). The interpreter should not hurry past such vivid images, for they are built upon the very patterns of life experienced in ancient times and had great power in their original settings. Jesus could hardly have conveyed better the contrast between His living concern and Jewish obduracy than in the Matthew 23:27 simile.

A metaphor is an implied, but in many ways even more direct, comparison because the reader is expected to identify the comparison without the "like" or "as"; for instance, "You are a shield around me, O Lord" (Ps. 3:3). There are two types of comparison.[8] A full or complete comparison states both items and the similarity between them.

The two may be contrasted directly ("I am weak but he is strong") or by degree ("he is stronger than I"). The resemblance may be relative ("I am strong and so is he") or absolute ("I am as strong as he"). An abbreviated comparison leaves the similarity implicit and the reader has to supply it, as in "You are the salt of the earth" (Matt. 5:13, metaphor) or "His eyes were like a flame of fire" (Rev. 1:14, simile). At other times the object of the image is unstated, as in "his sheep will be scattered" (Mark 14:27).

A metaphor or simile has three parts: the topic or item illustrated by the image, the image itself, and the point of similarity or comparison (the actual meaning of the metaphor or simile in the passage). Often all three are present in a comparison; for example, "The heavens [topic] shall vanish [point of comparison] like smoke [image]" (Isa. 51:6) or "Go rather to the lost [point of comparison] sheep [image] of the house of Israel [topic]" (Matt. 10:6). As Beekman and Callow point out, one or more of these can be missing and therefore must be supplied by the interpreter (1974, 128–31). The topic may be implied, as in "sheep among wolves" (Luke 10:3), where the "wolves" are the persecutors of the disciples. The point of similarity may be unstated, such as "and he is the head of the body, the church" (Col. 1:18), where the ruling function of Christ (the head) and the directed function of the church (the body) are assumed. Further, both topic and point of similarity may be omitted; for instance, in "beware the leaven of the Pharisees," which implies both the topic (their teachings) and the point of similarity (their permeating effect). Finally, the image and point of similarity can be missing, as in "it is hard for you to struggle against the goads," which assumes the ox and the point of similarity, namely, the struggle against guidance and control. The reader must be alert enough in such instances to supply the missing information; this demands a knowledge of the cultural background.

Above all, we must be careful not to overexegete figures of speech. Unlike modern metaphors, ancient figures of speech were inexact. They overlapped only at one point, and the modern reader often has trouble understanding that point. Caird provides an informative example:

> When the psalmist tells us that a united family is like oil dripping down Aaron's beard on to the skirts of his robe, he is not trying to persuade us that family unity is messy, greasy or volatile; he is thinking of the all-pervasive fragrance which has so deeply impressed itself on his memory at the anointing of the high priest (Ps. 133:2).[9]

We need help in unlocking such language, and for this the nonspecialist must turn to the better commentaries and background books.

This is especially true when the biblical writers pile image upon image, as in Psalm 92:10 (combining the "glory" of the strength of the ox with that of anointing the head) or Ephesians 4:14 (from infants to a helpless boat to a helpless bird to cheating at dice). Mixed metaphors were highly prized in ancient literature; rather than stress the ambiguity of the resultant statement (as we do today), classical writers emphasized the richness of the literary expression. We today must work behind the imagery to uncover the exact point accented in the compilation of metaphors. Often the image behind a metaphor is unknown. Numerous articles have been written on the "whitewashed sepulchre" of Matthew 23:27 or the "restrainer" of 2 Thessalonians 2:6–7. The actual thrust may never be known for certain before we get to heaven itself. The image also can be ambiguous, as in the many possible meanings of the "water" metaphor in John 3:5.

Finally, we should note the presence of live and dead metaphors in the biblical text. In a dead metaphor the image has become an idiom, understood directly by the hearer without producing a word-picture in the mind. A live metaphor is constructed on the occasion to teach a fresh point and force the hearer to recall both primary and associative meanings in order to understand the image. This distinction is critical because the interpreter can read too much into a dead metaphor by erroneously stressing its picture value.

The difficulty is that we have not grown up in the ancient culture and cannot easily identify such differences. Two criteria will help us understand the distinction. Etymologically, if the figurative thrust has been in existence for some time, it could well be a dead metaphor. According to BAGD, *sarx* ("flesh") was already used figuratively in the time of Epicurus, three centuries before Christ. When Paul contrasts "flesh" and "spirit," he is not trying to build a picture as an illustration of a truth but to use a semitechnical concept for the natural person. The same is true of *karpos* ("fruit"), also present in the time of Epicurus (BAGD). In passages on the "fruit of the Spirit" (Gal. 5:22–23) or "the fruit of lips which confess his name" (Heb. 13:15), the term has become an idiom and should simply be interpreted as "result." However, if the metaphor is elaborated in a series of pictures or its fresh image stressed in the context, it is more likely a live metaphor. This is true of *karpos* in several passages: Matthew 7:16–20, where "you will know them by their fruit" is expanded by successive images regarding grapes and thorns, figs and thistles, trees and the fire; John 15:1–8, where *karpos* is part of the vine-and-branches parable (a very live metaphor) and leads into the teaching on bearing fruit (vv. 4, 8); Jude 17, where it is part of the larger figure of "autumn trees—without fruit and uprooted—twice dead" (NIV). The context is the final arbiter in all such decisions.

## FIGURES OF ADDITION OR FULLNESS OF EXPRESSION

1. *Pleonasm* refers to the redundant addition of synonyms to emphasize a point. This was a favorite stylistic trait of ancient writers for clarification or emphasis, similar to the poetic device of synonymous parallelism. A major example is the constant use of "he answered and said" in the Gospels; others include "he did not remember but forgot" (Gen. 40:23), "the earthly house of this tent" (2 Cor. 5:1) and "the household master of the house" (Luke 22:11). The tendency of modern translations is to omit such phrases as in the New International Version on Luke 22:11, "the owner of the house." The reader must be careful not to read too much into such repetitive phrases; they are usually stylistic.

2. *Paronomasia* refers to words that are similar in sound and placed side-by-side in the text for emphasis. Often words are chosen to catch the original readers' attention and drive home the point. For instance, *tōhû wābōhû* ("waste and void"; Gen. 1:2) or *panti pantote pasan* ("all sufficiency in all things"; 2 Cor. 9:8) have a dramatic flair. Many times important theology is presented by means of paronomasia. Beitzel argues cogently that paronomasia was often used in the ancient Near East for solemn pronouncements and often in terms of divine names.[10] Rather than link *yhwh* (KJV "Jehovah"; Hebrew "Yahweh") with the verb "to be" (*hyh*), Beitzel argues that it is linked with the use of *yw* in Ugaritic, *yahwe/yiha* in Egyptian and *leuw* in Babylonian, all three instances of divine names. Therefore, *Yahweh* is connected with those and as a term has an "unknown lexicographic and ethnic origin." It derives its meaning not from etymology but from its paronomastic relation with *hayah* in Exodus 3:14, thus "He who causes to be [what is]" or "The Performer of the Promise."

3. *Epizeuxis* or *epanadiplosis* occurs when a crucial word is repeated for emphasis. John tends to employ this with the *amēn* ("truly, truly") formula; the Synoptic writers use only one. The use of the *amēn* formula has enormous implications for Christology, for it replaced the prophetic formula "thus says the Lord" and became a divine self-authentication by which Jesus was taking upon Himself the authority of Yahweh. By using epizeuxis John (1:51; 3:3, 5; twenty-five times in all) gives this solemn aspect special stress. Similar would be the threefold "holy, holy, holy" in Isaiah 6:3 and Revelation 4:8 to highlight the holiness of God.

4. *Hyperbole* is a conscious exaggeration or overstatement in order to drive home a truth. Jesus adopted this rabbinic ploy as one of His main teaching methods. Understanding it is critical to a proper interpretation of the Sermon on the Mount (Matt. 5:29, "If your right eye offends you, pluck it out"). Many serious errors have been made

by interpreting literally such statements as "turn the other cheek" or "if he asks your tunic, give him your cloak as well" (Matt. 5:39–40), as if those teachings defined the limits of a servant attitude. Jesus was talking generally of forgiveness and service rather than specifically, using these as hyperbolic examples. Similarly, when Jesus said the mustard seed was "the smallest seed" (Mark 4:31), He was not making a scientific statement but using a hyperbolic contrast (smallest-greatest); the mustard seed was the smallest seed that produced such a large plant (v. 32).

5. *Hendiadys* occurs when two or three terms are added to one another to express the same thing, such as "fire and brimstone"(Gen. 19:24), "blessed hope and glorious appearing" (Titus 2:13) or "kingdom and glory" (1 Thess. 2:12). The difficulty is deciding when there is one thought and when they express different aspects. For instance, "full of grace and truth" in John 1:17 may be hendiadys but more likely reflects the Jewish concepts of *ḥeseḏ* (covenant love) and *'ᵉmeṯ* (covenant faithfulness). The context and background of the terms must determine in individual cases.

## INCOMPLETE FIGURES OF SPEECH

This reverses the previous category, considering figures of speech that involve omission rather than addition.

1. *Ellipsis* is a grammatically incomplete expression requiring the reader to add concepts in order to finish the thought. Mickelsen mentions two types (1963, 189–90). In repetitional ellipsis the idea to be supplied is expressed earlier in the context or is clearly related to that which has been explicitly discussed; for example, "Does God give you his Spirit and work miracles among you because of the works of the law or . . ." (Gal. 3:5). The reader supplies the idea, "Did he do it?" (see also Rom. 11:22). In nonrepetitional ellipsis the concept to be supplied is not in the larger context. This is the more difficult, for the reader must speculate from the total message of the context. For instance, "Do we not have the right to eat and drink?" (1 Cor. 9:4). Nothing has been mentioned previously and only later statements about the apostle's right to be supported by the congregation help us to understand it. In Acts 18:6, "Your blood upon your head" could be "Your blood *be* upon your heads" (the traditional interpretation) or "May your blood *come* upon your head" (BDF par. 480[5]).

2. *Zeugma* is a special form of ellipsis in which two terms are combined that do not belong together and have to be separated by an added verb, as in 1 Timothy 4:3, "who forbid marriage [and order people] to abstain from certain foods." The statement has been

abbreviated in order to give it greater effect, and the reader must catch the intervening idea.

3. *Aposiopesis* occurs when a portion of the sentence is consciously omitted for reasons of emphasis. In John 1:22 the Jewish delegation to the Baptist queries, "Who are you? [We ask] so that we may give an answer to those who sent us." Mickelsen mentions an interesting example from the parable of the fig tree (Luke 13:9).[11] The caretaker, trying to save the tree, pleas for one more chance: "If indeed it bears fruit for the future [it should be allowed to grow]. Otherwise [if it does not produce fruit] then cut it down." Both clauses omit information for rhetorical effect.

## FIGURES INVOLVING CONTRAST OR UNDERSTATEMENT

1. *Irony* is an important rhetorical device that consists of stating one thing while meaning the direct opposite. It is most frequently employed in polemical contexts and is accompanied by sarcasm or ridicule, as in Michal's retort to David, "How the King of Israel has distinguished himself today" (2 Sam. 6:20), with open contempt for his dancing before the ark. Matthew 23 is filled with irony, as in Jesus' blistering denunciation of the Pharisees, "You fill up the measure of your fathers," referring to the murder of the prophets (v. 31). Many also see irony in the statement "The teachers of the law and the Pharisees sit in Moses' seat. So obey them and do what they tell you" (23:1–2). In such cases irony becomes biting sarcasm.

2. *Litotes* are phrases that understate or lessen one thing in order to magnify another. As Caird notes, the Old Testament contains few examples because Hebrew did not develop the form of understatement.[12] Two examples would be Genesis 18:22, "I am but dust and ashes" to demonstrate God's overwhelming greatness or "a drop of water" in Genesis 18:4 to wash the feet of the angels. More are found in the New Testament due to Hellenistic influence, such as Acts 21:39 ("a citizen of no ordinary city") or 1 Peter 2:10 ("those who are no people").

3. *Euphemism* substitutes a cultured or less offensive term for a harsh one. This is especially true with taboo or sexual items. For instance Judges 3:24 (compare 1 Sam. 24:3) has "surely he covers his feet," a euphemism for "goes to the bathroom." Several euphemisms describe sexual intercourse, such as "to know" and "to uncover nakedness." To "come near" is to entice sexually. Further, in Acts 2:39 "all who are afar off" refers to the Gentiles.

4. *Antithesis* is a direct contrast in which two sets of figures are set in opposition to one another. We see this in the Adam-Christ antithesis of Romans 5:12–21 and in the flesh/law versus Spirit opposition of

Romans 7–8. In fact Jesus' teachings about the differences between the "laws" of the new kingdom and of the Torah in Matthew 5:21–48 have been labeled "the Antitheses." The so-called dualism of the Gospel of John (light-darkness, above-below, death-life) also belongs to this category. We must interpret such oppositions carefully, for many have read later Gnostic teaching into John or Paul by overstating the contrasts. In actual fact the Johannine dualism is not Gnostic, for it is built upon Jewish-Christian rather than Gnostic patterns.

## FIGURES CENTERING UPON ASSOCIATION OR RELATION

1. *Metonymy* occurs when one noun is substituted for another that is closely associated with it. Modern examples include Jell-O for gelatin, saltines for crackers, the White House for the presidency, or the bottle for drunkenness. In the Old Testament "throne" (1 Chron. 17:12) stood for the kingship, "sword" (Isa. 51:19) for judgment or war, and "key" (Isa. 22:22) for authority. In the New Testament "principalities and powers" (Eph. 3:10; 6:12) refers to the demonic realm (some would say the demonic in government), "circumcision" (Gal. 2:7–9) to the Jews, and "Moses" (Luke 16:29) to the Torah.

2. *Synecdoche* is a figure of speech in which a part is substituted for the whole or vice versa. Since I have already dealt with this in some detail above on part-whole relations, I will simply mention it here for the sake of completeness.

## FIGURES STRESSING THE PERSONAL DIMENSION

1. *Personification* occurs when a thing or idea is represented as a person.[13] The most widely recognized example is "wisdom" in Proverbs, personified as a herald (1:20–21; 8:1–2), a creative force (3:19–20) and a hostess (9:1–2). In 9:13–18 wisdom is contrasted with "folly," itself personified as a hostess of a house of ill repute. We could note also *logos* ("word") in John 1:1–18. Similarly, the book of Revelation contains many personified symbols like the eagle (8:13), the locusts (9:3–11), the dragon (12:3–17) and the two beasts (13:1–17).

2. *Apostrophe* is a rhetorical device in which a statement is addressed to an imaginary object or person for effect; for instance, "Why gaze with envy, O rugged mountains, at the mountain where God chooses to reign" (Ps 68:16) or "Sing, O barren woman [for] your descendants will conquer nations" (Isa. 54:1–3). In Psalm 114:5–6 the seas, the mountains, and the hills are successively addressed. As we can see, most instances also involve personification, and the final result is a powerful and poignant message to God's people.

## CONCLUSION

Figures of speech are especially rich sources of imagery. While the discussion primarily has centered on the hermeneutical aspects, I want to note also their value for the sermon. It is my contention that some of the best illustrations come not just from cute stories or clever repartee but from the text itself and specifically from the background behind figurative language. Ricoeur's view of the world-referential value of metaphor (see above) is helpful in reminding us that our task is to immerse the audience not merely in entertaining anecdotes but in the Word itself. We are to help our congregation to live anew the message God has revealed in the text and to feel its power to change their situation as well. The starting reverberations of meaning inherent in the Bible's figurative language is the best place to start, for it is alive with powerful, colorful ideas. In recapturing the vitality and forceful presentation of the language, we will help our listeners to place themselves in the shoes of the original hearers and both to relive and to apply anew that eternal message.

# NINE

# AMBIGUITY IN THE BIBLE

## G. B. Caird

THE TIME HAS COME when we must examine more closely and distinguish more exactly those linguistic obstacles to communication which we have so far encountered only in a haphazard fashion. All such obstacles may be classified under three heads. The first of these, opacity, is integral to the very nature of language, and all we can do is come to terms with it. The second, vagueness, is in one sense an inescapable quality of language, in another sense a disease of language, and in a third sense a particular style of speech. The third, ambiguity, though frequently confused with polysemy, the multiple senses covered by the dictionary definition of words, is more usefully regarded as a characteristic of speech, being sometimes a defect in the use of language and sometimes a deliberate exploitation of multiple meaning.

### TRANSPARENCY AND OPACITY

A language is transparent insofar as its meaning lies open to any intelligent but uninstructed observer, and opaque insofar as it has to be learned; and anyone who has grappled with a hitherto unfamiliar language will be only too ready to believe that in all languages the opaque vastly exceeds the transparent. Transparency is of three kinds,[1] and it is important to note that languages vary both in the degree and in the incidence of their transparency.

1. *Phonetic transparency (onomatopoeia).* Total transparency occurs only where words reproduce the sounds they signify, as in the English "bang" or "fizzy." But onomatopoeia accounts for only a tiny proportion of the word-stock of any language and does not substantially qualify the general rule that the relation between words and what they signify is arbitrary or conventional. Even with the most obvious instances of onomatopoeia a certain element of convention enters in: the cock says "cockadoodledoo" in England, "cocorico" in France, and "kikeriki" in Germany and Greece. Classical Hebrew appears to offer comparatively

few instances of this deviation from arbitrariness.[2] This may be because the ear of the western lexicographer is not attuned to pick up assonances which would have been obvious to the native Hebrew-speaker. But a more probable reason is that onomatopoeia depends to a large extent on vowel sounds, and Hebrew is a language in which in most words only the consonants remain unchanged while the vowels are modified by inflexion. Examples do, however, occur, and some are readily recognizable by English readers: e.g., *has* (hush) and *yalal* (yell).

2. *Morphological transparency*. Much more important is the relative transparency effected by the two processes of inflexion and word-building. If we know the meaning of a root and the rules of inflexion and morphology, it is usually possible to work out for ourselves the meaning of cognate forms. In this respect English is more transparent than French and less transparent than agglutinative languages such as Greek or German. But all languages have their own areas both of transparency and of opacity.[3]

This is one of the many linguistic facts which have been overlooked by those who have tried to find in the Hebrew language evidence for some special quality of the Hebrew mind. J. Pedersen, for example, is one of those who have claimed that Hebrew is a primitive language because it is deficient in abstract terms, and that the Hebrew thinker did not think abstractly because he grasped each object or action in its undivided totality. "When we speak of going, going in, going out, going up or down, then it is for us the same action, only performed in a different manner and leading to different results, because we have the abstract idea, i.e. to 'go,' which may be supplemented now in one, now in another direction. To the Israelite these are perfectly different actions, seeing that he considers the totality-character of the action with its special stamp."[4] Barr has pointed out that Pedersen here confused general terms with abstract ones, and that French also uses a variety of terms for going in various directions (*monter, partir, sortir, entrer*, etc.), instead of qualifying the general term *aller* with directional markers.[5] The possession of general terms which can be the basis for word-building distinguishes transparent languages from opaque ones, not the developed from the primitive. The other point which Pedersen overlooked is that Hebrew has its own areas of transparency. The Hebrew word for "teach" (*limmad*) is a causative stem of the verb "learn" (*lamad*). The verb "to see" has a passive stem meaning "appear" and a causative stem meaning "show." Yet the absence of such verbal conveniences in English does not imply that we regard teaching and learning, or seeing and appearing, as totally unrelated processes.

The lack of congruence between any two languages in their areas of transparency can cause serious problems for the translator. What, for example, is the English translator to make of *dikaiosynē* (righteousness) in Romans. Greek, like Hebrew, possesses here a full range of cognate forms (verb, adjective, adverb, and noun), but English does not. The judge in a law court, faced with two litigants, justifies one of them, i.e., declares right to be on his side, gives the verdict in his favor. In the opening chapters of Romans Paul discusses on what grounds God justifies men and women or declares them to be in the right. English has the noun "justification" to connote the judicial act, but no cognate word to signify the character of the judge whose verdict is sound or the status of the person justified, and has to make do with "righteous" and "righteousness" instead. "Just" and "justice" will not do, because they are already preempted by long usage for quite a different meaning. But the traditional rendering is almost as unsatisfactory, since "righteous" has come to have a moral connotation, usually nowadays with a slightly disparaging tone, and certainly does not convey to the modern reader the notion of "being in the right" or "winning a lawsuit." R. Knox went further than this, dismissing "righteousness" as "a meaningless token word: "to use such a token word is to abrogate your duty as a translator."[6] The duty of the translator is to tell the reader what the original means, and this he cannot do by using token words which, like algebraical symbols, are devoid of semantic content. Yet if in Romans 1:17 we translate *dikaiosynē* in such a way as to explain what it means, shall we not be short-circuiting Paul's argument, since he takes four chapters to do precisely that?

A language, then, is transparent to the extent that the significance of its words may be deduced from a knowledge of their simpler elements. But there are two ways in which the importance of morphology can be overestimated. There is first a common human tendency to resent opacity and to try and enlarge the area of transparency. We have already seen that the writers of the Old Testament were not immune from it. . . . God took Adam from the ground—(*adamah*, Gen. 2:7). Naphtali was so called because Rachel wrestled (*naphal*) with Leah and won (Gen. 30:8). Even the more sophisticated writers take delight in exploring morphological links in ways that come near to punning. Isaiah's dictum to Ahaz, "Have firm faith, or you will not stand firm," plays upon the common etymology of two verbal forms which are not commonly related in sense (Isa. 7:9). Paul makes even more elaborate play out of simple and compound forms of the one verb *krinō* (1 Cor. 11:29–32). But such conceits have more to do with style than with meaning. It is well for the student of the Bible to recognize this stylistic tendency where it is in evidence, but he must not treat it as a warrant for indulging his own etymological fancies.

Even where a genuine etymological link exists, a word may grow away from its origins in the direction of opacity. The Greek *charis* (grace), for example, like *chara* (joy), is derived from the verbal root *chairein*, but none of its varied uses in the New Testament could be deduced from its etymology, and no New Testament writer ever attempts to establish a sibling link of sense between these two words of common ancestry.[7]

The second danger arising from morphology is less obvious, but no less important. The grammar of a language, at least as it is set out in elementary manuals of instruction, has traditionally been dictated by morphology. Nouns and adjectives are set out in declensions, verbs in conjugations. Inflected languages of the Indo-European family (e.g., Greek, Latin, French and German) roughly conform to a single pattern. English, a relatively uninflected language of the same family, fits the pattern less comfortably. But Hebrew is a Semitic language with a totally different grammatical structure. It is very easy therefore to draw the conclusion that Hebrew must be just as different from the European languages as a means of expressing thought, and this fallacy has had a good deal of support from those who ought to have known better.

a. Hebrew has been supposed deficient in adjectives. By the standard of Greek or Latin morphology this may be true, but the reason is that in Hebrew the function of the adjective is frequently discharged by two other grammatical forms: the stative verb (to be small, old, heavy, etc.) and the construct state of the noun ("my holy hill" is literally "the hill of my holiness"), both of which might properly be described as adjectival. Incidentally, the Hebrew noun does not morphologically have a genitive case, but the construct state shares most of the functions and, as we shall see later in this chapter, the ambiguities of the Greek and Latin genitive.

b. The Hebrew verb does not have tenses like those of Greek and Latin verbs. It has accordingly been argued that the Hebrew people had a different concept of time from ours.[8] But the users of Hebrew were quite capable of expressing the difference between past, present, and future by the use of other elements in their syntax.

c. With the majority of Hebrew roots the simplest form is that of the verb, from which noun and adjective are therefore said to be derived. In a Hebrew dictionary words are arranged wherever possible under the verbal form. So Hebrew grammarians have found it necessary to invent a technical term for verbs derived from nouns—denominative. . . . But the denominative verb is familiar enough in other languages, whose grammarians have not felt the need of a special name for it, e.g., in Greek *basileuein* (to be or act as king) or the English "to salt," "to chair," "to paper."

d. The Hebrew verb has a stem, the *niphal*, which can be either passive or reflexive, but has also a wide range of subsidiary uses, including the *niphal tolerativum*, which signifies allowing someone to do to you the action connoted by the verb. Thus *darash* means "to seek" and one of the senses of *nidrash* is "to allow oneself to be sought" (Isa. 65:1). But once this usage has been pointed out to us in Hebrew, we soon become aware that it exists without a name in other languages. Joseph went to Bethlehem "to get himself enrolled" (Luke 2:5). "Why," says Paul to the Colossians, "do you let yourselves be dictated to?" (Col. 2:21). It occurs in fact whenever a passive verb is used in the imperative. "Do not be bullied" is shorthand for "do not let anyone bully you."

Illustrations of this sort go far to substantiate the main point which is being made by linguists of the structuralist school, who maintain that beneath the surface structure dictated by the morphology of languages there is a deep structure which is common to all.[9]

3. *Analogical transparency (metaphor).* Most of the words in common use in any language have a wide range of metaphorical meaning which depends for intelligibility on an obvious similarity between the literal and the metaphorical referents. All we need to do is to identify the point of comparison. Much of this transparency can survive translation, provided that the objects or practices denoted by the literal sense exist in both cultures. We have no great difficulty with the following Hebrew metaphors:

> The head of Syria is Damascus and the head of Damascus is Rezin . . . the head of Ephraim is Samaria and the head of Samaria is Remaliah's son (Isa. 7:8–9).

> Harvest is past, summer is over, and we are not saved. I am wounded at the sight of my people's wound. . . . Is there no balm in Gilead, no physician there? Why has no new skin grown over their wound? (Jer. 8:20–22).

> Ephraim is a half-baked scone (Hos. 7:8).

Even when we discover that the ancient Israelite killed his enemies "with the mouth of the sword," the comparison of the sword with a ravenous beast overcomes any sense of unfamiliarity (e.g., Gen. 34:26).

One of the pitfalls for the biblical translator is that, in his eagerness to tell the reader exactly what the text before him means, he may ignore analogical transparency and quite unnecessarily unpack the metaphors, leaving the language flat and sterile. When, for example, Paul calls Christ "the firstfruits of the harvest of the dead" (1 Cor. 15:20 NEB), it can be assumed that the harvesting of crops is such a universal phenomenon that even the Translator's New Testament, produced as an aid for translators into a thousand tongues, hardly needed to resort to the paraphrase: "this is the guarantee that those who have died will be raised also."

## VAGUENESS

Vagueness covers three quite distinct aspects of linguistic usage, generalization, indeterminacy, and economy; and it is important not to confuse them.

1. *Generalization.* General terms are obviously less precise than particular ones: tree is less precise than cedar, weapon than sword, craftsman than potter, sin than covetousness. Yet general terms are, as we have seen, the indispensable means by which we organize and understand our experience. There is no truth in the claim that the Hebrew language is deficient in general terms, as anyone may demonstrate by running off a list of those which occur in the Old Testament.

It is, however, true that for a variety of reasons the biblical style avoids this type of vagueness. Much of the Bible is narrative, in which generalizations are inevitably sparse. The proverbial literature contains a fair number of vague moral commonplaces, but frequently prefers to teach by instance and illustration (e.g., Prov. 6:16–19). The poetical passages share with all other poetry a love of the particular (e.g., Isa. 11:6–8; 55:13). And the legal codes have at their core a body of case law (Ex. 21:1–23:19). In the interpretation of the law there was always a tendency to eliminate vagueness by exact definition. The commandment to love your neighbor as yourself invited the lawyer's question, "Who is my neighbor?" (Lev. 19:18; Luke 10:29). If the law forbade work on the Sabbath, the rabbis would naturally ask what the law intended by "work" and answer their own question with a list of thirty-nine categories (*Mishna*, Shab. 7.2).

Yet there can be dangers in too great precision. Jesus' reply to the lawyer denied him the right to limit his liabilities by definition. At other times Jesus attacked the Pharisees because, in their determination to know exactly what the Torah meant so that they might live in total obedience to it, they concentrated on the minor and practicable pieties, to the neglect of the broad and inexhaustible principles, "justice, mercy and good faith" (Matt. 23:23). A sound ethical system cannot dispense with the vague generality of the unattainable ideal.

2. *Indeterminacy.* In the examples cited above it will be obvious that
the distinction between particular and general applies equally to concrete and to abstract terms. But some abstract terms are of such a high
degree of generality that on close scrutiny they are found to have no
clearly defined referent. One of the reasons why Socrates annoyed his
contemporaries was that he pointed out to them how they used words
without knowing what it was they were talking about. "Socrates found
that his fellow-Athenians attached the greatest importance to *aretē* [vir-
tue, excellence], and each wanted his sons to be taught it; but, in ques-
tioning them closely, he again and again discovered that not one of them
knew what this prize was which they valued so highly. Neither did
Socrates; but, as he would genially point out to his interlocutors, there
was this difference between him and them—they thought that they knew,
but he knew that he did not."[10]

The causes of indeterminacy are various. Occasionally the weakness is congenital: "There is no ultimately correct and single meaning
to words like 'romanticism.'"[11] More often it happens that words,
which at other times and in other contexts can convey a clear meaning,
fall victim to careless or polemical use or to fashion, as did "wit" in
the eighteenth century. "It also suffered the worst fate any word has to
fear; it became the fashionable term of approval among critics. This
made it a prey to tactical definitions of a more than usually unscrupu-
lous type, and in the heat of controversy there was some danger of its
becoming a mere rallying-cry, semantically null."[12] For a similar cause
Jeremiah rebukes people for claiming to possess the law of the Lord
without considering what it is they are talking about, and complains
that prophets and priests say "Peace, peace," when there is nothing in
the contemporary situation to which the word can rightly apply (Jer.
8:8, 11).

In the Graeco-oriental background of early Christianity *gnōsis*
(knowledge) had become a fashionable term, annexed by the champions
of many incompatible cults, in which it was subjected to tactical
definition (1 Tim. 6:20). The New Testament writers combat its spurious
popularity in a variety of ways. With the "strong party" at Corinth
Paul sympathizes, but insists that knowledge shall be subordinate to
love (1 Cor. 8:1–11; 13:2, 8). To the Colossians he argues that the
only knowledge worth having is the knowledge of God revealed in
Christ (Col. 2:2). The author of 1 John denies that knowledge is the
monopoly of any esoteric sect (2:20); it is the common possession of
all who have inherited the apostolic tradition (1:1–4), and the test of
its possession is obedience (2:3). In all three communities there had
been a group using the fashionable word as a means of bullying their
less assertive fellow members. But the evidence of the three epistles

does not indicate that these groups had much else in common with each other, let alone with the developed Gnostic sects of the middle of the second century. It is therefore tendentious and confusing to use the word "Gnosticism" of the beliefs of these somewhat shadowy groups, as though they were the beginnings of a homogeneous and clearly defined movement, sharing all the marks of Gnosticism properly so-called.

3. *Economy*. Erich Auerbach has drawn attention to a striking difference between the epic styles of Homer and Genesis in his contrast between the stories of Odysseus' scar and the binding of Isaac. The old nurse Euryclea recognizes the returning Odysseus by a scar on his thigh, whereupon Homer spends more than seventy lines explaining how he came by the wound in a boar hunt. In this, as in other Homeric narratives, every detail of time, place, circumstance, feeling, and motive is explicit; all is foreground and every contour is sharply defined. In the biblical story we are not told why God gave Abraham the command to sacrifice Isaac, where Abraham was or what thoughts went through his mind. The story is told in starkest outline and all else is left to the imagination. "It would be difficult, then, to imagine styles more contrasted than of those two equally ancient and equally epic texts. On the one hand, externalized, uniformly illuminated phenomena, at a definite time and in a definite place, connected together without lacunae in a perpetual foreground; thoughts and feelings completely expressed; events taking place in a leisurely fashion and with very little suspense. On the other hand, the externalization of only so much of the phenomena as is necessary for the purpose of the narrative, all else left in obscurity; the decisive points of the narrative alone are emphasized, what lies behind is nonexistent; time and place are unidentified and call for interpretation; thoughts and feelings remain unexpressed, are only suggested by the silence and the fragmentary speeches; the whole, permeated with the most unrelieved suspense and directed toward a single goal (and to that extent far more of a unity), remains mysterious and "'fraught with background.'"[13]

I do not for a moment suggest that the vagueness of economy, which Auerbach finds so impressive and so redolent of mystery in this story, is peculiar to the Bible, or that it arises out of any unique properties of the Hebrew language. It is, as he himself says, a matter of style; and no doubt a similar economy of style may be found in the literature of other cultures. It is, however, characteristic of many other biblical narratives, and particularly of the stories in the Synoptic Gospels. In the parable of the Good Samaritan we are not told who the man was, what was the object of his journey or whether he ever in the end achieved it, what business brought the Samaritan to those parts, or the site of the inn. We do not need to know all this. Almost, it might be argued, we need not to know.[14]

Since the advent of Form Criticism it has been fashionable to attribute the absence of personal and circumstantial detail in the Gospels to the attritional effect of oral transmission, acting on each unit like the tide smoothing pebbles on a beach. No doubt the stories of Genesis too were orally transmitted before ever they were written down (see the reference to bards in Num. 21:27). But tradition is supposed also to have had something to do with the formation of the Homeric poems and their very different style. One cannot help wondering therefore whether too much has been ascribed to its influence.

## AMBIGUITY

Ambiguity is not a characteristic of language but of speech. It occurs when an utterance may bear more than one meaning and we are left in doubt which of the possible meanings is intended. Language is not ambiguous in itself, though it supplies the raw material for ambiguity; it becomes ambiguous in use, when neither context nor tone provide adequate clues to the speaker's intention. The types of ambiguity may thus be classified in two ways: (1) according to the linguistic area in which the doubt arises; and (2) according to the reason why that doubt is left unresolved.[15]

### Areas of Ambiguity

1. *Phonetic.* There are words of different sense which sound identical (homophons) and can therefore be mistaken for one another. Ambiguity of this kind occurs only in the spoken word, and it impinges on the study of the Bible only through variants in the text and through the constraints which it imposes on translation.

Manuscripts were frequently copied by dictation, and in this way homophony could cause errors of transcription. The chance of this happening in the text of the New Testament was considerably increased by the modification of vowels in Hellenistic Greek: the classical distinction between the long and the short O (omega and omicron) had been eroded, and three vowels (η, ι, υ) and three diphthongs (ει, οι, υι), which were phonetically distinct in classical times, were already, as in Modern Greek, pronounced alike (ēē as in the English "meet"). Thus in Romans 5:1, half the manuscripts read the indicative ("we have peace") and half the subjunctive ("let us have peace"), and the only difference between the two readings is the length of a vowel, which would not have been aurally discernible. In 1 Peter 2:3 the majority reading is "if you have tasted that the Lord is good (chrestos)," but one manuscript has "if you have tasted that the Lord is Christ (christos)." In this case there is no real doubt, since the clause is a quotation from Psalm 34:8, but the error is worth mentioning because of a probable parallel elsewhere. Aquila and Priscilla were expelled from Rome along with other Jews by an edict of Claudius (Acts 18:2), which Suetonius (*Claud.* 16) records in these terms: "he banned from Rome the Jews who were in a constant state of riot at the instigation of Chrestus."[16] There may have been a Jewish agitator named Chrestus, but it is much more likely that some Roman official got hold of the wrong end of the stick, and that the root of the trouble was anti-Christian rioting.

Because the Bible is regularly read and quoted in public, the translator has constantly to take note of phonetic ambiguity and avoid such words as "succor" for fear that they will be wrongly heard. A Roman Catholic priest told me that, when his church adopted a liturgy in the vernacular, in which the Lord's Prayer was introduced as "the prayer he taught us," some children asked to see the prairie tortoise.

2. *Lexical.* The commonest occasion for ambiguity is polysemy, which may leave us guessing which sense of a word is intended. Since in textbook descriptions of polysemy . . . the examples given tend to be nouns, it is important to note that multiple meaning may be found in any part of speech: pronoun, preposition, conjunction and interjection, as well as noun, verb, adjective and adverb. Hebrew, for instance, has a multipurpose preposition *b-*, which can mean in, during, at, against, down upon, with, by means of, through, for (at the cost of), on account of, in spite of, etc. In Hellenistic Greek the preposition ἐν was almost as versatile, and its range was even further enlarged in biblical Greek by its frequent use as the equivalent of *b-*.

With all this wealth of possibility it is remarkable how rarely lexical ambiguity in fact occurs, and how often the context enables us to settle upon a precise sense. Yet there remain enough instances which leave us in unresolved doubt. Does the prophet (Isa. 3:5) foresee the devastation of the whole land (AV, NEB) or of the whole earth (JB)? and are the meek to inherit the land (Ps. 37:11) or the earth (Matt. 5:4)? Is the steward in Jesus' parable called a bad steward because he was dishonest, or because he was incompetent, or because he had broken the law against usury by charging interest on his master's loans (Luke 16:8)? Does the "now" of Ephesians 3:5 denote the present of the Christian era, separated from former generations by the coming of Christ, or is the dividing line between past and present some more specific and more recent experience of revelation? When Paul says "we," is he referring to himself alone, to himself and his colleagues, to

Jewish Christians contrasted with "you Gentiles," or to all Christians without discrimination? Does Paul date the Last Supper on the night when Jesus was "betrayed" (AV), "arrested" (NEB), or "delivered up, (TNT)? When Paul says that God "chose to reveal his Son in me" (Gal. 1:16), does he mean "to me," "in my heart," "through me," or simply "in my case"? Does the conjunction "for" in Philippians 3:3 introduce the reason why the Philippians are to be on their guard or the reason why Paul has elected to use the opprobrious word "mutilation" to describe those who prided themselves on being "the Circumcision"? Is the interjection *ouai* (Luke 6:24–26; 11:42–52; Matt. 23:13–31) a term of imprecation ("woe to") or of lament ("alas for")?

3. *Grammatical.* Up to this point we have treated polysemy as though it were a property of words alone, but it is found not only in the eight parts of speech, but also in almost all of the much more numerous grammatical forms and syntactical constructions. The only grammatical form which appears to be wholly unequivocal is the vocative case. We may of course be left in doubt about the referent of a word in the vocative (are the people addressed in Gal. 3:1 north Galatians living in Ancyra and Pessinus, or south Galatians living in Antioch, Iconium, Lystra, and Derbe?), or about the degree of emotional intensity involved (John 2:4); but in neither instance does the doubt arise from the use of the vocative.

Some of the most important ambiguities arise in the uses of the Greek genitive. With the majority of these uses, particularly those in which the genitive is governed by a preposition or a verb, we need not be concerned.[17] But there are seven uses, enumerated below, which together constitute an area of ambiguity, and these are the more interesting for us in that most of them have their parallels in the Hebrew and English equivalents to the genitive, the Hebrew construct state and the English "of" or s with an apostrophe:

a.  The possessive genitive: "the mountain of the Lord" (Ps. 24:3); "the house of Simon and Andrew" (Mark 1:29).
b.  The genitive of relation: "Abner son of Ner" (2 Sam. 2:8); "Mary wife of Clopas" (John 19:25); "Mark cousin of Barnabas" (Col. 4:10).
c.  The subjective genitive: "the works of your father," i.e., such as your father would do (John 8:41); "your labor of love," i.e., the labor which love undertakes (1 Thess. 1:3).
d.  The objective genitive: "the fear of the Lord" (Job 28:28); "the zeal of your house" (Ps. 69:9; John 2:17).
e.  The partitive genitive: "the half of my goods" (Luke 19:8); "the firstfruits of them that sleep" (1 Cor. 15:20).
f.  The genitive of apposition or definition: "the cities of Sodom and Gomorrah" (2 Peter 2:6); "the shield of faith" (Eph. 6:16).

g.  The genitive of quality: "this body of death," i.e., this body beset by death as a physical and spiritual reality (Rom. 7:24). The genitive of quality is particularly common in the Old Testament because of the adjectival use of the construct state ("paths of righteousness" = right paths in Ps. 23:3), and because of the frequent use of *ben* (son) in the ben of classification ("sons of the prophets" = members of the prophetic guild; "sons of Belial" = riffraff). Hebraisms of both sorts are found in the New Testament: e.g., "the mammon of unrighteousness" (Luke 16:9) = worldly wealth (NEB), and "children of wrath" (Eph. 2:3) = those whose lives expose them to retribution.

Even within these categories there can be ambiguity. In English "Jane's Thomas" might, to anyone who did not know Jane, mean her husband, her son or her gardener. Was then "James's Judas' (Luke 6:16) his son (NEB) or his brother (AV)? More often ambiguity arises because the genitive might belong to either of two categories. "The love of God" is certainly subjective in the benediction of 2 Corinthians 13:14 and certainly objective in Luke 11:42. But is the love of God which the Spirit pours into Christian hearts God's love or love for God (Rom. 5:5; cf. 5:8; 8:28)? The same question must be asked about the love which Jesus finds lacking in His critics (John 5:42). Here the NEB decides for the objective: "you have no love for God in you." This may well be correct, though some slight doubt is raised when later we find Jesus praying to God for his friends "that the love you had for me may be in them" (John 7:26). Five times in his letters Paul uses the phrase "faith of (Jesus) Christ" (Rom. 3:22; Gal. 2:16 *bis*; 3:22; Phil. 3:9; cf. Eph. 3:12). In a literal English translation this sounds like a subjective genitive, referring to the faith which Jesus exemplified; and it has been argued that this is what Paul means, since elsewhere faith in Christ is expressed in prepositional phrases. But in Greek there is no difficulty at all in taking the genitive as objective, and the overwhelming majority of translators and commentators have held that this is in each case the sense required by the context.

Sometimes the choice is between the partitive and the appositive. When Paul describes Epaenetus as "the firstfruits of Asia" (Rom. 16:5), the household of Stephanas as firstfruits of Achaea (1 Cor. 16:15), and Christ as "the firstfruits of them that sleep" (1 Cor. 15:20), these are all beyond question examples of the partitive. But when he speaks of "the firstfruits of the Spirit" (Rom. 8:23), this may be either partitive (a first installment of the Spirit) or appositive (the Spirit as the first installment of a harvest to come). In another letter Paul twice uses the phrase "the downpayment of the Spirit," using the term *arrhabon* which we know from secular papyri to have been in common commercial use (2 Cor. 1:22; 5:5). Here the same doubt arises. But in Ephesians 1:14, where we are told that the Spirit is the *arrhabon* of our inheritance, the doubt is resolved in favor of apposition. We are faced with a similar choice in Ephesians 4:9, where "the lower regions of earth" can be either partitive (those regions of earth which are below, i.e., Hades) or appositive (the earth below). Over the centuries opinion has swung now this way, now that, always with a strong assertion that the one sense was correct and the other inadmissible. E. J. Goodspeed even used this verse as an argument against the Pauline authorship of Ephesians on the ground that Christ's descent into Hades is not mentioned in the other Pauline letters. It did not seem to occur to him that this might be an argument for adopting the alternative interpretation.[18]

From the possible ambiguities which may arise within the vast territory of syntax let us take as an example the simplest of all structures, predication . . . and in particular the uses of the verb "to be." In English, as in Greek and Latin, the verb "to be" may be used either in statements of existence or as a copula linking two ideas in statements which may be of four kinds: identity, attribute, sequence or cause, resemblance or equivalence. It is sometimes inaccurately stated that the Hebrew language has no verb "to be." It is more accurate to say that it has a verb (*yesh*) for use in statements of existence, but does not commonly employ any verb as copula, except in the future tense where the sense approximates to "become" (e.g., 2 Sam. 7:14: "I will be father to him and he shall be son to me"). The confusion between statements of existence and statements involving the use of a copula, which so bedeviled Greek philosophy that even Plato and Aristotle barely fought their way free of it, could not readily have occurred in Hebrew. The only places in the Bible where we meet anything like it are those which refer to pagan gods. Sometimes it is far from clear whether the prophet or apostle intends to deny their existence or merely that they have the attributes of deity. Deutero-Isaiah appears explicit enough. "I am the Lord, there is no other; there is no god beside me" (45:5). Apart from the one Creator, the word "god" has no referent other than the manmade images to which other nations look in vain for help (45:20). But does this hold also for Jeremiah when he calls pagan deities no-gods (2:11; 5:7)? Paul can on occasion be as absolute as Deutero-Isaiah: "a false god has no existence in the real world" (1 Cor. 8:4; cf. Eph. 2:12). Yet in another context he can speak of pagan religion as slavery "to beings which in their nature are no gods," and appears to identify these with "the weak and beggarly elementals," the powers of the old world order (Gal. 4:8–9).

We turn then to look more closely at copular predication, noting that Hebrew is not alone in being able to achieve this without the actual use of the copula. Here is an example of each of the main types with the copula suppressed in Greek:

a.  Identity. "Is the law sin?" (Rom. 7:7).
b.  Attribute. "No one is good except God alone" (Mark 10:18).
c.  Cause. "To be carnally minded is death" (Rom. 8:6).
d.  Resemblance. "The tongue is a fire" (James 3:6).

Ambiguity sets in when we are unable to determine which of these types of predication was intended.

If we may judge by the acrimonious debates and mutual recrimina-tions it has engendered, the sentence "this is my body" (Matt. 26:26; Mark 14:22; Luke 22:19; 1 Cor. 11:24) must be one of the most ambiguous in the New Testament. There are those who print the words THIS IS in large capitals in their prayer books, as though to assert that this particular instance of predication is unique, not to be compared with any other use of the verb "to be." Yet they are only marginally more naive than those (of whom I myself have been one) who accuse them of absurdity on the ground that Hebrew and Aramaic possess no copula, as though that debarred speakers in those languages from predi-cation altogether. The statement cannot be one of identity, since Jesus cannot be supposed to have identified the bread in his hands with the living body of which those hands were part; and if it be claimed that the word "body" in this instance has a different referent, then it is being used metaphorically, and all metaphorical statements belong to class "d." But if we conclude that "is" here stands for "represents" or "symbolizes," the traditional riposte is that the eucharistic elements are not to be regarded as "mere symbols." The fallacy in this objection lies in the assumption that symbols are invariably substitutes for the reality they signify, bearing the same relation to it as a still-life paint-ing to real fruit and fish, whetting but not satisfying the appetite. But many symbols, such as a kiss, a handshake and the presentation of a latchkey, are a means, or even the means, of conveying what they represent. The most natural way of taking the copula in the eucharistic saying, therefore, is "represents," with the understanding that Jesus intended the gift of bread to convey the reality it symbolized.

Another verse of notorious difficulty is the opening sentence of the Fourth Gospel: "In the beginning the Logos already existed, and the Logos was in God's presence, and the Logos was God." The third clause looks like a statement of identity, yet the second denies the possibility of taking it so. The NEB has attempted to take it as attributive ("what God was the Word was"); but, since God is a class of one, whoever has all the attributes of God is God, so that the attributive converts into a statement of identity. Is it possible, then, that we have manufactured our own difficulty by leaving Logos untranslated, as though it were a proper noun, and that bold translation would resolve the problem? "In the beginning was a purpose, a purpose in the mind of God, a purpose which was God's own being." It is surely a conceivable thought that God is wholly identified with His purpose of love, and that this purpose took human form in Jesus of Nazareth. Yet by this resort we have only postponed our difficulty to the prayer in which Jesus speaks of the glory He had and the love with which the Father loved Him before the world began (17:5, 24). Perhaps in the end it is best to conclude that John intended to write an opening sentence which would "tease us out of thought as doth eternity."

4. *Functional*. Further ambiguities may arise out of the use to which words are put, and of these it is unnecessary at this point to give illustrations.

## Causes of Ambiguity

The reasons why ambiguity may be unresolved are of three kinds: accidental, historical, and deliberate. That is to say, a speaker may have intended to be unambiguous and yet have failed to notice that what he said could be taken in a way he did not intend; his utterance may have been unambiguous to his original audience and have become ambiguous to us because, with the passage of time, we lack the contextual knowledge available to them; or he may have intended the ambiguity, and that in a variety of ways which we may classify as oracular, ironic, parabolic, exploratory, and associative.

Accidental and historical ambiguities are straightforward and need not delay us. Paul in 1 Corinthians has to correct a false impression given by a previous letter, in which he had warned his converts not to associate with immoral persons, not intending to refer to pagans, since "to avoid them you would have to get out of the world altogether" (5:10). Both his letters to the Thessalonians contain passages written because they (in common with some modern scholars) had wrongly taken his preaching about the coming of Christ from heaven to mean that he expected the world to end shortly. Much of Corinthians can be taken in more than one way because it was an answer to a letter from Corinth of which we know neither the exact content nor the tenor (1 Cor. 7:1). In two of his letters Paul refers to "the elements of the world" (Gal. 4:3, 9; Col. 2:8, 20), which can mean either "the elemental powers controlling the present world order" or "the elementary teaching characteristic of this world"; and the original readers were probably familiar enough with the term to be in no doubt which sense was intended whereas we have to make our choice on a calculation of probabilities. But the deliberate exploitation of ambiguity requires closer attention.

1. Oracular ambiguity is commonly associated with Delphi and Sibyl. When Croesus consulted the Delphic oracle, he was told, "if Croesus crosses the Halys, he will destroy a great empire"; and with this equivocal encouragement he destroyed his own (Aristotle, *Rhet.* iii.5). Maxentius, on the eve of his death in battle against Constantine, consulted the Sibylline books and was told that the enemy of Rome would die (Lactantius, *M.P.* 44). The Old Testament prophets did not as a rule indulge in this hedging of bets, though we might perhaps assign to this category Jeremiah's prediction of destruction at the hands of an enemy from the north (Jer. 1:13; 4:6). Brewer's *Dictionary of Phrase and Fable* cites as a parallel Micaiah's prophecy to Ahab (1 Kings 22:15), but there it is not the sense or the referent of the oracle that is ambiguous, but the intention: Ahab is meant to think that God intends him to conquer, whereas in fact God means him to die. A better instance would be Joseph's interpretation of the dreams of the head butler and head baker, both of whom are told that "within three days Pharaoh will lift up your head," though in the one case this means restoration to favor and in the other hanging (Gen. 40:12, 19). The evasive responses of the Pythian priestess and the Sibyl were of course designed to protect the oracle against recrimination, and it is possible that John thought Pilate to be covering himself in a similar fashion in causing the title "King of the Jews" to be nailed to the cross. This could be taken either as a statement of the charge of which he had been found guilty or as a simple designation, and Pilate refused to remove the ambiguity (John 19:19–22).

2. The prophecy of Caiaphas, on the other hand, is not oracular but ironical. Dramatic irony is a form of speech which assumes a double audience, the first understanding nothing beyond the face value of the words, the second seeing both the deeper meaning and the incomprehension of the first. It is well exemplified in the conversation between Joseph and his brothers, where the reader knows the identity of Joseph and the brothers do not (Gen. 42). Similarly when Caiaphas declares that it is expedient that one man should die for the people and not the whole nation perish (John 11:50), his is the voice of *Realpolitik*, but John attributes a deeper, theological meaning to his words and credits him with the unwitting faculty of prophecy on the strength of his priestly office. Dramatic irony is one of the most prominent stylistic features of the Fourth Gospel, based on the evangelist's belief that all earthly things are capable of being symbols of things heavenly, and

that this is preeminently so in the words and works of Jesus (3:12). In one incident after another the interlocutor takes the words of Jesus at the earthly level, and his sights, or those of the reader at least, have to be raised to the heavenly. The bystanders who hear Jesus say "Destroy this temple, and in three days I will raise it again" remonstrate that it has already been forty-six years under construction; and John's comment is that "the temple he was speaking of was his body" (John 2:19–21). Nicodemus has to be taught that rebirth is not reentry into the womb but spiritual renewal (3:3–8), the Samaritan woman that living water is an inner spring which cannot be piped into her house (4:10–15), Martha that resurrection is not an event at the end of time but a recreative power already present in Jesus (11:23–26).

3. Parabolic ambiguity is well illustrated by Nathan's parable (2 Sam. 12:1–10). Nathan tells David the story of the rich man who took the poor man's ewe lamb, and asks him as head of the judiciary to give his official ruling on the case, with the intention that his own verdict on the hypothetical situation may be seen to apply to the real offense of his treatment of Uriah. Many of the parables of Jesus contain, explicitly or implicitly, a similar invitation to the hearer to judge, and incidentally to judge himself. "What will the owner of the vineyard do?" (Mark 12:9). "Which of the two did as his father wished?" (Matt. 21:31). "Which of the three do you think was neighbor to the man who fell into the hands of the robbers?" (Luke 10:36).

4. Some deliberate uses of ambiguity must be called exploratory, because the speaker has not made up his mind between two senses, but is discovering a new truth by investigating the interconnection between them. In our study of the genitive case above we have seen that the phrase "the love of God" can be either subjective or objective, and that both uses are found in the New Testament. In 1 John this ambiguity is exploited to the full. The letter was written to encourage the faithful survivors of a schismatic split, caused by the departure of an influential group who had been making startling claims for themselves (2:19): they knew God with an esoteric knowledge not vouchsafed to other members, and they loved Him with an intensity which put them beyond sin and gave them a share in His divine life (1:6, 8; 2:4; 4:20). Since, then, the author writes to controvert the schismatics' claim that they love God, we may assume that the objective sense of "the love of God" is the starting point of his argument, and in one passage this is unambiguously expressed. "When we love God and obey his commands we love his children too. For this is the love of God, that we keep his commands" (5:2–3). In three other passages it is doubtful whether the objective or the subjective is meant. "If anyone keeps his word, in him the love of

God comes to its perfection" (2:5). "If anyone loves the world, the love of the Father is not in him" (2:15). "If anyone has enough to live on and yet when he sees his brother in need shuts up his heart against him, how can it be said that the love of God dwells in him?" (3:17). In a fifth passage the sense intended is clearly the subjective. "God himself dwells in us if we love one another; his love is brought to perfection within us" (4:12). In the light of the two unambiguous passages it appears probable that in the three ambiguous ones both senses are being intended at once. For John's argument is that love for God entails love for our fellows, so that the one cannot exist without the other; and that when we love our fellows, it is not merely we who love, but God who loves through us; so that all human love which is genuine is the indwelling of God. God is love, and only by the experience of loving can one have experience of God (4:7–9).

The teaching attributed to Jesus in the Gospels strongly suggests that he used this device of deliberate ambiguity to provoke His hearers into thought about ultimate questions. Consider the following passage, which is quoted in the first instance from the RV.

> If any man would come after me, let him deny himself and take up his cross and follow me. For whosoever would save his life shall lose it; and whosoever shall lose his life for my sake and the gospel's shall save it. For what doth it profit a man, to gain the whole world and forfeit his life? For what should a man give in exchange for his life? (Mark 8:34–37).

Here the Greek word *psyche* is used four times in quick succession, and the revisers decided to render it uniformly by "life." But *psyche* can mean life is a wide variety of senses, ranging from "being alive" through "life that is worth living" to "true self" or "soul." Ought not the translation then to be more explicit? The opening reference to the cross, the Roman method of execution, indicates that the starting point of the discussion is the risk of physical death entailed in discipleship. Yet it simply is not true that to lose one's life in this sense is to save it. And is there not a curious clash between the warning against saving one's life and the warning against forfeiting it? It was considerations such as these that had prompted the AV to render *psyche* in verse 35 by "life" and in verses 36–37 by "soul": "what shall it profit a man, if he gain the whole world and lose his own soul? Or what shall a man give in exchange for his soul?" But this has the double disadvantage of breaking the verbal link without solving the problem. Accordingly the NEB made a bolder attempt at giving the sense of the passage.

Anyone who wishes to be a follower of mine must leave self behind: he must take up his cross, and come with me. Whoever cares for his own safety is lost; but if a man will let himself be lost for my sake and for the gospel, that man is safe. What does a man gain by winning the whole world at the cost of his true self? What can he give to buy that self back?

The intention was excellent; but it did not produce such an increase in clarity as to compensate for the loss of directness and force. The commentator may of course cut the knot with the scissors of Form Criticism, by arguing that the four sayings in this passage came to Mark as independent units of tradition which he threaded together by the catchword *psychē*, much as the three sayings of 9:50 are threaded together by the catchword "salt"; but that extreme and improbable view is no help to the translator, who has to try and make sense of the passage as it stands. I would suggest, rather, that Jesus was deliberately exploiting the ambiguity of "life," and this view finds some support in other parts of the Gospel tradition. "I bid you put away anxious thoughts about food and drink to keep you alive, and clothes to cover your body. Surely life is more than food, the body more than clothes" (Matt. 6:25). But if that is so, this is one of those rare passages where a word of many meanings must be rendered by a single English word throughout.

5. Closely akin to the exploratory is that use of ambiguity known as associative thinking. This device is more popular with creative thinkers than with logicians, who tend to look askance at it, since in it the argument does not proceed by logical and compelling steps, but by the exploitation of polysemy. Nathan's prophecy, for example, which was the ground of later belief in the eternity of David's dynasty, and therefore also, once that dynasty had been interrupted, of the confidence that God would one day restore it by the sending of a Messiah, was constructed out of a word-play on two meanings of the word "house." David is not to build a house (temple) for God; God will build a house (dynasty) for David (2 Sam. 7:5–11). An even more elaborate play on the same word is found in Ephesians 2:19–22. The church is God's house (household), in which Gentile Christians have now joined Jewish Christians as members of the one family. They are therefore built as living stones into a house (building) of which Christ is the cornerstone, and which grows into a temple or house (dwelling place) for God.

This kind of associative link was particularly important in the exegesis of Scripture. Jewish exegetes had a name for it, *gᵉzerah shᵉwa*, which signified the explication of one text by cross-reference to another which had some verbal link with it; and Christian exegetes followed their example. The author of 1 Peter has brought together three Old

Testament texts which have in common only the word "stone" (Isa. 8:14; 28:16; Ps. 118:22), and out of them has fashioned the sonorous and impressive declaration that Christ is the precious stone set by God in Zion, a foundation stone to those who believe and are built as living stones into the same temple, but to unbelievers the stone which the builders rejected and which is therefore left lying around for them and others to trip over.[19]

# TEN

# THE USE OF WORDS IN
# VARIOUS CONTEXTS

### Milton S. Terry

SOME WORDS HAVE A variety of significations, and hence, whatever their
primitive meaning, we are obliged to gather from the context, and from
familiarity with the usage of the language, the particular sense which
they bear in a given passage of Scripture. Many a word in common use
has lost its original meaning. How few of those who daily use the word
*sincere* are aware that it was originally applied to pure honey, from which
all wax was purged. Composed of the Latin words *sine*, without, and
*cera*, wax, it appears to have been first used of honey strained or separated from the wax-like comb. The word *cunning* no longer means knowledge, or honorable skill, but is generally used in a bad sense, as implying
artful trickery; the verb *let* has come to mean the very opposite of what
it once did, namely to *hinder*; and *prevent*, which was formerly used in
the sense of *going before*, so as to prepare the way or assist one, now
means to intercept or obstruct. Hence the importance of attending to
what is commonly called the *usus loquendi*, or current usage of words as
employed by a particular writer, or prevalent in a particular age. It often
happens, also, that a writer uses a common word in some special and
peculiar sense, and then his own definitions must be taken, or the context and scope must be consulted, in order to determine the precise meaning intended.

There are many ways by which the *usus loquendi* of a writer may
be ascertained. The first and simplest is when he himself defines the
terms he uses. Thus the word ἄρτιος, *perfect, complete*, occurring
only in 2 Timothy 3:17, is defined by what immediately follows:
"That the man of God may be perfect, thoroughly furnished unto
every good work." That is, he is made perfect or complete in this, that
he is thoroughly furnished and fitted, by the varied uses of the inspired
Scripture, to go forward to the accomplishment of every good work.
We also find the word τέλειοι, commonly rendered *perfect*, defined in

Hebrews 5:14, as those "who by practice have the senses trained unto a discrimination of good and evil." They are, accordingly, the mature and experienced Christians as distinguished from *babes*, νήπιοι.

Compare verse 13, and 1 Corinthians 2:6. So also, in Romans 2:28–29, the apostle defines the genuine Jew and genuine circumcision as follows: "For he is not a Jew, who is one outwardly (ἐν τῷ φανερῷ); nor is that circumcision, which is outward in the flesh: but he is a Jew, who is one inwardly (ἐν τῷ κρυπτῷ); and circumcision is that of the heart, in the spirit, not in the letter; whose praise is not of men, but of God."

But the immediate context, no less than the writer's own definitions, generally serves to exhibit any peculiar usage of words. Thus, πνεῦμα, *wind, spirit*, is used in the New Testament to denote the wind (John 3:8), the vital breath (Rev. 11:11), the natural disposition or temper of mind (Luke 9:55; Gal. 6:1), the life principle or immortal nature of man (John 6:63), the perfected spirit of a saint in the heavenly life (Heb. 12:23), the unclean spirits of demons (Matt. 10:1; Luke 4:36), and the Holy Spirit of God (John 4:24; Matt. 28:19; Rom. 8:9–11). It needs but a simple attention to the context, in any of these passages, to determine the particular sense in which the word is used. In John 3:8, we note the two different meanings of πνεῦμα in one and the same verse. "The wind (τὸ πνεῦμα) blows where it will, and the sound of it thou hearest; but thou knowest not whence it comes and whither it goes; so is every one who is born of the Spirit" (ἐκ τοῦ πνεύματος). Bengel holds, indeed, that we should here render πνεῦμα in both instances by spirit, and he urges that the divine Spirit, and not the wind, has a *will* and a *voice*.[1] But the great body of interpreters maintain the common version. Nicodemus was curious and perplexed to know the *how* (πῶς, vv. 4, 9) of the Holy Spirit's workings, and as the Almighty of old spoke to Job out of the whirlwind, and appealed to the manifold mysteries of nature in vindication of his ways, so here the Son of God appeals to the mystery in the motion of the wind. "Wouldst thou know the whence and whither of the Spirit, and yet thou knowest not the origin and the end of the common wind? Wherefore dost thou not marvel concerning the air which breathes around thee, and of which thou livest?"[2] "Our Lord," says Alford, "might have chosen any of the mysteries of nature to illustrate the point. He takes that one which is above others symbolic of the action of the Spirit, and which in both languages, that in which he spoke, as well as that in which his speech is reported, is expressed by the same word. So that the words as they stand apply themselves at once to the Spirit and His working, without any figure."[3]

The word στοιχεῖον, used in classical Greek for the upright post of a sundial, then for an elementary sound in language (from letters standing in rows), came to be used almost solely in the plural, τὰ στοιχεῖα, in the sense of *elements* or *rudiments*. In 2 Peter 3:10 it evidently denotes the elements of nature, the component parts of the physical universe; but in Galatians 4:3, 9, as the immediate context shows, it denotes the ceremonials of Judaism, considered as elementary object lessons, adapted to the capacity of children. In this sense the word may also denote the ceremonial elements in the religious cults of the heathen world (compare v. 8).[4] The enlightened Christian should grow out of these, and pass beyond them, for otherwise they trammel, and become a system of bondage. Compare also the use of the word in Colossians 2:8, 20 and Hebrews 5:12.

In connection with the immediate context, the nature of the subject may also determine the usage of a word. Thus, in 2 Corinthians 5:1–2, the reference of the words οἰκία, *house*, σκῆος, *tabernacle*, οἰκοδομή, *building*, and οἰκητήριον, *habitation*, to the body as a covering of the soul hardly admits of question. The whole passage (vv. 1–4) reads literally thus: "For we know that if our house of the tabernacle upon earth were dissolved, a building from God we have, a house not made with hands, eternal, in the heavens. For also in this we groan, yearning to be clothed upon with our habitation which is from heaven, since indeed also (εἴγε καὶ) being clothed we shall not be found naked. For, indeed, we who are in the tabernacle groan, being burdened, in that we would not be unclothed, but clothed upon, to the end that that which is mortal may be swallowed up by the life." Hodge holds that the "building from God" is heaven itself, and argues that in John 14:2, heaven is compared to a house of many mansions; in Luke 16:9, to a habitation; and in Hebrews 11:10, and Revelation 21:10, to a city of dwellings.[5] But the scripture in question is too explicit, and the nature of the subject too limited, to allow other scriptures, like those cited, to determine its meaning. No one doubts that the phrase, "our house of the tabernacle upon earth," refers to the human body, which is liable to dissolution. It is compared to a tent, or tabernacle (σκῆος), and also to a vesture, thus presenting its with a double metaphor. "The word tent," says Stanley, "lent itself to this imagery, from being used in later Greek writers for the human body, especially in medical writers, who seem to have been led to adopt the word from the *skin*-materials of which tents were composed. The explanation of this abrupt transition from the figure of a house or tent to that of a garment, may be found in the image, familiar to the apostle, both from his occupations and his birthplace, of the tent of Cilician haircloth, which might almost equally suggest the idea of a habitation and of a vesture. Compare the same union of metaphors in Psalm 104:2, 'Who coverest thyself with light as with a garment; who stretchest out the heavens like a curtain' (of a tent).''[6]

The main subject, then, is the present body considered as an earthly house, a tabernacle upon earth. In it we groan; in it we are under burden; in it we endure "the momentary lightness of our affliction" (τὸ παραυτίκα ἐλαφρὸν τῆς θλίψεως), which is mentioned in 4:17, and which is there set in contrast with an "eternal weight of glory" (αἰώνιον βάρος δόξης) To this earthly house, heaven itself, whether considered as the house of many mansions (John 14:2) or the city of God (Rev. 21:10), affords no true antithesis. The true antithesis is the heavenly body, the vesture of immortality, which is from God. For the opposite of *our house* is the *building from God*; the one may be *dissolved*, the other is *eternal*, the one is *upon earth* (ἐπίγειος), the other is (not heaven itself, but) *in the heavens*. The true parallel to the entire passage before us is 1 Corinthians 15:47–54, where the earthly and the heavenly bodies are contrasted, and it is said (v. 53) "this corruptible must be clothed with incorruption, and this mortal must be clothed with immortality."

The above example also illustrates how antithesis, contrast, or opposition, may serve to determine the meaning of words. A further instance may be cited from Romans 8:5–8. In verse 4 the apostle has introduced the antithetic expressions κατὰ σάρκα, and κατὰ πνεῦμα, *according to the flesh* and *according to the spirit*. He then proceeds to define, as by contrast, the two characters. "For they who are according to the flesh the things of the flesh do mind (φρονοῦσιν, *think of, care for*), but they, according to the spirit, the things of the spirit. For the mind of the flesh is death, but the mind of the spirit life and peace. Because the mind of the flesh is enmity toward God, for to the law of God it does not submit itself, for it is not able; and they who are in the flesh are not able to please God." The spirit, throughout this passage, is to be understood of the Holy Spirit: "the Spirit of life in Christ Jesus," mentioned in verse 2, which delivers the sinner "from the law of sin and of death." The being *according to the flesh*, and the being *in the flesh*, are to be understood of unregenerate and unsanctified human life, conditioned and controlled by carnal principles and motives. This Scripture, and more that might be cited, indicates, by detailed opposition and contrast, the essential and eternal antagonism between sinful carnality and redeemed spirituality in human life and character.

The *usus loquendi* of many words may be seen in the parallelisms of Hebrew poetry. Whether the parallelism be synonymous or antithetic, it may serve to exhibit in an unmistakable way the general import of the terms employed. Take, for example, the following passage from Psalm 18:6–15 (Heb. 7–16):

6   In my distress I call Jehovah,
    And to my God I cry;
    He hears from his sanctuary my voice,
    And my cry before him comes into his ears.
7   Then shakes and quakes the land,
    And the foundations of the mountains tremble,
    And they shake themselves, for he was angry.
8   There went up a smoke in his nostril,
    And fire from his mouth devours;
    Hot coals glowed from him.
9   And he bows the heavens and comes down,
    And a dense gloom under his feet;
10  And he rides upon a cherub, and flies,
    And soars upon the wings of the wind.
11  He sets darkness his covering,
    His pavilion round about him,
    A darkness of waters, thick clouds of the skies.
12  From the brightness before him his thick clouds passed away,
    Hail, and hot coals of fire.
13  Then Jehovah thunders in the heavens,
    And the Most High gives forth his voice,
    Hail, and hot coals of fire.
14  And he sends forth his arrows and scatters them,
    And lightnings he shot, and puts them in commotion.
15  And the beds of the waters are seen,
    And the foundations of the world are uncovered,
    From thy rebuke, O Jehovah!
    From the breath of the wind of thy nostril.

It requires but little attention here to observe how such words as *call, cry, he hears my voice,* and *my cry comes into his ears* (v. 6), mutually explain and illustrate one another. The same may be said of the words *shakes, quakes, tremble,* and *shake themselves,* in verse 7; *smoke, fire,* and *coals* in verse 8; *rides, flies,* and *soars* in verse 10; *arrows* and *lightnings, scatters,* and *puts in commotion,* in verse 14; and so to some extent of the varied expressions of nearly every verse.

Here, too, may be seen how subject and predicate serve to explain one another. Thus, in verse 8, above, *smoke goes up, fire devours, hot coals glow.* So in Matthew 5:13: "if the salt become tasteless," the sense of the verb μωρανθῇ, *become tasteless,* is determined by the subject ἅλας, *salt.* But in Romans 1:22, the import of this same verb is *to become foolish,* as the whole sentence shows: "Professing to be wise, they become foolish," i.e., made fools of themselves. The word is used in a similar signification in 1 Corinthians 1:20: "Did not God make foolish the wisdom of the world?" The extent to which qualifying words, as adjectives and adverbs, serve to limit or define the meaning is too apparent to call for special illustration.

A further and most important method of ascertaining the *usus loquendi* is an extensive and careful comparison similar or parallel passages of Scripture. When a writer has treated a given subject in different parts of his writings or when different writers have treated the same subject, it is both justice to the writers, and important in interpretation, to collate and compare all that is written. The obscure or doubtful passages are to be explained by what is plain and simple. A subject may be only incidentally noticed in one place, but be treated with extensive fullness in another. Thus, in Romans 13:12, we have the exhortation, "Let us put on the armor of light," set forth merely in contrast with "cast off the works of darkness"; but if we inquire into this "armor of light," how much more fully and forcibly does it impress us when we compare the detailed description given in Ephesians 6:13–17: "Take up the whole armor of God. . . . Stand, therefore, having girded your loins with truth, and having put on the breastplate of righteousness, and having shod your feet with the preparation of the gospel of peace; withal taking up the shield of faith wherewith ye shall be able to quench all the fiery darts of the evil one. And take the helmet of salvation, and the sword of the Spirit, which is the word of God." Compare also 1 Thessalonians 5:8.

The meaning of the word אָנֻשׁ (compare the Greek νόσος) in Jeremiah 17:9, must be determined by ascertaining its use in other passages. The common version translates it "desperately wicked," but usage does not sustain this meaning. The primary sense of the word appears to be *incurably sick*, or *diseased*. It is used in 2 Samuel 12:15, to describe the condition of David's child when smitten of the Lord so that it *became very sick* (וַיֵּאָנַשׁ). It is used in reference to the lamentable idolatry of the kingdom of Israel (Micah 1:9), where the common version renders, "Her wound is *incurable*," and gives in the margin, "She is grievously sick of her wounds." The same signification appears also in Job 34:6: "My wound (חִצִּי, wound caused by an arrow) is incurable." In Isaiah 17:11, we have the thought of "incurable pain," and in Jeremiah 15:18, we read, "Wherefore has my pain been enduring, and my stroke incurable?" Compare also Jeremiah 30:12, 15. In Jeremiah 17:16, the prophet uses this word to characterize the day of grievous calamity as *a day of mortal sickness* (יוֹם אָנוּשׁ). In the ninth verse, therefore, of the same chapter, where the deceitful heart is characterized by this word, which everywhere else maintains its original sense of a *diseased and incurable condition*, we should also adhere to the main idea made manifest by all these parallels: "Deceitful is the heart above every thing; and *incurably diseased* is it; who knows it?"

The *usus loquendi* of common words is, of course, to be ascertained by the manner and the connection in which they are generally used. We feel at once the incongruity of saying, "Adriansz or Lippersheim discovered the telescope, and Harvey invented the circulation of the blood." We know from familiar usage that *discover* applies to the finding out or uncovering of that which was in existence before, but was hidden from our view or knowledge, while the word *invent* is applicable to the contriving and constructing of something which had no actual existence before. Thus, the astronomer invents a telescope, and by its aid discovers the motions of the stars. The passage in 1 Corinthians 14:34–35 has been wrested to mean something else than the prohibition of women's speaking in the public assemblies of churches. Some have assumed that the words *churches* and *church* in these verses are to be understood of the business meetings of the Christians, in which it was not proper for the women to take part. But the entire context shows that the apostle has especially in mind the worshiping assembly. Others have sought in the word λαλεῖν a peculiar sense, and, finding that it bears in classic Greek writers the meaning of *babble, prattle*, they have strangely taught that Paul means to say: "Let your women keep silence in the churches; for it is not permitted them to *babble*. . . . For it is a shame for a woman to *babble* in church!" A slight examination shows that in this same chapter the word λαλεῖν, *to speak*, occurs more than twenty times, and in no instance is there any necessity or reason to understand it in other than its ordinary sense of *discoursing, speaking*. Who, for instance, would accuse Paul of saying, "I thank God, I *babble* with tongues more than ye all" (v. 18); or "let two or three of the prophets *babble*, and the others judge" (v. 29)? Hence appears the necessity, in interpretation, of observing the general usage rather than the etymology of words.

In ascertaining the meaning of rare words, ἅπαξ λεγόμενα, or words which occur but once, and words of doubtful import, the ancient versions of Scripture furnish an important aid. For, as Davidson well observes, "An interpreter cannot arrive at the right meaning of every part of the Bible by the Bible itself. Many portions are dark and ambiguous. Even in discovering the correct sense, no less than in defending the truth, other means are needed. Numerous passages will be absolutely unintelligible without such helps as lie out of the Scriptures. The usages of the Hebrew and Hebrew-Greek languages cannot be fully known by their existing remains."[7]

In the elucidation of difficult words and phrases the Septuagint translation of the Old Testament holds the first rank among the ancient versions. It antedates all existing Hebrew manuscripts; and parts of it, especially the Pentateuch, belong, without much doubt, to the third century before the Christian era. Philo and Josephus appear to have made more use of it than they did of the Hebrew original; the Hellenistic Jews used it in their synagogues, and the New Testament writers frequently quote from it. Being made by Jewish scholars, it serves to show how before the time of Christ the Jews interpreted their Scriptures. Next in importance to the Septuagint is the Vulgate, or Latin Version, largely prepared in its present form by St. Jerome, who derived much knowledge and assistance from the Jews of his time. After these we place the Peshito-Syriac Version, the Targums, or Chaldee Paraphrases of the Old Testament, especially that of Onkelos on the Pentateuch, and Jonathan Ben Uzziel on the Prophets, and the Greek versions of Aquila, Symmachus, and Theodotion.[8] The other ancient versions, such as the Arabic, Coptic, Æthiopic, Armenian, and Gothic, are of less value, and, in determining the meaning of rare words, cannot be relied on as having any considerable weight or authority.

A study and comparison of these ancient versions will show that they often differ very widely. In many instances it is easy to see, in the light of modern researches, that the old translators fell into grave errors, and were often at a loss to determine the meaning of rare and doubtful words. When the context, parallel passages, and several of the versions agree in giving the same signification to a word, that signification may generally be relied upon as the true one. But when the word is an ἅπαξ λεγόμενον, and the passage has no parallel, and the versions vary, great caution is necessary lest we allow too much authority to one or more versions, which, after all, may have been only conjectural.

The following examples will illustrate the use, and the interest attaching to the study, of the ancient versions. In the Authorized English Version of Genesis 1:2, the words תֹהוּ וָבֹהוּ are translated, *without form and void*. The Targum of Onkelos has צָדְיָא וְרֵיקַנְיָא, *waste and empty*; the Vulgate: *inanis et vacua, empty and void*; Aquila: κένωμα καὶ οὐδέν, *emptiness and nothing*. Thus, all these versions substantially agree, and the meaning of the Hebrew words is now allowed to be *desolation and emptiness*. The Syriac merely repeats the Hebrew words, but the Septuagint reads ἀόρατος καὶ ἀκατασκεύαστος, *invisible and unformed*, and cannot be allowed to set aside the meaning presented in all the other versions.

In Genesis 49:6, the Septuagint gives the more correct translation of עִקְּרוּ שׁוֹר, *they houghed an ox*, ἐνευροκόπησαν ταῦρον; but the Chaldee, Syriac, Vulgate, Aquila, and Symmachus read, like the Authorized Version, *they digged down a wall*. Here, however, the authority of versions is outweighed by the fact that, in all other passages where the Piel of this word occurs, it means to *hamstring* or *hough* an animal. Compare Joshua 11:6, 9; 2 Samuel 8:4; 1 Chronicles 18:4. Where the *usus loquendi* can thus be determined from the language itself, it has more weight than the testimony of many versions.

The versions also differ in the rendering of עַצְּבֹת in Psalm 16:4. This word elsewhere (Job 9:28; Ps. 147:3; Prov. 10:10; 15:13) always means *sorrow*; but the form עָצָב means *idols*, and the Chaldee, Symmachus, and Theodotion so render עַצְּבֹת in Psalm 16:4: *they multiply their idols*, or *many are their idols*. But the Septuagint, Vulgate, Syriac, Arabic, Ethiopic, and Aquila, render the word *sorrows*, and this meaning is best sustained by the usage of the language.

In Cant. 2:12, עֵת הַזָּמִיר is rendered by the Septuagint καιρὸς τῆς τομῆς, *time of the cutting*; Symmachus, *time of the pruning* (κλαδεύσεως); so also the Vulgate, *tempus putationis*. Most modern interpreters, however; discard these ancient versions here, and understand the words to mean, *the time of song is come*; not merely or particularly *the singing of birds*, as the English version, but all the glad songs of springtime, in which shepherds and husbandmen alike rejoice. In this interpretation they are governed by the consideration that זָמִיר and זְמִירוֹת signify *song* and *songs* in 2 Samuel 23:1; Job 35:10; Psalms 95:2; 119:54; Isaiah 24:16; 25:5, and that when "the blossoms have been seen in the land" the pruning time is altogether past.

In Isaiah 52:13 all the ancient versions except the Chaldee render the word יַשְׂבִּיל in the sense of *acting wisely*. This fact gives great weight to that interpretation of the word, and it ought not to be set aside by the testimony of one version, and by the opinion, which is open to question, that יַשְׂבִּיל is in some passages equivalent to הִצְלִיחַ, to *prosper*.

From the above examples it may be seen what judgment and caution are necessary in the use of the ancient versions of the Bible. In fact, no specific rules can safely be laid down to govern us in the use of them. Sometimes the etymology of a word, or the context, or a parallel passage may have more weight than all the versions combined; while in other instances the reverse may be true. Where the versions are conflicting, the context and the analogy of the language must generally be allowed to take the precedence.

In ascertaining the meaning of many Greek words the ancient and glossaries of Hesychius, Suidas, Photius, and others are useful; but as they treat very few of the obscure words of the New Testament, they are of comparatively little value to the biblical interpreter. Scholia, or brief critical notes on portions of the New Testament, extracted chiefly from the writings of the Greek Fathers, such as Origen and Chrysostom, occasionally serve a good purpose,[9] but they have been superseded by the more thorough and scholarly researches of modern times, and the results of this research are embodied in the leading critical commentaries and biblical lexicons of the present day. The Rabbinical commentaries of Aben-Ezra, Jarchi, Kimchi, and Tanchum are often found serviceable in the exposition of the Old Testament.

# ELEVEN

# THE RELATION OF PURPOSE AND MEANING IN INTERPRETING SCRIPTURE

## Norman L. Geisler

DOES PURPOSE DETERMINE meaning or does meaning determine purpose? Which is the cart and which is the horse? It is common among evangelicals to appeal to the purpose of the author to determine the meaning of a passage. Is this legitimate? Are there any dangers in so doing?

In this study I propose two theses in answer to these important questions: (1) Purpose does not determine meaning. Rather, meaning determines purpose. (2) Using purpose to determine meaning sometimes leads to unorthodox conclusions, including a denial of the full verbal inspiration (inerrancy) of Scripture.

## THE MEANING OF THE WORD *INTENTION*

### Several Meanings of the Word *Intention*

Evangelicals often refer to the *intention* of the biblical author in order to determine the meaning of a passage. According to one meaning of the word *intention*, this is certainly important, for surely the meaning resides in what the author intended by the passage as opposed to what the readers may take it to mean to them.[1] However, the word *intention*, like most words, has several meanings. Not all of these usages are legitimate in this connection. The following sentences provide examples of four different meanings of the word *intention*. *Intention* may mean:

1. *plan*, as in: "I intend to go tomorrow";
2. *purpose*, as in: "My intention was to help you";
3. *thought in one's mind*, as in: "I didn't intend to say that";
4. *expressed meaning*, as in: "The truth intended in John 3:16 is clear."

143

## The Legitimate Sense of the Word *Intention*
## in the Context of Hermeneutics

First, evangelicals who believe in verbal[2] inspiration of Scripture should not use *intention* in the third sense when referring to the meaning of Scripture, for the locus of meaning (and truth) is not in the author's mind behind the text of Scripture. What the author meant is expressed *in* the text. The writings (γραφή) are inspired, not the thoughts in the author's mind.

Second, when we speak of understanding the meaning of a text we do not refer to some *plan* which the author had to express this meaning, whether or not it got expressed (no. 1 above). All we know of the author's intention is what the author did express in the text, not what he planned to say but did not express. Our knowledge of the author's plan (intention) is limited to the inspired text itself. So to speak of an intention which did not get expressed is to shift the locus of authority from the text to the author's mind behind the text.[3]

Third, the word intention can mean purpose (no. 3 above). This raises the question of whether we should look for the purpose of the author when we seek to find out what he really meant. Before we can answer this question properly we must define what is meant by the word *purpose* in this connection. The following contrast will clarify how we are using these terms:

1. Meaning is *what* the author expressed.
2. Purpose is *why* the author expressed it.

If this is so, then the question we pose is this: does the purpose (why) of the author determine his meaning (what)? Or, does the meaning determine the purpose? Our thesis is that purpose does not determine meaning. Actually, as I shall show later, the reverse is true, namely, meaning determines purpose.

Finally, the proper meaning of the *intention* of the author is the *expressed meaning* in the text (no. 4). Just as we do not say that the beauty is behind the painting, so the hermeneutically discoverable meaning is not located *behind* the text in the author's intention (no. 3). Rather, the meaning (*intention* no. 4) is expressed *in* the text the way beauty is expressed in the pigments on the canvas of a painting.[4]

The misuse of the word *intention*, to stand for the purpose (why) of the author, rather than for the meaning (what) of the author, often leads to unorthodox conclusions. One such conclusion is the denial of the full inspiration (inerrancy) of Scripture. This will become apparent in the discussion of the relation between meaning and purpose which follows.

## THE RELATION OF MEANING AND PURPOSE

Meaning can be known independently of knowing the author's purpose. Of course, there is a sense in which one always knows the purpose of an author: his purpose is to convey his meaning. But in this sense it would be circular to claim that purpose determines meaning, for *purpose* in this sense simply means to convey the meaning. One can know the meaning (what) of a passage (including what we should *do* as a result of knowing the meaning) apart from knowing the purpose (why) the author had in mind for expressing that meaning. If this is so, then purpose could not possibly determine meaning, for if it did, then one could not know the meaning unless he first knew the purpose.

### Select Passages Illustrating the Relation of Meaning and Purpose

Some "difficult" passages of Scripture will serve as illustrations of the point that purpose does not determine meaning. Exodus 23:19 is a good test case: "Do not boil a kid in its mother's milk." Checking only three commentaries (Lange, Keil and Delitzsch, and Ellicott) yielded numerous different suggestions as to why the author said this. But despite the lack of unanimity or clarity as to the *purpose* of the author there is absolutely no question as to the *meaning* of the author.

The *meaning* (what) of Exodus 23:19 is simply this: Do not put a baby goat into a kettle of its mother's milk and heat it up to the boiling point. There is no word in the passage of doubtful meaning (usage), and every Hebrew who could read (or hear) this command knew exactly what it meant. And they knew precisely what he/she should do in obedience to this command.

Furthermore, the *meaning* would not be different, even if this statement were found in a cookbook. It would still mean that baby goat's meat should not be boiled in goat's milk. Of course, if it were found in a cookbook the *significance* would be different. Its significance is gained from the fact that it is a command of God in Scripture, not merely a human recipe, and from the overall context of this command in the Levitical legislation, which imparts theocratic significance that it would not have in a cookbook. However, the *meaning* is the same in both cases; only the *significance* differs. The *affirmation* (or command) is the same; only the *implications* differ. Further, even these broader implications are not determined by purpose; they are determined by the overall context of *who* said it, to *whom* it was said, and under *what* circumstances, etc. But *why* it was said (other than the purpose to communicate this *meaning*, what) has no determinative effect on the meaning of what was said.

However, despite the perfect clarity of the *meaning* of this passage, it is not at all clear what purpose the author of Exodus (Moses) had in giving this command. Here are seven of the speculations about purpose found within a few minutes in three commentaries. The prohibition of boiling a kid in its mother's milk was given:

1. because this was an idolatrous practice;
2. because it was a magical practice to make the land more productive;
3. because it was cruel to destroy an offspring in the very means (milk) which sustained it;
4. because it showed contempt for the parent-child relation;
5. because it would profane (symbolically) the Feast of Ingathering;
6. because God wanted them to use olive oil, not butter, for cooking;
7. because it was too luxurious or Epicurean.

The truth of the matter is that we do not know for sure the purpose of this text. In fact, it doesn't really matter what the purpose is. The meaning is clear, and this is all that matters. Meaning stands apart from purpose. Understanding purpose is not necessary for knowing the meaning of a passage. One can know what is meant (and what to do) without knowing why God gave this command.

The same point can be made from numerous "difficult" passages. The meaning in these passages is clear even if the purpose is not. Note the following Old Testament examples:

1. Do not eat shrimp (Lev. 11:10).
2. Do not wear a garment which mixes wool and linen (Deut. 22:11).
3. Do not have sex during the woman's menstrual period (Lev. 20:18).

Despite the fact that we do not know the purpose for these commands, the *meaning* is perfectly clear. The fact is that knowing their meaning is not dependent on knowing their purpose.

## Several Reasons Why Purpose Does Not Determine Meaning

The thesis that purpose does not determine meaning can now be supported by several additional arguments.

First, if purpose determined meaning, then we could not know the meaning (what) of a passage apart from knowing its purpose (why). But the above illustrations show clearly that meaning can be known apart from knowing purpose. So in spite of whatever added light may be cast on a passage by knowing one or more of the author's purposes, in no sense is the basic meaning of the passage dependent on knowing these purposes. Knowing the purpose can help illuminate the significance(s) of a passage, but it does not determine its meaning.

That is, knowing the purpose(s) may aid understanding *how* the author intended the meaning to be applied to the original readers (hearers), but it no more determines meaning than *application* (how) determines *interpretation* (what). In short, *how* does not determine *what* any more than *why* the author said it determines *what* is meant. What is meant stands independently of the many ways a truth may be applied, for a single interpretation may have many applications as well as many implications. For example, the meaning (what) of the great commands is to love God with all our heart and our neighbor as ourselves. But this meaning does not limit us in the many *ways* (hows) this love can be expressed. Nor does our understanding of this meaning guarantee that we see all the implications of this love. The significance of love is deeper than the meaning.

The second reason that purpose cannot be used to determine meaning is that there are often many purposes for a text. If meaning were determined by a specific purpose of a text, then we would have to know which of the many purposes of a text is *the* purpose. That is, how do we know which purpose is hermeneutically determinative? Take, for example, the book of Philippians: there are at least four purposes for which it was written: (1) to thank them for their gift (4:16–17); (2) to inform them of Paul's well-being (1:12–26); (3) to encourage them to rejoice in their faith (3:1; 4:4); and (4) to help resolve the conflict between two feuding women (4:1–3). Now which of these is *the* purpose? How do we know for sure? Which purpose would we use to determine the meaning of the text? This leads to the next reason.

Third, many times we do not know what purpose(s) the author had in mind. Not all authors state their purpose as clearly as John did (John 20:30–31). Thus, the purpose of an author is often only a matter of conjecture. But if it is conjecture, then understanding the meaning of the passage is dependent on our guesses! Surely God did not plan that the meaning of so much Scripture should be subject to our widely divergent guesses. At any rate, to claim that purpose determines meaning and to acknowledge (as finitude and humility demand) that much of the time it is possible only to conjecture as to the central purpose is to admit that frequently we cannot know what the meaning of Scripture is.

Fourth, if our conjectures about purpose are often based on extra-biblical data (such as conditions, beliefs, or practices of the group addressed), then the meaning of Scripture is not self-contained. The meaning of Scripture would in fact be dependent on factors not found in the biblical text.[5] This is unacceptable for several reasons. First of all, it would sacrifice the very heart of Protestant hermeneutics, for it would make extra-biblical Protestant scholarship into a kind of teaching magisterium of its own. Further, it would make it practically impossible for the "laity" to understand the Scripture without the aid of "professional" interpretation, since only the latter are in command of the extra-biblical data on which the interpretation would depend.

Fifth, if purpose determines meaning there can be no systematic theology. For example, it would be impossible to treat traditional subjects, such as angelology and demonology. It is probably correct to say that it is not the central purpose of any book or section of Scripture to teach about angels or demons. But if the central purpose determines the meaning, then systematic theology is wrongly collecting and systematizing all of the incidental aspects of various passages which were not part of the determinative meaning of the passage. Not only is this true of angels and demons but it is true in most passages of Scripture relating to pneumatology, anthropology, and eschatology, for few passages have these subjects as their central purpose. In point of fact, the very concept of *systematizing* various truths is contrary to the purpose of most (if not all) passages of Scripture. In short, the bulk (if not whole) of systematic theology would be built on teachings which were not meant (purposed) by any author in any passage of Scripture. So if purpose determines meaning, then systematic theology would be meaningless.[6]

Finally, if knowing the purpose (apart from what the text affirms) determines the meaning of that text, then we cannot know the meaning of any passage of Scripture. Since human interpreters do not have supra-human knowledge, their understanding of the author's meaning is limited to *what* is expressed in the text. But purpose is not *what*; it is *why*. If all we know is what is expressed, then we can never really know why. And if knowing what a text means is determined by knowing why it was written, then we can never know what it means.

In summary, if purpose determines meaning then the final authority for determining meaning does not reside in the text itself but in factors outside the text, such as the alleged purpose of the author. In this case we would not have a firm objective basis for knowing the absolute truth of God on which man's eternal destiny is dependent. If, on the contrary, meaning is not determined by purpose, but is expressed objectively in the text, then all men who can read (or understand by hearing) are capable of knowing the basic message from God in Holy Scripture.

## HOW STRESSING PURPOSE
## LEADS TO UNORTHODOX CONCLUSIONS

A brief survey of the use of the principle that purpose determines meaning brings some sobering results for orthodox believers. Several examples will suffice.

## Non-literal Interpretation of Genesis 1 and 2

Evangelicals have always claimed that Genesis 1 and 2 convey information about God's creative acts in the space-time world. While evangelicals differ about the details of the time of creation and number of the kinds of animals created, there is general agreement that cosmological truths about creation are expressed in these chapters, not simply religious truth.

Some interpreters of Genesis 1 and 2, however, have generally not recognized the scientific and historical nature of the early chapters of Genesis.[7] Why? Often the answer seems to be in their acceptance of the principle that purpose determines meaning. It is sometimes alleged that the purpose of Genesis 1 and 2 is to describe God's creative acts in a way that will lead men to worship Him. This *conjectured* purpose is used then in a hermeneutically definitive way to explain away the obvious affirmations about the creation of animals and humans and to open the door for an evolutionary view of origins. In other words, if purpose *determines* meaning, then what seems to be a description of literal creation does not really mean this; it is simply a "myth" of origin to evoke our worship of God. Thus, by using purpose to determine meaning such interpreters have effectively obscured the literal meaning of the text of Genesis 1–2.

The same procedure is used by pro-homosexual interpreters of verses like Leviticus 18:22. The text says, "You shall not be with a male as one lies with a female; it is an abomination." But according to a pro-homosexual understanding of this verse, one must view this obvious prohibition against homosexual acts in view of the purpose of the author. Just what was this purpose? According to some pro-gay interpreters, the purpose was to preserve ritual purity or to avoid idolatry. It was not to make moral pronouncements about the wrongness of homosexual acts.[8] Thus, we are told that when one "understands" the prohibition *in the light of this purpose* there is, in fact, no moral condemnation here against homosexual acts.

Rudolph Bultmann's methodology is another example of the purpose-determines-meaning hermeneutic in operation. Bultmann acknowledged that the New Testament documents present the life of Christ in terms of miraculous stories culminating in the story of the resurrection of Christ. However, when these stories are seen in the light of the central purpose of the author, which is to evoke an existential commitment to the Transcendent, then they must be understood as myths.[9] These myths do not describe space-time events, but rather, they are religious stories designed to evoke an existential commitment to the Transcendent. Here again, using purpose to determine meaning has led to a distortion and negation of the true meaning of the text.

Let us take an example of the same procedure practiced by someone less liberal. Jack Rogers is well known for his attacks on the doctrine of inerrancy. What is not as well known is that he launched his attack from this same purpose-determines-meaning basis.[10] Rogers has not carried it as far as others have, but he has used it to deny the historic biblical teaching about the inerrancy of Scripture. Rogers's view is particularly dangerous because he not only claims to be orthodox, but he also claims to believe in the inspiration and authority of Scripture. He even insists that in one sense the whole Bible is true and without errors."[11] If this is so, then how is it that he can also insist that some of the scientific and historical statements of Scripture can be mistaken? He can do so because he practices a purpose-determines-meaning hermeneutic. According to Rogers, interpreting in view of the purpose of the author enables one to accept modern higher criticism. He wrote: "Because of his conviction that the purpose of Scripture was to bring us to salvation in Christ, Berkouwer, like Kuyper and Bavinck, was open to the results of critical scholarship in a way that the Princeton theology was not."[12] Here again when purpose is used as hermeneutically determinative of meaning the real meaning of Scripture can be obscured or negated.

Not all evangelicals carry this principle as far as in the foregoing examples. However, the same principle seems to be at work even among evangelicals who believe inerrancy and all major orthodox doctrines. Illustrations of this can be found in interpretations of how the New Testament uses the Old Testament. One example is Psalm 8:5, which reads: מֵאֱלֹהִים וַתְּחַסְּרֵהוּ מְעַט, "and you made him a little lower than God (מֵאֱלֹהִים)." The New Testament quotes this verse, following the LXX: ἠλάττωσας αὐτὸν βραχύ τι παρ' ἀγγέλους, "You made him a little lower than the angels" (Heb. 2:7). Some Hebrew scholars prefer to translate מֵאֱלֹהִים in the psalm as "God," but at the same time to maintain that the usage of the LXX translation's ἀγγέλους is appropriate, though not hermeneutically determinative for the interpretation of the Old Testament passage itself.[13] How then can one believe in the truthfulness of all Scripture (including Hebrews 2) and yet explain how this LXX translation is included in the inspired text of Hebrews 2? According to some evangelicals this can be accomplished as long as we remember "that the author of Hebrews did not intend to say anything about the temporary or permanent inferiority of Christ to angels. His sole purpose in using Psalm 8 was . . . to identify Jesus with man."[14] So it is claimed that the purpose of the writer of Hebrews is not to teach anything about angels in this passage, but is solely to stress the humanity (and humiliation) of Christ.[15] Thus, if this passage is interpreted in the light of its central *purpose* there is no problem.

For if this is so then the author is not stressing the mistaken part of the quotation but only the true part. In this way some believe they have retained a belief in inerrancy of Scripture and yet have explained the difference between the Hebrew of Psalm 8 and the inspired text of Hebrews 2. In fact, other inerrantists, including John Calvin, are cited in support of this position.[16] Calvin wrote: "The apostles were not so scrupulous, provided they perverted not Scripture to their own purpose. We must always have a regard to the end for which they quote passages. . . ."[17]

Laying aside this debatable statement from Calvin,[18] *in principle* there is no difference between this conclusion and that of the above examples where purpose determines meaning. In each of the above cases there are the following similarities:

1.  The text says something is so.
2.  But for some reason it is believed that this is not so.
3.  Yet the complete truthfulness of Scripture is claimed.
4.  This conclusion is justified by an appeal to the purpose of the author as the key to what the text really means.

In short the purpose-determines-meaning hermeneutic is used to explain a "mistake" in the text. For what is not so is believed to be outside the purpose of the text and therefore not contrary to inerrancy.

Of course there is a difference in the "size" or importance of the mistakes thus explained from person to person in the above examples. Bultmann uses the purpose-determines-meaning procedure to deny the essentials of the Faith, and homosexuals use it to justify immoral activity. Others use it to explain minor difficulties in the text. But for everyone there are places in which what the text actually says is considered wrong. So regardless of the size of the error in the various examples, the fact is that in each one the purpose of the author (and the interpreter sees it) is used to justify rejecting what the text actually affirms.

This next example does not fit the above pattern, but it does reveal a misuse of the purpose of the author. It is generally agreed that John states his purpose for writing his Gospel when he says "that you might believe that Jesus is the Christ" (John 20:31). So in this case we do not have to guess; we know for sure what his overall purpose is. Since this is the case, if purpose determines meaning, then it would follow that whenever there is any difficulty in knowing what a given passage means one could appeal to this purpose to help explain the difficulty. One writer takes this to imply that we should limit our application of the truths of the Gospel to what the author intended (purposed).[19] For example, some claim that how Jesus approached the woman at the well should not be used to teach how we can witness to others about Christ. For they say the author did not so intend this passage. They insist John intended this passage not to teach us how to witness but to show us that Jesus was the Messiah who could give living water.

Several things seem evident about this understanding of John. First, purpose is being used as hermeneutically determinative meaning. Second, *why* the passage was written is used to limit *how* the passage can be legitimately applied. In short, there is a twofold confusion. There is the already familiar problem of using the purpose (why) to determine meaning (what). But there is the additional confusion of using purpose (why) to limit application (how). But this is wrong. For simply because an author may have envisioned a particular application of the truth he affirmed does not mean that this is the only appropriate application of that meaning.

This hermeneutical mistake violates several principles. First, it is contrary to the inspired usage of one Scripture by other Scripture. For example, the meaning (what) of Hosea 11:1 ("Out of Egypt have I called my son") has its application in Hosea to the nation of Israel. However, in Matthew 2:15 its application is different; it is to the return of Christ from Egypt. Now if application must be limited to the way the original author applied it, then the divinely authoritative apostle Matthew made a mistake in his inspired writing. Some would justify this kind of error by appealing to a so-called inspired liberty of a biblical writer or to imply that he took leave of the Holy Spirit to change the intended meaning of the author expressed in the text.[20] But it seems to me this negates the whole evangelical hermeneutic. The inspired writings of the New Testament cannot be mistaken in how they use the Old Testament.

Further, if the application (how) of a passage is limited to the purpose (why), which really determines the meaning (what), then there is no way to preach (and apply) much of the Bible to most believers in the world today. For how a passage is applied will depend on the culture in which the person lives. "Lift holy hands [in prayer]" (1 Tim. 2:8); "Greet the brethren with a holy kiss" (1 Thess. 5:26); and women praying with a veil over their face (1 Cor. 11:13) are only a few of the examples which come to mind. In each case the *what* (meaning) is absolute but the *how* (application) is relative to the culture. For example, 1 Thessalonians 5:26 is an absolute obligation to greet fellow believers. Precisely what means (how) this greeting should take will depend on the culture. For some it will be a kiss, for others a hug, and for still others a handshake. The interpretation (what) is the same for all cultures but the application (how) will be different from culture to culture. There is another way to view the fallacy of tying the application to the purpose (and meaning). If the application is tied to the meaning, when the application changes, the meaning must change with it. But if the meaning changes then so does the truth which that meaning expresses also change. And if truth changes then it is not absolute but in process. Thus, we have a denial of the absolute or unchangeable truth of Scripture.

Finally, if application is inseparably connected with the purpose (and meaning) of the author then we have placed a straitjacket on the Holy Spirit. This would mean that we must apply all Scripture the same way the original author did. Besides the already noted problem that we are usually only guessing as to what the author's intended application was, this would make some passages of Scripture unpreachable in most churches. How many churches have drunkards at the Lord's Table (1 Cor. 11:21)? Or sons cohabiting with their stepmothers (1 Cor. 5:1)? Must we limit the Holy Spirit in *applying* the same truth (of the wrongness of these and numerous other acts) to the same kind of situations which occasioned the apostles' original exhortations? Surely a more sensible approach is to concentrate our hermeneutical efforts on getting the right *interpretation* of the passage. Once we are assured of this, then any application of *that* truth to anyone who in anyway needs that truth will be legitimate. Let us not hermetically seal the Holy Spirit into the container of our hermeneutics so as to suffocate the fresh breath He wishes to breathe on our lives as He applies the unchanging truth of Scripture to our changing situations. Those who oppose this method are ignoring the numerous divinely authorized examples of the same truth being applied in different ways within the Scripture itself.[21]

## AN ALTERNATIVE VIEW:
## LOOK FOR MEANING NOT PURPOSE

If we are not to use purpose to determine meaning then what does determine meaning? In order to answer this question properly, we must first make an important distinction. Technically speaking, the interpreter does not determine (cause) meaning by any hermeneutical procedure. Meaning is determined by the author; it is *discovered* by the reader (listener). Only minds cause meaning by (in) a medium of expression which other minds are thereby able to discern. So when we speak loosely of "determining" the meaning of the author we refer to the active hermeneutical process by which we discover the meaning which the author expressed. But since the process of interpretation is an active one there is some sense in which the reader is "determining" what the writer meant.

154 Rightly Divided: Readings in Biblical Hermeneutics

## Context Determines (Helps Us to Discover) Meaning

Purpose does not determine meaning; context determines meaning. First, this can be seen with respect to how a word is used in a sentence. Although we speak of the different meanings of words, technically speaking, words do not have any meaning. Words have different *usages* in sentences; sentences have meaning. There is no intrinsic meaning to isolated entities such as words any more than there is a meaning to letters of which words are composed. Like broken pieces of colored glass, words have no meaning unless they are formed into an overall picture or framework which expresses some thought or feeling. When the broken glass is formed into a cathedral window or the individual words structured into a poem they are given meaning by the overall *Gestalt* or order expressed by the mind. The meaning, however, is not in the individual words (or pieces of glass) but in the overall mosaic or structure into which they are intentionally shaped. Thus, it is their form or context which determines their meaning; the whole determines the parts.

What is true of the relation of individual words in a sentence is similarly true of the relation of individual sentences in a paragraph, and of a paragraph in a whole book. That is to say, the same series of words can have a different meaning in a different context. For example, the sentence "love the world" has a different meaning when used in the context of an exhortation against lust than it has in a paragraph about our need for compassion for the lost.

In the final analysis, the meaning of the smaller unit is determined by the broader context. This same principle applies as we move from word to sentence to paragraph to book to the whole Bible. But in each case it is not why (purpose) the author used the smaller unit in the larger, but how it fits into the overall picture (or meaning) he is portraying. It is misleading to inquire about the purpose for which (why) an artist used a triangular piece of blue glass to portray the sky in an unfilled triangular hole in the section of the mosaic portraying a sky. He used it because of how it fits into that position which conveys the desired meaning he wished to express. Thus the real question leading to the discovery of the meaning of the parts in relation to the whole is how the part fits into the overall picture, not the purpose for which it is there. It is obviously there because the author put it there. And he put it there because of how it fitted into the picture of the overall meaning it was his purpose to express. The question is: how do the small meaning units (m) fit into the larger unit of meaning (M)? The question is never, how does purpose (P) determine meaning? It is, how does overall meaning (M) determine particular meaning (m)?

The situation may be diagrammed as follows:

| Wrong View | Right View |
|---|---|
| Purpose determines meaning | Meaning determines purpose |
| P → M | M → P |

Or to put it all together—including the smaller units of meaning, the overall meaning, and the purpose—the situation could be diagrammed as follows:

AUTHOR → M → PURPOSE (end)

This raises the question of the "hermeneutical circle," for the whole is made up of the parts. Yet the parts are made up by the whole. Is this not a vicious circle, an impossible situation? It certainly would be if the parts determined the whole in the same sense that the whole determined the parts. Fortunately this is not the case. The following diagram illustrates how the parts relate to the whole in a different way than the whole relates to the parts.

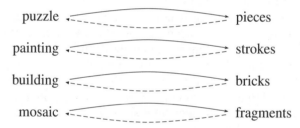

puzzle ⬅ ⟶ pieces

painting ⬅ ⟶ strokes

building ⬅ ⟶ bricks

mosaic ⬅ ⟶ fragments

It is obvious from these illustrations that the whole is related to the parts by way of *determination*, but the parts merely make a *contribution* to the whole. That is, the whole gives *structure* to the parts, whereas the parts provide the *stuff* for that form. In short, the parts are the *material* cause but the whole is the *formal* cause of the overall meaning (M). So it is that the small units of meaning (m) contribute to the larger meaning (M) in Scripture, whereas the larger meaning provides the determinative context for understanding the smaller units. It is in this sense that overall meaning (M) determines particular meanings (m). But purpose does not determine meaning.

## Meaning Determines Purpose

Not only does purpose *not* determine meaning, but just the reverse is true. There is a real sense in which the meaning of a passage determines its purpose. For once we know *what* God said in Scripture, we automatically know *why* He said it. He said it for the purpose of expressing this truth to us so that we could know and obey it. The purpose of all Scripture is for us to *understand* (and obey) the mind of God on the matter revealed. The purpose (why) of Scripture is always to convey the meaning (what). So, contrary to a widely accepted hermeneutic, meaning is the "horse" and purpose is the "cart." To claim that purpose determines the meaning is to get the cart before the horse.

## Where Does the Central Unity of a Passage Reside?

Many students of Scripture are so accustomed to looking for the central purpose of a book that they feel that the method proposed here will rob them of the primary objective of looking for the central purpose of a book. If we should not look for purpose of a passage, then for what should we look? In brief, the answer is, we should look for the *unifying theme* of the book. We should ask what it is that holds the whole book together the way the picture unifies all the pieces of a puzzle. That overall order is the unifying theme.

To put it another way, we should look for the *overall argument* of the author. This can be done by tracing the premises, by observing how they build, and by noting the conclusions the author draws from them. But whether we call it unifying theme or overall argument we are looking for the *what* (meaning), not the *why* (purpose) of a book. Herein lies the key to understanding the Word of God. On the contrary, seeking the alleged purpose of the author and interpreting the parts in the light of it will be both confusing and misleading. It will inevitably lead to a distortion of the very meaning which we allegedly seek to understand, no matter how sincere or scholarly the approach may be.

## Relating Purpose and Meaning: A Summary

1. Purpose is not hermeneutically determinative of meaning. *Why* something is said never determines the meaning of *what* is said.
2. Purpose is formally independent of meaning. One can understand what is meant, even if he does not understand why it was said.
3. Using purpose to determine meaning leads to a distortion of the true meaning by reshaping the meaning to fit the purpose.
4. Using purpose to determine meaning confuses *application* (why) with *interpretation* (what). It confuses the content of the message with the *behavioral* change in the lives of the readers envisioned by the author.
5. Using purpose to determine meaning is a hermeneutical form of "the end (purpose) justifies (validates) the means (meaning)" principle. It is hermeneutical utilitarianism.[22]

This is not to deny that understanding purpose is often interesting and even illuminating. For *how* a passage is applied or *why* an author wrote it (that is, what changes he purposed in the readers) can be helpful in understanding the significance of the passage. However, to limit the application of the passage to our conjectures about the author's purpose, or to eliminate certain aspects of truth in the passage because they are not believed to be necessary to the central purpose, is hermeneutically illegitimate. It in fact may lead to a denial of the full inspiration and inerrancy of Scripture, as well as other teachings.

# TWELVE

# THE SINGLE INTENT
# OF SCRIPTURE

### Walter C. Kaiser, Jr.

EVEN BEFORE T. S. ELIOT, Ezra Pound, and their associates began to argue on literary grounds that the meaning of a biblical text was independent of an author's verbal meanings, evangelical exegetical practice had likewise begun to slip into an easygoing subjectivism. Words, events, persons, places, and things in Scripture were allowed to signify all they could be made to signify apart from any authorial controls of those prophets and apostles who claimed to have stood in the divine council and received this intelligible revelation.

Almost as if to prepare for the banishment of the author in later theories of literary criticism, evangelicals began to excuse their multiple interpretations of a single text as logical outgrowths of the fact that: (1) Scripture had two authors (God and the human writer); (2) prophecy had at least two meanings (the prophet's understanding and God's surprise meaning in the distant fulfillment); and (3) interpreters are divided into two groups: the natural man who fails to "receive the things of God" (1 Cor. 2:14) and the spiritual man who understands the deep things of God.

But such views were so antithetical to the actual statements and claims of Scripture that if any or all of them were consistently pressed, they would lead to outright departure from the concept of an intelligible revelation from God. Bishop Ryle likewise commented:

> I hold it to be a most dangerous mode of interpreting Scripture, to regard everything which its words may be tortured into meaning as a lawful interpretation of the words. I hold undoubtedly that there is a mighty depth in all Scripture, and that in this respect it stands alone. But I also hold that the words of Scripture were intended to have one definite sense, and that our first object should be to discover that sense, and adhere rigidly to it. I believe that, as a general rule, the words of

Scripture are intended to have, like all other language, one plain definite meaning, and that to say that words *do* mean a thing, merely because they *can* be tortured into meaning it, is a most dishonourable
and dangerous way of handling Scripture.[1]

While few would directly challenge the general legitimacy of Ryle's
principles, many would conveniently escape its full application to personal Bible study and the practical needs of the professional ministry.
For this group of unconvinced evangelical exegetes, there are parts of
the Bible that are given in terms unintelligible to the sacred writers
themselves and, as a consequence, to their original listeners. Accordingly, on this line of reasoning, there must be parts of the Bible incapable of being interpreted by the ordinary aids and procedures of
exegesis. These texts then become the exceptions that prove the rule
that, by and large, biblical exegesis is to be placed outside the pale of
the ordinary conventions of literary interpretation. Therefore, before
any progress can be made in the area of general hermeneutics or any
practical applications can be implemented in preaching and teaching,
an examination must be made of a representative number of texts that
point to the biblical writers' alleged ignorance, passivity, or mundane
apprehension of the messages they were receiving and delivering to
Israel and the church.

## ALLEGED PROOF TEXTS FOR "DOUBLE MEANING"

### 1 Peter 1:10–12

No text has appeared more frequently in the argument against the
single meaning of the text as found in the author's verbal meanings
than 1 Peter 1:10–12. I have treated this text at some length already,[2]
but it must be included here because of its central place in the debate.

Of which salvation the prophets have enquired and searched diligently,
who prophesied of the grace that should come unto you:
Searching what, or what manner of time the Spirit of Christ which
was in them did signify, when it testified beforehand the sufferings of
Christ, and the glory that should follow.
Unto whom it was revealed, that not unto themselves, but unto us
they did minister the things, which are now reported unto you by them
that have preached the gospel unto you with the Holy Ghost sent down
from heaven; which things the angels desire to look into.

Does this text teach that the writers of Scripture "wrote better than
they knew"? Indeed it does not. On the contrary, it decisively affirms

that the prophets spoke knowingly on five rather precise topics: (1) the Messiah, (2) His sufferings, (3) His glory, (4) the sequence of events (for example, suffering was followed by the Messiah's glorification), and (5) that the salvation announced in those pre-Christian days was not limited to the prophets' audiences, but it also included the readers of Peter's day (v. 12).

What they "enquired and searched diligently for" without any success was the *time* when these things would take place. The Greek phrase that gives the object of their searchings was "what" [time] or "what manner of time" [*eis tina ē poion kairon*] this salvation would be accomplished. In no case can the first interrogative "what" [*tina*] be translated as the RSV, NASB, the Berkeley, the Amplified, and the NEB footnote have it—"what person." Greek grammarians such as A. T. Robertson;[3] Blass, DeBrunner, and Funk;[4] the lexicon by Bauer, Arndt, and Gingrich;[5] and Moulton, along with such important commentaries as Charles Briggs and Edward G. Selwyn,[6] are all emphatic on the point: *tina* and *poion* are "a tautology for emphasis"[7] and both modify the word "time."

This passage does not teach that these men were curious and often ignorant of the exact meaning of what they wrote and predicted. Theirs was not a search for the *meaning* of what they wrote; it was an inquiry into the *temporal* aspects of the *subject*, which went beyond what they wrote. Let it be noted then that the *subject* is invariably larger than the verbal meaning communicated on any subject; nevertheless, one can know *adequately* and truly even if he does not know comprehensively and totally all the pans of a subject.

### Daniel 12:6–8

> And one said to the man clothed in linen, which was upon the waters of the river, How long shall it be to the end of these wonders?
>
> And I heard the man clothed in linen, which was upon the waters of the river, when he held up his right hand and his left hand unto heaven, and sware by him that liveth for ever that it shall be for a time, times, and an half; and when he shall have accomplished to scatter the power of the holy people, all these things shall be finished.
>
> And I heard, but I understood not: then said I, O my Lord, what shall be the end of these things?

Attention usually moves from 2 Peter 1:10–12 to this statement of Daniel. "I heard, but I understood not." But again, what was it that Daniel did not understand? Was it the words he was speaking? Not at all; the words he did not understand were those of the angel, not his own! Furthermore, the fact that these words of the angel were to be "closed up and sealed until the time of the end" was no more a sign that these events were to remain *unexplained* until the end time than was the equivalent expression used in Isaiah 8:16, "Bind up the testimony, seal the law." There, as here, the "sealing" of the testimonies was a reference primarily to the certainty of the predicted events.

Moreover, Daniel's question in verse 8 involved the temporal aspect and consequences of the angel's prophecy: "What shall be the end of these things?" One of the angels had asked in verse 6, "How long shall it be to the end of these wonders?" But Daniel asked a different question: "What" would be the state of affairs at the close of "the time, times, and an half"? Concerning this question he was given no further revelation. Therefore the "sealing up" of the prophecy only indicated its *certainty*, not its hiddenness.

Let it be admitted, however, that whenever the prophet received his revelation in a vision (for example, Dan. 8 or Zech. 1–6), the objects presented to his mind's eye were usually a preparation for the verbal prediction that accompanied that vision. Thus, in those cases the interpreting angel did not refuse to clarify the prophecy. So clear was Daniel's understanding of the meaning of his prophecy and so dramatic was its effect on him that he "was overcome and lay sick for some days" (Dan. 8:27, RSV).

To say that we now understand the predictions of the apostles and prophets better than they did contributes nothing to the present debate about authorial controls over meanings. Certainly a man who visits a country can understand the description of a place better than one who never personally saw it. But this is to confuse fullness of consequences or fullness of a total subject with the validity, truthfulness, and accuracy of contributions to that subject. And should this lead to the argument that God is the real Author of Scripture, it would still make no important difference. God did not make the writers omniscient. Rather, He imparted just as much as they needed to make their message effective for that moment in history and for the future contribution to the whole progress of revelation.[8]

### John 11:49–52

And one of them, named Caiaphas, being the high priest that same year, said unto them, Ye know nothing at all,

Nor consider that it is expedient for us, that one man should die for the people, and that the whole nation perish not.

And this spake he not of himself: but being high priest that year, he prophesied that Jesus should die for that nation;

And not for that nation only, but that also he should gather together in one the children of God that were scattered abroad.

Relentlessly the argument is pressed into the New Testament. There it is hoped that Caiaphas could be a witness for the double-author theory of hermeneutics.

Caiaphas pronounced an accurate judgment on his colleagues, "You know nothing at all" (John 11:49). But as Rudolf Stier asked, "What better, then, [did Caiaphas] know?"[9] His suggestion was one of political expediency: it is better to let one man be a sacrificial lamb to save the Jewish cause than to have everyone implicated, with Rome's wrath falling on the whole body politic.

John's comment on Caiaphas's speech was: "And this spake he not of himself: but being high priest that year, he prophesied . . ."

Now, several things must be observed:

1. These words are not to be classed along with later rabbinic alleged examples of unintentional prophecy, as cited by Strack and Billerbeck on John 11:51 and 2 Peter 1:20–21(II, 546). Nor is this proof that the earlier prophets belonged to such a category as Rabbi Eleazar (ca. A.D. 270), who argued, "No prophets have known what they prophesied. Only Moses and Elijah knew." Indeed, according to the same line of logic, even "Samuel, the master of the prophets, did not know what he prophesied."[10] Thus it is argued that Caiaphas illustrates the same process. But Caiaphas said what he wanted to say and mean. There was no compulsion or constraint here any more than there was in the superscription Pilate put over Jesus' cross. Rather, in these words John immediately saw there was "a grand irony of a most special Providence"[11] in the case of both Pilate and Caiaphas.[12]

2. The truth-intention of Caiaphas (v. 50) is to be sharply contrasted with the *significance* (v. 51) John found in these words, especially since Caiaphas was high priest when he uttered his cynical estimate of the situation. For John there was a strong contrast (note John's word, "on the contrary" [*alla*]) between what Caiaphas said and meant and what John under the inspiration of the Spirit of God disclosed by using many of the same words.

3. With that John *corrected* Caiaphas's provincial statement with its ethnocentricities and turned it into a comprehensive statement of the universal implications of Jesus' death (v. 52). Whereas Caiaphas had used the expression, "on behalf of the people" (v. 50), John corrected those words of cynical political expediency and expanded them to match the value of Jesus' death; it was now, "on behalf of the nation" (v. 51) and on behalf of the "children of God scattered abroad" (v. 52). Caiaphas had said that the nation was going to perish—therefore Jesus must die. John said that the people and nation were perishing—therefore Jesus must die to unite all the children of God, including the nation,

into the true "people" of God as Jesus had proclaimed in John 10:15–16 and as Paul would later describe in Ephesians 2:14.

4. John's evaluation of Caiaphas's speech was that "he did not speak on his own authority, but being high priest that year, he prophesied." The expression "on his own authority" is unique to John and occurs in six passages (John 5:19; 7:18; 11:51; 15:4; 16:13; 18:34). In three of the instances, it clearly means to say something on one's own authority: "The Son can do nothing on his own authority" (5:19), "a person who speaks on his own authority" (7:18), and "The Spirit . . . will not speak on his own authority" (16:13). If this meaning is also correct for John 11:51—and we believe it is—then John's point was not the method in which Caiaphas spoke (unconscious or involuntary prediction), but that since he was in the office of high priest when he gave this somewhat bitter proverb, it had the significance of an official prediction.[13] One cannot miss the repeated emphasis of verses 49 and 51, "He being high priest that year."

5. When verse 51 comments that he (Caiaphas) was prophesying *that* [*hoti*] Jesus was about to die, John is not giving us the contents of Caiaphas's prophecy, but only that the significance of his otherwise witty speech could be found in *reference to the fact that* Jesus was about to die. In Caiaphas we do not have the words of a true prophet coming with authority from God. Instead we see an erring high priest giving wicked counsel. However, God was pleased to turn this advice back on the speaker as a most appropriate explication of the very principle he was intent on denying.

Thus we conclude that if Caiaphas had prophesied in the ordinary sense of the word, there would have been no need for any immediate corrections on John's part. But when an official like himself or Pilate gave a verdict that could take on a proverbial status and significance which accorded with the plan of God, only the God of providence could be praised, for now the wrath of men had been turned into the glory of God. But such examples could not be used to support a double-author view of normative revelation. Even if every part of our previous argument failed, it still remains true that Caiaphas never belonged to the class of the apostle and prophets who received revelation.

## 2 Peter 1:19–21

We have also a more sure word of prophecy; whereunto ye do well that ye take heed, as unto a light that shineth in a dark place, until the day dawn, and the day star arise in your hearts:

Knowing this first, that no prophecy of the scripture is of any private interpretation.

> For the prophecy came not in old time by the will of man: but holy
> men of God spake as they were moved by the Holy Ghost.

Scholars of the standing and stature of E. W. Hengstenberg have appealed to 2 Peter 1:19–21 to show that the prophets did not always understand nor could they always interpret their own words. But Peter makes the opposite point. Christians, he argues, "have not followed cleverly devised fables" (v. 16), for not only was Peter among those eyewitnesses who saw Jesus' glory on the mount of Transfiguration (2 Peter 1:16–18), but "we have the stronger or more secure prophetic word" found in the Old Testament prophecies (v. 19a). If readers would attentively contemplate what was said in these Old Testament prophecies, they would find the day dawning and the day star rising in their own minds; they would become instructed, illuminated, and satisfied by means of the light shed from these prophecies (v. 19b).

These Old Testament Scriptures were not a matter of one's own "loosing" (*epiluseōs* v. 20), "because prophecy came not in old time by the will of man, but holy men of God spoke as they were moved by the Holy Spirit" (v. 21).

To make the word *epiluseōs* mean in this context an "explanation" or "interpretation," as some do, would be to argue that no prophet can interpret his own message—hence he had to write better than he knew. So argued Hengstenberg.

However, the claim is too bold for the following reasons:

1. The substantive *epilusis* in classical usage is a "freeing, loosing" or "destroying"; in other words, it is an unleashing from life. The only example of this form in the New Testament is 2 Peter 1:20; the Septuagint exhibits no instances of its usage either. However, the verbal form in its original meaning would appear to be "to set at liberty, to let go, to loose," while secondarily it came to mean "to explain, unfold, or interpret," as in Mark 4:34.

2. Even if that secondary meaning were intended by Peter here, it would claim too much. Can it be said that *all* prophetic writings were closed to their writers?

3. Peter's readers are urged to give heed to the Old Testament prophecies, "as unto a light that shineth in a dark place" because the Spirit of God has revealed through these prophets what is certain, plain, and intelligible. The light offered in the text came not from the ability of men, but from the "Father of lights" above. Had Peter's logic been, "Give heed to the light shining in a dark place since no prophet understood or could even explain what he said, but wrote as

he was carried along by the Holy Spirit," then the light would have been darkness and how could any, including the prophet, give heed to that enigmatic word? No, since the prophets were enlightened, instructed, and carried along by the Holy Spirit, they too were thus enabled to understand what they wrote. Otherwise we must ask for a second miracle—the inspiration of the interpreter.

### John 14:25–26; 15:26–27; 16:12–15

Some, of course, will not shrink from following this last suggestion to its ultimate end. After all, they say, did not the Spirit promise to "teach us all things" (John 14:26) and then take what was His and declare it to us (John 16:15)?

But as any serious New Testament student will immediately recognize, the "you" intended in these passages was not the body of believers at large but the future writers of the New Testament. This is clear from its larger contextual setting (the "upper room discourse") and from the immediate contextual notations such as:

| John 14:26 | He will teach you all things, and bring to your remembrance all that I have said to you when I was with you (RSV). |
| John 15:27 | You also are witnesses, because you have been with me from the beginning [of my earthly ministry] (RSV). |
| John 16:12–13 | I have yet many things to say to you, but you cannot bear them now [while I am still on earth with you men]. When the Spirit of truth comes, we will guide you into all the truth . . . (RSV). |

Therefore, believers must refrain from using these texts as proofs of their own inspired interpretations as against those meanings derived through the hard labor of exegesis. Almost every cult or aberration from historical Christian doctrine has appealed at one time or another to these three texts as their grounds for adding to the inscripturated Word of God, but all have failed to meet the demands of the text. They have never personally walked with the Lord while He was on the earth. They have never heard from His lips His instruction, and they were not witnesses from the start of His three-year ministry. But the apostles were! Therefore, that special band of men could record the life, words, and works of Christ in the Gospels with the Spirit's aid of recollection (John 14:26); teach doctrine ("what is mine"—John 16:14–15); and predict the future (John 16:12). They were eyewitnesses of what had happened to the Christ (John 15:26–27).

If believers complain that this principle, if applied consistently, could signal the rain of the Great Commission (Matt. 28:18–20) for contemporary believers, let it be noted that this was the precise problem William Carey faced when he launched the modern impetus for missions. Believers resisted the appeal to "go and make disciples" by arguing that that command was delivered to the disciples alone. But Carey answered wisely that the principle was extended to all, for that same text also said: "And lo, I am with you always even to the end of the age"! Hence the divine intention would admit no such easy excuses as the one Carey's generation offered at first. Such is also the solution to our texts; where the extension is made, it must be observed.

## 2 Corinthians 3:6; Romans 2:29; 7:6

As a final line of defense, some will appeal to the contrast between the dead exegesis of the "letter" of Scripture (according to them, the author's verbal meanings) versus the freedom of viewing the text under the fresh and immediate aid of the "Spirit."[14] But this stems from a false dichotomy that pretends to use the method it assails in order to substantiate the validity of its practice, only to depart from it once it is aloft. However, it is wrongheaded on both counts.

| 2 Corinthians 3:6 | The letter kills, but the spirit gives life (NASB). |
| Romans 2:29 | But he is a Jew, which is one inwardly; and circumcision is that of the heart, in the spirit, and not in the letter. |
| Romans 7:6 | We serve in newness of the Spirit and not in oldness of the letter (NASB). |

The Pauline word for "letter" in these verses is *gramma*, not *graphē*. Paul assails outward, fleshly, uncommitted "letterism"—a perfunctory external observance of the law which has no antecedent commitment of the life by faith to the God who has given the law. Such ceremonialism was a "serving in the oldness of the letter." But the *graphē* was sacred to Paul: it was the very Word of God.

Paul's complaint is not about the inadequacy of what was written or about what the words of the text meant grammatically and syntactically as used by individual writers. His complaint was rather with those who *by means of* observing the outward letter of the law and *by means of* [instrumental use of *dia* in Rom. 2:20] circumcision were actually breaking the law. Circumcision was really a matter of the heart *by means of* the Spirit and not a matter of letter-keeping (*gramma*).[15]

Once again, Scripture is abused if such contrasts as "the letter kills, but the Spirit makes alive" is turned into a slogan to allow so-called Spirit-led interpreters to bypass the authorial verbal meanings in each text in favor of more practical, personal, relational, spiritual, or sensational meanings obtained allegedly from the Holy Spirit as promised in these three texts. But the promise is nonexistent and the method is therefore subbiblical and ultimately heretical.

The work of the Holy Spirit in 2 Corinthians 3:14ff. must not be used in a dialectical way that relates understanding to an existential response or to the tension that exists between the "letter" and the "Spirit" as Peter Richardson and others have proposed. The source of our understanding in 2 Corinthians 3:14 is still located in our "reading." What Paul prescribed for the removal of the veil that prevented a personal reception and application of either Moses' or Paul's words was that men should "turn to the Lord" (v. 16), who is the Spirit (v. 17).

Now does the Spirit set us free from the verbal meanings of the Word of the text (supposedly the *gramma*)? We answer with a decisive no! The Spirit is the Unveiler of significance, relevance, personal application, but not the Releaser of additional or delayed verbal meanings. This latter ministry of the Spirit was focalized in the apostles and prophets. They received the gifts of revelation, truth, verbal meanings, and valid teachings; their readers, on the other hand, received the ministry of reception, application, and significance—sometimes called "meaning-for-me." To confuse meaning and significance is to reduce all hermeneutics to shambles.[16]

## EVANGELICAL EXEGETICAL PROCEDURE

If each of the above arguments can be successfully sustained (and we believe they will bear even more intense scrutiny than is possible in the short scope of this chapter), then all alleged biblical grounds for finding some sort of *superadditum* or *sensus plenior* in addition to the human writers' supposed nominal or prosaic meanings is cut away. We are back to searching for God's revelation for our generation through the verbal meanings and contexts supplied by the ancient writers of Scripture.

That is exactly where the Pauline claim of 1 Corinthians 2:9–16 figures so prominently. Indeed, this may be one of the most neglected, yet most significant texts in the whole inspiration-hermeneutical debate. Paul located the source of his inscripturated wisdom in God. It was altogether different from that wisdom found in empirical sources or from pockets of political savvy (1 Cor. 2:9). And this wisdom God had revealed (aorist tense) to the apostle (the "us" of v. 10 and "we" of vv. 12–13 are used editorially; cf. 3:1, "I") by means of the Holy Spirit. The words Paul wrote, then, were not merely the result of his own human intelligence, but the result of "*words* taught by the Spirit" as he "explained spiritual truths with *words* given by the Spirit" (note the Greek grammar here versus the misunderstanding of most modern translations on 1 Corinthians 2:13). An identical claim was repeated again in 1 Thessalonians 2:13: ". . . you received the word of God which you heard from us . . . not as the word of men but as what it really is, the *word* of God" (RSV, italics mine).

But it is the organic unity between the words of the writer and the work of the Holy Spirit that is the key point of the 1 Corinthians 2:13 reference. There the Holy Spirit *teaches* the apostle in words. Consequently, the writer was not oblivious to the import or verbal meaning of his terms: he himself was taught by the Holy Spirit. Such a claim can only mean there was a living assimilation of God's intended truth into the verbalizations of the writers of Scripture, rather than a mere mechanical printout of semi-understandable verbiage.

Therefore evangelicals are urged to begin a new "hermeneutical reformation" to correct this type of growing malpractice our profession has allowed in recent years. As a contribution toward that end, it is urged that the following axioms be adopted and implemented in our preparation of lectures, sermons, home Bible studies, and personal devotions:

1. God's meaning and revelatory-intention in any passage of Scripture may be accurately and confidently ascertained only by studying the verbal meanings of the divinely delegated and inspired human writers.

2. Only one verbal meaning is to be connected with any passage of Scripture unless the writer of the text gives literary and contextual clues that he has several aims in view for this exceptional passage (for example, the two or three questions asked at the beginning of the Olivet Discourse).

3. That single, original verbal meaning of the human author may be ascertained by heeding the usual literary conventions of history, culture, grammar, syntax, and accumulated theological context. And if it cannot be ascertained by these means then it cannot be ascertained at all.

4. This authorial meaning can be understood by all readers who will allow the writer to first say what he wants to say without introducing conservative or liberal prejudices as a preunderstanding.

5. The personal impact, significance, application, reception, and

value this text has for particular individuals or situations is directly linked to the illuminating ministry of the Holy Spirit. The Spirit takes the single truth-intention of the author and in His convicting, comforting, teaching, and motivating power urges us to apply the principle taught in this text to scores of different situations.

In addition to these axioms, the following clarifications should be added if exegetical practice is to be worthy of the Bible:

1. The "original meaning" of any text can be defined, as John F. A. Sawyer reminds us, in two different ways: "original" in an etymological sense, and "original" in the meaning it had in its original context.[17] Exegesis is interested in this second usage. The object of exegesis is to discern the original meaning of the present canonical shape of the text rather than the root meaning of words or even the original meaning of the text's separate units (if indeed it had such a prehistory).

2. "Theological exegesis" of a passage is most important if we are to transcend the chasm between the scientific dissecting of the text into its philological components, complete with parsings and grammatical notes. However, a premature use of the *analogia fidei*, "analogy of faith," is as destructive of true meaning as no interaction with the accumulated and antecedent theology that "informed" that text. The "analogy of faith" is the sum of the prominent teachings of Scripture gathered from all its parts without regard to any diachronic considerations. This "rule of faith" was first set forth by Augustine and further defined by men like Chemnitz (*Examen*, VIII, I) to say that the articles of faith were to be derived from clear passages and in no case was a clear passage to be set in opposition to a difficult or problematic passage. Hence a principle of harmonization or proportionality was introduced.[18]

But can the analogy of faith function as a "preunderstanding" with which the interpreter approaches his task of exegesis in a distinctively Christian way? I believe not! The interpreter must not even carry such high and worthy goods as these to his task. Only the doctrine and the theology prior to the time of the writer's composition of his revelation (which theology we propose to call here the "Analogy of Scripture")[19] may be legitimately used in the task of theological exegesis, in other words, where the writer directly cites or obviously alludes to the theology that preceded his writing and formed a backdrop against which he cast his own message. Only the discipline of biblical theology, if it traces the buildup of doctrine from era to era within each of the Testaments, will supply the extremely important theological data necessary to rescue an otherwise dull philological and grammatical exercise.[20]

The "analogy of Scripture" then was the "preunderstanding" of both the writer and of those in his audience who were alert to what God had revealed prior to this new word of revelation. Likewise, the interpreter must employ the identical method if he is to be successful in aiding modern hearers to hear the total word in a text.

Having arrived at the original historical, cultural, grammatical, syntactical, theological meaning of the text, the exegete may *now* use the analogy of faith (of the whole of Scripture) in the summaries and conclusions he offers to each section of his exegesis and to the whole message, for what is learned in this context may relate to what was later revealed in Scripture. However, our methodology must be clean and there must be no confusion about these two methods in the name of orthodox or pragmatic results.

Nowhere, then, does Scripture support the view that the Bible has a multi-track concept of meanings. If the human author did not receive by revelation the meaning in question, then exegetes and readers have no right to identify their meanings with God. Only by following the careful distinctions set forth in the authorial autonomy view can the Word of God be preserved for future generations and be handled as what it is indeed—the powerful and authoritative Word from God.

# THIRTEEN

# DUAL AUTHORSHIP AND THE SINGLE INTENDED MEANING OF SCRIPTURE

## Elliott E. Johnson

CHRISTIAN HERMENEUTICS HAS long wrestled with the perplexing problem of the dual authorship—divine and human—of Scripture. This dual authorship seems to imply that a given passage may have more than one meaning. Yet in order to maintain the determinate nature of interpretation, Protestant hermeneutics has often affirmed the maxim of one meaning and many applications.

In response to the hermeneutical problem of how many meanings a passage may have, two solutions have been proposed in current evangelical discussions. These two will be evaluated briefly and then a third alternative will be proposed.

### SINGLE MEANING

Kaiser presents a view held by many evangelicals.[1] He writes:

> Evangelicals are urged to begin a new "hermeneutical reformation" . . .
> it is urged that the following axioms be adopted and implemented. . . .
> 1. God's meaning and revelatory-intention in any passage of Scripture
> may be accurately and confidently ascertained only by studying *the
> verbal meanings of* the divinely delegated and inspired *writers*. . . .
> 2. That single, original *verbal meaning of the human author* may be
> ascertained by heeding the usual literary conventions of history, culture, grammar, syntax, and accumulated theological context.[2]

This is certainly accurate as far as it goes. The divine meanings are expressed in the human authors' words. But in other writings Kaiser states the issue in this question: "*Could* God see or intend a sense in a particular text *separate* and *different* from that conceived and intended

171

by His human instrument?"[3] The issue turns on the words "separate" and "different." How is the divine meaning separate and different from the human author's meaning? Kaiser affirms that there is no difference. In fact he says the human authors of Scripture fully knew and expressed the divine meaning. So he concludes. "God did not exceed the intention of the human author."[4]

In discussing 1 Peter 1:10–12, Kaiser rightly argues that the passage does not support "double meaning." But he also argues that the ignorance of the human authors was an ignorance, not of the *subject matter* of the Old Testament prophecies, but of the *times* when those prophecies would be fulfilled. "This passage does not teach that these men were curious and often ignorant of the exact meaning of what they wrote and predicted. Theirs was not a search for the *meaning* of what they wrote; it was inquiry into the *temporal* aspects of the *subject*, which went beyond what they wrote."[5]

His argument seems to be dealt a fatal blow, however, if temporal aspects are stated in some of the prophets' writings. And such is certainly the case in Daniel 9:24–27. A period of time was decreed against Israel that is related to the 70 years predicted by Jeremiah (Jer. 25:11). So Peter's general summary could legitimately include Daniel's ignorance of all the *implications* of what he wrote. This ignorance seems to be referred to in other passages as well. Daniel repeatedly prayed for understanding of the visions he saw (Dan. 7:15–16; 8:15–16; 10:12–14).

After Daniel was given understanding, he was told to "seal up the book until the end of time" (Dan. 12:4). God spoke through Daniel to later generations who would understand more fully what Daniel wrote on the scroll. Their understanding would not arise, however, because of new, special revelation but because they could recognize the correspondence between what Daniel had written and what was happening in their day in its historical fulfillment. So Simeon had a prophetic understanding and expectation: He was "looking for the consolation of Israel" (Luke 2:25). Similarly John the Baptist understood his ministry in terms of the prophetic Word and described it as such (3:4–5). Jesus likewise presented Himself as fulfilling the prophetic expectation (4:17–19), and the people of His day recognized Him in terms defined by Old Testament prophets (9:19–20). In each case it is possible that those who lived when prophecies of Jesus were fulfilled understood the prophecies better than the prophets themselves understood their writings, and the later understanding was based not on further revelation but on correspondence between the prophecies and their fulfillments. (Of course in some situations additional revelation did provide the basis for understanding earlier prophecies.)

Though Kaiser's work[6] is appreciated for his insistence on the single meaning of Scripture, his limiting the biblical meaning to what the human author consciously perceived must be rejected.

## ONE LITERAL MEANING
## AND SEVERAL SPIRITUAL MEANINGS

A second evangelical alternative is presented by LaSor.[7] He forthrightly affirms that "the literal meaning of the text, then, is the basic meaning and the basis for interpretation. Without the literal sense we have no control of any other sense."[8] This literal sense is the product of the grammatical-historical method. Then LaSor writes:

> Starting from the premise that the Bible is the Word of God to the people of His covenant, it follows that this word is applicable according to His will to all generations. Since He is a spiritual being and since His purpose is redemptive, it follows that His word is spiritual and redemptive. There is therefore a spiritual meaning—or possibly more than one spiritual meaning—implicit in His word. Discovering the spiritual message in, rather than imposing it on, the Scripture is a serious task; and the believing community has attempted various methods.[9]

On the surface the approaches of Kaiser and LaSor seem directly opposite. While Kaiser argues for single meaning and single intent, LaSor readily acknowledges a literal meaning and one or more spiritual meanings. In part the difference is one of emphasis. Kaiser acknowledges the importance of recognizing several factors in interpreting a passage's single meaning, including history, culture, grammar, syntax, and accumulated theological teaching. LaSor limits the literal meaning to two contexts: grammatical and historical. At this point it is clear that Kaiser's view of "single meaning" differs from LaSor's view of "literal meaning." But in this author's opinion, LaSor has lost control on the determination of limits to meaning in his discussion of *sensus plenior*.

In discussing the Davidic Covenant, LaSor criticizes the literal meaning as being inaccurate. "Israel did not continue to live 'in their own place, and be disturbed no more' ([2 Sam.] 7:10). . . . The throne of David was not 'made sure forever'" (7:16).[10] Then he turns to the New Testament writers' view of the Davidic Covenant and concludes, "It becomes obvious that, for the New Testament writers (and for Jesus), at least, the Old Testament passage must have *some* deeper meaning."[11] Concluding the discussion with these remarks, LaSor leaves a number of questions unanswered. If the literal meaning is inaccurate, in what sense is it a controlling base for the *sensus plenior?* If a passage has some deeper meaning, what limits exist for that deeper meaning? How are those limits recognized? These two approaches introduce the need for parameters in interpreting the Bible. The first parameter is *determinate limits* that enable meaning to be known and recognized as known. The second parameter is *flexibility in the fullness of meaning* so that some distinction may be acknowledged between the textual sense understood in the historic context and this same sense understood in its future fulfillment.

At stake here is the very tradition of literal interpretation that both Kaiser[12] and LaSor acknowledge as basic to accurate and controlled interpretation. At issue is the question of whether there is a *sensus plenior* that is legitimate and one that is illegitimate. Could God intend a sense *separate* and *different* from that intended by the human author? LaSor argues for a *sensus plenior* that is built on the literal sense.

## ONE SINGLE MEANING
## THAT INCLUDES RELATED SUBMEANINGS

In Kaiser's view the "control" for interpretation is that each text has a single meaning that is textually determined. He properly recognizes historical and cultural contexts with emphasis on lexical, grammatical, and syntactical considerations. In addition the theological context is limited to the accumulated theological revelation at the time of the human writer. The textual context determines the meanings expressed, and the theological context may inform his written textual usage. It is clear that the stated text was understood sufficiently by the human author to express the message. But are there unstated meanings that are also necessarily intended meanings? Clearly in cases where there is dictation of the message, as in the case of the "70 sevens." Daniel may not have understood the full sense of what he wrote. In his case the decree to rebuild Jerusalem had not yet been given. Who can say that Daniel knew the date of the future decree? The date that would initiate the period of the "70 sevens" was unknown. Thus a definition of literal sense that rests on the indeterminate aspect of the human author's awareness results in a literal sense that is ultimately indeterminate itself.

Another view of "controls" in interpretation is that the sense of a passage is textually indeterminate. This is the traditional allegorical interpretation. In this view a text may have a literal sense and also several other senses determined by other factors such as theology, church tradition, or spiritual practice. Since the textual form may be interpreted within any conceivable context brought by the interpreter no controls are within the text itself. This is the danger in LaSor's treatment of the Davidic Covenant.

A third view is proposed by this writer. In this view the sense of a passage is textually determined as a single meaning that includes any *related* submeanings or implications of the meaning expressed by the human author. This statement of literal sense has the advantage of being textually determined. The sense expressed by the author in the text is a *single* meaning that includes any unstated yet *related* submeaning, a meaning that is a necessary trait of that type of meaning as a whole. It follows that the determinate nature of literal meaning must be defined not at the word level but at the level of a unit of text in which the author expresses a single message or proposition. Each message expressed by the author involves a distinct unit. The most clearly distinguished unit expressed by a human author is the composition of the whole piece of literature. However, this includes many other subunits of thought, such as sentences, paragraphs, and chapters. The propositions so expressed must also be recognized as distinct "types of meaning" subsumed by the overall type of meaning.

This recognized type of meaning determines the limits of a literal meaning. In this model the textual meaning consists of (a) a type of meaning as a whole and (b) component traits of meaning. This rests on a knowledge of categories of meaning shared between an author and his reader. When an author expresses a new type of meaning in the text, the reader recognizes that meaning as he reads. The meanings of the text are necessary or associated traits of the type of meaning expressed. This model describing the communication of textual meanings explains both the implications of the textual sense and the implications of historical reference. It does not rest on determining those meanings the human author is aware of or on distinguishing which meanings the divine Author knows beyond the human author. Meaning is determined by the text and by considering the historical reference about which the Author spoke.

This model of the literal meaning can be supported because it accounts for test cases in which the biblical writers interpreted the Bible. The divine and human authors shared the textually expressed meanings. How many additional unstated submeanings the human author consciously knew is unnecessary to determine. At the same time God, since He is omniscient, intended all the submeanings necessary to this expressed type of meaning. The interpreter may not know or recognize all these submeanings until the divinely intended reference appears in history. But such recognition of submeanings is not a "consequent" sense.[13] Nor are they "separate" in the sense of *unrelated*. They are separate only in the sense of being *unstated*. Nor are they "different" in the sense of being *conflicting*. They are different only in the sense of being *unexpressed*. They are necessary submeanings of a category of meaning. They are necessary because, though they are unstated, they still define that type of meaning. In addition there are associated traits which, though not defining, are commonly associated with this type of meaning. But associated traits must be stated for them to be determined.

Without identifying this model of type and trait of meaning. Marshall exhibits the same concept. He imagines the Apostle John responding. "I hadn't consciously thought of the story like that, but now that you suggest it to me, I would agree that you could also understand it in that way."[14] This approach also helps clarify passages that are difficult to interpret.

## THE VIEWS ILLUSTRATED IN ISAIAH 7:14

As illustrated in Isaiah 7:14, submeanings or implications are not an "elusive surplussage."[15] Two questions focus on the central issues in this *crux interpretum*. What is the meaning of Isaiah 7:14, and what is the correspondence between Isaiah 7:14 and the sign to Ahaz? Three views have been given in answer to these questions. (1) The verse refers to a natural conception, and the birth of a son was the sign to Ahaz. (2) The verse refers to a natural conception followed by the birth of a son, which was a sign to Ahaz; and at the same time the verse typologically refers to the supernatural conception of Christ to which Matthew refers. (3) The verse refers to the supernatural conception and birth of Christ, and the sign refers either to the growth of this future "Son" or more likely, to the statement of promise given to Ahaz.

Support for the meaning of a natural conception rests in the broad semantic range of the word עַלְמָה. In Hebrew usage this word means "young woman." Koehler and Baumgartner say the word means a girl of marriageable age, a young woman (until the birth of her first child).[16]

However, some would seek to limit the range by specifying the trait of virginity. "Since *b<sup>e</sup>tulâ* is used many times in the Old Testament as a specific word for 'virgin,' it seems reasonable to consider that the feminine form of *'almâ* is not a technical word for virgin but represents a young woman, one of whose characteristics is virginity."[17] This limited sense rests on biblical usage where the sense can be determined, but not all cases are clear. And since עַלְמָה is not the technical term in Old Testament usage, Wilson draws the following conclusion: "Since the presumption of common law and usage was and is, that every *'almah* is virgin and virtuous until she is proven not to be we have the right in assuming that Rebecca and the *'almah* of Isaiah 7:14 were virgins until and unless it shall be proven that they were not."[18]

Because of the difficulty in limiting the meaning of עַלְמָה to "virgin," various commentators have concluded that Isaiah's promise refers to a historic woman, either Isaiah's bride-to-be or Ahaz's wife, who conceived in a natural fashion and not as a virgin. Isaiah's prophecy then concerned the timing of the conception and the birth of the boy. The determinate limits of the condition of the young woman are settled in the broader semantic range of the word in its usage.

This interpretation is certainly legitimate, but it conflicts with Matthew's interpretation. In Matthew, the angel quoted Isaiah to satisfy Joseph's concern, since Isaiah anticipated a "virgin conception." Mary's pregnancy, which came by the Holy Spirit, was a historic realization of what Isaiah prophesied. So Joseph need not put her away but could take her as a his wife without any sense of guilt or any concern. This sense of "virgin conception" is not the same as "natural conception." Thus in light of the broader biblical context the limited historic view (view 1) must be rejected.

Therefore some have taken the historic sense to have also a typological meaning that anticipates a future conception. Hoekema holds to this interpretation. "Obviously, this [Isa. 7:14] was fulfilled in the immediate future in the birth of a child as a sign to King Ahaz [but] the greater fulfillment of these words to Ahaz occurred when Jesus was born of the virgin Mary."[19] In typology there are shared traits as well as traits distinguishing the type from the antitype. In this case the shared traits must be the same kind of conception and birth. In this typology view the conception by a woman in Isaiah's day anticipated and was fulfilled in Christ's conception. But in what way is a natural conception a type of a virgin conception? In fact this example of double reference involves two meanings that are unrelated in the text. A natural conception corresponds to a virgin conception only in that both are conceptions. In this interpreter's judgment the single textual meaning is violated in the two unrelated types of conception, natural and virgin. The natural conception was miraculous only in *timing*, and that timing does not adequately typify the virgin conception by Mary.

Rather than being established by usage, the meaning of the kind of conception is determined in the contextual type of meaning expressed by Isaiah. The meaning builds on the legitimate semantic range of עַלְמָה but the determining limits are found in the type of meaning expressed in the context. While there may be some question about the defining components of a type of meaning, it is clear that a subject and complement define important components of the textual meaning. The immediate textual unit is Isaiah 7:10–17. Isaiah proclaimed a sign that is two-edged. This is the subject. The Lord granted evidence (signs) that accompany His Word and vouch for its validity and reliability. At issue in the context is the Lord's warning of the certain and near demise of Damascus and Ephraim (7:7–9a). Included as well is a warning concerning Ahaz's own future (7:9b). His future rested on his faith in response to the Lord's warning.

Isaiah offered a sign to verify his warnings. When Ahaz refused to believe (7:12), the sign did two things. It guaranteed the house of David in spite of the threat of attack from Israel and Syria, and at the same time it assured the king of his coming demise.

The Hebrew word אוֹת ("sign") "either signifies the unusual event itself (miraculous display) or in some way points to that unusual event."[20] Beecher has argued with force that the syntax of the stated prophecy reflects the syntax of the promise formulation of a divinely enabled birth as it was first spoken to Abraham and Sarah.[21] When this promise was clarified (Gen. 15:4–5), Abram asked how he might know it would happen. In response God confirmed the promise in the form of a covenant formulation. In the initial expression, the covenant gave evidence of fulfillment. The sign then was in the restatement of the divine Word that promised a divinely enabled birth. In Isaiah's prophecy the sign[22] was in the statement of the promise that pointed to an unusual miracle in the future. The complement expressed something about that two-edged sign. It denied Ahaz, who rejected the sign, a future in the royal line. And yet it affirmed the glorious climax of the Davidic line in spite of imminent judgment by Assyria. If this is stated about the עַלְמָה conception, then the conception must necessarily be a virgin conception. Only a virgin conception would exclude Ahaz or his heir from participating in the royal line of David. Thus the type of meaning expresses limits and determines the sense of עַלְמָה and harmonizes completely with the Matthean usage.

But what about the historical elements in the sign? A prediction of a future miraculous conception does not seem at first to relate to the events in Ahaz's day. The antecedent of "He" in 7:15 seems to anticipate some historic figure. This difficulty may be surmounted either by saying that "He" refers to the future born Son in anticipation of His growth[23] or by saying that "He" refers to "Shear-Jashub" (7:3), whom Isaiah was told to bring with him during his prophecy. This second alternative would introduce a break in thought between 7:14 and 7:15, as a new subject is introduced.

This model of literal interpretation meets the criteria demanded by the biblical usage and data. First, it establishes a determinate sense expressed in the text. This determinate meaning is shared by the human author who expressed the text and by the divine Author who authored the text. Recognized as a type of meaning, it determines both the proposition (subject and complement) and any unstated but necessary submeanings. Isaiah knew that his prophecy anticipated an עַלְמָה, a virgin who conceives and who bears a son who is named Immanuel. Did Isaiah know it referred to and meant Mary? One has no way of knowing. Did God know it meant Mary? There is no way of denying that. If Isaiah could have been transported to the time of Mary's experience and he had no further information beyond his own prophecy, he could identify her as the girl God said would conceive. This is the understanding of the angel, of Joseph, and of Matthew who recorded the prediction. The construction of biblical meaning and its interpretation recognizes determinate textual limits and possible components of meaning in the progress of revelation. Thus this model of literal interpretation is valid because it corresponds with the data of Scripture and because it meets the demands of literal interpretation.

# THE OLD TESTAMENT IN THE NEW

# FOURTEEN

# NEW TESTAMENT USE OF THE OLD TESTAMENT

## Roger Nicole

THE NEW TESTAMENT contains an extraordinarily large number of Old Testament quotations. It is difficult to give an accurate figure since the variation in use ranges all the way from a distant allusion to a definite quotation introduced by an explicit formula stating the citation's source. As a result, the figures given by various authors often reflect a startling discrepancy.

### RANGE OF OLD TESTAMENT REFERENCES

The present writer has counted 224 direct citations introduced by a definite formula indicating the writer purposed to quote. To these must be added seven cases where a second quotation is introduced by the conjunction "and," and 19 cases where a paraphrase or summary rather than a direct quotation follows the introductory formula. We may further note at least 45 instances where the similarity with certain Old Testament passages is so pronounced that, although no explicit indication is given that the New Testament author was referring to Old Testament Scripture, his intention to do so can scarcely be doubted. Thus a very conservative count discloses unquestionably at least 295 separate references to the Old Testament. These occupy some 352 verses of the New Testament, or more than 4.4 percent. Therefore one verse in 22.5 of the New Testament is a quotation.

If clear allusions are taken into consideration, the figures are much higher: C. H. Toy lists 613 such instances, Wilhelm Dittmar goes as high as 1640, while Eugen Huehn indicates 4105 passages reminiscent of Old Testament Scripture. It can therefore be asserted, without exaggeration, that more than 10 percent of the New Testament text is made up of citations or direct allusions to the Old Testament. The recorded words of Jesus disclose a similar percentage. Certain books like Revelation, Hebrews, Romans are well nigh saturated with Old Testament forms of language, allusions, and quotations. Perusal of Nestle's edition of the Greek New Testament, in which the Old Testament material is printed in bold face type, will reveal at a glance the extent of this practice. These facts appear even more impressive when one remembers that in New Testament times the Old Testament was not as today duplicated by the million but could be obtained only in expensive handwritten copies.

If we limit ourselves to the specific quotations and direct allusions which form the basis of our previous reckoning, we shall note that 278 different Old Testament verses are cited in the New Testament: 94 from the Pentateuch, 99 from the Prophets, and 85 from the Writings. Out of the 22 books in the Hebrew reckoning of the Canon only six (Judges-Ruth, Song of Solomon, Ecclesiastes, Esther, Ezra-Nehemiah, Chronicles) are not explicitly referred to. The more extensive lists of Dittmar and Huehn show passages reminiscent of all Old Testament books without exception.

It is to be noted that the whole New Testament contains not even one explicit citation of any of the Old Testament Apocrypha which are considered as canonical by the Roman Catholic Church. This omission can scarcely be viewed as accidental.

## AUTHORITY OF OLD TESTAMENT REFERENCES

From beginning to end, the New Testament authors ascribe unqualified authority to Old Testament Scripture. Whenever advanced, a quotation is viewed as normative. Nowhere do we find a tendency to question, argue, or repudiate the truth of any Scripture utterance. Passages sometimes alleged to prove that the Lord and His apostles challenged at times the authority of the Old Testament, when carefully examined, turn out to bolster rather than to impair the evidence for their acceptance of Scripture as the Word of God. In Matthew 5:21–43 and 19:3–9, our Lord, far from setting aside the commandments of the Old Testament, really engages in a searching analysis of the spiritual meaning and original intent of the divine precept, and from this vantage point He applies it in a deeper and broader way than had been done before Him. In some passages in which comparison is made between the revelation of the Old Testament and that of the New (John 1:17; 2 Cor. 3:6; Gal. 3:19ff.; Heb. 1:1–2, and so forth), the superior glory of the New Testament is emphasized, not as in conflict with the Old, but as the perfect fulfillment of a revelation still incomplete, yet sanctioned by divine authority.

It is noteworthy that the New Testament writers and the Lord Jesus Himself did not hesitate on occasion to base their whole argumentation upon one single word of Old Testament Scripture (Matt. 2:15;

4:10; 13:35; 22:44; Mark 12:36; Luke 4:8; 20:42–43; John 8:17; 10:34;
19:37; Acts 23:5; Rom. 4:3, 9, 23; 15:9–12; 1 Cor. 6:16; Gal. 3:8, 10,
13; Heb. 1:7; 2:12; 3:13; 4:7; 12:26), or even on the grammatical form
of one word (Gal. 3:16).

Of special interest are the formulas by which the New Testament
writers introduce their quotations. In a particularly significant way
these formulas reflect their view of the Old Testament Scriptures,
since they do not manifest any design to set forth a doctrine of Scripture, but are rather the instinctive expression of their approach to the
sacred writings.

The formulas emphasize strongly the divine origin of the Old Testament, and commonly (at least 56 times) refer to God as the author. In
a number of passages God is represented as the speaker when the
quotation is not a saying of God recorded as such in the Old Testament, but the word of Scripture itself, in fact, at times a word addressed to God by man (Matt. 19:5; Acts 4:25; 13:35; Heb. 1:5–8, 13;
3:7; 4:4). These "can be treated as a declaration of God's only on the
hypothesis that all Scripture is a declaration of God's."[1]

Often passages of the Old Testament are simply attributed to the
Scripture, which is thus personified as speaking (John 7:38, 42; 15:25;
19:37; Rom. 4:3; 7:7; 9:17; 10:11; 11:2; 1 Cor. 14:24; 2 Cor. 6:2; Gal.
3:8; 4:30; 1 Tim. 5:18; James 2:23; 4:5). In Romans 9:17 and Galatians
3:8 the identification between the text of Scripture and God as speaking is carried so far that the actions of God are actually ascribed to
Scripture, which is represented as speaking to Pharaoh and as foresee-
ing justification by faith. Warfield urges that "These acts could be
attributed to Scripture only as the result of such a habitual identification, in the mind of the writer, of the text of Scripture with God as
speaking that it became natural to use the term 'Scripture says,' when
what was really intended was 'God, as recorded in Scripture, said.'"[2]

The collaboration of man in the writing of Scripture is also emphasized. The names of Moses, David, Isaiah, Jeremiah, Daniel, Joel and
Hosea appear in the formulas of quotation. It is noteworthy that, in the
majority of the cases where the human author is named, reference is
made not to a personal statement recorded in Scripture but to an utterance of God, which the writer was commissioned to transmit as such.
In a number of passages both the divine and the human authorship
appear side by side.

> . . . which was spoken by the Lord through the prophet . . . (Matt.
> 1:22).

> David himself said in the Holy Spirit (Mark 12:36; cf. Matt. 22:43).

... the Holy Spirit spake before by the mouth of David (Acts 1:16; cf. 4:25).

Well spake the Holy Spirit through Isaiah the prophet (Acts 28:25).

He saith also in Hosea . . . (Rom. 9:25).

These passages supply clear evidence that the divine superintendence was not viewed as obliterating the human agency and characteristics of the writers, but rather, that God secured a perfectly adequate presentation of the truth through the responsible and personal agency of the men He called and prepared for this sacred task.

"It is written" is one of the frequent formulas of introduction, the one, in fact, which our Lord used three times in His temptation (Matt. 4:4, 7, 10). This expression does not connote merely that an appeal is made to the written text of Scripture but, as Warfield so aptly has said, "The simple adduction in this solemn and decisive manner of a written authority carries with it the implication that the appeal is made to the indefectible authority of the Scriptures of God, which in all their parts and in every one of their declarations are clothed with the authority of God Himself."[3]

The use of the terms "law" (John 10:34; 15:25; Rom. 3:19; 1 Cor. 14:21), or "prophets" (Matt. 13:35), where reference is made to passages belonging, strictly speaking, to other parts of the Hebrew Canon, indicates that the New Testament writers viewed the whole Old Testament Scripture as having legal authority and prophetic character.

In their formulas of quotation the New Testament writers give expression to their conviction as to the eternal contemporaneity of Scripture. This is manifest in particular in the many (41) instances where the introductory verb is in the present: "He says," and not "he said." This is reinforced by the use of the pronouns "we," "you," in connection with ancient sayings: "That which was spoken unto you by God" (Matt. 22:31); "The Holy Spirit also beareth witness to us" (Heb. 10:15; cf. also Matt. 15:7; Mark 7:6; 12:19; Acts 4:11; 13:47; Heb. 12:5). This implication gains explicit statement in Romans 15:4: "Whatsoever things were written aforetime were written for our learning" (cf. also Rom. 4:23–24; 1 Cor. 9:10; 10:11).

The New Testament writers used quotations in their sermons, in their histories, in their letters, in their prayers. They used them when addressing Jews or Gentiles, churches or individuals, friends or antagonists, new converts or seasoned Christians. They used them for argumentation, for illustration, for instruction, for documentation, for prophecy, for reproof. They used them in times of stress and in hours of mature thinking, in liberty and in prison, at home and abroad. Everywhere and always they were ready to refer to the impregnable authority of Scripture.

Jesus Christ Himself provides a most arresting example in this respect. At the very threshold of His public ministry, our Lord, in His dramatic victory over Satan's threefold onslaught, rested His whole defense on the authority of three passages of Scripture. He quoted the Old Testament in support of His teaching to the crowds; He quoted it in His discussions with antagonistic Jews; He quoted it in answer to questions both captious and sincere; He quoted it in instructing the disciples who would have readily accepted His teaching on His own authority; He referred to it in His prayers, when alone in the presence of the Father; He quoted it on the cross, when His sufferings could easily have drawn His attention elsewhere; He quoted it in His resurrection glory, when any limitation, real or alleged, of the days of His flesh was clearly superseded. Whatever may be the differences between the pictures of Jesus drawn by the four Gospels, they certainly agree in their representation of our Lord's attitude toward the Old Testament: one of constant use and of unquestioning endorsement of its authority.

### ACCURACY OF OLD TESTAMENT REFERENCES

A difficulty comes to the fore, however, when the New Testament citations are carefully compared with the original Old Testament texts.[4] In their quotations the New Testament writers, it would appear, use considerable freedom, touching both the letter and the meaning of the Old Testament passages.

Opponents of verbal inspiration repeatedly have brought forward this objection mainly in two forms:

1.  The New Testament writers, not having taken care to quote in absolute agreement with the original text of the Old Testament, it is urged, cannot have held the doctrine of plenary inspiration. Otherwise they would have shown greater respect for the letter of Scripture.

2.  The New Testament writer, in quoting the Old "inaccurately" as to its letter, or "improperly" as to its sense, or both, cannot have been directed to do so by the Spirit of God.

The first argument impugns mainly the inspiration of the Old Testament, the second mainly that of the New. Both will be met if it can be shown that the New Testament method of quotation is entirely proper and consistent with the highest regard for the texts cited. In the present treatment it is possible only to delineate the main principles involved, without showing their application to particular cases. We

shall consider first, principles involved in the solution of difficulties
arising from the New Testament manner of quoting, after which brief
comments will be offered regarding the methods of interpretation
exhibited by the New Testament authors in their application of Old
Testament passages.

## Form of Quotation

It must be recognized that each of the following principles does not
find application in every case, but the writer is of the opinion that,
singly or in combination, as the case may be, they provide a very
satisfactory explanation of apparent discrepancies in almost all cases,
and a possible solution in all cases.

1. *The New Testament writers had to translate their quotations.* They
wrote in Greek and their source of quotations was in Hebrew. They needed
therefore either to translate for themselves or to use existing translations. Now no translation can give a completely adequate and coexten-
sive rendering of the original. A certain measure of change is inevitable,
even when one is quoting by divine inspiration.

When the New Testament writers wrote, there was one Greek version
of the Old Testament, the LXX. It was widespread, well known, and
respected in spite of some obvious defects when appraised from the
standpoint of modern scholarship. In most cases, it was a fair translation
of the Hebrew text, and possessed distinctive literary qualities. Its
position in the ancient world is comparable to that of the Authorized
Version before the Revised was published. A conscientious scholar
writing nowadays in a certain language will use for his quotations
from foreign sources the translations which his readers generally use.
He will not attempt to correct or change them unless some mistake
bears directly on his point. When slight errors or mistranslations occur,
generally he will neither discuss them, for in so doing he would tend
to direct the reader's attention away from his point, nor correct them
without giving notice, for this might tend to arouse the reader's
suspicion. This practice is followed by many preachers and writers
who use the Authorized Version in English or Luther's translation in
German. They are often well aware that some verses rather inadequately
render the Hebrew or the Greek, but no blame can be laid on them as
long as they base no argument on what is mistaken in the translation.
Similarly, the writers of the New Testament could use the LXX, the
only Greek version then existing, in spite of its occasional inaccuracy,
and even quote passages which were somewhat inaccurately translated.
To take advantage of its errors, however, would have been inadmissible.
We do not find any example of a New Testament deduction or

application logically inferred from the LXX and which cannot be maintained on the basis of the Hebrew text.

Some of the recently discovered Dead Sea scrolls at times provide the Hebrew text which underlay the LXX where it differs from the Massoretic text. This is the case, for instance, in Isaiah 53:11, where the scroll Isaiah A reads, "He shall see light," thus supporting the LXX rendering. While great caution is still necessary in any textual emendation of the Massoretic text, the possibility that in some divergent translations the LXX occasionally represents the primitive Hebrew original may be held to have received some support from these discoveries. In such cases, of course, it would not only have been proper for the New Testament writers to quote from the LXX, but this would actually have been preferable.

The use of the LXX in quoting does not indicate that the New Testament writers have thought of this version as inspired in itself. *A fortiori* they did not confer inspiration upon the translation of the passages they have used. Samuel Davidson was laboring under a regrettable confusion when he wrote: "It will ever remain inexplicable by the supporters of verbal inspiration that the words of the LXX became literally inspired as soon as they were taken from that version and transferred to the New Testament pages."[5] This statement misconstrues verbal inspiration. When the New Testament authors appealed to Scripture as the Word of God, it is not claimed that they viewed anything but the original communication as vested in full with divine inerrancy. Yet their willingness to make use of the LXX, in spite of its occasional defects, teaches the important lesson that the basic message which God purposed to deliver can be conveyed even through a translation, and that appeal can be made to a version insofar as it agrees with the original. It would be precarious, however, to rest an argument on any part of the LXX quotations which appears not to be conformed to the Hebrew original nor to the point of the New Testament writers, for the mere fact that the quotation was adduced in this fashion was not meant as a divine sanction upon incidental departures from the autographs. In the quotations made from the LXX we have indeed God's seal of approval upon the contents of the Old Testament passage, but the form of the citation is affected by the language and conditions of those to whom the New Testament was first addressed. Such use of the LXX was not a case of objectionable accommodation. That the inspired Word is accommodated to humanity is an obvious fact: it is written in human languages, uses human comparisons, its parts are conditioned by the circumstances of those to whom they were at first destined, and so forth. But we cannot admit of an accommodation in which inspired writers would give formal assent to error.

In their use of the LXX, however, the New Testament authors were so far from actual endorsement of error that the best scholars of all times have used similar methods in adducing translated quotations, as noted above.[6]

The frequent use of the LXX, it must also be noted, did not impose upon the New Testament authors the obligation to quote always in accordance with this version. Whenever they wanted to emphasize an idea which was insufficiently or inadequately rendered in the LXX, they may have retranslated in whole or in part the passage in question. In certain cases the reason for their introduction of changes may remain unknown to us, but we are not on that account in a position to say either that a careful reproduction of the LXX is illegitimate or that a modification of that text is unjustifiable.

2. *The New Testament writers did not have the same rules for quotations as are nowadays enforced in works of a scientific character.* In particular, they did not have any punctuation signs which are so important in modern usage.

  a. They did not have any quotation marks, and thus it is not always possible to ascertain the exact beginning, or the real extent of quotations. They were not obliged to start actual citations immediately after an introductory formula, nor have we a right to affirm that their quotations do not end until every resemblance with the Old Testament text disappears. In certain cases they may very well have made shorter citations than is generally believed, and also may have added developments of their own, retaining some words taken from the original source but not actually intended as part of a quotation. Criticism of such passages if they were not intended as actual citations is manifestly unfair.

  b. They did not have any ellipsis marks. Thus special attention is not drawn to the numerous omissions they made. These ellipses, however, are not to be considered as illegitimate on that account.

  c. They did not have any brackets to indicate editorial comments introduced in the quotation. Thus we should not be surprised to find intentional additions, sometimes merely of one word, sometimes more extended (cf. Eph. 6:2).

  d. They did not have any footnote references by which to differentiate quotations from various sources. Sometimes we find a mixture of passages of analogous content or wording, but we are not justified on that account in charging the writers with mishandling or misusing the Old Testament.

We readily recognize that the New Testament writers fell into these patterns, whose legitimacy is universally granted, much more than a

present-day author would. Modern punctuation rules make such practices tiresome and awkward. One tries nowadays to omit, insert or
modify as little as possible in quotations, in order to avoid the complexity of repeated quotation marks, ellipsis marks, brackets, and so
forth. Yet this common present usage is by no means a standard by
which to judge the ancient writers.

3. *The New Testament writers sometimes paraphrased their quotations.*
   a. Under this heading we might first mention certain cases where
      we find a free translation of the Hebrew rather than a real para-
      phrase. Such a procedure certainly needs no justification, since
      a free translation sometimes renders the sense and impression
      of the original better than a more literal one.
   b. Slight modifications, such as a change of pronouns, a substitu-
      tion of a noun for a pronoun or vice versa, transformations in
      the person, the tense, the mood or the voice of verbs, are some-
      times introduced in order to better suit the connection in the
      New Testament. These paraphrases are perhaps the most obvi-
      ously legitimate of all.
   c. There are cases in which the New Testament writers obviously
      forsake the actual tenor of the Old Testament passage in order to
      manifest more clearly in what sense they were construing it. In
      this they are quite in agreement with the best modern usage, as
      represented, for example, in W. G. Campbell, *A Form Book for
      Thesis Writing*: "A careful paraphrase that does complete jus-
      tice to the source is preferable to a long quotation."[7]
   d. In certain cases the New Testament writers do not refer to a
      single passage, but rather summarize the general teaching of the
      canonical books on certain subjects in phrasing appropriate to
      the New Testament, although as to the essential thought they
      express indebtedness to, or agreement with, the Old Testament.
      This method of referring to the Old Testament teaching is
      obviously legitimate. The following passages might be viewed
      as examples of "quotations of substance," as Franklin Johnson
      calls them in his able treatise on *The Quotations of the New
      Testament from the Old Considered in the Light of General
      Literature*: Matthew 2:23; 5:31, 33; 12:3, 5; 19:7; 22:24; 24:15;
      26:24, 54, 56; Mark 2:25; 9:12–13; 10:4; 12:19; 14:21, 49; Luke
      2:22; 6:3; 11:49; 18:31; 20:28; 21:22; 24:27, 32, 44–46; John
      1:45; 5:39, 46; 7:38, 42; 8:17; 17:12; 19:7, 28; 20:9; Acts 1:16;
      3:18; 7:51; 13:22, 29; 17:2–3; Romans 3:10; 1 Corinthians 2:9;
      14:34; 15:3–4, 25–27; 2 Corinthians 4:6; Galatians 3:22; 4:22;
      Ephesians 5:14; James 4:5; 2 Peter 3:12–13.[8]

e.  Finally, we must consider the possibility that the writers of the New
    Testament, writing or speaking for people well acquainted with the
    Old, may in certain cases have intended simply to refer their readers
    or hearers to a well-known passage of Scripture. Then, in order to
    suggest it to their memory they may have accurately cited therefrom
    some expressions, which they then placed in a general frame differ-
    ent from that of the original. At times the actual words quoted may
    have been intended merely or primarily to indicate the location of a
    passage, as the general context of the Old Testament in which the
    stipulated truth could be found, rather than as an express citation.

4. *The New Testament writers often simply alluded to Old Testament
passages without intending to quote them.* It was quite natural that people
nurtured and steeped in the oracles of God should instinctively use forms
of language and turns of thought reminiscent of Old Testament Scripture.

> The speakers or writers, in such cases, do not profess to give forth the
> precise words and meaning of former revelations; their thoughts and
> language merely derived from these the form and direction, which by
> a kind of sacred instinct they took; and it does not matter for any
> purpose, for which the inspired oracles were given, whether the portions
> thus appropriated might or might not be very closely followed, and
> used in connections somewhat different from those in which they
> originally stood.[9]

Only in cases where the New Testament authors definitely manifest the
intention of citing by the use of a formula of introduction can we require
any strong degree of conformity.

With respect to what might be viewed as formulas of introduction,
the following remarks may be made:

a.  Only a quotation which immediately follows such a formula is to
    be certainly considered as a formal citation. In cases of succes-
    sive quotations "and again" always introduces an actual citation
    (Rom. 15:11; 1 Cor. 3:20; Heb. 1:5; 2:13; 10:30), but in the case
    of "and" or "but," or of successive quotations without any inter-
    vening link, criticisms are quite precarious, since no formal quo-
    tation may be intended.
b.  Even when a definite formula points directly to an Old Testament
    passage, we may not expect strict adherence to the letter of the
    source when this quotation is recorded in indirect rather than in
    direct discourse. In such cases we often find remarkable verbal
    accuracy, but we cannot criticize departure from the original when
    the very form of the sentence so naturally allows for it.

c. When what may appear to be a citation is introduced by a form of the verbs "say" or "speak," it is not always certain that the writer actually intended to quote. Rather, the possibility must at times be taken into consideration that we are facing an informal reference to some saying recorded in Scripture. Perhaps some of the clearest examples along this line may be found in the discourse of Stephen in Acts 7, in which free references are made to sayings of God, of Moses, and of the Jews, woven in the survey of covenant history presented by the first martyr. In Acts 7:26, a declaration of Moses is mentioned which is not found at all in the Old Testament and obviously was not intended as an actual quotation. In all cases of this type it must certainly be acknowledged that a considerable measure of freedom is legitimate and that one could scarcely expect here the exactness looked for in actual citations. The following may belong to this category: Matthew 2:23; 15:4; 22:32; 24:15; Mark 12:26; Acts 3:25; 7:3, 5–7, 26–28, 32–35, 40; 13:22; Rom. 9:15; 11:4; 2 Cor. 4:6; Gal. 3:8; Heb. 1:5, 13; 6:14; 8:5; 10:30; 12:21, 26; 13:5; James 2:11; 1 Peter 3:6; Jude 14.

5. *The New Testament authors sometimes recorded quotations made by others.* Not all quotations in the New Testament are introduced by the writers themselves for the purpose of illustrating their narrative or bolstering their argument. Sometimes they record quotations made by the personalities who appear in the history, as by Jesus, Paul, Peter, James, Stephen, the Jews, and Satan. In two cases we have a record of a reading— Luke 4:18–19 and Acts 8:32–33. The New Testament writers had at their disposal at least three legitimate methods of recording such quotations:
   a. They could translate them directly from the original text;
   b. They could use the existing LXX and quote according to this version, as suggested earlier;
   c. They could translate directly from the form used by the person quoting, often presumably an Aramaic translation of the Hebrew text. A few words are needed here only with reference to the last possibility. Of course, we expect the persons quoting, at least those who were inspired (Jesus, Paul, Peter, James, and probably Stephen), to quote accurately, so that in these cases no divergence from the original can be explained by the mere fact that somebody else's quotation is recorded. Since, however, probably most of these quotations were originally made in Aramaic according to a current oral or written Aramaic translation, certain discrepancies between the Old Testament and the New, which cannot be accounted for on the basis of the LXX, may have their true explanation in the use of this probable Aramaic version.

6. *Other principles whose application must be limited.* Under this heading we need to consider briefly three additional principles of explanation of apparent discrepancies between the text of the Old Testament and that of the New. These principles, in the writer's opinion, may well be at times the ground of a legitimate explanation, but they ought to be handled with utmost discrimination, lest the assured present authority of Scripture appear to be placed in jeopardy.

    a.  The texts may have been altered in the process of transmission. We have ample reasons to be grateful for the marvelous state of conservation of the text of Scripture: the New Testament possesses a degree of certainty no doubt unequaled by any other ancient text transmitted to us by manuscript; the Hebrew Old Testament has been the object of the loving and painstaking watchcare of the Jews and the accuracy of the Massoretic text has been confirmed in a striking way by the Dead Sea scrolls. Nevertheless, it is conceivable that at times an early mistake in copying may have vitiated our texts, thereby introducing a discrepancy which was not present in the autographs. Still, it would be very injudicious to indulge in unrestrained corrections of the texts on the ground of the quotations, and the present writer has not found any instance in the New Testament where such a correction might appear as the only possible legitimate explanation of a quotation difficulty.

    b.  In the quotations, as well in other inspired texts, the personality of the writers has been respected. It is an unsearchable mystery that the Holy Spirit could inspire the sacred writings so as to communicate his inerrancy to their very words and, at the same time, respect the freedom and personality of the writers so that we might easily recognize their style and their characteristics. The same thing is true of the quotations, for there also we may discern the individuality of the writers in their use of them, in the sources quoted, and in the method of quoting. There is, however, a dangerous distortion of this principle in the appeal made by some to slips of memory in order to explain certain difficulties in the quotations. Now the very idea of a slip of memory undermines seriously the whole structure of inerrancy and is therefore out of keeping with a consistent upholding of plenary verbal inspiration. In fact, as C. H. Toy himself recognized—and he cannot easily be charged with undue bias in favor of the conservative view of Scripture!— so many quotations show verbal agreement with the LXX "that we must suppose either that they were made from a written text, or, if not, that the memory of the writers was very accurate."[10]

c. The Spirit of God was free to modify the expressions that He inspired in the Old Testament. While this is no doubt true with respect to the interpretation of Old Testament passages and with respect to allusions or distant references, the statement should not be made too glibly with respect to quotations, and some conservative writers may have been too prone to advocate this approach when other less precarious solutions might be advanced. Nevertheless, in this connection, one may well give assent to the judgment of Patrick Fairbairn:

> Even in those cases in which, for anything we can see, a closer translation would have served equally well the purpose of the writer, it may have been worthy of the inspiring Spirit, and perfectly consistent with the fullest inspiration of the original Scriptures, that the sense should have been given in a free current translation; for the principle was thereby sanctioned of a rational freedom in the handling of Scripture, as opposed to the rigid formalism and superstitious regard to the letter, which prevailed among the Rabbinical Jews. . . . The stress occasionally laid in the New Testament upon particular words in passages of the Old . . . sufficiently proves what a value attaches to the very form of the Divine communication, and how necessary it is to connect the element of inspiration with the written record as it stands. It shows that God's words are pure words, and that, if fairly interpreted, they cannot be too closely pressed. But in other cases, when nothing depended upon a rigid adherence to the letter, the practice of the sacred writers, not scrupulously to stickle about this, but to give prominence simply to the substance of the revelation, is fraught also with an important lesson; since it teaches us, that the letter is valuable only for the truth couched in it, and that the one is no further to be prized and contended for, than may be required for the exhibition of the other.[11]

## Meaning of the Old Testament Passages

It has been urged at times that the New Testament writers have flouted the proper laws of hermeneutics, have been guilty of artificial and rabbinical exegesis, and thus have repeatedly distorted the meaning of the Old Testament passages which they quote.

1. This type of objection may appear at first more weighty than those which affect merely the wording of the quotation, since an alleged discrepancy in meaning is more grievous than a mere divergence of form. Yet the problems raised in this area are probably less embarrassing to the advocates of plenary inspiration, since a verbal comparison is largely

a matter of plain fact, while the assessment of the full extent of the meaning of a passage calls for the exercise of human individual judgment and fallible opinion. Few Christians, it is hoped, will have the presumption of setting forth their own interpretation as normative, when it runs directly counter to that of the Lord Jesus or of His apostles.

2. There is obviously a deep underlying relationship between the Old Testament and the New: one purpose pervades the whole Bible and also the various phases of human history, more especially of Israel. Thus the Old Testament can and must be considered, even in its historical narratives, as a source of prefigurements and of prophecies. It has been widely acknowledged that, in spite of certain difficult passages, the New Testament interpretation of the Old manifests a strikingly illuminating understanding of Old Testament Scripture. C. H. Dodd, although not a defender of verbal inspiration, could write: "In general . . . the writers of the New Testament, in making use of passages from the Old Testament, remain true to the main intention of their writers."[12] And again: "We have before us a considerable intellectual feat. The various scriptures are acutely interpreted along lines already discernible within the Old Testament canon itself or in preChristian Judaism—in many cases, I believe, lines which start from their first, historical, intention—and these lines are carried forward to fresh results."[13]

3. There are certain Old Testament passages in which the connection with the New Testament is so clear that there can hardly be doubt about their applicability and about the fact that the Old Testament writers foresaw some events or some principles of the new covenant. This is not necessary in every case, however, and the Spirit of God may very well have inspired expressions which potentially transcended the thoughts of the sacred writers and of those to whom they addressed themselves. This certainly occurred in the case of Caiaphas (John 11:49–52), and there is no ground to deny the possibility of such a process in the inspiration of the Old Testament Scripture.

4. While the doctrine of verbal inspiration requires that we should accept any New Testament interpretation of an Old Testament text as legitimate, it does not require that such interpretation be necessarily viewed as exclusive or exhaustive of the full Old Testament meaning. In many cases the New Testament makes a particular application of principles stated in the Old, whose fulfillment is accomplished in more than a single event. Thus certain Old Testament prophecies may have conveyed to the original hearers a meaning more restricted than the perspective opened in the New Testament pages. The original understanding was a legitimate interpretation of the prophecy, yet one which does not preclude the propriety of the larger vistas, authoritatively revealed in the New Testament.

5. Not all the passages quoted in the New Testament are necessarily to be considered as definite prophecies, but many are cited as simply characterizing in a striking way the New Testament situation. At times the New Testament writers may have simply used Old Testament language without intending to imply that there is a distinct relationship of prophecy to fulfillment, or of antitype to type.

6. Writing about this subject, C. H. Toy makes a remark which he apparently intends only with respect to apostolic times, but which may well be viewed as having more general reference: "The deeper the reverence for the departed Lord and for the divine word, the greater the disposition to find him everywhere."[14] Conservatives hope that, judged by this standard, they will not be found to have less reverence for their Lord and for the divine Word than the New Testament writers!

## CONCLUSION

One could wish to quote at length some remarks of B. B. Warfield,[15] which for the sake of brevity we shall be constrained to summarize here. The student of Scripture is not bound to provide the solution of all the difficulties which he encounters in the Bible. It is better to leave matters unharmonized than to have recourse to strained or artificial exegesis. Even when no solution of a difficulty is offered, we are not thereby driven to assume that the problem is insoluble.

> Every unharmonized passage remains a case of difficult harmony and does not pass into the category of objections to plenary inspiration. It can pass into the category of objections only if we are prepared to affirm that we clearly see that it is, on any conceivable hypothesis of its meaning, clearly inconsistent with the Biblical doctrine of inspiration. In that case we would no doubt need to give up the Biblical doctrine of inspiration; but with it we must also give up our confidence in the Biblical writers as teachers of doctrine.[16]

It has been the writer's privilege to devote substantial time to the consideration of all quotations of the Old Testament in the New. This study has led him to the conclusion that the principles mentioned above can provide in every case a possible explanation of the difficulties at hand in perfect harmony with the doctrine of the inerrancy of Scripture. There is no claim here that all the difficulties are readily dispelled, or that we are in possession of the final solution of every problem. Nevertheless, possible if not plausible explanations are at hand in every case known to the present writer. It is therefore with some confidence that this presentation is made. In fact, the quotations, which are often spoken of as raising one of the major difficulties against the view of plenary inspiration, upon examination turn out to be a confirmation of this doctrine rather than an invalidation of it. To this concurs the judgment of men who can surely be quoted as impartial witnesses, in statements such as the following, made precisely with reference to Old Testament quotations in the New:

> We know, from the general tone of the New Testament, that it regards the Old Testament, as all the Jews then did, as the revealed and inspired word of God, and clothed with his authority.[17]

> Our authors view the words of the Old Testament as *immediate* words of God, and introduce them explicitly as such, even those which are not in the least related as sayings of God. They see nothing in the sacred book, which is merely the word of the human authors and not at the same time the very word of God Himself. In everything that stands "written," God Himself is speaking to them.[18]

> In quoting the Old Testament, the New Testament writers proceed consistently from the presupposition that they have Holy Scripture in hand. . . . The actual author is God or the Holy Spirit, and both, as also frequently the *graphe*, are represented as speaking either directly or through the Old Testament writers.[19]

Such statements, coming as they are from the pen of men who were not at all inclined to favor the conservative approach to the Scripture, are no doubt more impressive than anything a conservative scholar could say. They may be allowed to stand at the end of this study as expressing in a striking way the writer's own conclusions on the subject.

# FIFTEEN

# OLD TESTAMENT QUOTATIONS IN THE NEW TESTAMENT

### Ronald F. Youngblood

SO MUCH OF THE NEW TESTAMENT consists of references to or quotations from the Old Testament that the so-called New Testament Christian is biblically illiterate if he knows little or nothing about the Old Testament. Reading the New Testament without knowledge of its Old Testament background is like starting to watch a two-act play at the beginning of the second act.[1] The latter experience would be supremely unsatisfying—for most of us, at least. We want to know how the play began—in its entirety, not just in its second half.

The Bible is the most dramatic literary production of all time. The preparation and promise of the Old Testament find their completion and fulfillment in the New Testament. Each half of Scripture needs the other for its fullest understanding. As Augustine put it: "The New Testament is in the Old Testament concealed, the Old Testament is in the New Testament revealed." Such a close relationship between the two Testaments is reason enough to warrant frequent examination of the ever-fascinating and always-important topic, "Old Testament Quotations in the New Testament." Each of the major elements in that title, however, is fraught with its own dangers.

## PRELIMINARY QUESTIONS

1. *What is meant by "New Testament"?* The so-called *Textus Receptus* ("Received Text") is the Greek form of the New Testament that underlies the KJV translation. It is now almost universally recognized that the *Textus Receptus* (TR) contains so many significant departures from the original manuscripts of the various New Testament books that it cannot be relied on as a basis for translation into other languages.

An example of the effect that this has on quotations of the Old Testament in the New Testament is the way Luke 4:18–19 cites Isaiah 61:1–2. The phrase "to bind up the brokenhearted" (Isa. 61:1) was omitted by Jesus in the synagogue at Nazareth (Luke 4:18 NIV), as the best Greek manuscripts attest. The KJV of Luke 4:18, however, includes the phrase (translating "to heal the brokenhearted") because it used the inferior TR as its basic manuscript. This is not to say, of course, that the TR is always wrong and that other Greek manuscripts are always right, because each variant between texts must be judged on its own merits.[2] It is simply to point out that in most cases the readings found in older manuscripts, particularly the Greek uncials Vaticanus and Sinaiticus of the fourth century A.D., are to be preferred to those found in later manuscripts, such as those that reflect the TR.

By making full use of the discipline known as textual criticism, the NIV translators attempted to employ the most accurate and original Greek text for every given New Testament passage. Such a procedure results in what is called an "eclectic" text[3] and ensures that we are reading and studying a New Testament that is as close to the divinely inspired original as is humanly possible.

2. *What is meant by "Old Testament"?* It hardly needs to be stated that "the NT reacts to the OT as the OT was experienced in the first century."[4] Our present knowledge, however, leads us to believe that more than one version of the Hebrew Old Testament was available to the first-century reader who "experienced" it. In addition one or more Greek translations of the Hebrew Old Testament were circulating at that time, and Aramaic Targums ("translations," "paraphrases," "interpretations")—whether written or oral were also current.[5] It is to be expected, then, that the New Testament writers would quote sometimes from one Old Testament version or translation, sometimes from another.[6] In every case, however, we can be sure that the inspired author quoted from or alluded to a version that did not distort the truth being asserted.

3 *What is meant by "quotations"?* Roger Nicole reminds us that the New Testament writers did not have the same rules for quoting that we take for granted today. They neither had nor used quotation marks, ellipsis marks, brackets, or footnote references.[7] They were therefore unable to indicate readily where quotations began and ended, whether omissions occurred in their citations, whether editorial comments were being inserted or intercalated, whether more than one Old Testament passage was being quoted, etc.

In addition "quotations" should be understood to include allusions and paraphrases, since the New Testament writers often quoted from memory and therefore with greater or lesser degrees of freedom.[8] The minds of the New Testament authors were so saturated with Old Testament texts and teachings that they referred to the Old Testament in a variety of ways—now quoting precisely, now alluding to this or that passage, now paraphrasing—but never deviating from its life-transforming message.

## THE QUOTATIONS THEMSELVES

1. *How many quotations are there?* Unanimity on the question of statistics is notably lacking. New Testament verses or passages introduced by a formula designating that what follows is indeed an Old Testament quotation number 224 according to Nicole,[9] 239 according to Shires.[10] If we add to these the Old Testament citations that are not formally introduced but are nevertheless clearly intended as quotations, the manner is 255,[11] "at least 295,"[12] etc. (According to my own count, in the NIV there are 296 New Testament footnote references to Old Testament citations.)

If we include allusions, the total rises dramatically, with tallies ranging from 442[13] to 4,105.[14] But since "the gradation from quotation to allusion is so imperceptible that it is almost impossible to draw any certain line,"[15] it is perhaps best to content ourselves with round numbers and rough estimates. S. Lewis Johnson summarizes: "There are over three hundred explicit quotations of the Old Testament in the New, and there are literally thousands of allusions."[16] Nicole is thus able to assert that "more than 10 per cent of the New Testament text is made up of citations or direct allusions to the Old Testament."[17]

2. *What New Testament books quote the Old Testament, and what Old Testament books are quoted in the New Testament?* The New Testament authors were by no means the first to quote from the Old Testament. In fact a later Old Testament author sometimes quoted from or alluded to one or more earlier Old Testament authors. Wenham points out:

> We have an instance of a later prophet quoting an earlier prophet in Daniel 9:2, where Jeremiah is quoted; references to the former prophets collectively by Zechariah (1:4–6; 7:7, 12); and an instance of earlier prophets being quoted as authoritatively by the elders of the land in Jeremiah 26;17 [*sic*].[18]

The Daniel and Zechariah references noted here are not footnoted in the NIV since it was not our normal policy to footnote general allusions. But the Jeremiah 26:18 reference, which cites Micah 3:12, is duly footnoted.

The Old Testament quotes and/or alludes to itself far more than we usually realize. The NIV footnotes call attention to the following additional citations: Genesis 50:25 in Exodus 13:19; Deuteronomy 1:36 in Joshua 14:9; 1 Kings 21:19 in 2 Kings 9:26; 1 Kings 21:23[19] in 2 Kings

9:36; Deuteronomy 24:16 in 2 King 14:6;[20] 2 Kings 10:30 in 15:12; Exodus 20:4–5 in 2 Kings 17:12; 1 Kings 8:29 in 2 Kings 23:27; Deuteronomy 24:16 in 2 Chronicles 25:4; Leviticus 23:37–40 in Nehemiah 8:15; Deuteronomy 15:12 in Jeremiah 34:14; 1 Samuel 5:5 in Zephaniah 1:9. An example of an important allusion not footnoted by the NIV is Exodus 20:25 in Joshua 8:31.

It is generally agreed that the New Testament never quotes from the Apocrypha, though some have detected apocryphal allusions here and there. Jude 14 quotes the pseudepigraphal 1 Enoch (also known as Ethiopic Enoch) 1:9. Such quotations and allusions do not confer canonical status on the Apocrypha and Pseudepigrapha, however, any more than Paul's quotation of Aratus in Acts 17:28, Menander in 1 Corinthians 15:33, or Epimenides in Titus 1:12 turns the writings of pagan poets into inspired Scripture.[21] NIV footnote policy does not include references to nonbiblical or extrabiblical sources.

As to which of the New Testament books quote from the Old Testament, the NIV footnotes omit from consideration Philippians through 2 Thessalonians, Titus, Philemon, and 1 John through Jude. Romans occupies pride of place with 58 footnotes, while Matthew and Hebrews are second and third (47 and 39 footnotes respectively). Needless to say, all the New Testament books without exception make allusion to the Old Testament, however generally.

In this respect the book of Revelation holds its own unique fascination. "That museum of rough Old Testament allusions"[22] cites or refers to the Old Testament "about 331" times, nearly a third of the total New Testament tally of "rather over 1,020 direct quotations or verbal allusions to the Old."[23] At the same time it is commonly asserted that, however many allusions it may have, Revelation exhibits no direct quotations at all.[24] The NIV footnotes rightly disagree, however, by specifying that Revelation 2:27; 19:15 quote Psalm 2:9 in whole or in part and that Revelation 1:13; 14:14 quote the phrase "like a son of man" from Daniel 7:13.[25]

Of Old Testament books quoted in the New Testament, it is generally agreed that Ruth, Ezra, Nehemiah, Esther, Ecclesiastes, and Song of Songs are not explicitly cited. To this list some would add Lamentations,[26] others Chronicles.[27] But just as all the New Testament books make at least general allusion to the Old Testament, so also the New Testament contains "passages reminiscent of all Old Testament books without exception."[28] And the Old Testament verse most frequently cited in the New Testament is Psalm 110:1.[29]

In a very few cases, no suitable Old Testament passage can be found as the source for what clearly seems to be direct citations of Scripture in the New Testament. In such instances it would seem that the New Testament writer was freely summarizing Old Testament teaching and did not intend to quote—either *verbatim ad litteratim* or *ad sensum*—a specific Old Testament verse.

3. *What Old Testament versions do the New Testament authors quote?* Most of the New Testament citations of the Old Testament are from the Septuagint (LXX), the Greek translation in common use in first-century Palestine.[30] Various forms of the Hebrew text were sometimes cited as well especially in books such as Matthew and Hebrews, which had Hebrew-Christian audiences in view.[31] A third source for New Testament quotations are the various Aramaic Targums whether written or oral on the Old Testament. Earlier opinions held that written Targums did not make their appearance until the second century A.D. or later,[32] but the discovery of a number of Aramaic documents (including Targums) among the Dead Sea Scrolls has increased the likelihood of the existence of written Aramaic Targums at a much earlier date. In any case a more pervasive influence of such material on the New Testament writers has become more plausible in the light of recent research.[33]

At one time it was thought that first-century Christian missionaries may have compiled one or more books of notes on the Old Testament texts most useful to them in their evangelistic endeavors. Such a "testimony book" then became the source of many New Testament citations.[34] Although this idea at first attracted a few adherents and has even gained a certain documentary credibility by virtue of the discovery of *testimonia* fragments among the Dead Sea Scrolls, its weaknesses outweigh its strengths and have caused it to fall into disfavor. Other related theories, while somewhat promising, have not gained the same kind of widespread consensus that sees the LXX version(s), Hebrew text(s), and Aramaic Targums as the major (if not exclusive) sources of New Testament quotations from the Old Testament.[35]

4. *Why do New Testament writers quote from the Old Testament?* The Old Testament was the Bible of first-century believers. They quoted from it as an indispensable aid to their ministry and mission, and they made primary use of the LXX—even when it disagreed with the Hebrew[36]—because it was such a widely disseminated version and could be read and understood by large numbers of people.[37]

When New Testament writers cited the Old Testament, they were often alluding not only to the specific passage quoted but also to its context, whether near or remote.[38] An excellent example is Hebrews 12:21: "The sight was so terrifying that Moses said, 'I am trembling with fear.'" The NIV correctly footnotes Deuteronomy 9:19 as the closest Old Testament parallel, but the previous footnote recognizes Exodus 9:19 as the overall contextual setting. It was to be expected that most first-century readers and hearers, steeped in the Old Testament Scriptures, would see in their mind's eye the entire context of any Old Testament verse or two brought to their attention.

Finally New Testament writers quoted from the Old Testament because they believed that it pointed to the Messiah, whom they had come to know and love as Jesus Christ (Luke 24:25–27, 44–49; Acts 3:17–26; 2 Cor. 1:20; 3:14). They read the Old Testament in the light of what Christ had done for them and for the whole world—and so should we.[39]

5. *How do New Testament writers quote from the Old Testament?* Wenham maintains:

> We have . . . no right to demand of believers in verbal inspiration that they always quote Scripture verbatim, particularly when the Scriptures are not written in the native language of either writer or reader. As with the word preached, we have a right to expect that quotations should be sufficiently accurate not to misrepresent the passage quoted; but, unless the speaker makes it clear that his quotation is meant to be verbatim, we have no right to demand that it should be so. In the nature of the case, the modern scholarly practice of meticulously accurate citation, with the verification of all references, was out of the question.[40]

Given these parameters it is possible, with R. T. France,[41] to distinguish the following five forms of Old Testament text quoted or alluded to in the New Testament: (1) those that agree with both LXX and Hebrew, constituting more than half the total number;[42] (2) those that agree with one LXX text against another; (3) those that agree with the LXX against the Hebrew; (4) those that agree with the Hebrew against the LXX; (5) those that differ from both the LXX and the Hebrew. The latter would include citations from one or more Aramaic Targums (oral or written), free renderings[43] of the substance of a passage, etc.

Various combinations of passages cited from two or more Old Testament books are not uncommon in the New Testament. A fine example is Romans 3:10–18, which, according to the NIV footnotes there, quotes from the Psalms, Isaiah, and (perhaps) Ecclesiastes. A noteworthy variation of this phenomenon is the so-called *haraz* ("chain," "necklace"; the same Hebrew root is used in Song of Songs 1:10, where it is translated "strings of jewels"), which intersperses a series of quotations with conjunctions, introductory formulas, and the like (see, e.g., Rom. 9:25–29[44] and NIV footnotes there).

When a New Testament writer quoted an Old Testament prophecy or promise, he was not necessarily saying that the Old Testament text in question was a direct prophetic prediction being fulfilled in his own time.[45] In a substantial number of cases the relationship of the Old Testament text to its New Testament citation is that of type to antitype, and the Old Testament passage is an example of what I have elsewhere called "typological prefiguration."[46] The New Testament writers' approach to the Old Testament was not as one-dimensional as it is often made out to be. "The early church looked upon the OT as a Prophecy, as a history (the book of preparation), as a promise, and as the book of prefigurations."[47]

Typology is almost universally recognized as a legitimate hermeneutical method that can be used to clarify the relationship between the Old Testament and the New Testament.[48] "Typology connotes two factors: a set of correspondences between objects or actions in both Testaments, and an indication that their interrelations are God-willed."[49] As long as the first is controlled by the second—and we can be reasonably sure of that only as we rely on the insights expressed in the words of the apostolic authors of the New Testament—only then can we prevent typological method from vaporizing into flights of fancy.

## CONCLUSION

Jean Levie gave to his book on biblical criticism and exegesis the perceptive title *The Bible: Word of God in Words of Men.*[50] The subtle symbiosis between divine and human authorship in Scripture is present in such a way as to give us divine truth without admixture of human error. This fact is nonetheless true with respect to Old Testament quotations in the New Testament than with respect to any other biblical phenomenon.[51]

At the same time, "when the Holy Ghost in the New Testament quotes something He said in the Old, He is completely independent of all human versions. He is His own infallible interpreter."[52] Since "all Scripture is God-breathed," Old Testament quotations in the New Testament are—like the rest of the Bible—"useful for teaching, rebuking, correcting and training in righteousness" (2 Tim. 3:16). The NIV thus performs a useful service for its readers by setting off in quotation marks almost three hundred citations of the Old Testament in the New Testament and by footnoting each Old Testament reference at the appropriate New Testament location.

# SIXTEEN

# EVANGELICALS AND THE USE OF THE OLD TESTAMENT IN THE NEW

### PART ONE

## Darrell L. Bock

FOR EVANGELICALS, WHOSE distinctive characteristic is their commitment to a high view of Scripture, perhaps no hermeneutical area engenders more discussion than the relationship between the Testaments. Within this discussion, a particularly important issue is the use made of the Old Testament by the New Testament. For evangelicals this issue is of high importance since both Christological claims and theories of biblical inspiration are tied to the conclusions made about how the phenomena of these passages are related to one another. The hermeneutics of the New Testament's use of the Old is a live topic for discussion within evangelicalism. In fact one could characterize the discussion as one of the major issues of debate in current evangelicalism. In short, the subject of the use of the Old Testament in the New Testament is a "hot" issue in evangelical circles, as many recent works in the area suggest.[1]

Despite all the discussion, no consensus has emerged. That main reason for the absence of consensus is the complex nature of the discussion both hermeneutically and historically. Major theological issues often involve multifaceted questions and this area is no exception. The goal of this article is to discuss the hermeneutical issues that are raised in the debate. The article seeks to describe four schools of approach that have emerged recently in evangelicalism. letting each view define its perspective on these complex issues. A second article will discuss four major hermeneutical issues which each school is attempting to handle in dealing with the phenomena of certain passages. The merits and weaknesses of each hermeneutical area will be evaluated briefly. Also a framework for dealing with the Old Testament in the New will be presented that reflects consideration of these key hermeneutical issues and draws from the contributions of each of these schools. Hopefully this two-part discussion will lead to a better understanding of the debate in this complex area and will provide a basis for better dialogue.[2] It is also hoped that the proposed framework in the second article can serve as a functional working model for a way to approach the subject of the Old Testament in the New.

## FOUR SCHOOLS WITHIN EVANGELICALISM

The following outline of the four approaches to the use of the Old Testament in the New is an attempt to group together the various evangelical approaches to this area. None of these groups has consciously attempted to form a "school"; but the term is used simply for convenience. The titles given to each school represent an attempt to summarize their distinctive qualities. All the approaches have one thing in common: they all recognize that the way to discuss the use of the Old Testament in the New is not on a "pure prophetic" model, in which one takes the Old Testament passage in its context and simply joins it directly to its New Testament fulfillment without any consideration of the historical situation of the Old Testament passage. In fact Kaiser explicitly makes the point that the best term to summarize the prophetic connection between the Old Testament and the New is not "prediction" but "promise."[3] This point is well taken.

The relationship between certain Old Testament texts and their New Testament fulfillments is often more than just a mere linear relationship between the Old Testament text and New Testament fulfillment. As helpful as charts are which simply lay Old and New Testament passages beside one another, the hermeneutics of how the passages are tied together is often more complex than a direct line-exclusive fulfillment. All the schools mentioned in this article agree on that fundamental point.[4]

### The Full Human Intent School (Walter C. Kaiser, Jr.)

The basic premise of this school is that if hermeneutics is to have validity then all that is asserted in the Old Testament passage must have been a part of the *human author's intended meaning*. Thus the Old Testament prophets are portrayed as having a fairly comprehensive understanding of what it is they are declaring about the ultimate consummation of God's promise.[5] So Kaiser rejects *sensus plenior*, dual sense, double fulfillment, or double meaning. He rejects any bifurcation between the divine author's intended meaning and the human author's intended meaning, though he recognizes that God has a better recognition of the fuller significance of a promise. He believes that to portray the relationship between the human and divine author as in some way divided is to create hidden secret meanings, something that is not a disclosure, something that cannot be called a revelation. Kaiser does have a place for typology which he sees as having four elements: historical correspondence, escalation, divine intent, and prefigurement. Typology, however, is not prophetic nor does it deal with issues of meaning; rather it is merely applicational.

The key point of Kaiser's view is his appeal to "generic promise," drawn from Beecher's "generic prediction."[6] Beecher defines it this way:

> A generic prediction is one which regards an event as occurring in a series of parts, separated by intervals, and expresses itself in language that may apply indifferently to the nearest part, or to the remoter parts or to the whole—in other words, a prediction which, in applying to the whole of a complex event, also applies to some of its parts.[7]

Kaiser comments:

> The fundamental idea here is that many prophecies begin with a word that ushers in not just a climatic fulfillment, but a series of events, all of which participate in and lead up to that climactic or ultimate event in a protracted series that belong together as a unit because of their corporate or collective solidarity. In this way, the whole set of events makes up one collective totality and constitutes *only one idea* even though the events may be spread over a large segment of history by the deliberate plan of God.[8]

Kaiser's key point is that in generic prediction *only one meaning* is expressed and also that *the human author is aware of all the stages* in the sequence from the first event to the last. The only factor the prophet does not know is the time when those events will occur, *especially the time of the final fulfillment.* Kaiser does identify features by which one can spot a generic promise. These textual features include: (1) collective singular nouns (e.g., "seed," "servant"); (2) shifts between singular and plural pronominal suffixes in an Old Testament passage (e.g., Servant as Israel in Isa. 44:1 and as an individual, the Messiah, in Isa. 52:13–53:12; reference to the monarchy and to the Davidic ruler through a pronoun shift in Amos 9:11–12); and (3) analogies that are expressed on the basis of *antecedent* (italics his) theology (e.g., either a use of technical terms already revealed like "kingdom," "seed," "rest," or a quotation or allusion to an earlier old Testament text, event, or promise). Thus the human author can intend in one message to address two or more audiences at once and have in view two or more events at once. It is important to recognize that for Kaiser generic promise does not equal typology, a distinction which others might not make. Kaiser sees typology as a nonprophetic, analogous phenomenon.

His view may be diagrammed as follows:

### HUMAN INTENT SCHOOL

**Intention of
prophet in
God's revelation:**

**One sense,
many events:**

**1 sense, meaning (generic promise)**

Again the point of Kaiser's model is that "the truth-intention of the present was always singular and never double or multiple in sense."[9] The key distinctive of this view is that the human author had the whole picture in view as part of his own intention and understanding, with the one exception of the time frame.

### The Divine Intent-Human Words School
### (S. Lewis Johnson, James I. Packer, Elliott E. Johnson)

The key emphasis of this school of thought is that prophetic passages all draw on the human author's words but that the human author did not always fully intend or comprehend the prophetic reference, while God did intend the full reference.[10] In a real sense, according to this view God speaks through the prophet's words. The terminology used to describe how this distinction is made and maintained differs between the adherents in the school even though they express basically the same view. S. Lewis Johnson and James I. Packer refer to *sensus plenior* while Elliott E. Johnson prefers the term *references plenior*. The meaning of these terms is disputed and will be discussed later in making the distinction between the human author's intention and God's intention, all three proponents seek to maintain a connection between the human author's words and meaning and God's intention and meaning in order to avoid the appearance of arbitrary fulfillment. Thus the fulfillment does not give the Old Testament text a meaning foreign to its wording and conceptual sense.[11]

Both Johnsons allude to the work of E. D. Hirsch for support.[12] S. Lewis Johnson says directly that "we may agree with Hirsch"—by which he means he can agree with Hirsch's thesis that meaning is to be located in *the author's willed meaning*—provided "that it is understood that the 'authorial will' we are seeking as interpreters is God's intended sense." He continues, "we should not be surprised to find that the authorial will of God goes beyond human authorial will, particularly in those sections of the Word of God that belong to the earlier states in the historical process of special revelation."[13] This introduces a key issue, namely, how the progress of revelation affects the understanding of these passages and their relationship to one another. (More will be said about this factor later.)

One objection that could be leveled against this school is the charge of the arbitrariness of a fulfillment that distinguishes between what God knows and what the human author does not know. How does this school deal with this problem? S. Lewis Johnson cites Packer as follows in defining their concept of *sensus plenior*:

> If, as in one sense is invariably the case, God's meaning and message through each passage, *when set in its total biblical context*, exceeds what the human author had in mind, that further meaning is *only an extension* and development of his [i.e., of the human author's meaning], a drawing out of implications and an establishing of relationships between his words and the other, perhaps later, biblical declarations in a way that the writer himself, in the nature of the case [i.e., because of the limits of the progress of revelation to that point] could not do. Think, for example, how messianic prophecy is declared to have been fulfilled in the New Testament, or how the sacrificial system of Leviticus is explained as typical in Hebrews. The point here is that the *sensus plenior* which texts acquire in their wider biblical context *remains an extrapolation on the grammatico-historical plane, not a new projection onto the plane of allegory*. And, though God may have more to say to us from each text than its human author had in mind, *God's meaning is never less than his*. What he means, God means.[14]

Packer stresses the role of the progress of revelation and the connection between the human author's meaning and God's meaning.

Elliott E. Johnson emphasizes some important semantic issues in his article which among other things discusses his concept of *references plenior*.[15] In defining meaning he notes the distinction between sense and reference.[16] "Sense" refers to the verbal meaning of language expressed in the text regardless of the reference, that is, "sense" involves the definition of a term, not what the term refers to. "Reference" indicates what specifically is referred to through the sense meaning. There is a difference between what is described and meant (sense) and to whom or what it refers (reference). For example, the word "Paraclete" is defined as "comforter" (the sense), but in John 14–16 it *refers* to the Holy Spirit (reference). The human and the divine authors share the sense of a prophetic passage but God may have more referents in mind than the human author had. Thus Johnson's designation of *references plenior* is to him a more accurate term than *sensus plenior*. For Johnson, there is always a fundamental connection between the sense the human author intends and what God intends. He writes,

> What we are therefore proposing is that the *author's intention* expresses a *single, defining textual sense of the whole*. This single sense is capable of implying a fullness of reference. This is not *sensus plenior* but *sensus singular* as expressed in the affirmation of the text. But it also recognizes the characteristic of *references plenior*. In Psalm 16 . . . the words of verse 10 apply to both David and Christ in their proper sense, yet in a fuller sense to Christ who rose from the dead, while David's body knew corruption but will not be subject to eternal corruption.[17]

Johnson's illustration of Psalm 16 argues that the idea of the passage, the "sense" of the author, is this: "Rejoicing in God, His portion brings His Holy One hope for resurrection." The passage applies both to David (at the final resurrection) and to Christ (at His resurrection). Thus the term "Holy One" has two referents: David and Christ. Though David spoke of his own hope, his language prophetically pointed to Christ. This Psalm 16 passage illustrates how this school sees these kinds of texts.[18]

The point of the previous discussion is that within the divine intent-human words school two sets of terms are used to protect the connection between the human author's intention and God's intention. Appeal is made either to *sensus plenior* (Packer and S. L. Johnson) or to *references plenior* (E. Johnson). There is a small but potentially significant difference in nuance between the two terms. Packer's *sensus plenior* sees the limitation that prevents an arbitrary fulfillment as residing in "the *implications* of the words" in the light of the progress of revelation, while Elliott Johnson's limitation is found in the *non-alteration* of the "defining sense" of the human author's words. Thus Packer's limitation is slightly more open-ended than Johnson's. In other words Packer has more room for the amount of extension of meaning between the Old and New Testaments than does Elliott

Johnson. This school, despite this internal distinction, has many other nuances hermeneutically, but the preceding paragraphs have surfaced its basic characteristic.

The view of this school may be diagrammed as follows:

**HUMAN WORDS SCHOOL**

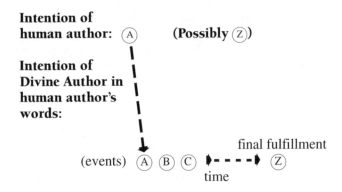

**1 sense, multiple reference with extension**

For this school, typology is prophetic because the pattern of God's activity is designed by God to be repetitive and the correspondences are identifiable from details in the Old Testament text. In identifying typology as prophetic, this school differs from Kaiser's view. This represents a second divergence, the first being its refusal to identify human intent with divine intent totally, as Kaiser does. The key distinctive of this school is its defense of a distinction between the human author's intent and God's intent, while trying to maintain a connection between the meaning which both express in the words of the text.

### The Historical Progress of Revelation and Jewish Hermeneutic School (Earle E. Ellis, Richard Longenecker, Walter Dunnett)

The main characteristic of this school of thought is its utilization of historical factors in assessing the hermeneutics of the relationship of the two Testaments. As the title of Longenecker's work suggests, *Biblical Exegesis in the Apostolic Period*, this school attempts to present the New Testament use of the Old as a reflection of the progress of revelation in Jesus Christ ("the Christological glasses" of the New Testament writers) and as especially making use of methods of first-century Jewish interpretation and exegesis (concepts such as midrash, pesher, and Hillel's rules of interpretation).[19] Longenecker speaks of the "Christocentric exegesis" that permeates the New Testament. He argues that the "Jewish roots of Christianity make it *a priori* likely that the exegetical procedures of the New Testament would resemble to some extent those of then contemporary Judaism."[20] He argues that New Testament writers neither (a) mechanically "prooftexted" the Old Testament nor (b) illegitimately twisted or distorted the ancient text. The New Testament writers got their perspective from Jewish exegetical techniques and from Jesus. Their exegesis could be characterized as "charismatic" in the sense that they saw events and declared them to fulfill the Old Testament in the "this is that" language reminiscent of pesher exegesis at Qumran. Some of these pesher treatments of the text may not conform to historical-grammatical exegesis as it is practiced today; but it was the basic way in which the Bible was read in the first century and therefore was a legitimate way to read the Old Testament. Often an important element in the pesher handling of the text is the rewording of the Old Testament passage so that it more nearly conforms to the New Testament situation in light of larger biblical and theological understanding.[21] One can readily see the historical stress in the argument of this school. Also appeal is often made to *sensus plenior*, as a way to describe this phenomena.[22]

This view also emphasizes that when the New Testament writers read the Old Testament, they did so out of a developed theological picture both of messianic expectation and salvation history.[23] Thus the theology of the Old Testament and in some cases that theology's development in intertestamental Judaism affect these writers.[24] Proponents of this view argue that one's understanding of the New Testament writers' hermeneutic should be less concerned with abstract issues of legitimacy and be more sensitive to the historical factors that can explain this type of exegesis.

A few citations from Longenecker serve to summarize the approach of this school.

> It is hardly surprising to find that the exegesis of the New Testament is heavily dependent upon Jewish procedural precedents, for, theoretically, one would expect a divine redemption that is worked out *in the categories of a particular history* . . . [and] to express itself in terms of the concepts and methods of that particular people and day. And this is, as we have tried to show, what was in fact done—the appreciation of which throws a great deal of light upon the exegetical methodology of the New Testament. But the Jewish context in which the New Testament came to birth, significant though it was, is not what was distinctive or formative in the exegesis of the earliest believers. At the heart

of their biblical interpretation is a Christology and a Christological perspective.[25]

Longenecker also writes:

> Thus it was that Jesus became the direct historical source for much of the early church's understanding of the Old Testament. But in addition, the early Christians continued to explicate Scripture *along the lines laid out by Him and under the direction of the Spirit.* . . . But the Christocentric perspective of the earliest Christians not only caused them to take Jesus' own employment of Scripture as normative and to look to Him for guidance in the ongoing exegetical tasks, it also gave them a new understanding of the course of redemptive history and of their own place in it. . . . From such a perspective, therefore, and employing concepts of corporate solidarity and correspondences in history [i.e., typology], all the Old Testament became part-and-parcel of God's preparation for the Messiah.[26]

While this view will be evaluated later, two potentially negative responses to it are addressed now: (1) This view seems too open to historical parallels from outside Christianity, and (2) this approach seems to lessen the concept of prophecy by setting its recognition largely in the fulfillment period, rather than at the time of the original revelation. The view, however, need not seem as unusual or negative as it may appear at first. For example, any New Testament passage where Yahweh in the Old Testament becomes Christ in the New Testament (e.g., Rom. 10:13 and its use of Joel 2:32) follows this principle of reading the Old Testament in light of New Testament realizations about the nature of the Messiah (where Jesus as Messiah is recognized as Lord and God Himself). Even Christianity's interpretation of a gap in Isaiah 61:1–2—in which part of the passage refers to Jesus' first coming (Luke 4:18) and the other part refers to Jesus' return—is possible only because of the New Testament teaching about Jesus' two comings. This "refractory" and reflective use of the New Testament on the Old is a key factor that must be evaluated in the use of the Old Testament by the New. As new revelation was given (in the life of Jesus and in the teaching from Him), the Old Testament was elucidated with greater detail.[27]

Again the distinctive of this school is its attempt to be historically sensitive to factors operating in the interpretation of Scripture in the first century. It could be diagrammed as follows:

## JEWISH HERMENEUTIC SCHOOL

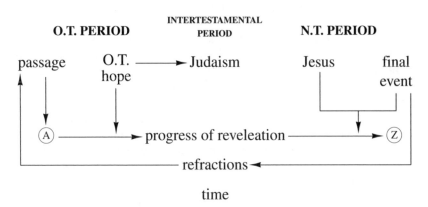

time

Obviously the diagram for this school is more complicated than the other diagrams. Advocates of this view still see a "prophetic" element in the fulfillment even though it is realized mainly with the event itself. Their appeal for a prophetic meaning is grounded in (a) the sovereign design of God in which the patterns of salvation history reoccur and aim for fulfillment and in (b) the appeal to the wording of the text in conjunction with God's revelation in Christ. However, it is also crucial to note that the event is the key dynamic that leads to the realization of the prophetic meaning. Most realization of fulfillment works toward and from the New Testament event.

### The Canonical Approach and New Testament
### Priority School (Bruce K. Waltke)

The discussion of this fourth approach will be brief since the writings propounding this point of view are not so numerous.[28] Waltke defines his approach as follows:

> By the canonical process approach I mean the recognition that the text's intention became deeper and clearer as the parameters of the canon were expanded. Just as redemption itself has progressive history, so also older texts in the canon underwent a correlative progressive perception of meaning as they became part of a growing canonical literature.[29]

While noting his indebtedness to Brevard Childs's work, *Introduction to the Old Testament as Scripture*, Waltke distances himself from all the details of Childs's approach. Waltke also states that his approach, though similar to *sensus plenior* is distinct from it in that he asserts *the unity between the Old Testament writers' ideal language and God's intention.* This agreement of intention is possible because the human authors spoke in ideal language. For him, progressive revelation made more clear the exact shape of the ideal, which was always pregnant in the vision. What is unclear from Waltke's writing is what the human authors understood of their intention. The lack of clarity on this point distinguishes his view from Kaiser's view. Waltke rejects a *sensus plenior* that "wins" new meanings from the text and sees New Testament writers as "supernaturally" discovering the fuller sense. Waltke and Kaiser are close in their denial of *sensus plenior*. The difference between them is how they handle later revelation in relationship to earlier revelation.[30] Waltke appeals to it openly while Kaiser refuses to refer to subsequent revelation as relevant to this discussion.

Waltke's appeal to the refractory role of the progress of revelation sounds like Longenecker's view. The difference is in the widespread application of this method and the assertion of the unity of authorial intent. For Waltke, all of the Psalter was ultimately the prayerbook of Jesus Christ. All the Psalms can ultimately be applied to Him.[31] In addition, New Testament fulfillments of earthly Old Testament promises have the effect of taking priority over the Old Testament promise and "unpacking" its literal meaning. An illustration of this approach can be seen in the following quote:

> If the Lord Jesus Christ and his church fulfill the promises of the Old Testament, as the New Testament affirms (see Acts 3:24–25), then those promises expressed in terms appropriate for the earthly form of God's kingdom in the old dispensation, find their *literal* fulfillment in the spiritual form of the kingdom in the New dispensation. Thus if Psalm 2:7 refers to Jesus Christ in his first coming, *so also the reference to Psalm 2:6 and Mt. Zion* does not refer to a location in Palestine; but rather refers to heavenly Mt. Zion and Christ's taking possession of the nations.[32]

So Waltke's position is that the whole of the Old Testament is to be reread ultimately in light of the New Testament; as a result the original expression of meaning within the Old Testament passage is over-ridden and redefined by the New Testament. Though Waltke would probably not describe the result of his method in this manner, such a conclusion seems fair. This description of Waltke's method is argued for as a result of his shift from earthly to heavenly referents in his understanding of Psalm 2. Such a wholesale shift of referents to the exclusion of the original sense is actually a shift of meaning. This writer is not able to supply a good functional diagram for this view.

The key to this view is its desire ultimately to read the Old Testament so thoroughly in light of the New.

## SUMMARY

This survey of recent evangelical views on the Old Testament in the New has demonstrated the variety of approaches which this area of debate has produced among conservatives. Four distinct schools exist. Some share overlapping concerns while they diverge from each other at other key points. What key hermeneutical issues are isolated by this debate? The second and concluding article in this series will state and evaluate four key issues involved in the debate. That article will discuss the differences among the schools and isolate the key points in the discussion, highlighting the four key areas of debate. The writer will then seek to offer an eclectic approach to the hermeneutical problems raised by suggesting lines of approach for the evangelical handling of each of these four areas. This eclectic approach will draw on the best points of each of these schools of thought.

# SEVENTEEN

# EVANGELICALS AND THE USE OF THE OLD TESTAMENT IN THE NEW TESTAMENT

## PART TWO

### Darrell L. Bock

IN THE PREVIOUS CHAPTER[1] this writer discussed four schools of approach within evangelicalism with regard to the use of the Old Testament by the New. In the interaction between these schools of thought four tension points will be raised in this chapter concerning dual authorship, language-referent, the progress of revelation, and the problem of the differing texts used in Old Testament citations by their New Testament fulfillment(s). In isolating these four areas of concern, it is important to recall that in any passage being discussed all these concerns interact with one another. That is why this area of hermeneutics is so difficult to discuss. Nevertheless by isolating the key issues, discussion of problem texts may become more manageable since the area of concern can be more easily identified. In this chapter the state of the debate will be evaluated and a suggested approach will be offered.

## DUAL AUTHORSHIP

The question of dual authorship is the basic one to be considered. Can God intend more in a passage than the human author intended? For Kaiser and also, it seems, for Waltke the answer to this question is no.[2] What the prophet intended, God intended; and He intended no more than what the prophet intended. God may have a greater understanding about the intention of the passage; but the prophet must understand what he was trying to say. The concept of "generic promise" is especially important to this view.

For those who make a distinction between the human author's intention and God's intention, a variety of approaches exist. Appeal is made to *sensus plenior* or *references plenior*. S. Lewis Johnson and

Elliott E. Johnson try to establish a firm link between God's intention and the human author's intention so that the Old Testament prophet's message remains demonstrably the basis for the divine New Testament fulfillment. This limitation prevents a charge of arbitrary fulfillment being raised against the New Testament. Their limitation is either "the implication of the words" in light of the progress of revelation (S. Lewis Johnson) or the "defining sense" of the human author's words (Elliott E. Johnson).

Those who emphasize the historical perspective of the use of the Old Testament in the New (the third school of thought) generally do not discuss dual authorship in any detail. They simply regard this distinction as established. This omission is a major weakness of the historical school. Dunnett is an exception within this approach and attempts to suggest limitations under which a distinction of authorship can be maintained. He initially appeals to the vague category of "other criteria" as he discusses *sensus plenior*. Later he refers to the "other criteria."[3] These criteria seem similar to an appeal to the progress of revelation. He also insists on an "organic connection" between the two meanings. In describing texts like Isaiah 7:14; Isaiah 53; and Hosea 11:1, Dunnett summarizes by saying:

> These kinds of texts may illustrate for us a *sensus plenior*. Yet to maintain some control in exegesis one should begin with the literal sense of the text, observe the total context, realize that the divine purpose in history is certain of fulfillment (on God's terms), and include both Old and New Testaments to have a measure for interpretation.[4]

How is this question of dual authorship to be evaluated? A fair summary would be to say that God wrote to His people at a point in history and to His people throughout time, while the human author wrote to his people at a point in history and/or, as a prophet, wrote to his people with hope as he expressed God's ultimate deliverance, either (a) in full human consciousness (direct prophecy, full human intent; Dan. 7:9–14), (b) in the ideal language of the passage itself(many of the psalms such as 16; 22; 110; and Isa. 53), (c) in language capable of expansion of reference into a new context through progressive revelation (Gen. 2:7; 3:15; Pss. 2:1–2; 8; 16:10; Isa. 61:1–2; Old Testament kingdom texts; texts about Yahweh in the Old Testament that refer to Christ in the New Testament), or (d) in language that involves a "pattern" of fulfillment but with less than full human authorial understanding of each referent in the pattern (typology that is typico-prophetic, Gen. 2:7; Pss. 8; 95:7–11; Isa. 7:14; 40; Hos. 11:1).[5]

The reason this writer rejects a "total" identification between the divine intent and the human author's intent is that in certain psalms, as well as in other Old Testament passages, theological revelation had not yet developed to the point where the full thrust of God's intention was capable of being understood by the human author. For example the divine nature of messianic kingship was nowhere so explicitly stated in the Old Testament that it became a basic tenet of ancient Jewish eschatological hope. Psalm 110 suggests it strongly, but it is not entirely clear that the Davidic Covenant by itself *at the time it was given* required a divine son for fulfillment. Apparently David thought Solomon could be that son. One must also reckon with the fact that Old Testament prophets sometimes admitted that they did not understand their utterances (Dan. 12:6–8; John 11:44–52; and esp. 1 Peter 1:10–12). Kaiser has admirably tried to deal with these passages; but his explanations have failed to convince most scholars that he is correct in uniting the authorial intent of the human and divine authors. Kaiser's concept of generic prophecy is a helpful one for this discussion; but what is unclear is whether the human author *always* intended *all* the sense that emerges from the promise in the New Testament and whether the human author always understood all the referents in the promise. The four qualifications stated in the preceding paragraph concerning the human author's language are an attempt to describe the various ways human and divine intent can be joined without being a violation of the sense and promise of a passage.

So to try to limit the meaning to the human author's intention seems to be too narrow a view. However, to say that there is a clear and definable connection between the expression of the human author and God's intention seems necessary or else the text can be made to say anything whatsoever in its fulfillment. Another important point is that the nature of the connection between the two passages can manifest itself *in a variety of ways*, including a human author's full intent. To try to limit the nature of the connection to one specific type of relationship seems to place a limitation on the text that its phenomena may not sustain. Broadly speaking, such a view places this writer in agreement with those of the second school (the human words school) and with some of those of the third school (the progress of revelation or Jewish hermeneutics school), who affirm that God could intend more than the human author did but never at the expense of the thrust of his wording. The New Testament fulfillment will either agree with or expand by natural implication the human author's wording. Whether it is better to call this relationship *sensus plenior* or *references plenior* or some other term, should still be discussed by evangelicals after a renewed study of several sample passages from different authors of the New Testament.[6] The variety of relationships between the divine and human authors naturally leads to a discussion of meaning in these texts and the role of language, that is, it leads to semantic issues of language and referent.

## LANGUAGE-REFERENT

This specific hermeneutical issue deals with the question, Where does meaning reside in a given utterance? Is it at the level of sense (the definitions of the words within a passage) or at the level of the referents? Is it at the level of the word or at the level of the word in its context? This question raises the complex area of semantics. Elliott E. Johnson grapples seriously with this area. The works of Moo and of this writer have also attempted to raise issues in this area.[7] In general the other schools have not dealt with it in any detail. The area still needs much study, especially in light of the acknowledged fact that words gain their sense not in and of themselves but from their literary context, that is, from the sentence, paragraph, and larger setting in which they are contained.[8] So the role of the context of a passage is crucial in determining the passage's meaning.

An additional question is this: As the biblical theological context of a passage is deepened, how is the meaning of that passage affected? Much of the debate among evangelicals about eschatology falls in this semantic area. Does a "heavenly" referent for the New Testament fulfillment of passages like Psalms 2 and 110 nullify what appears to be an "earthly" reference in the original Old Testament contexts? Amillenarians will answer yes to this question, while dispensationalists answer no and covenant premillenarians vacillate.[9] Are New Testament fulfillments final, initial, or decisive-but-not-final?

If the "seed" example from Genesis 3 cited in the previous chapter is any guide, then meaning deals primarily with the sense, not always with the referent, of a passage as that meaning is defined by its literary context. For Kaiser the literary context is limited to antecedent revelation. For the other schools, the literary context of all of Scripture is to be used. But it is important to state that when appealing to the whole of Scripture *an awareness of what is antecedent to the given passage and what is subsequent must be maintained.*[10]

Within the Scriptures the following sense-referent relationships can occur:

1. Referents of passages were made more specific, as in the "seed" example.
2. Motifs were reapplied. For example the Exodus imagery was re-used and reapplied, sometimes with changes, by Isaiah and by some New Testament writers; also Adam is introduced as the "first Adam" by Paul, a change made in light of Jesus' coming.

3. Language that was "earthly" in the Old Testament was expanded to include a "heavenly thrust." For example, the king as "son" in a nonontological sense in the Old Testament is "the Son" in an ontological sense in the New Testament (Heb. 1); "kingdom" in some New Testament texts along with "Jesus as King" refer to something other than an earthly rule (Luke 17:20–21; Acts 2:32–36). The eschatological debate turns on the question whether the Old Testament earthly sense is removed by the heavenly thrust of some New Testament texts. Premillennialists answer this question with a firm no.

4. Language that was figurative became literal. Examples are (a) the righteous sufferer in Psalm 22 is described with figurative language that Jesus, the righteous Sufferer par excellence, fulfills literally; (b) Psalm 69; and (c) "the right hand" of Psalm 110.

5. Language that is literal becomes figurative. For example literal lambs were sacrificed in the Old Testament but Christ was "the Passover lamb" in the New (1 Cor. 5:7), and the literal firstfruits in the Old Testament refer in 1 Corinthians 15:20 figuratively to resurrected saints.

Though a variety of relationships exist at the level of the referent, the basic sense of the passage is maintained.[11] At what level is the basic sense of the original passage determined? Is it at the level of the word, the phrase, the sentence, or the paragraph? This question still needs to be dealt with in detail by evangelicals.

Meaning as it relates to the use of the Old Testament in the New and as it relates to the language of these passages is vitally concerned with issues of sense versus issues of referent; but the exact limits of any approach to this issue are still unclear. One area that obviously touches on this discussion is the progress of revelation, the next area of concern.

## THE PROGRESS OF REVELATION

This issue deals with historical concerns. The question here is this: What effect did the history of Jesus' life and ministry, especially His resurrection and ascension, have on the church's understanding and the apostolic understanding of Scripture? The revelation of Jesus, the living Word of God, helps specify the referents in the Scriptures and the exact focus of their promises. John 2:22; 12:16; and 20:9 confirm this. The life of Christ did help the disciples understand what the Scriptures taught. What they did not realize about the Old Testament before, the life of Christ made clear to them.

As stated in the previous chapter, knowing that there are two comings of Christ and seeing Jesus as Lord in Old Testament texts that referred to Yahweh are two examples of the effect of this factor. These show an interaction between the life of Christ and the Old Testament in which the revelation of the Person helped make clear the revelation of the Book, by showing how the promise came to fruition. It is here that the concept of pattern and generic promise are helpful, because with the coming of the *pattern* and the *promise*, many seemingly loose ends in the Scriptures were tied together in one Person, bringing a unity to the whole plan. Patterns were completed and promises were fulfilled in ways that reflected a connection to Old Testament persons or events, or in ways that heightened them. The "refraction" principle, which was mentioned earlier,[12] rightfully belongs here.

Longenecker correctly takes the role of this historical factor seriously in explaining how the New Testament authors saw some of these texts as fulfillments. In short, they saw in the relation of Jesus Christ a revelation on revelation. Two points can be made to those who object that such an approach seems to demean prophecy because the realization of a prophecy's full presence is limited to the time of its fulfillment. First, a passage may not have been recognized as a prophecy until it was fulfilled. So one must distinguish, then, between what the passage initially declared and what one comes to realize later was ultimately meant by the passage. This distinction does not mean, however, that the passage did not originally *suggest* the prophetic meaning the reader now understands it to have. Through the progress of revelation, he can come to understand what he could not originally comprehend, because the Old Testament passage or larger Old Testament context only hinted at that meaning. This is much like a play in the second quarter of a football game that many come to realize in the fourth quarter was the turning point of the game.

Second, many of the Old Testament passages the New Testament appeals to were recognized as prophetic in Judaism, but the referent of those passages was disputed.[13] The force of the passage was seen as prophetic, but who or what fulfilled it was an issue in the first century. In the context of the progress of revelation, the disciples could point to recent historical events in the life of Jesus that fulfilled these passages and completed the promises. This is something that even the Qumran writings could not do with most of their "pesher" fulfillments which still looked to future and thus unverifiable events. The clear strength of New Testament proclamation about fulfillment was its *historical and textual* base.

A more controversial aspect of the historical emphasis school is the role of noncanonical phenomena, specifically Jewish intertestamental theology and Jewish hermeneutics. Evangelicals have often neglected the role of Jewish theology as the framework of theological discussion in the first century. On the other hand *the New Testament use of terms from Jewish theology does not necessarily mean the terms were appropriated without any change in meaning in the New Testament.* Careful historical-grammatical exegesis should trace both this background and any modification of it in the New Testament. As stated in the earlier chapter,[14] certain developments in Jewish theology may well have reflected divine reality, not because Jewish theology as a whole was true and authoritative, but because on certain issues they accurately expressed or developed the teaching of Scripture. In a more extreme example Paul cited the Greek poet Aratus without endorsing his pagan world view (Acts 17:28). God is sovereign enough to prepare the world for Christ in the conceptual realm of first-century Jewish religious expression as well as in the social-political realm of the first century with its Pax Romana.

The techniques of Jewish hermeneutics do appear in the New Testament. The use of key words to link certain passages is clearly seen in 1 Peter 2:4–10 and in 2 Corinthians 3:1–18. These are two of many examples. Longenecker demonstrates the repeated use of these techniques in the New Testament. What is debated is (a) *how* much the perspective of this hermeneutic *has influenced* the interpretations of the New Testament and (b) how proper it is to refer to New Testament quotations in Jewish terms such as "pesher" or "midrash." With regard to the first issue, it is fair to say that the key hermeneutical perspectives of New Testament interpretation (its Christological focus, corporate solidarity, and the presence of pattern) all emerge either from the events of Jesus' life (Christology) or from perspectives already present in the Old Testament (corporate solidarity and the use of pattern).[15] So the key elements in the New Testament approach to hermeneutics, according to Longenecker are not found in Jewish hermeneutics but rather in the history and theology of the Old Testament and Jesus' first advent.

Much confusion exists with regard to the use of the terms "pesher" and "midrash." The definitions of these terms are not fixed even in the technical literature.[16] Often when these terms are used, they are not clearly defined. Longenecker's repeated use of the term "pesher exegesis" suffers from this problem. Is he referring to an "eschatologically fulfilled and presently fulfilled" text or to a "technical style" of exegesis? Also is he using "pesher" in a descriptive-analogical sense (in which the New Testament use *is parallel to* this Jewish technique *but with important distinctions*) or is he using "pesher" to refer to a New Testament technique in which the *technique and the theological approach* of the two systems are *so identified* that they are treated as *virtually synonymous* hermeneutical systems?

Much of the reaction against this ancient hermeneutical terminology grows out of a sense of excessive identification between the Jewish and New Testament approaches in the writings of the progressive revelation school, without careful qualification or without a strong enough stress on the differences between the Jewish and Christian approaches to the Old Testament. More important than the choice of descriptive terms is what is meant by their use. If the terms are merely descriptive and analogical, then a problem does not seem to exist with their use; but if an identification of hermeneutical approach is asserted, then the distinctives of the New Testament perspective are minimized.

In summary the role of the progress of revelation in this discussion is a major one. Consequently a careful reader will seek to avoid being insensitive to the historical progress of God's revelation. Wrong emphasis exists on all sides of this issue, including the denial of the original Old Testament meaning, the denial of the influence of the events of Christ's life on the New Testament author's reading of the Old Testament, and an excessive or unclear identification between the hermeneutics of early Christianity and first-century Judaism.

## DIFFERING TEXTS

This issue is one about which the majority of evangelicals are most aware. The question is this: Do not certain New Testament uses of the Old Testament require an altering of the Hebrew text in which a way that fulfillments are possible only because the text has been altered? The alterations are often used by nonevangelicals to show the nonprophetic, haphazard, and nonauthentic use of the Old Testament by the New, especially in passages attributed to Jesus and the earliest church.[17]

Evangelicals have usually answered this charge in one of two ways. One reply is to assert that since first-century Palestine was multilingual, Jesus and the early church on occasion used the Greek text. This reply avoids the basic issue, which is this: If the inspired text is the original text (which is usually reflected in the Hebrew version), then how could the New Testament authors have cited a flawed translation? A second reply is to argue that whenever the Greek text is cited against the Hebrew text, then *ipso facto* the Greek text represents the original text or the Greek text represents what was an original but now lost Hebrew text.[18]

Another approach is to wrestle with the change by working at the hermeneutical and semantic level. Alteration of wording can be seen in one of several ways. The first is to distinguish between the *textual form* of the citation (i.e., what Old Testament text was used) and the *conceptual form* of the citation (i.e., what point the text is making). In making this distinction, a basic question needs to be asked: Could the point of the passage be made from the Hebrew text, given the speaker's understanding of Old Testament biblical theology and his understanding of the events of Jesus' life up to the point in question? In all the passages treated in Luke-Acts, the answer to this question was that the theological point could have emerged from an understanding of the Hebrew wording, so the fact that Luke used a *Greek* Old Testament text is irrelevant as a charge against the historicity of the event.[19]

Second, in other cases alteration of wording has clearly occurred and the above basic question about a Hebrew origin for the text can still be answered positively, and yet a question remains as to the legitimacy of the change (e.g., the use of Ps. 68 in Eph. 4, the dual use of χύριος for two distinct Hebrew terms in Ps. 110, or the change of μετα ταῦτα from Joel 2:28 to ἐν ταῖς ἐσχάταις ἡμέραις in Acts 2:17). Acts 2:17 is a good example of an interpretive biblical theological change, in which the "after this" in Joel is interpreted correctly as "the last days." No first-century Jew would deny that Joel 2 dealt with the *eschaton*. His question would have been, Is today that time? And that was the point Peter was trying to argue. So a change may be interpretively grounded in larger *biblical theological* concerns of *history*.

Third, sometimes the wording was changed because a larger literary context, either around the passage itself or around the theme of the passage, was being invoked without citing all the verses.[20] So alterations could occur in New Testament texts for biblical theological grounds (whether this biblical theology emerges from historical events or other biblical texts or motifs) that were broader than the verses being cited. The area of differing texts is a complex one, but this need not raise charges of arbitrary hermeneutics or a lack of historicity in these citations.[21]

## CONCLUSION

Recent discussions on the use of the Old Testament in the New have resulted in four distinct evangelical approaches to this issue. Also the debate has isolated four areas of concern for evangelical hermeneutics: dual authorship, language-referent, the progress of revelation, and the problem of differing texts. Work still remains to be done, especially in the area of semantics, in historical issues related to the progress of revelation, and in handling in detail all the specific passages with these concerns in mind. But this outline of the discussion shows that the framework for an overall satisfaction approach to this issue does exist, even if some details still need working out.

The theses of this chapter are four: (1) A distinction between divine intention and the intent of the human author is to be made; but both intentions are related in their basic meaning and that relationship can be articulated. (2) Meaning involves the sense of a passage and not primarily the referents of a passage; but the language of an Old Testament passage and its New Testament fulfillment can be related in terms of referents in one of several ways. (3) The progress of revelation affects the detailed understanding of Old Testament passages in specifying details about the completion of the promise and the completion of salvific patterns in God's' revelation. But one should always be aware of (a) what was originally understood by the human author at the time of the original revelation and (b) what God disclosed about the details of that revelation through later revelation or through events in Jesus' life. (4) New Testament alterations of Old Testament texts were neither arbitrary changes to create fulfillment in the New Testament nor reflections of later church theology placed back anachronistically into the lips of Jesus or the early church; rather they reflect accurate biblical theological considerations of the New Testament authors on the original Old Testament text.

Of course the test of such theses is whether they can be related to all the specific examples from the text. Several supporting examples have been supplied, usually in notes or parentheses, for consideration in evaluating this approach. It is hoped that this overview has helped (a) present fairly the different approaches to this area within evangelicalism, (b) distinguish clearly the key issues facing evangelicals in this area of hermeneutics, and (c) suggest avenues of solutions for these issues, while recognizing the recent valuable work and contributions of many evangelicals of different persuasions who have worked so diligently on these matters. The author also hopes that in being rather eclectic with the various approaches, the wheat has been successfully retained from each view while the chaff has been left behind.

# CULTURAL RELEVANCE
# AND PERSONAL APPLICATION

# EIGHTEEN

# A PROPOSAL FOR THE TRANSCULTURAL PROBLEM

## Henry A. Virkler

WHAT WAS THE AUTHOR'S MEANING when he wrote a particular text? And what are the implications of that meaning for us in a different time and culture?

There are two main categories of Scripture to which the above questions must be addressed. The first are the narrative portions of Scripture. How can we make these portions of the Bible useful for teaching, reproof, correction, and instruction in righteousness in a hermeneutically valid way?

Second, how do we apply the normative commands of Scripture? Do we transfer them wholesale into our time and culture, regardless of how archaic or peculiar they might seem to us? Or should we transform them? What guidelines do we follow to answer these questions?

This chapter is divided into two parts. The first part describes a method—principlizing—that is a hermeneutically legitimate way of showing the relevance of the narrative portions of Scripture for contemporary believers. The second half of the chapter proposes a model for translating biblical commands from one culture to another.

## PRINCIPLIZING: AN ALTERNATIVE TO ALLEGORIZING BIBLICAL NARRATIVES

Allegorism developed from a proper motive: the desire to make Old Testament passages relevant to the New Testament believer. Allegorism has been rejected, however, because it imports meaning on to the text which the author never intended to be there. Thus a method is needed for making the long historical sections of Scripture relevant for the contemporary believer.[1]

A simple recounting of the narrative is an insufficient and ineffective expository method. By itself such a method leads to a "B.C. message," a message that may have possessed relevance for believers at the time of the writing, but fails to seem applicable to believers today.

What is needed, then, is an expository method that makes the narrative portions of Scripture relevant for contemporary believers without making the text say something the original author did not intend it to say. One method of doing this is called principlizing.

*Principlizing* is an attempt to discover in a narrative the spiritual, moral, or theological principles that have relevance for the contemporary believer. It is based on the assumption that the Holy Spirit chose those historical incidents that are recorded in Scripture for a purpose: to give information, to make a point, to illustrate an important truth, etc. Principlizing is a method of trying to understand a story in such a way that we can recognize the original reason it was included in Scripture, the principles it was meant to teach.

Unlike allegorizing, which gives a story new meaning by assigning its details symbolic significance not intended by the original author, principlizing recognizes the validity of both the historical details of narrative and the principles those details attempt to teach.

Methodologically, the approach is the same as in the exegesis of any biblical passage. The historical circumstances and the cultural customs that illuminate the significance of various actions and commands are carefully observed. The purpose of the book within which the narrative occurs is studied, as well as the narrower context of the passages immediately preceding and following the section under examination. The state of theological knowledge and commitment is also surveyed.

When these things have all been done, the interpreter is then in a position to understand the significance of the narrative in its original setting. Finally, based on this understanding and using a process of deduction, the interpreter attempts to articulate the principle(s) illustrated by the story, principles that continue to possess relevance for the contemporary believer. We will look at two narratives to illustrate this process of principlizing.

## Example 1: The "Unholy Fire" of Nadab and Abihu (Lev. 10:1–11)

The story of Nadab and Abihu is interesting both because of its brevity and because of the sternness and uniqueness of the judgment on them. It raises curiosity because it is not immediately apparent what the "strange fire" (NASB) was, nor why it brought such a quick and forceful response from God.

### The Actions of the Narrative

Aaron and his sons had just been consecrated to the priesthood (Lev. 8); after commanding that the fire be kept burning continually

(6:13), God had confirmed their sacrificial offering by kindling it miraculously (9:24).

Nadab and Abihu, Aaron's two oldest sons, took "strange fire" and made an incense offering to the Lord. Immediately they were struck dead by fire from God. Moses uttered a prophecy, and then commanded Aaron's relatives to take the dead bodies of Nadab and Abihu from the camp. Aaron and his two remaining sons, who were also priests, were commanded not to show the traditional signs of mourning (letting their hair hang loose and tearing their clothes), although their relatives were allowed to do so.

God then gave Aaron three commands (Lev. 10:8–10): (1) neither he nor any of his priestly descendants were to use fermented beverages before entering their sacred duties; (2) they were to distinguish between the holy and the common, the clean and the unclean; and (3) they were to teach the people all of the Lord's statutes.

### Significance or Meaning of the Actions

*Historical-cultural analysis.* Israel had just come out of, and continued to be surrounded by, idolatrous worship. There was an ever-present danger of syncretism, i.e., combining the worship of the true God with the practices of pagan worship.

*Contextual analysis.* This was the inauguration day of Aaron and his sons as initiators of the Levitical priesthood. Their actions would undoubtedly be regarded as precedents for those who followed. Similarly, God's acceptance or rejection of these actions would affect further developments of the priesthood itself and the priestly activities.

*Lexical-syntactical and theological analysis.* Fire was regarded as a divine symbol in almost all ancient religions, including Judaism. The unholy or "strange" fire which Nadab and Abihu offered is explained as fire which God had not commanded them to offer (v. 1). A similar expression is found in Exodus 30:9, where incense that had not been prepared according to the directions of the Lord is called "strange incense."

Further analysis of the time sequence of chapters 9 and 10 suggests that Nadab and Abihu offered the incense of offering between the sacrificial offering (9:24) and the sacrificial meal which was to have followed it (10:12–20), i.e., at a time other than the time designated for an incense offering. Keil and Delitzsch suggest that it is not improbable that

> Nadab and Abihu intended to accompany the shouts of the people with an incense-offering to the praise and glory of God, and presented an incense-offering not only at an improper time, but not prepared from

the altar-fire, and committed such a sin by this will-worship, that they
were smitten by the fire which came forth from Jehovah. . . . The fire
of the holy God (Ex. 14:18), which had just sanctified the service of
Aaron as well-pleasing to God, brought destruction upon his two el-
dest sons, because they had not sanctified Jehovah in their hearts, but
had taken upon themselves a self-willed service.[2]

This interpretation is further borne out by God's prophecy through Moses
to Aaron immediately after fire had consumed Nadab and Abihu. "This
is what the Lord spoke of when he said: 'Among those who approach me
I will show myself holy; in the sight of all the people I will be honored'"
(v. 3).
    Shortly after this, God spoke directly to Aaron, saying:

You and your sons are not to drink wine or other fermented drink
whenever you go into the Tent of Meeting, or you will die. This is a
lasting ordinance for the generations to come. You must distinguish
between the holy and the profane, between the unclean and the clean
(vv. 9–10).

Some commentators have inferred from these verses that Nadab and
Abihu were under the influence of intoxicating beverages when they
offered the strange fire. The text does not allow us to assert that with
absolute certainty, although it is probable that God was giving commands
related to the offense which had just brought the judgment of death upon
Nadab and Abihu.
    The principal lesson of the three commands is clear: God had care-
fully shown the way by which the Israelites might receive atonement
for their sins and maintain a right relationship with Himself. The distinctions between holy and unholy, clean and unclean, had been clearly
demonstrated by God to Aaron and his sons, who had been instructed
to teach these things to the people. Nadab and Abihu, in an act of self-
will, had substituted their own form of worship, obscuring the distinction between the holy (God's commands), and the profane (man's
self-initiated religious actions). These actions, had they not been quickly
rebuked, might easily have led to the assimilation of all kinds of
personal pagan practices in the worship of God.
    A second lesson is found in the fact that reconciliation and atone-
ment had been given by God. Nadab and Abihu attempted to add
something to God's means of reconciliation. As such they stand as an
example to all people and all religions that substitute their own actions
for God's grace as a means of reconciliation and salvation.

## *Application*

God is the initiator of His mercy and grace in the divine-human relationship; we are the respondents to that grace. Believers, particularly those in positions of leadership within the believing community, have a God-given responsibility to teach carefully that salvation comes by God's grace, not through man's works, and to distinguish between the holy and the profane (v. 10). To believe and to act as if we are the initiators rather than the respondents in our relationship with God, particularly if we are in positions where others are likely to model their behavior on ours, as in the case of Nadab and Abihu, is to invite God's displeasure on ourselves.

## Example 2: An Analysis of the Temptation Process

Sometimes a narrative provides several principles or truths that continue to possess relevance, as does the narrative of the first temptation, found in Genesis 3:1–6. The actions of the narrative are found in a straightforward recounting of the text:

> Now the serpent was more crafty than any of the wild animals the Lord God had made. He said to the woman, "Did God really say, 'You must not eat from any tree in the garden'?"
>
> The woman said to the serpent, "We may eat fruit from the trees in the garden, but God did say, 'You must not eat fruit from the tree that is in the middle of the garden, and you must not touch it, or you will die.'"
>
> "You will not surely die," the serpent said to the woman. "For God knows that when you eat of it your eyes will be opened, and you will be like God, knowing good and evil."
>
> When the woman saw that the fruit of the tree was good for food and pleasing to the eye, and also desirable for gaining wisdom, she took some and ate it. She also gave some to her husband, who was with her, and he ate it.

## *Significance of the Actions*

Satan's temptation of Eve can be conceptualized in six steps, steps that can be seen in Satan's temptation of believers today. Step one is found in the first verse. The Hebrew may be paraphrased in the following way: "Now the serpent was more crafty than any wild creature that the Lord God had made. He said to the woman: 'Is it really a fact that God has prohibited you from eating of *all* the trees of the garden'?"

What is the dynamic here? Why did Satan ask this question? He obviously knew what God had said to Adam and Eve, or he would not have been able to ask what he did. Furthermore, he deliberately distorted what God had said. "Is it really a fact that God has prohibited you from eating of *all* the trees of the garden?" Satan's ploy is rather obvious: he was getting Eve to take her eyes off all the things God had given her to enjoy, and to focus on the one thing that God had forbidden. There were probably a thousand pleasurable things Eve could have done in the garden, but now all her attention was focused on the one thing she could not do. We might call this first step *maximizing the restriction.*

Eve was now prepared for Satan's next step. In response to Eve's statement that God said that eating of the fruit of the tree would result in death, Satan boldly declared: "You will not surely die." The results of such-and-such an action won't really be as bad as God has said. This might be called *minimizing the consequences* of sin. Satan minimized the consequences of sin in two ways: first, by telling Eve that the consequences of sin would not be as bad as they had been stated to be, and second, by eventually focusing her attention so completely on the tree that she forgot about the consequences entirely (v. 6).

The third step Satan took might be called *relabeling the action.* In verse 5 he says: "For God knows that when you eat of it your eyes will be opened, and you will be like God, knowing good and evil." Here Satan planted the suspicion in Eve's mind that it was not because the fruit of the tree would injure her that God had forbidden her to eat it, but because He did not wish her to be like Himself. Satan deftly tried to remove his temptation from the category of sin by relabeling it. In this particular instance, partaking of the fruit was relabeled as a way of expanding her consciousness. She would become a more complete person if she tried it once. Before this time Eve had thought of the forbidden action as disobedience: now she sees it as a necessity if she is to become a complete and mature person.

Satan then quickly added another aspect to his temptation, an aspect which might be called *mixing good and evil*: Verse 6 reads: "The woman saw that the fruit of the tree was good for food." C. S. Lewis has commented that evil is often a perversion of something good that God has created. In this instance Satan added potency to his temptation by mixing good with evil: Eve saw that the tree *was* good for food.

The fifth aspect of Eve's temptation is found in the middle part of verse 6: "She saw that the fruit of the tree was . . . pleasing to the eyes." This might be called mixing *sin with beauty.* Temptation often comes wrapped in the form of something beautiful, something that appeals to our sense and desires. It is often necessary to think twice before we recognize that a beautiful object or goal is really sin in disguise. In this incident Even failed to discriminate between the beautiful package and the sinful contents that the package contained.

Finally Eve took a sixth step: the narrative tells us that "she saw that the fruit of the tree was . . . desirable for gaining wisdom." In essence she swallowed the Devil's lie. This step might be called *misunderstanding the implications*. Although this may seem like a less significant point in the temptation process, it is perhaps the most crucial. In effect, by accepting Satan's statement, Eve was calling God a liar, even though she might not have recognized those implications of her action. She accepted Satan as the truth-teller and God as the prevaricator: by partaking of the fruit she was implicitly stating her belief that Satan was more interested in her welfare than God was. Yielding to the temptation implied that she accepted Satan's analysis of the situation instead of God's.

### *Application*
Many of the same dynamics of Eve's temptation are often present in Satan's temptations of believers today. With only brief introspection his tactics of maximizing the restriction, minimizing the consequences, relabeling the action, mixing good and evil, and mixing sin with beauty can frequently be found operating in our own lives.

### Guidelines for Principlizing
1. Principlizing focuses on those principles implicit in a story that are applicable across times and cultures. The details may change, but the principles remain the same: e.g., Satan may continue to tempt us by maximizing a restriction, but is not likely to do so by using a fruit tree.
2. When deriving the meaning of a story as a basis for principlizing, the meaning must always be developed from a careful historical, lexical analysis: the meaning must be the author's intended one.
3. From a theological standpoint, the meaning and principles derived from a story must be consistent with all other teachings of Scripture. A deductive principle drawn from a narrative which contradicts the teaching of some other scriptural passage is invalid.
4. Principles derived by this method may be either normative or nonnormative. For example, it is valid to say that Satan sometimes uses the above methods to tempt believers today, but it would be invalid to say that he *always* uses these methods, or that he uses *only* these methods.
5. Texts have only one meaning, but may have many applications. Principlizing is a method of application. The meaning is the author's intended one, but the applications of that meaning may refer to situations which the author, in a different time and culture, never envisioned. For example, the author of Genesis intended to

give us a narrative account of the first temptation—not a psychological analysis of the temptation process. In order for our application of the text (through principlizing) to be valid, it must be firmly grounded in, and thoroughly consistent with, the author's intention. Thus if the author's intention in a narrative passage was to describe an event of temptation, it is valid to analyze that passage deductively in order to understand the sequence and process of that particular temptation and then see how it might apply to our lives. It would not be valid to generalize from the same text principles about the way temptation always takes place, since the author did not intend the text to be the basis for normative doctrine.

## TRANSLATING BIBLICAL COMMANDS FROM ONE CULTURE TO ANOTHER

In 1967 the United Presbyterian Church in the U.S.A. adopted a new confession of faith which contained the following statement.

> The Scriptures, given under the guidance of the Holy Spirit, are nevertheless the words of men, conditioned by the language, thought forms, and literary fashions of the places and times at which they were written. They reflect views of life, history, and the cosmos which were then current. The church, therefore, has an obligation to approach the Scriptures with literary and historical understanding. As God has spoken his word in diverse cultural situations, the church is confident that he will continue to speak through the Scriptures in a changing world and in every form of human culture.

While this statement obviously addresses some very basic cultural issues, it does not give specific guidelines for interpreting the Scriptures in "diverse cultural situations." Two important questions it does not answer are: (1) To what extent are biblical commands to be understood as culturally conditioned and thus not normative for believers today? and (2) What kind of methodology should be applied to translate biblical commands from that culture to our own?

At one end of the spectrum are those interpreters who believe that often both the scriptural principle and the behavioral command which expresses that principle should be modified in light of historical changes. At the other end of the spectrum are those who believe that scriptural principles and their accompanying behavioral commands always should be applied literally within the church today. Many believers adopt a position somewhere between these two views.

The majority of evangelical churches have, by their actions, implicitly agreed that some biblical commands are not to be adopted wholesale into our time and culture. For example, the command to greet one another with the holy kiss is made five times in the New Testament,[3] yet very few churches observe this command today. Likewise, few Protestant churches observe the command for women to wear veils when praying (1 Cor. 11:5). Few churches continue the practice of footwashing spoken of in John 13:14, because the changing cultures and times have lessened the need and significance of the practice.

More controversially, some evangelical churches now have women who preach, although Paul stated in 1 Timothy 2:12 that he permitted no woman to teach or have authority over men. Many evangelicals, men and women alike, are wondering whether the traditional husband-wife roles delineated in Ephesians 5 and other passages are to be continued in our culture and time. Similar questions are being raised on a number of other issues as well.

In 1973 a conference was convened by the Ligonier Valley Study Center to address the question "Is Scripture culturally bound?" Speakers at this conference included some of the leading contemporary evangelical scholars. The difficulty and complexity of the issue is demonstrated by the fact that the major outcome of the conference was refinement of the question, rather than any substantive answers. Thus the question is one of immense importance, yet one that has no easy nor agreed-on answers at this time.

If we adopt, as most evangelical Christians have, the view that some scriptural commands are culturally limited while others are not, then it becomes necessary to develop some criteria for distinguishing between those commands which apply literally and those that do not. If our procedure is not to be simply an arbitrary one, where we dismiss those commands and principles with which we disagree and retain those with which we agree, we must develop criteria, (a) the logic of which can be demonstrated, (b) which can be consistently applied to a variety of issues and questions, and (c) the nature of which is either drawn from Scripture or, at least, is consistent with Scripture.

### Establishing a Theoretical Framework for Analyzing Behavior and Behavioral Commands

First postulate: A single behavior usually has ambiguous significance for the observer. For example, if I look out my study window and see a man walking up the street, I do not know whether he is (a) getting some exercise by taking a walk, (b) on his way to catch a bus, or (c) leaving home after an argument with his wife.

Second postulate: Behavior takes on more meaning for the observer as he ascertains more about its context. As I observe the man in the above example more closely, I hypothesize that he is a student on his way to a class because of his age, dress, briefcase, and books. However, I also observe a woman, apparently his wife (because of similar clothing styles) following about fifteen feet behind him, walking with her head down. I immediately wonder if they have been fighting, and she is following him in an attempt to pacify him after he left the house in anger. I quickly dismiss this hypothesis when I recognize that the clothing styles indicate this couple is from a culture where it is normal and expected that the wife walk a certain distance behind her husband whenever they are together in public.

Third postulate: Behavior that has a certain meaning in one culture may have a totally different significance in another culture. In American society, for a woman to follow her husband at a distance of fifteen feet, with her head down, would usually indicate a problem in their relationship. In another culture, this same behavior may be considered normal and expected.[4]

Let us examine the implications of these three postulates.

*First,* the meaning of a single behavior cannot be ascertained apart from its context. Analogously, the meaning of (and principle behind) a behavioral command in Scripture cannot be ascertained apart from the context of that command.

*Second,* the meaning behind a given behavior can be more accurately ascertained the more one knows about the context of that behavior. Similarly, the more we know of the context of a behavioral command, other things being equal, the more we will be able to ascertain accurately the meaning of (and the principle expressed by) that command.

*Third,* since a given behavior in one culture may have a different meaning in another culture, it may be necessary to change the behavioral expression of a scriptural command in order to translate the principle behind that command from one culture and time to another.

Two aspects of biblical command need to be differentiated: the behavior specified, and the principle expressed through the specified behavior. For example, the holy kiss greeting (behavior) expressed brotherly love (principle).

In making transcultural applications of biblical commands, three alternatives can be considered:

1. Retain both the principle and its behavioral expression.
2. Retain the principle but suggest a change in the way that principle is behaviorally expressed in our culture.
3. Change both the principle and its behavioral expression, assuming that both were culture-bound and are therefore no longer applicable.

As an example, let us look at the custom of the veiling of wives as an expression of voluntary submission to their husbands (1 Cor. 11:2–16). Three approaches have been taken by various commentators:

1. Retain both the principle of submission and its expressions through the use of veils.
2. Retain the principle of submission but replace veiling with some other behavior that more meaningfully expresses submission in our culture.
3. Replace both the principle of submission and all expressions of submission with a more egalitarian philosophy, believing that the concept of hierarchy within the family is a culture-bound one.[5]

Thus the analysis of biblical commands into (a) principles, and (b) behaviors that express those principles, possesses little worth unless there are some means for differentiating between those principles and behaviors that are culture-bound and those that are transcultural.

## Some Preliminary Guidelines for Differentiating Culture-Bound from Transcultural Principles and Commands

The following guidelines are called preliminary for two reasons: First, they are incomplete in that they do not cover every biblical command and principle, and second, they are at this point tentative, intended to initiate discussion and further exploration of the issue.

### Guidelines for Discerning Whether Principles Are Transcultural or Culture-Bound

*First*, determine the reason given for the principle. For example, we are to love one another *because* God first loved us (1 John 4:19). We are not to love the world and its values, *because* love of the world and love of God are mutually exclusive (1 John 2:15).

*Second*, if the reason for a principle is culture-bound, then the principle may be also. If the reason has its basis in God's unchanging nature (His grace, His love, His moral nature, or His created order), then the principle itself should probably not be changed.

### Guidelines for Discerning Whether Commands (Applications of Principles) Are Transcultural or Culture-Bound

*First*, when a transcultural principle is embodied in a form that was part of the common cultural habits of the time, the form *may* be modified, even though the principle remains unchanged. For example, Jesus demonstrated the principle that we should have an attitude of humility and willingness to serve one another (Mark 10:42–44) by washing the disciples' feet (John 13:12–16), a familiar custom of the day. We retain the principle, although it is possible that there are other ways to express that principle more meaningfully in our culture.

Again, James argued that believers should not show partiality within the church meeting by having the rich sit in chairs and the poor sit on the floor (James 2:1–9). We retain the principle of nonpartiality, but the application of the principle takes on different dimensions in our time and culture.

*Second*, when a practice that was an accepted part of a pagan culture was forbidden in Scripture, this is probably to be forbidden in contemporary culture as well, particularly if the command is grounded in God's moral nature. Examples of practices that were accepted parts of pagan cultures but were forbidden in Scripture include fornication, adultery, spiritism, divorce and homosexual behavior.

*Third*, it is important to define the intended recipients of a command, and to apply the command discriminately to other groups. If a command was given to only one church, this *may* indicate that it was meant to be only a local rather than a universal practice.

## Some Suggested Steps in Translating Biblical Commands from One Culture and Time to Another

1. *Discern as accurately as possible the principle behind the given behavioral command.* For example, Christians are to judge individual sin within their local community of believers because, if unchecked, evil will have an effect upon the entire community (1 Cor. 5:1–13, especially v. 6).

2. *Discern whether the principle is timeless or time-bound (transcultural or culture-bound).* Some suggestions for doing this were offered in the last section. Since most biblical principles are rooted in God's unchanging nature, it seems to follow that a principle should be considered to be transcultural unless there is evidence to the contrary.

3. *If a principle is transcultural, study the nature of its behavioral application within our culture.* Will the behavioral application given be appropriate now, or will it be an anachronistic oddity?

The danger of conforming the biblical message to our cultural mold is very great. There are times when the expression of a God-given principle will cause Christians to behave in a way different from non-Christians (Rom. 12:2), but not needlessly so, not for the sake of the difference itself. The criterion for whether a behavioral command should be applied in our culture should *not* be whether or not it conforms to modern cultural practices, but whether or not it adequately and accurately expresses the God-given principle that was intended.

4. *If the behavioral expression of a principle should be changed,*

*suggest a cultural equivalent that would adequately express the God-given principle behind the original command.* For example, J. B. Phillips suggests that "Greet one another with a hearty handshake" may be a good cultural equivalent to "Greet one another with the holy kiss."[6]

If there is no cultural equivalent, it might be worthwhile to consider *creating* a new cultural behavior that would meaningfully express the principles involved. (In a similar but not strictly analogous manner, some of the newer wedding ceremonies express the same principles as more traditional ones, but in very creative and meaningful new ways.)

5. *If after careful study the nature of the biblical principle and its attendant command remain in question, apply the biblical precept of humility.* There may be occasions when even after careful study of a given principle and its behavioral expression, we still may remain uncertain about whether it should be considered transcultural or culture-bound. If we must decide to treat the command one way or the other but have no conclusive means to make the decision, the biblical principle of humility can be helpful. After all, would it be better to treat a principle as transcultural and be guilty of being overscrupulous in our desire to obey God? Or would it be better to treat a transcultural principle as culture-bound and be guilty of breaking a transcendent requirement of God? The answer should be obvious.

If this humility principle is isolated from the other guidelines mentioned above, it could easily be misconstrued as ground for unnecessary conservatism. The principle should be applied only after we have carefully tried to determine whether a principle is transcultural or culture-bound, and despite our best efforts, the issue still is uncertain. This is a guideline of last resort and would be destructive if used as a first resort.[7]

### SUMMARY

1. Principlizing: Based on a historical-cultural, contextual, lexical-syntactical, and theological analysis of the narrative portion, ascertain by deductive study (a) the principle(s) that passage was intended to teach, or (b) the principles (descriptive truths) illustrated within the passage that remain relevant for the contemporary believer.

2. Transcultural transmission of biblical commands:
   a. Discern as accurately as possible the principle behind the command.
   b. Discern whether the principle is transcultural or culture-bound by examining the reason given for the principle.
   c. If a principle is transcultural, determine whether or not the same behavioral application in our culture will express the principle as adequately and accurately as the biblical one.

d.  If the behavioral expression of a principle should be changed,
    suggest a cultural equivalent that will express the God-given
    principle behind the original command.

e.  If, after careful study, the nature of the biblical principle and
    its attendant command remain in question, apply the biblical
    precept of humility.

# NINETEEN

# INTERPRETING IN CULTURAL CONTEXT

## Charles H. Kraft

AT THE START OF THIS chapter I would like to briefly introduce myself. First of all I am an evangelical Christian, committed to God through Jesus Christ as revealed in the written Word. I have been trained in an evangelical college and seminary and now, as a professor in an evangelical seminary, I endeavor to maintain in all that I do a commitment to the authority of the Scriptures as interpreted from an evangelical perspective. I am, furthermore, a missionary and trainer of missionaries. I am thus committed to the communication of the revealed message of God to the ends of the earth. Additionally I am an anthropologist, linguist, and communicologist. From these disciplinary involvements I am committed to studying and analyzing the Word and the communication of God's message from a Christ-centered, cross-cultural perspective.

An evangelical anthropologist should have something to say about culture and the Bible, and I feel that my evangelical commitment to the inspired Word of God and my attempts to integrate that commitment with my academic disciplines enable me to at least take a stab at certain of the cultural issues that affect our attempts to interpret the Bible. Many, however, consider the disciplines that I represent to be basically antagonistic to an evangelical commitment. I do not find them so. Indeed, I feel that my involvement in cultural, linguistic, and communicational studies has deepened and strengthened my commitment to God's inspired Word. I find that these perspectives continually illumine for me the Scriptural message for which I have given my life. For the Bible is a cross-cultural book, and to interpret it properly we need the sharpest tools available to enable us to deal reverently— and yet precisely—with the inspired message that comes to us in cultural forms that are not our own.

The matter of interpretation in culture is a weighty concern. For the Word has come to us via the forms of Hebrew, Aramaic, and Greek cultures. We are immersed in a culture far different from any of these. We cannot, therefore, always trust our culturally-conditioned reflexes to give us the proper interpretation of Scripture. We trust the Holy Spirit to keep us from going too far astray in our interpretations. Yet we are often puzzled that God's Spirit does not lead us all to the same answer concerning every issue.

In this chapter I have selected four areas where insight into the influences of culture can assist us in our understanding of how the Scriptures are to be interpreted. Underlying my discussion is an assumption that I have examined in another place.[1] This assumption is that God communicates via culture and language in essentially the same way that human beings do. If this is true, the insights into culture and language provided by my disciplines are going to be very helpful with respect to our understanding of what it means to interpret the Bible in context.

Evangelical biblical theologians have for some time focused on the need to interpret the Bible in context. The context that has been largely in view has been that of the whole Bible. "The Bible is its own best interpreter" is a statement that is often made to emphasize the importance of this context. Without denying the necessity to focus strongly on the whole Bible as context, evangelical biblical theologians have also been coming to recognize more and more the importance of the individual cultural context in which each portion of the Bible has been written. Largely through the input of the grammatico-historical method, evangelical scholars have begun to pay more and more attention to the interrelationships between the ways in which things are stated in Scripture and the ways in which things were stated in the wider cultural context in which the people and events recorded in Scripture participated. When it comes to the analysis of such cultural contexts, however, it is likely that contemporary disciplines such as anthropology and linguistics, dedicated as they are to a primary focus on these issues, may be able to provide us with sharper tools for analysis than the disciplines of history and philology have provided.[2] On this assumption, I am attempting to develop an approach that may be labeled culturolinguistic (or, better, ethnolinguistic) as a contemporary evangelical modification and amplification of the grammatico-historical method. This method depends greatly on the pioneering insights of Bible translation theorists such as Eugene Nida and John Beekman, who have for some time now been forced to wrestle with the cultural and linguistic dimensions of the Bible at a deeper level than most theologians have felt to be necessary.

The basic difference here centers around the matter of whether the interpreter has two or more than two cultural contexts in view. If he only considers the biblical cultural context and his own cultural context (the latter usually being that of the academic interpreter), the problems (and the insights) are significantly less than if the interpreter must, in addition to these two contexts, consider a third cultural context into which he must intelligibly render the message. In the latter case the interpreter is forced to develop what may be called a "cross-cultural perspective" as opposed to a "mono-cultural perspective" on the problems of biblical interpretation. A mono-cultural perspective may assume, as many historically oriented interpreters do, that when one attempts to move the biblical message from the biblical cultures into Euro-American language and culture he is moving from less adequate cultures and languages into more adequate cultures and languages. This was one of the mistakes that Bultmann made. A cross-cultural perspective, however, is one that has learned that all cultures and languages, like all varieties of human being, are potentially adequate vehicles for the communication of the biblical message. It is not, therefore, quite so prone to be ethnocentric in its approach to the relationship between the messages and the cultural context in which they are presented. Though I will not be able to develop the implications of these statements in this presentation,[3] there often seems to be a large gap in understanding between those who have experience with only one receptor culture (their own) and those who have experience with many receptor cultures. The latter are, I believe, usually in a much better position to understand and interpret the relationships between the message and its cultural context. It is this kind of insight that I see as the basic difference between what I am calling the ethnolinguistic approach to biblical interpretation and the grammatico-historical approach. To illustrate this approach I would like to focus on four specific areas, each of which has its contribution to make to a deepened evangelical understanding of the relationship of culture to biblical interpretation. These areas are (1) the definition of meaning, (2) communication within a range, (3) culture and interpretational reflexes, and (4) levels of abstraction in interpretation.

## DEFINITION OF MEANING

The first of these areas, and in many senses the most basic, has to do with how meanings are arrived at. By "meaning" I do not mean the same thing as "message." Meaning is, from this point of view, that which the receiver of a message constructs within his head and responds to. We know, of course, that there is often a wide discrepancy between the meanings that the communicator seeks to get across and those meanings that the receptor understands. The process seems to be one in which the communicator has certain meanings in his mind that he encodes in cultural symbols (primarily linguistic symbols) and transmits in the form of a message to one or more receptors. The receptors, for their part, decode the message in their heads and thereby derive the meanings on the basis of which they act.

Culture provides the matrix in terms of which such meanings are both encoded by communicators and decoded by receptors. The symbols used for the transmission of such meanings are all defined and interpreted culturally. We may say, therefore, that words and all other cultural symbols derive their meanings only from their participation in the cultural context of which they are a part. There are, apparently, no symbols that mean exactly the same thing in all cultures and few, if any, that mean exactly the same thing in two or more cultures.

The crucial thing in the transmission of messages via such culturally defined symbols is the extent of agreement between the communicator and the receptor concerning what the cultural symbols signify. If the communicator and the receptor have been taught by means of their participation in the same culture that such-and-such a word has such-and-such a meaning, the degree of difficulty that they experience in understanding each other will be minimal. If, however, communicator and receptor have been taught different meanings for the same word, the degree of difficulty will be large. We may say that common agreements concerning cultural and linguistic symbols minimize the difficulty of communication between participants in a communicational event, while lack of such agreements makes difficult or even blocks communication. The same can be said for interpretation of materials such as the biblical materials. The fact that we who live in Euro-American culture attempt to interpret the Bible, none of which was spoken or written in Euro-American culture, raises great difficulty for us. For we are unlikely to share with the original authors many, if any, of the agreements concerning the meanings of the concepts that they use, since our cultural conditioning is so different from theirs.

## COMMUNICATION WITHIN A RANGE

Considerations of how cultural symbols convey meanings lead to the recognition that all communication (including interpretation) is approximate. I believe we can state boldly that no receiver of a message ever understands exactly what the communicator intends—even when both communicator and receiver participate in the same culture. The lack of correspondence between intent and interpretation is even greater, of course, when there is a culture gap and/or a time gap between the communicator and his receptor(s).

In ordinary communicational interaction we attempt to compensate for this fact in two ways. (1) The communicator attempts to elicit "feedback" from the receptors to see how well they are getting his message. If he finds out that they are not understanding him well, he adjusts his message by rephrasing, providing additional information, explaining more elaborately, and so forth, in order to bring about greater correspondence between his intent and the receptors' understanding. Such was the process that Paul and Barnabas went through in Acts 14 when the people of Lystra interpreted their healing as the act of gods and began to worship them. Paul and Barnabas, through feedback, discovered their miscommunication and took steps to straighten it out. (2) The second method of compensation in communication is the fact that human beings settle for approximate understandings of what they seek to communicate, as long as they are reasonably close to what is intended. We make a statement and the receptor restates in his own words roughly what we intend and we settle for that.

In interpreting the Scriptures we are, of course, cut off from the possibility of asking the original authors to clarify their meanings for us. So the first of these techniques for compensating for communicational impreciseness is not available to us. The fact that messages can be interpreted within a range is, however, of great significance to our attempts to understand the Bible from within another culture. I believe that the Holy Spirit, as He assists us in interpreting His Word, works in terms of such an allowable range.

At one level, of course, the God-allowed range of acceptable interpretation is very narrow. The fact that God exists, that Jesus is the Mediator between God and man, that human beings are sinful, and so on, are either assumed or continually asserted by Scripture. These matters are not debatable, at least at that deep level. At another more surface level, though, there is—even within Scripture—a range of allowable understanding that is culturally conditioned. This fact raises the hope that additional interpretations developed by God-led people within contemporary cultures may also fall within the range allowed by Scripture.

Though the existence of God is not debatable (Heb. 11:6), we see in Scripture a range of understandings of Him allowed. Likewise with sin, the understanding of the nature of man (one, two, or three parts), understandings of the spirit world, and so forth. The problem is, of course, to determine which contemporary understandings of these things fit within the scripturally-allowed range and which fall outside. Within the allowed range fall both the intent of the author and the intent of God, but these are not always the same. In prophetic utterances, for example, the human author was often unaware of the later use God would make of those utterances.

Accuracy of interpretation is, therefore, a matter of coming to understand what is said or written within an allowable range.

## CULTURE AND INTERPRETATIONAL REFLEXES

This recognition, coupled with the recognition of how meanings are
arrived at, leads to our next point: the consideration of our ability to
accurately interpret the Scriptures. The major problem here stems from
the fact that those who agree on large areas of cultural experience
seldom discuss these areas of agreement. What everyone in a given
situation assumes is not mentioned.

The Hebrew people, for example, assumed that God exists. They
did not, therefore, attempt to prove His existence. Jesus assumed that
His hearers understood what a mustard bush and its seeds looked like,
that those who sowed seed scattered them around broadcast, that sheep
could be led by the shepherd, and so on.

The interpretational reflexes of Jesus' hearers were conditioned by
the same culture as His were. They therefore did not need explanation
of the assumptions and agreements underlying the things that Jesus
said and did. Our interpretational reflexes are, however, conditioned
by quite a different culture. We are therefore subject to several pitfalls
that accompany the cross-cultural transmission of materials such as
that in the Scriptures.

We may, for example, not understand major portions of what is
going on at all, since we do not know the cultural agreements. In the
story of the woman at the well, for example, we are likely to entirely
miss the significance of such things as Jesus' going through Samaria,
His talking to a woman, the fact that the woman was at the well at
midday, the necessity that she go back to get her supposed husband
before she could make a decision, and so forth. For us to understand
such things we need large doses of explanation by those who study the
cultural background. We cannot simply trust our culturally-conditioned
interpretational reflexes. For the Scriptures are specific to the cultural
settings of the original events. Sheep, mustard seeds and bushes, broadcast sowing, levirate marriage, and many other aspects of the life of
biblical cultures fit into this category.

A much bigger problem of interpretation lies in those areas where
the Scriptures use cultural symbols that are familiar to us but for
which our cultural agreements are different. We are tempted to simply
interpret according to what seems to be the "plain meaning"—as if we
could get the proper meaning of Scripture as we would from a document originally written in English. It is to avoid this pitfall that many
translation theorists are now contending that a faithful translation of
the Scriptures must involve enough interpretation to protect the reader

from being seriously misled at points such as these. Our interpretational reflexes tell us, for example, that a fox is sly and cunning. So,
when Jesus refers to Herod as a fox (Luke 13:32) we misinterpret the
symbol to mean sly when, in fact, on the basis of the Hebrew cultural
agreement it was intended to signify treachery. Our cultural reflexes
tell us that plural marriage is primarily a sexual matter, though in
nonwestern cultures it seldom is. Our cultural reflexes tell us that
Jesus was impolite to His mother when He addressed her the way He
did in the temple and at the wedding feast. Our culturally-conditioned
interpretational reflexes lead us to understand "the faith once for all
delivered to the saints" (Jude 3) to be a system of doctrine rather than
a relationship to God. The culturally-conditioned interpretational reflexes of the Nigerians I worked among misled them into thinking that
Psalm 23 presented Jesus as insane, since in their culture only young
boys and insane men tend sheep. The interpretational reflexes of the
Sawi of New Guinea misled them into admiring the treacherous Judas
even more than Jesus, and those of the Chinese into regarding positively the dragon of the book of Revelation.

The point is that for cultural reasons we who are not a part of the
biblical cultures cannot trust our interpretational reflexes to give us the
meanings that the original authors intended. What to us are the "plain
meanings" are almost certain to be the wrong meanings unless the
statements are very general (see below). We must, therefore, engage in
exegesis to discover what the original utterances meant to those whose
interpretational reflexes were the same as those of the authors.

With respect to interpretational reflexes there seem to be four
principles.

1. If the culture of the original is at any given point very similar to
ours, our reflexes are going to serve us fairly well. In these instances the
interpretational principle that says that "the plain meaning is the true
meaning" is a good principle. Such a situation is rarely the case between
Euro-American culture and the Hebrew and Aramaic portions of Scripture. Certain Greek customs do, however, seem to be similar enough to
Euro-American customs that our interpretational reflexes will give us
the correct meaning. I think in this regard of the language of the race
track that Paul uses in Philippians 3. The same may be true of the language of economics that Paul uses earlier in that same chapter. The amount
of biblical material where there is such close cultural similarity to our
agreements is, however, distressingly small. And the fact that we cannot
trust our interpretational reflexes in most places means that we can never
be sure of them unless we have independent evidence that this is a place
where their custom is close to ours.

2. If the Scriptural statement is a cultural universal, however, our interpretational reflexes will enable us to get close to the intended meaning. Statements such as those in the Ten Commandments that exist, as far as we know, in every one of the world's cultures are easy to interpret relatively accurately. There is a slight problem in the fact that each culture defines murder, adultery, and so on, in its own way. But the fact that such commands occur in all cultures means that these statements are elevated out of the most difficult interpretational category—that of the culturally specific. Other parts of Scripture such as those dealing with eating together, such injunctions as "love your neighbor," and many of the proverbs of Scripture are also in the cultural universal category.

3. Similarly, if a Scriptural statement relates to experiences that are common to all mankind our culturally-conditioned interpretational reflexes can be of considerable help. When the Scriptures say "go," "come," "trust," "be patient," and the like, they are dealing with experiences that are common to all human beings and therefore readily interpretable. Likewise with respect to illness and death, childbirth and rearing, obtaining and preparing food, and the like.

4. But as indicated above, much of the biblical material is presented in cultural forms that are very specific to cultural practices quite different from ours. These materials, because of their specificity to the cultural agreements of the original hearers, communicated with maximum impact to them. This is, I believe, a major part of the genius of God and of His Word—that He speaks specifically to people where they are and in terms of the culture in which they are immersed. This fact does, however, enormously complicate the task of the one immersed in another culture who seeks to interpret the Scriptures.

The fact that our interpretational reflexes are so limited when dealing with biblical materials argues strongly for the application of the sharpest tools available to the study of the cultural matrices through which God revealed His Word. The harnessing of the perspectives of anthropology and linguistics to this end of the interpretational task (as well as to the communication end) could be a real boon to the evangelical exegete. One important result of such harnessing is the development of faithful dynamic-equivalence translations and highly interpretive "transculturations" of God's Word. These aim to communicate God's message as specifically as possible in today's languages and cultures so that the members of these cultures will be able to trust their interpretational reflexes when they study the Scriptures.

## LEVELS OF ABSTRACTION IN INTERPRETATION

The fact that so much of the biblical material is presented in a form that is specific to the biblical cultures but distant in its forms from our cultural matrix presents us with the major problem in our search to discover a principled way of interpretation. And yet, as I have endeavored to point out, not all the scriptural material is at this culturally specific, distant-from-us level. What we find is, rather, a mixture of materials, some of which require a great deal of expert exegesis and some of which are readily interpretable even by twentieth-century American laymen. We need, therefore, an approach to interpretation that will sort out which is which.

I came to feel this need deeply as a result of the question directed to me by one of the Nigerian church leaders whom I was assisting. He pointed out to me that the Bible commands both that we not steal and that we not allow women to pray with their heads uncovered. He then asked, "Why is it that you missionaries teach us that we are to obey the one command and to ignore the other?" I do not feel that I was able to give him a very good answer at that time. But I have been able, I believe, to get closer to a satisfying approach since then.

My suggestion is that we recognize that when people speak they continually mix levels of abstraction. In this presentation I have mixed general statements with very specific illustrations. The Bible does the same. The statement, "God is love," and the statement, "The Lord is my shepherd," say much the same thing. But one is at a general level of abstraction, while the other is rather specific to Hebrew culture.

With respect to the head-covering versus the "do not steal" commands, likewise, we have statements at two different levels of abstraction. "Do not steal" is a general command that occurs in every culture. Analysis of the meaning of this command from culture to culture yields slight culturally-conditioned alternative understandings within a fairly narrow range. With respect to the head-covering command, however, analysis of the meaning of the custom in its cultural context does not simply lead to an alternative understanding of the same command. It leads, rather, to a meaning that demands expression via a different cultural form if it is to be understood in English. In the Greek culture of that day, apparently, the cultural form "female praying in public without head covering" would have been interpreted to mean that "this female is immoral"—or, at least, that "she is not showing proper respect to men" (see commentaries on 1 Cor. 11:10–12). Since that meaning was not consonant with the witness that Christians ought to make, Paul commands against the use of the head-uncovered symbol in favor of its opposite, the head-covered symbol. For only this latter symbol conveyed the proper Christian meaning in that culture—that Christian women were not immoral and/or were properly subject to their men. The theological truth, then—a truth just as relevant today as in the first century—is that Christian women should not behave in such a way that people judge them to be "out of line" (whether morally or with respect to authority).[4]

Such cross-cultural analysis shows that in comparing the two commands we are not comparing sames. The commands are given at different levels of abstraction—that is, the relative importance of the specific cultural context to the meaning of the utterances differs. Those utterances that relate most specifically to their particular cultural contexts are here termed "at a lower level of abstraction." Those utterances in which the specific context is less important to the meaning and which, therefore, relate to pancultural human commonality are termed "at a higher level of abstraction." That the stealing command is at a higher level of abstraction is evident from the fact that it does not refer to a specific cultural act but to a category of cultural behavior. The command is general rather than specific. Note, by way of contrast, the specificity of the tenth command. That command is at a lower level of abstraction (like the head-covering command) in that it specifies the prescribed cultural acts rather than (until the final phrase) generalizing them into an overall principle as we do when we refer to that command as the command against "coveteousness" in general. Note the wording: "Do not desire another man's house; do not desire his wife, his slaves, his cattle, his donkeys, or anything else that he owns" (Ex. 20:17 TEV).

The head-covering command is at this more specific level, where the particular cultural context is very important to the meaning. A corresponding specific stealing command would be something like this: "Do not take your neighbor's donkey without his permission." A head-covering command at the same level of generality as the stealing command would be something like this: "Do not appear out of line with respect to immorality or authority." Thus we see a specific cultural form/symbol level with context contributing relatively more to the meaning, and a deeper "general principle" level in which the context contributes relatively less. "Seesaw" diagrams illustrating these two possibilities are as follows:

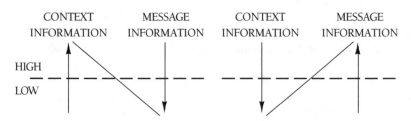

| At the "culture-specific" level of abstraction the contribution of the context to the meaning is high. | At the "general principle" level of abstraction the contribution of the context to the meaning is low. |

There seems in Scripture to be yet a deeper level of abstraction, however. This is made explicit by Jesus when He summarizes the teaching of the law and the prophets in two statements:

> "Love the Lord your God with all your heart, with all your soul, and with all your mind." This is the greatest and the most important commandment. The second most important commandment is like it: "Love your neighbor as you love yourself." The whole law of Moses and the teachings of the prophets depend on these two commandments (Matt. 22:37–40; cf. Deut. 6:5; Mark 12:29–31; Luke 10:27 TEV).

In such a three-level scheme there are occasional problems with respect to which of the levels to assign certain of the general statements of Scripture. We may, however, advance the following chart as a step in the direction of developing this model more precisely. Note that a complete chart would show (even more than this one does) the fact that there are fewer categories at the basic ideal level, more at the general principle level and an enormous number at the specific cultural form level.

| 1. BASIC IDEAL LEVEL | 2. GENERAL PRINCIPLE LEVEL | 3. SPECIFIC CULTURAL FORM/SYMBOL LEVEL |
|---|---|---|
| ◄ · · · · · · More General ◄――――► More Specific · · · · · · ► | | |
| A. Love your neighbor as you love yourself (Matt. 22:39) | 1. Do not steal (Ex. 20:17) | a. Do not take your neighbor's donkey (Hebrew) <br> b. Do not take your employer's money (U.S.A.) |
| | 2. Do not covet | a. Do not desire another man's house . . . (Ex. 20:17) <br> b. Same for U.S.A. |
| | 3. Be free from partiality (1 Tim. 5:21; James 3:17) | a. Treat Gentiles/blacks/women as human beings <br> b. Rebuke whoever needs it (1 Tim. 5:20) |
| B. Love the Lord your God with all your heart . . . (Matt. 22:37) | 1. Worship no God but me (Ex. 20:3) | a. Do not bow down to any idol or worship it (Ex. 20:5) <br> b. Do not pledge primary allegiance to material wealth (U.S.A.) |
| | 2. Seek by all means to save people (1 Cor. 9:22) | a. Live as a Jew to win Jews (1 Cor. 9:20) <br> b. Live as a Gentile to win Gentiles (1 Cor. 9:21) <br> c. Live as an African to win Africans |

| C. Everything must be done in a proper and orderly way (1 Cor. 14:40) | 1. Leaders should be beyond reproach (1 Tim. 3:2; Titus 1:6) | a. They must be self-controlled, etc. (1 Tim. 3:2) |
| --- | --- | --- |
| | 2. Christian women should not appear out of line | a. They should cover their heads when praying in Greek culture (1 Cor. 11:10)<br>b. They should not wear their clothes too tight (U.S.A.) |
| | 3. Christians should live according to the rules of the culture (as long as they do not conflict with Christian principles) | a. Women should learn in silence in Greek culture (1 Tim. 2:11)<br>b. Women may speak up in mixed groups in U.S.A.<br>c. Pay the government what belongs to it (Matt. 22:21)<br>d. Obey governmental authorities (Rom. 13:1)<br>e. Wives, submit to your husbands in Greek and many segments of U.S.A. culture (Eph. 5:22; Col. 3:18; etc.) |

D. Other ideals?

In such expositions as the Ten Commandments (especially as Jesus summarizes them in Matt. 22:37–40), the Sermon on the Mount, the listing of the fruits of the Spirit (Gal 5:22–23) and the many similar statements, the Scriptures seem to come closest to a clear statement of a portion of the supracultural will of God for man's conduct. The reason for the apparent clarity of these portions is that they are phrased at a level of abstraction that largely extricates them from specific application to the original cultures in which they were uttered. As one moves from specific cultural applications of supracultural truth (as with the head-covering command) back toward the most general statements of the truth, however, the statements require less understanding of the original cultural context to be accurately understood. They therefore have more immediate (though general) meaning to us in another culture. The "plain meaning" principle is therefore often adequate for interpreting information presented at this deeper level of abstraction.

Note, however, that the effectiveness of the communicational impact is a matter of cultural perception. For the original hearers, it was presentations of supracultural truth in terms of specific applications (abstraction level three) that communicated most effectively. For us, likewise, it would be specific applications of Scriptural generalizations that most effectively communicate. But since the Scriptures were written in terms of cultures other than ours, we are denied inscripturated applications of supracultural truth in our culture. The general statements, therefore, make more sense to us than the specific cultural forms through which these principles were applied in biblical cultures. And the more specific applications in the Scriptures are often the most confusing to us.

Throughout the Scriptures we are provided with glimpses of supracultural truth, clothed in specific events taking place within specific cultures at specific times. Frequently, as with statements at the general principle or basic ideal level, we get the impression that we are looking at such truth with a minimum of cultural conditioning. More frequently, however, we are exposed to supracultural truth applied in a specific situation in a specific biblical culture. The record of this, then, comes to us only in translation, so that we see such truth as "puzzling reflections in a mirror" (1 Cor. 13:12, *Phillips*). Among these "reflections" William Smalley feels that

> those parts of Scripture which give us evaluations of human motives and emotions, human attitudes and personalities, give us the deepest insight into God's ultimate will, and that to understand the revelation in terms of God's will for our behavior we will have to learn to look behind the cultural facade to see as much as we can of what the Word indicates about those questions. The cultural examples given us are thereby not lost. They provide most valuable examples of the way in which God's will was performed in another cultural setting to help us see how we may perform it in ours.[5]

In this way it is possible for Christians to learn something of supracultural truth even though this, like all human knowledge, is perceived by us in terms of the cultural grid in which we operate. Though often puzzling and never total or absolute, such knowledge is adequate for God's purposes—the salvation and spiritual growth of all who give themselves to him in faith.[6] We may, then, under the leading of the Spirit come to know something of how He desires us to live out these truths in terms of our cultural forms.

## CONCLUSION

I have attempted to raise four closely interdependent issues that relate to the matter of scriptural interpretation on which my fields (anthropology, linguistics, and communicology) cast some light. I am hopeful that these considerations will make some contribution and/or stimulate my readers to greater insight into faithful scriptural interpretation in culture.

# IDENTIFYING THE AUDIENCE GOD INTENDED

J. Robertson McQuilkin

## WRONG APPROACHES FOR LIMITING THE AUDIENCE AND DETERMINING APPLICATION

SOME HOLD THAT IF THE Bible is correct it must be believed and obeyed, but where it errs it is not normative. When the Bible speaks of the creation of the first couple, when Christ treated demons as if they existed, when Paul gave a distinct role in marriage to the husband, those teachings were in error and therefore are not binding for faith and behavior. An even more radical approach is taken by liberation theologians, who do theology by beginning with what God is doing in the world today. This activity of God in history, as, for example, in social revolution, is the revelation of His will. The Bible is then used only as a source book for other examples of God's activity in history. Although those approaches set aside the authority of Scripture, each has been advocated by people who call themselves evangelicals.

There are other approaches that are not so obviously nonbiblical. We cannot consider all of them, but we should identify those which seem to have the greatest influence among Bible-believing people. We will examine briefly two approaches that use cultural factors to define meaning, limit the audience, or determine application. Then we will consider two that use certain principles to define meaning, limit the audience, or determine application.

### Use of Culture to Define Meaning, Limit the Audience, or Determine Application

*The response God desires today.* This approach examines the words of Scripture to determine the meaning, as we do. It is interested in getting behind the meaning of a passage to discern what response the author desired from his original audience. When that response is identified, through a process called "dynamic equivalence interpretation," the present-day interpreter then asks, "How can I reproduce that response in my audience today?" The answer to this question will be the revelation of God's will. It will be the authoritative message for today.

To those who take this approach, the words of Scripture are not accurate, and the concepts are, as they say, culture-bound. The task of the interpreter is to discern the cultural universal in the biblical data and reproduce, in contemporary society, the impact God intended.

Since all Scripture—as all other human writing—reflects the culture of the writer, the task of the Bible student is to set the truth free from its cultural wrappings so that it can be applied to contemporary life. To do this, all the tools of cultural anthropology are used. When it is clear what the author intended to happen in his cultural setting as a result of what he wrote, we are then prepared to seek the same response in our audience today in a way that fits our culture.

For example, Paul taught that spiritual leaders should have only one wife (1 Tim. 3:2; Titus 1:6). That is what he said. In fact, that is what he seemed to mean. But what was he trying to accomplish? One interpreter will say he was trying to make sure that the church had leaders who were qualified, in the eyes of their fellow believers, to lead. He was setting criteria for leadership that were culturally relevant to their society. What about today? Well, in a particular African tribe, the requirements for leadership are just the opposite. A man is not fit to lead until he can afford and acquire at least a second wife. So how is one true to the command of Paul to Timothy and Titus? He must require that to serve as elders of the church, men must have at least two wives. No matter that this is the opposite of what Paul said. The purpose of the command must be discovered through cultural analysis and applied today in some culturally equivalent way.

In this approach to Scripture, current cultural understanding has displaced the apostle as the authority for church life. The end result is not merely that the church is free to baptize or not, as the culture may demand, or that one may arrange church government in accordance with local cultural norms. Far more basic theological teaching is modified through cultural understanding. For example, it is taught that people can be saved without knowledge of Jesus Christ through faith in what they do know of God and that which their culture will permit them to receive.

*Universal cultural pattern.* Only Bible teaching that reflects a universal cultural pattern is normative for all people in all societies. This position accepts for application today (with authority as God's certain will) only those teachings in Scripture that reflect universal cultural norms. The command, "You shall not steal" (Ex.. 20:15), is sometimes given as an example. The rest of biblical teaching is culture-bond, speaking to cultural specifics.

The task of the interpreter is to set the teaching free from its cultural bondage to determine a universal truth or principle. Depending upon the interpreter, Christ's teaching against divorce, Paul's teaching against homosexuality, and biblical norms for the role of the woman in marriage are all culturally bound teachings and not normative. Therefore, they do not demand obedience in every culture of every age.

This position is similar to the preceding one except that the interpreter does not try to get behind the meaning of a passage to discover the impact intended by the author, but rather seeks the enduring principle in the meaning itself. In this position, the meaning itself is valid, but is normative (applicable universally) only when a culturally universal truth is being taught.

I once was seated across the luncheon table from a leading biblical linguist. We were discussing the question of what teachings in Scripture are normative.

"What do you think," I asked, "should be required of all people in every tribe and culture?"

He responded immediately, "Those teachings which are culturally universal."

"For example?"

"Well—" He hesitated. "I'm not altogether sure."

I suggested, "Something like the forbidding of murder?"

"Why yes," he said, "that would be a cultural universal."

"I am surprised to hear that," I replied. "I would have thought that killing, and perhaps even eating the victim, would be a virtue in some societies."

"Well, I guess you're right."

The conversation continued in the same vein with considerable uncertainty as to whether there were *any* universally valid cultural norms. Since the Bible itself makes no distinction between cultural universals and cultural specifics, for us to seek to make that distinction and undertake the enormous task of positively identifying any cultural universals is well nigh impossible. And to attempt the distinction will result in making culturally relative teaching out of most Scripture. Thus, the independent authority of Scripture is set aside.

Those arguments by which the audience or application is limited through cultural understanding are similar to the approach I advocated earlier in this chapter—limiting the audience because of the historic setting.

## LEGITIMATE AND ILLEGITIMATE USE OF CULTURE

Consider the distinction between the legitimate and illegitimate uses of culture.

## History and Culture

Is there a legitimate distinction between history and culture? Is history not the record of behavior as well as of events? Is culture not a part of history? There is a great deal of overlap and interplay so that they are sometimes hard to distinguish. But I believe the distinction is crucial for biblical interpretations.

What is culture? Although there are many definitions of *culture*, contemporary interpreters are using the term in the technical sense of all human language, behavior, morals, values, and ways of doing things in any particular group of people.

Let us agree at the outset that unevaluated and uninterpreted cultural elements in Scripture may be no more normative than unevaluated and uninterpreted historic events. But the difference between the two is vast. Much of history in Scripture is unevaluated and uninterpreted, and therefore, should not be made normative for other people in other times and places. However, virtually all the teachings of Scripture give cultural evaluation. Human behavior, morals, values, and ways of doing things are constantly evaluated, prohibited, or commanded. It is not too much to say that the purpose of divine revelation is to create a culture, a special people of God. He is out to *change* culture; although, at the same time, He uses human culture as a vehicle for revealing Himself and His truth. The teachings of Scripture are not often "aimed at" history. True, historical events are often demonstrated to be the acts of God, but revelation simply records the setting, whereas most biblical teaching is directly "aimed at" culture, for human behavior is the object of revelation.

My contention is that the historical context of teaching is normative *only* if Scripture treats it that way, whereas the cultural context is normative *unless* Scripture treats it as limited. As we have seen, history is often recorded without any evaluation as to whether the behavior is good or bad. God must take the initiative through revelation to make it normative. David's polygamy, uncondemned in Scripture, should not be taken as a normative model today, nor should Paul's taking a Jewish religious vow. But the apostles' response, "We must obey God rather than men" (Acts 5:29), although unevaluated in the immediate context, is obviously viewed as a model to follow because of abundant teaching in other parts of Scripture.

It is true that culture may also be recorded without an evaluation as to whether it is to be taken as normative. In such cases, culture is no more normative than a historical record. Was the behavior of the slaveholder in making his slaves serve tables after working the fields all day—and giving them no thanks—a normative model to be followed in labor-management relations (Luke 17)? But unevaluated cultural behavior is far less common than unevaluated historical events because the purpose of revelation is to create a way of behavior, a culture. Therefore, value-free or culturally relative records of behavior are not typical. Rather, cultural change is the point of revelation, and God must take the initiative through revelation to make cultural teaching not normative. So the teachings of God concerning human behavior are final in authority and are to be set aside only if Scripture itself limits the audience intended or the response God desires. If anyone else sets such "cultural" teaching aside, he has become the authority sitting in judgment on Scripture.

Most of us might agree that washing another's feet at mealtime, leaving ladies' hair uncut, and other such commands are culturally specific and therefore do not apply universally. Specifically they do not apply to us! However, we have discovered that the same principle can apply to virtually any teaching of Scripture. But to set aside any Scripture simply on the basis that it is cultural, and therefore valid for only one specific cultural setting, is to establish a principle that can be used to set aside any or even all biblical teaching. With such a view, the interpreter becomes the authority over Scripture, establishing as normative for human belief or behavior only those elements of Bible teaching or those principles deduced from Bible teaching that prove universally valid according to some cultural criteria.

Because of the difference between historical record and culturally based teaching, it is legitimate to say of a historical event that Scripture does not evaluate that it should not be made normative. But of teaching concerning human behavior (what *should* happen as distinct from what *did* happen) it must be said that it is normative unless Scripture itself limits the recipient or application. No, Scripture is not a prisoner of culture. Rather culture, in the language of biblical authors and the context in which they wrote, is the vehicle of revelation, and at the same time, that very culture is the object of change demanded by Scripture. To disallow any teaching of the Bible because it is cultural is to make all Scripture vulnerable to this relativistic approach.

## Valid Cultural Argument

Is the cultural context of no value at all? Can culture never be used to determine the audience or the response God desires? Perhaps culture is significant when the *Bible itself* gives a culturally based reason for a particular teaching. For example, Paul used a cultural argument to support His injunction to work with one's hands (1 Thess. 1:11). Scripture may not give a reason for a teaching, but if it does, the reason becomes a part of the teaching. Here, the reason given is not some eternal moral principle, but a cultural argument: "so that you may behave *properly* toward outsiders and not be in any need" (4:12). In other words, the enduring principle is given that Christians should earn their livelihood as a testimony to non-Christians. It reflects the cultural pattern ("properly") which, for Christians in Thessalonica, would mean manual labor. Since the argument is based on culture, if that cultural situation is not present, only the principle (not the command) should be made normative. In this case, the cultural factor is not imposed externally but is part of Paul's argument. Paul does not make the cultural context of the command a universal norm, and we are not obliged to duplicate the cultural context of the command to work.

There is another case in which the cultural factor may be considered in designating the recipient without usurping the authority of Scripture. The Bible may address people in cultural settings or historical situations that are not present in other cultures. If Scripture expresses no moral injunction that the situation be recreated, the generic principle that undergirds the biblical injunction rather than the culturally or historically limited injunction itself, should be applied to other situations. That is a legitimate guideline to follow unless the cultural form itself is treated by Scripture as having enduring significance.

For example, biblical commands requiring kind treatment for animals or slaves do not require a person to have either animals or slaves. The principle of kindness must be applied to any people or sentient beings that are dependent on the twentieth-century believer. But he does not need to become a farmer or slaveholder to obey the command.

## Discerning the Meaning Intended by the Author

Understanding cultural factors that provide the setting of a biblical text may be helpful in clarifying the meaning of a passage if it is unclear or contains an apparent inconsistency with other clearer biblical teachings. But cultural insight may not be used to modify the plain meaning intended by the author; nor may it be used to determine the God-intended recipient of a passage. The data of Scripture must control those decisions because the Bible itself is our authority.

## Current Culture

An understanding of current cultural forms is helpful in two ways. First, present realities challenge the Bible student to reexamine accepted interpretations. For example, scientific theory has driven us to take a closer look at traditional understandings of Genesis. A sociological movement has forced reexamination of the role of women, just as a movement required our forefathers to reevaluate God's will concerning slavery.

Second, an accurate understanding of present cultural factors is essential if one is to make correct application of eternal truth to his culture. But contemporary customs and anthropological theory may not be used as the norm to which the plain meaning of Scripture is forced to adapt. For example, the command to love and cherish one's wife (Eph. 5:25, 28–29) must be applied differently in different cultures. In America, if a man never praises his wife before others, and refuses to embrace her when saying good-bye in the lobby of an airport, he is probably disobeying the apostolic command. But for the Japanese husband to do those things might not be so much an expression of love as a public scandal bringing shame on the name of the family. The truth must be applied authentically in each cultural context, but in doing that, the plain teaching of Scripture may not be set aside.

Finally, we must exercise modesty in using cultural tools inasmuch as we are far removed by language, history, culture, and geography from the setting in which the original revelation was given. We must use these tools but refuse to be used by them.

## USE OF CERTAIN PRINCIPLES TO DEFINE MEANING, LIMIT AUDIENCE, OR DETERMINE APPLICATION

### Only Principles Are Valid

"Only principles are valid, not the specific teaching itself." This position is the opposite of a commonly held view that *only* direct commands and injunctions are authoritative for present Christian behavior. Of course, that latter contention is invalid, since the Bible is filled with teaching in the form of general principles, rather than specific commands. In fact, far more than a collection of maxims, formula, and specific rules, the Bible is a book of principles. However, the opposite contention seems to be gaining ground: specific teaching and direct commands are not universally applicable, but only the principle that lies behind the direct teaching.

This approach is very appealing, not only because it makes life easier, in a sense, but because there is a strong element in the approach that is true to the authority of Scripture. The approach of limiting normative teaching to principles derived from biblical specifics need not be an attempt to subvert or get around Scripture, but can serve to implement the authority of Scripture.

However, where in the Bible is such an approach taught? Where in Scripture are we told that the specific declarations of God's truth and God's will for men are not normative, but only the principles that lie behind them? The explicit declarations of Scripture are treated as normative both in the Old Testament and the New Testament. To disallow the authority of explicit statements on that ground is not to permit Scripture to make the choice. The Bible gives both specifics and generic principles.

It is quite legitimate to derive generic principles from specific teaching. But the principle must not then be turned on the specific teaching to modify it or disallow it for application today. To set aside any specific teaching of Scripture, allowing only the principle deduced to be normative, is to impose an extrabiblical notion, and violate the authority of Scripture.

## Only Teaching Based on the Nature of God Is Normative

"Only teaching that is based on the nature of God or on the order of creation is universally normative." This position does not establish the idea of principles alone as the only abiding norm. In addition to principles, specific teachings that fit the above criteria are considered normative. Other teachings may be transient, that is, not applicable to the believer today. The problem here is the same as in the preceding case, if Scripture itself does not identify which teaching is founded upon the nature of God or upon the order of creation, and which teaching is purely culture-based. On what grounds I make such a distinction is important, for those grounds become my authority.

Furthermore, there is a problem in applying this principle. Is the fall of man based on the nature of God or on the order of creation? It does not seem to be based on either although it is inherently theological. Or is it? Is teaching concerning the Lord's Supper and its observance grounded in anything other than the authoritative word of Christ? It does not seem to be grounded in the nature of God or in the order of creation. It was a cultural form that He made normative. What of the command that the wife should be in subjection to the authority of her husband, or that homosexual behavior is wrong? If all explicit teaching not limited by Scripture itself is taken as normative, those teachings are normative. However, if only those teachings which can be demonstrated to be theological in nature or to be certainly grounded in the nature of God or in the order of creation are considered normative, those teachings, along with many others, become legitimate questions for debate.

Seeking the theological basis of any teaching or searching for its foundation in the nature of God or in the order of creation is very helpful in several ways. To demonstrate that kind of foundation may reinforce or clarify specific teaching. It helps in discerning general principles lying behind specific teaching. This approach may be used along with other indicators in the text itself to ferret out that which Scripture did not intend as a universal norm. But to set aside any specific teaching simply because its theological nature cannot be proved, is to introduce an extrabiblical hermeneutical principle that violates the independent authority of Scripture.

## SUMMARY

Scripture itself must determine whom God would have believe and obey a given teaching. If the context itself does not make that clear, appeal may be made to other passages. But in the end, external criteria may not be imposed on Scripture to disallow its applicability to contemporary life.

To summarize, since the Bible is God's revelation of His will for all mankind, any teaching of Scripture should be taken as normative for contemporary faith and living unless Scripture itself indicates otherwise. Yet, to identify the intended recipient of a teaching does not automatically indicate the specific implications for faithful discipleship.

# TWENTY-ONE

# THE DEVOTIONAL AND PRACTICAL USE OF THE BIBLE

### Bernard Ramm

## THE GENERAL USE OF
## THE BIBLE FOR CHRISTIAN LIVING

THE FIRST PURPOSE OF THE Holy Bible is to make men "wise unto salvation through faith which is in Christ Jesus" (2 Tim. 3:15). After a man has received this salvation, then we are told that "All Scripture is given by inspiration of God and is profitable for doctrine, for reproof, for correction, for instruction in righteousness that the man of God may be perfect, throughly furnished unto all good works" (2 Tim. 3:16–17). Most of the material of the Bible is for the Christian, and specifically for his growth in knowledge, holiness, and spirituality. Doctrine and theology are in primary intention aimed at making sinners into saints, and immature Christians into Christian men. The Bible and its study is one of the prime requisites for every Christian in order that he may lead an effective and genuine Christian life.

In using the Bible for moral, ethical, spiritual, and devotional purposes aimed at our spiritual growth, we suggest the following principles:

1. *All practical lessons, all applications of Scripture, all devotional material, must be governed by general Protestant hermeneutics.*
More pointedly it could be stated this way: all such usages of the Bible must be based upon sound exegetical principles. The notorious dictum: "The ends justifies the means," is frequently baptized into the Christian fold under the guise of: "The blessing justifies the means."

If a blessing is derived from an improper interpretation of Scripture, the blessing has come not because of improper interpretation, but in spite of the misinterpretation. If a passage does not yield the help and strength the interpreter is seeking, he ought not to distort it until he does get a blessing from it, but he ought to go elsewhere in the Scripture where a blessing can be derived from the native meaning of the text.

In the intense desire to find something practical or devotional in Scripture, we are in danger of obscuring the literal or genuine meaning of the passage. It may sound harsh to so speak, but not too infrequently a very devotional message is conjured up from the Scriptures by a method of interpretation which is nothing short of trifling or tampering with Scripture.

Never should we handle a passage of Scripture in such a way as to distort its original meaning simply because we feel under pressure to find something devotional or spiritual or especially edifying in *every* passage we are called upon to teach or explain. Let the truth of God be its own blessedness.

2. *The Bible is more a book of principles than a catalog of specific directions.*

The Bible does contain an excellent blend of the general and the specific with reference to principles for Christian living. If the Bible were never specific we would be somewhat disconcerted in attempting a specific application of its principles. If the Bible were entirely specific in its principles, we would be adrift whenever confronted with a situation in life not covered by a specific principle. The *emphasis* in Scripture is on moral and spiritual principles, not upon specific and itemized lists of rules for moral or spiritual conduct. There are two very important reasons for this:

a.   If it were entirely specific in its practical teachings, then it would be provincial and relative. If Paul had classified sin solely in terms of specifics and therefore in terms of the culture of his day, then as new ways of sinning were devised by man, and as culture changed, Paul's teaching would no longer be relevant. As we study the terminology of Paul we are amazed how he was able to put his finger on the universal element of human sin, and so provide every generation in all cultures with a reliable guide to moral and spiritual behavior.

b.   If it were a legal code of rules, then the Bible would foster an artificial spirituality, and indirectly sponsor hypocrisy. If the directions were all specific, a man could live up to the letter of the rules, and yet miss the spirit of true godliness. Real spiritual progress is made only if we are put on our own. Unless we must take a principle and interpret its meaning for a given situation in life, we do not spiritually mature. It is this general nature of New Testament ethics which helps prevent hypocrisy. As long as there is a specific code to obey, men can conform without change of heart. Obedience to a moral code with no change of heart may result in the discrepancy between inner life and outward conduct which is one of the characteristics of hypocrisy. But inasmuch as we must govern ourselves by principle, we are put on our own mettle. In each important decision we shall ask ourselves: *What is the spiritual principle involved?* From this consideration we may then proceed to: *What ought I do?* If we so treat our moral and spiritual decisions we develop in spiritual insight and moral strength. Such development is central to a mature spirituality.

3. *The Bible emphasizes the inner spirit rather than the outward religious cloak.*

The moral teaching of the Old Testament contains many rules about kinds of food permitted and banned; types of clothing which may be worn, and types prohibited. The basic purpose of these *material* regulations was to inculcate in the Jewish people a sense of *discrimination.* Right and wrong had to be learned on the obvious level of the material to help the mind to learn to discern right and wrong in the more subtle level of the spiritual. In the New Testament morality and spirituality are lifted to a higher level by being inward and spiritual.

The New Testament does not, however, condemn only improper motives, but it also condemns external acts. Gluttony, drunkenness, and reveling are specifically forbidden, and chaste, honorable behavior before men is taught. But the emphasis is upon the inner spiritual life rather than upon a mere social circumspection.

Measuring spirituality entirely by outward appearances is not just to the person being judged. Judging spirituality by external matters (diet, dress, sanctimonious acts) fails to consider that our Lord taught that true spirituality was a secret activity. The external parade of piety as made by the Pharisees is specifically condemned. Prayer is to be in the secret of the closet. Giving is to be such that the right hand does not know what the left hand is doing. Fasting is to be hidden by grooming one's self before one appears in public and so to appear as if one were not fasting.

Negations ("touch not, taste not, handle not," Col. 2:21) do not measure piety; they prepare the way for true piety. True piety is faith, hope, and love. The church has had a constant battle with asceticism. If man is born a legalist in soteriology, he is a born asceticist in sanctification. Asceticism is the belief that the body and the material world are in some sense evil and that victory over them is both by abstinence from the world and by bodily suffering. That there is a measure of truth to asceticism is evident from the biblical teaching about fasting and sexual abstinence (1 Cor. 7:5). But that asceticism as practiced at times in the history of the church is unscriptural is also evident from the words of our Lord (Luke 11:24ff.) and of Paul (Col. 2:20ff.).

The Bible is to be used to develop a true inner life. The Beatitudes

inform us that happiness is an inner quality of life. Spirituality is
striving toward correct attitudes, spiritual graces, the fruit of the Spirit
(Gal. 5:22–23). The emphasis on outward religious show and manifest
badges or banners of religious profession is not in keeping with the
biblical perspective on spirituality.

4. *In some statements it is the spirit of the statement that is to be
our guide.*

We are enjoined to cut off our hands and pluck out our eyes if they
offend (Matt. 5:29–30). People who have had the courage to conform
to this literally do not impress their contemporaries with their spirituality but with their foolhardiness. Is not the spirit of the command that
we should not pamper or nurse our sins, but deal with them with the
utmost severity? If life and death are the issues, then sin certainly must
be treated with the greatest dispatch and severity.

Certainly when our Lord told Peter to forgive his brother seventy
times seven He was not prescribing the number of times we are to
forgive a brother, but He was prescribing the *spirit* of forgiveness
(Matt. 18:21ff.). The same holds true for commands to turn the other
cheek, to go the second mile, to yield the second garment. Certainly, if
taken literally they become mechanical or external guides to conduct
the very thing they are intended to correct. But if the inner spirit of the
command be taken, these passages teach us lessons of generosity, of
kindness, of helpfulness. Rather than being covetous we ought to be
generous; rather than being goaded by a spirit of vengeance we should
be prompted by a spirit of love; rather than being tightfisted we
should be merciful to the destitute.

5. *Commands in terms of one culture must be translated into our
culture.*

When our Lord and His apostles gave exhortations and teachings
they spoke in terms of the prevailing culture. Otherwise they could not
have communicated effectually with their audience. Paul's statements
about women (1 Tim. 2:9) must be reinterpreted for our culture. The
same applies for Paul's statements about cutting the hair and wearing the
veil. Cutting the hair was associated with paramours, and wearing
a veil (not some modern perky hat) was the sign of a decorous woman.
In modern terms this means that Christian women should avoid all
appearances of immodesty, and should be chaste and dignified in dress
and behavior.[1]

## GUIDANCE FROM EXAMPLES

The lives of the great men of the Bible provide a great story of
spiritual guidance, and the great events of the Bible provide a vast
amount of practical wisdom for godly living. We learn, too, by the

mistakes of good men or by the sinful careers of bad men.[2] Events in the lives of great men are often recorded without an express comment by the biblical writers. Therefore guides are necessary so that we may benefit from their examples without making needless mistakes.

1. *We must make a distinction between what the Bible records and what it approves.*[3]

Men frequently make the mistake of assuming that whatever is written in the Bible is thereby approved. Therefore, there is a rather uncritical justification of their activities on the basis that they parallel the activity of men in an inspired document. *The fact* of divine inspiration does not mean that *all* which is in the Bible is the will of God. The Bible no more morally approves of all that it records than an editor approves of all that he prints in his newspaper.

Records of lying, adultery, incest, cruelty,[4] and deceit are found in the Bible, but on each occasion the sacred writer does not necessarily add his word of condemnation. There are not only sinful acts but erroneous notions recorded. The voice of the Devil is heard, the voice of Judas, the voice of demons, the voice of the opponents of Christ, and of the enemies of the apostles. Inspiration here extends only to fidelity of recording. Such words do not constitute either the will of God or the approval of God. Therefore, in every example from a man's life or from Israel's history it must be determined if in any Scripture there is approval or disapproval of this specific situation. If there is none, then we must analyze the passage to see if it is approved or disapproved by other clear teaching of the Bible.[5]

2. *We may take direct application from all of those incidents that the Bible directly censures or approves.*

The woman who poured out the valuable incense was censured by Judas but approved by Christ, and made an example for all church history (John 12:1ff.). The equivocal behavior of Peter at Antioch was expressly condemned by Paul writing under inspiration, and is a lesson to all not to be guided by opinion but by principle (Gal. 2:11ff.). Certainly the rebellion of Saul, the immorality of David, the pride of Absalom, the treachery of Judas, the denials of Peter, and the lying of Ananias and Sapphira stand as examples of what not to do. So the faith of Abraham, the obedience of Moses, the loyalty of Elijah, and the love of John the Apostle stand out as great examples to follow.

3. *Express commands to individuals are not the will of God for us.*

Abraham was commanded to offer up his son; that is not a standing order for each father. Joshua was commanded to slay all in his military campaign; that is not instruction for Christian soldiers. A passage of great instruction is found in the closing part of John's Gospel. Our

Lord tells Peter that he will suffer a violent death (John 21:18–19). Misery loves company, so looking at John, Peter said, "what shall this man do?" (v. 21) as if to say "haven't you something equally as painful for him?" Our Lord says that if He wills it, John might never die! Two disciples are offered utterly contrasting experiences, yet both within the will of Christ. It behooves us to be unusually careful that we do not try to apply uncritically the commands given to good men of the Bible. Paul's trip to Arabia is not the will of God for some, nor is Peter's call to the apostleship the will of God for others, even though both of these activities were the will of God for Paul and Peter respectively.

4. *In the lives of men in the Scriptures determine what the outstanding spiritual principle is.*

Hebrews 11 is a remarkable example of going through the Old Testament and isolating from the lives of its great men a great spiritual virtue for our benefit. There is a danger of becoming too particular in our lessons from great men, and unconsciously engaging in double-sense interpretations. But if the essential spiritual principles are the goal of our investigations, we derive positive food for the soul, and avoid the mistakes of trying to find too much meaning in trivial details.

5. *In the application of examples to our lives we do not need a literal reproduction of the biblical situation.*

Baptism need not be done in the river Jordan nor in the land of Palestine to be scriptural baptism. Neither do we need to go to an upper room in Jerusalem to have the Lord's Table.

### PROMISES

"Every promise in the book is mine" is one of the overstatements of the century. Few Bible promises partake of such universality. In applying the promises of the Bible to our specific situations we need to exercise great care. If we apply promises to ourselves that are not for us, we may suffer severe disappointment. Also, promises must not be used to tempt God. A reserve and a patience should temper all our usages of promises.

1. *Note whether the promise is universal in scope.*

The classic example of a universal promise is "and whosoever will, let him take the water of life freely" (Rev. 22:18). General invitations to salvation are for all men, but invitations to prayer or to special blessings are only for the company of the saved.

2. *Note whether the promise is personal.*

When God said to Paul, "Be not afraid, but speak, and hold not thy peace: for I am with thee, and no man shall set on thee to hurt thee"

(Acts 18:10), that was personal to Paul and may not be used generally. Missionaries in difficult situations may hope for this type of deliverance but may not command it.

3. *Note whether the promise is conditional.*

When it says "Draw nigh unto God and he will draw nigh to you" (James 4:8), there is a human condition to be fulfilled before the promise is received.

4. *Note whether the promise is for our time.*

Some promises pertain just to the Jews in their land and have ceased with the coming of the New Testament. Some promises refer to future conditions that shall prevail upon the earth at the close of the age. Evidently, in Revelation 2 and 3 certain promises were restricted to different churches.

In connection with the rise of promises some have used the Bible on the same principle of animistic divination. Divination is the means whereby primitives decide whether they should undergo a proposed adventure such as hunting, fishing, or battle. Common methods among primitives to decide the portent of future events are to read the entrails of pigs or chickens; to crack a bone in the heat of the fire and decide what to do from the nature of the crack; to throw an egg on a grass roof to see if it breaks or not; to use the fire-test to determine guilt. On the sillier level divination is predicting one's future by the reading of cards or tea leaves.

Whenever we force the Bible to say something on specific items of our life, we are in danger of divination. If we do this we leave the sensible, intelligent use of the Bible for that which borders on primitive divination. Most notorious is the custom of opening the Bible and putting the finger on a verse and taking that verse as divine guidance. This method dishonors the intelligence of God, the sobriety of the Bible, puts the Christian faith in a ridiculous light, and places the method of determining the will of God on a superstitious, magical basis. It ought to be added: *no promise of the Bible is to be used that is not in keeping with sane, exegetical principles.*

The type of divination mentioned above exists on a more sophisticated level with those who every day try to find specific guidance from the Bible—not guidance in the sense of getting truth, soul-food, and principles, but in finding one particular verse that tells them exactly what to do that day, or how to resolve a given situation. To do this they have to admit that God can give a message through the Bible that is completely divorced from the native, grammatical meaning of the verse. If this is permitted, then what is to prevent the interpreter from finding anything he wishes in the Bible?

To be specific, at the outbreak of World War II, a certain individual could not decide what his course of action should be—enlist? join the merchant marines? get a theological waiver? He went to his Bible and, finding a reference to those who go down to the seas in ships, he took it as his orders from God to enlist in the United States Navy. The action could not be based upon any sensible exegetical principle, nor upon any spiritual principle; it was a haphazard coincidence between the verse that had the word *seas* in it and the United States Navy.

The will of God is determined from the Bible only in terms of what it says in its first grammatical sense, or what can be derived from it in terms of great spiritual principles. To use the Bible as in the above example is in direct violation of the nature of inspiration and of the character of the Bible. God does not "double-talk" when He speaks in Scripture, i.e., He does not have a historical, common-sense meaning, plus some special message to us in a given situation. If God speaks to us in a given situation, it must be in terms of the sound exegesis of the passage.[6]

## THE USE OF THE BIBLE IN PREACHING OR TEACHING

The preaching and teaching ministry in the church is applied hermeneutics and exegesis and comes under the discussion of the practical use of the Bible. The *basic theory* of the ministry must be understood if the correct ministry of preaching will be done by the preacher or teacher. The preacher is *a minister of the Word of God*. He is not a person who has a full and free right of sermonizing before a group of people. If he is a true minister of God *he is bound to the ministry of the Word of God*. He has only one claim to the right to preach and demand decision, and that is that he is *declaring the truth of God*. It is impossible to separate the man from his calling, but as much as possible the minister must realize preaching is not *his* opportunity to express *his* religious views. His fundamental task in preaching is not to be clever or sermonic or profound but *to minister the truth of God*. The apostles were called *ministers of the word* (Luke 1:2). The apostles were ordained as *witnesses of Jesus Christ* (Acts 1:8). Their task was to preach what they heard and saw with reference to the life, death, and resurrection of Jesus Christ. The elder (pastor) is to labor *in word and doctrine* (1 Tim. 5:17). What Timothy is to hand on to others is not apostolic succession but *the truth of Christianity* which he heard from many Christians (2 Tim. 2:2). Paul instructs Timothy not to sermonize but to "preach *the message*" (2 Tim. 4:2. Grk: *kērukson ton logon*). Peter says he is an elder by virtue of having *witnessed* the sufferings of our Lord (1 Peter 5:1).

The New Testament servant of Christ was not one free to preach as he wished, but one bound to minister the truth of Christianity, to preach the Word of God, and to be a witness of the Gospel. This is very far removed from much of our contemporary preaching which is hardly more than popular, superficial, and personal discourses on religious themes.

One of the mighty issues of the Reformation was the nature of the Christian ministry. Martin Luther and John Calvin both opposed the notion of the ministry as a priesthood. The doctrine of justification by faith alone meant the end of Catholic priestcraft and sacerdotalism. What then was a minister? He was according to both Luther and Calvin *a minister of the Word of God*. In place of the liturgy and sacrament was put the singing of hymns and the preaching of the Word of God. No longer was the altar the focal point of attention, but the open Bible with the man of God preaching forth its meaning and content. The magnificent and thrilling singing of hymns was the spirited way in which the Reformed movement expressed its new joy in Jesus Christ and its freedom from the ritual and liturgy. The mass, so central to Catholic piety and ministry, was replaced by *the preaching of the Word of God*.

Again it is painful to note how these great Reformation convictions have been forgotten, and how the great emphasis on the ministry of the Word of God as God's supreme method of blessing His people has given way to popular, ephemeral sermonizing.

The rules for the practical use of the Bible in preaching are basically derived from (a) general hermeneutic theory, and (b) the conviction about the nature of the Christian ministry.

1. *The minister must realize he is a servant of the Lord and bound to the Word of the Lord.*

His basic motivation in preaching must be to convey to people the truth of God's Word. This means he should publicly read the Bible which is evidently the meaning of "give attendance to reading" (1 Tim. 4:13). He should teach God's Word for one of the requirements of a pastor is "apt to teach" (1 Tim. 3:2). He should *herald* or *preach* the Word of God.

2. *The preacher must use all Scripture in accordance with the rules of hermeneutics.*

It is felt too frequently by preachers that preaching is of such a nature as to exempt the preacher from close adherence to the rules of exegesis. Proper exegesis is necessary for commentators and theologians but preachers—it is argued—have a "poetic license" with reference to Scripture. This is most unfortunate reasoning. If the preacher's duty is to minister the Word of God, hermeneutics is the means whereby he determines the meaning of the Word of God. To ask for exemptions from the strict rules of hermeneutics is then to ask for an exemption from preaching the true meaning of the Word of God. This is precisely a repudiation of what a man is called to preach, namely, the truth of God's Word.

This does not mean that preaching is nothing but public exegesis or drab commenting on the Sacred Text. There must be energy, life, imagination, relevancy, illustration, and passion to all preaching. Bookish, dry, technical exposition is not necessarily preaching the Word of God. But whenever Scripture is used, it must be used according to sound rules of hermeneutics.

The principal mistakes in preaching in violating the meaning of Scripture are:

a.   Taking a phrase from a text because of its attractive wording. The preacher does not actually expound the meaning of the text, but uses the felicitous wording of it as the basis for his own sermonizing. Broadus says that this is not preaching Scripture, but merely the words of Scripture.[7] No matter how literary the expression nor how catchy to the ear, a phrase must not be wrenched from its content and preached upon with no real interpretation of its meaning. This is not preaching the Word of God.

b.   A preacher may choose a text but rather than explaining it sermonize on it. The remarks in a sermon need not be as narrow as the text, but if a text or passage is employed then the preacher is under holy obligation to explain its meaning. Either the preacher ignores the text save for the topic it suggests, or else he misinterprets it altogether. This is not a willful perversion of Scripture but a negligent or careless or ignorant method of treating the inspired Text. Broadus is not too strong when writing on this sort of an abuse of a text when he says: "It is a mournful fact that Universalists, Romanists, Mormons, can find an apparent support for their heresies in Scripture, without interpreting more loosely, without doing greater violence to the meaning and connection of the Sacred Text than is sometimes done by orthodoxy, devout, and even intelligent men."[8]

c.   A preacher may "spiritualize" a text or a passage and so impose a meaning on the text that is not there. This is usually done under the sincere pretense that the preacher is seeking a deeper meaning of the Bible. It is actually a species of patristic allegorization, and it is astounding how many of the patristic allegories are taught in Protestantism under the guise of typology.

One of the primary causes of this Protestant allegorizing is the proper notice to be edifying. Some Scripture is plain historical narrative and it is not especially edifying for the preacher to summarize so many historical incidents. But if he can read into the passage something about Christ, or the Gospel, or spiritual life, then he can make the passage very interesting. But he does so at the expense of its true meaning. He then is no longer preaching the Word of God but engaging in allegorization. Again we cite with much approval the judgment of Broadus about this sort of treatment of the Sacred Text:

> Among Baptists, for instance, the influence of Fuller, Hall, and others, and the wider diffusion of ministerial education, have wrought a gratifying change. But there is still much ignorance to overcome, and too many able and honored ministers continue sometimes to sanction by their potent example the old-fashioned spiritualizing [really, allegorizing]. It is so easy and pleasant for men of fertile fancy to break away from laborious study of phraseology and connection, to cease plodding along the rough and homely paths of earth, and sport, free and rejoicing, in the open heaven; the people are so charmed by ingenious novelties, so carried away with imaginative flights, so delighted to find everywhere types of Christ and likenesses to the spiritual life; it is so common to think that whatever kindles the imagination and touches the heart must be good preaching, and so easy to insist that the doctrines of the sermon are in themselves true and Scriptural, though they be not actually taught in the text—that preachers often lose sight of their fundamental and inexcusable error, of *saying that a passage of God's Word means what it does not mean.* So independent, too, one may feel; so original he may think himself. Commentaries, he can sneer at them all; other preachers, he has little need of comparing views with them. No need of anything but the resources of his own imagination, for such preaching is too often only building castles in the air.[9]

The proper alternative to spiritualizing the Old Testament is to *principlize* the Old Testament. To *principlize* is to discover in any narrative the basic spiritual, moral, or theological principles. These principles are latent in the text and it is the process of deduction which brings them to the surface. It is not an imposition on the text. Allegorizing is the imputation to the text of a meaning which is not there, but *principlizing* is not so guilty. By principlizing we are able to obtain devotional and spiritual truth from Scripture and avoid the charge of eisegesis.

When David repeatedly refuses to slay Saul we see the principle of obedience to powers that be. When Saul is not patient with God's prophet we see the principle of disobedience. When Isaiah prays for the shadow to retreat on the sundial we see the principle of great spiritual courage. In truth, Hebrews 11 is a magnificent example of principlizing. The great faith of a multitude of men is set before us as the true principle of their lives.

# TWENTY-TWO

# APPLICATION IN BIBLICAL HERMENEUTICS AND EXPOSITION

### Roy B. Zuck

## IS BIBLE KNOWLEDGE ENOUGH?

SEVERAL YEARS AGO I passed by a partially constructed apartment building twice daily on my way to and from my place of employment. For some reason the construction work, once begun, had been discontinued. Many months later, however, the project was finally resumed and the building was completed.

Similarly many people, having begun the process of Bible study, fail to finish the task. Neglecting to apply the Scriptures to their lives makes their study of God's Word incomplete and deficient.

This short-circuited approach to the Bible reduces God's Word to a mere object or antique "museum piece" to be examined by scientific inquiry, relegates Bible study to an academic exercise, and restricts the Scriptures to being only a sourcebook of information with little regard for its life-changing relevance.[1]

Theoretical knowledge of the content of the Bible, while absolutely indispensable, does not in itself automatically guarantee spiritual development. More is needed—a responsive heart with a willingness to appropriate the truths of the Scriptures into one's own experience. As Sterrett has well stated, "The Bible has spiritual dimensions that can be grasped only when the will responds to what God says, not simply when the mind analyzes the language."[2]

This deficiency is one of the greatest problems in Christianity today. The popular home Bible class movement reveals that many people desire to acquire more Bible facts and to amass more scriptural knowledge. And yet many Christians with extensive comprehension of the truth of God are not putting that truth into action. They know more than they live, and that borders on hypocrisy.

Furthermore, when believers possess the truth without letting the truth possess them, non-Christians question the authenticity and value of Christianity. Elwell urges churches to "find ways to help people turn their religious beliefs into action," for, as he concludes, "the world needs to see life in action."[3] Without such a personal appropriation of the truth, the Christian life remains sterile and fruitless.

## WHY DOES THIS PROBLEM EXIST?

Several factors may account for this problem of Christians' mastering the Book without the Book mastering them.

### "Application Will Follow Automatically"

Failure to apply the truth is often caused by assuming that if one knows the meaning of the Scriptures, correct application will follow. Christian leaders often feel that their responsibility in expounding the Bible ends when the text is explained. They apparently believe that somehow their people, by knowing the content, will thereby act in accord with its standards and precepts. Consequently, application is missing from many Bible messages and from many lessons in Bible teaching.

This is a dangerous assumption, for the meaning of the Scriptures to its original audience may or may not be the same for today's audiences. The expositor must therefore determine how to transfer the meaning to current life. This involves answering several questions: Are the experiences and precepts that are explicated in a given Bible passage repeatable today? If not, why not? How does one determine whether they are universally applicable or limited to ancient cultures and conditions? To what extent is the Old Testament relevant for contemporary times? Do all biblical commands, promises, and examples have present-day relevance? How does one bridge the gaps that exist between the Bible and today, including the geographical, chronological, cultural, linguistic, and literary gaps?

Application, then, in Bible preaching and teaching and in personal Bible study involves determining how the relevance of a passage for hearers/readers today may or may not differ from its relevance for its original hearers/readers. Unless this is done, some rather unwarranted points of relevance may be taught. For example, should Christians today be stoned if they pick up sticks on the Sabbath (Num. 15:32–36)? Should Christians in church gatherings today give each other a holy kiss (Rom. 16:16; 1 Cor. 16:20; 2 Cor. 13:12; 1 Thess. 5:26; 1 Peter 5:14)? Obviously the first of these has been abrogated by a dispensational change, and the second has been altered by a cultural difference.

### "Only the Hearer and the Holy Spirit Can Apply the Bible"

Some assume that because the Holy Spirit applies the truth a Bible teacher is incapable of applying it. Clines argues that "the aim of the expositor should be to lay bare the text so that it can apply itself to the listeners"[4] and that "to apply is the task of the hearer and of the Holy Spirit and not of the preacher-expositor."[5] He seeks to support this view in several ways.

First, "the expositor does not usually know how the text applies to each of his hearers, except perhaps in the most general way."[6] But would not at least a general kind of application help one's hearers sense the Scriptures' relevance? And should not an expositor seek to know his audience's needs?

Second, Clines suggests, "There is no such thing as *the* application of the text; each text is capable of manifold applications."[7] This is granted, but why should that mean the expositor can therefore eliminate application entirely?

Third, according to Clines, the expositor's "application and not the text is the message, for the application is the point at which the hearer is personally addressed."[8] This is an unfortunate confusing of terms. The *purpose* of the message—to "change lives in some specific way"[9]— differs from the message (the explication of the text) itself. Application does not replace the message of the text; it builds on it.

Fourth, Clines writes that if an expositor gives an application he should explain that it is not binding ("prescriptive," to use his term) on the individuals since that limits the ways the text can be used.[10] It is agreed that the specific applications made by an expositor do not carry divine authority as do the biblical texts. However, citing examples of spiritual relevance hardly limits that relevance. To say, "These are examples of how a text touches on today's living" is not the same as saying, "This is the only way this text touches on today's living."

Fifth, it is argued by Clines that application to contemporary issues should be avoided by the expositor because he probably does not know enough about those issues to make such a judgment.[11] Is this not like saying that if one does not know how to preach, he should not try or seek to find out how?

The notion that the Holy Spirit and not the Bible teacher applies the truth overlooks the several ways in which the word *apply* may be used. *The expositor or teacher applies* in the sense that he points out ways (some, if not all) in which the passages may be applied. *The hearer applies* in the sense that he selects from those possible applications or others he thinks of and decides how and when to carry out that application and follows that with the actual doing of it. And *the Holy Spirit applies* because He prompts and enables the hearer to live out that truth in the area of his conduct where the truth is needed.[12]

## "The Bible Is Already Relevant"

Several Christian leaders and laypersons deliberately avoid pointing out applications of the Scriptures because, they reason, the Bible is already relevant in itself. "The Word need not be made relevant because it is relevant," Greidanus asserts.[13] According to Veenhof, since "Scripture is applied" it is only necessary "to pass on its message in its 'applicatory' character."[14] Veenhof affirms that "the only application which the minister of the Word must make is the *choice of the text*."[15]

Two observations may be made in response to this view. (1) It is agreed that the Bible is life-relevant. It confronts man in his areas of deepest need and meets his greatest problems. This will be discussed more later. (2) Seeing the relevance of the biblical text is not the same as pointing out how that passage may be applied or carried out specifically in one's life. Thus, if Greidanus, Veenhof, and others mean that one need not "apply" the Bible in the sense that he need not add a relevancy to the Scriptures that is already there, their view is acceptable. However, if they mean that no attempt should be made to suggest specific courses of action one may take in order to appropriate a biblical text to one's experience, then that, to me, is unacceptable. The latter view seems to be what Greidanus is suggesting for he says that the preacher "should not add a subjective application."[16]

## WHAT THEN IS APPLICATION?

Application in Bible exposition (preaching or teaching) may be defined as the process of communicating the present-day relevance of a biblical text, specifying how that relevance may be translated into action, and inviting and urging the hearers to make that transference. Stated in another way, the application process involves communicating the Bible's relevance in both a general way and in a specific way, and then calling for a response.

In personal Bible study the application process is similar, but the difference is twofold: (1) Instead of a preacher or teacher stating the general and specific aspects of relevance, the student himself observes those points of relatedness. (2) Instead of a preacher or teacher inviting and urging his congregation or class to put into action the biblical truths, the student himself makes the decision to respond and actually carries out the truths in his experience.

In a congregation or class, application involves the communicator and the hearers. A preacher or teacher is thus a channel for motivating his people to respond and it is their responsibility to transfer the truth to their experience as needed. On the other hand, in personal Bible study the student is responsible both for observing the life-relatedness of the scriptural material and for deciding how to apply it to his needs.

Many times the applicational relevance of a Bible passage is explicitly evident in the text itself. This is especially true in the New Testament epistles, in which commands are clearly relevant to all Christians. Other times, however (e.g., in Old Testament narratives), the relevance may be implicit, not explicit, and the relevance may need to be spelled out. (How this can be done will be discussed later.)

Greidanus suggests, however, that the latter is undesirable, that preaching is not to be dualistic in the sense that it contains explication and application.[17] Following Van Dijk, he prefers not to think of application as separate from exposition, and thus he calls preaching "the applicatory explication of God's Word."[18]

If Greidanus means by this that the exposition of a text is to include both meaning and relevance, then that is acceptable. However, if Greidanus means that implicit relevance is not to be made explicit, then that is unacceptable. And if he means to exclude stating how the audience can respond to the truth and if he means to exclude appealing for response, then that too is undesirable.

To exclude any of these aspects—general life-relevance, specific relevance, and action response—means that application is missing. Application in this essay may be thought of as *relevance* (both general and specific) *plus response*. This concept may be summarized by the equation R+R=A.

## WHY IS RELEVANCE-AND-RESPONSE APPLICATION ESSENTIAL?

Applying the Bible to life is an essential step in Bible study and exposition for five reasons.

### The Nature of the Spiritual Life

Growth in the spiritual life comes not merely from hearing but from hearing and doing. This is why James wrote, "But prove yourselves doers of the word, and not merely hearers who delude themselves" (James 1:22). If a person hears (or reads) the Bible and does nothing about its implications for his attitudes and conduct, he deceives himself into thinking he has fulfilled his obligations when actually he has not.

Whereas deception comes from not heeding the Word, blessing stems from obeying it. The "effectual doer . . . shall be blessed in what he does" (James 1:25). "If you know these things, you are blessed if you do them" (John 13:17).

The Bible emphasizes that head knowledge, although crucial to the spiritual life, is not enough. Continually, obedience is enjoined, development of the inner quality of life is encouraged, and outward conduct consistent with God's standards is commanded. The New Testament, for example, frequently encourages Christians to "walk" (conduct themselves) in a manner that is pleasing to God (Rom. 13:13; Gal. 5:16–25; Eph. 4:1; 5:2, 8; Phil. 3:16; Col. 1:10; 2:6; 4:5;1 Thess. 2:12; 1 John 1:7; 2:6; 2 John 6; 3 John 4).

Those who "profess to know God" but who "by their deeds deny Him" (Titus 1:16) are strongly condemned. Scriptural depth is measured by a demonstration of "good behavior . . . in the gentleness of wisdom" (James 3:13), not by the extent of one's knowledge of the Scriptures. That is why Ezra was determined (he "set his heart") not only "to study the law of the LORD," but also "to practice it" (Ezra 7:10).

The Christian is to grow, not merely to know (1 Peter 2:2). Since he is God's "workmanship, created in Christ Jesus for good works" (Eph. 2:10), he is to be "zealous for good deeds" (Titus 2:14) and to "be careful to engage in good deeds" (Titus 3:8).

Those "good deeds" in the life of the Christian stem from an inner quality of life. "Spirituality," as Ramm explains, "is striving toward correct attitudes, spiritual graces, the fruit of the Spirit (Gal. 5:22–23)."[19]

Luther wrote that the Bible "is not merely to be repeated or known, but to be lived and felt."[20]

## The Purpose of the Scriptures

The reason God has given the Scriptures is to change man's basic nature, including his attitudes and actions, thus making him more Christlike.

This purpose is spelled out in Paul's classic statement on the inspiration of the Scriptures. "All Scripture is inspired by God and profitable for teaching, for reproof, for correction, for training in righteousness: that the man of God may be adequate, equipped for every good work" (2 Tim. 3:16–17). The inspired Word teaches man the ways of God, rebukes him when he fails to heed those ways, restores him back to those ways, and gives him training (*paideia*, "child nurture") in righteous living. The ultimate result of these immediate purposes is that the believer (the "man of God") may be "adequate" and "equipped." Interestingly, these two words (*artios*, an adjective, and *exērtismenos*, a participial adjective) are related and thus are close in meaning. Lenski suggests that the first word means "in fit shape or condition" and the second word means "altogether fit."[21] Each word occurs only here in the New Testament. In the Greek papyri the second word refers to a boat "supplied" with two oars and an oil-press in working order and "completely finished."[22]

The practical nature of the Bible is seen in that it convicts (Heb. 4:12–13), regenerates (2 Tim. 3:15; 1 Peter 1:23), nurtures (1 Peter 2:2), cleanses (Ps. 119:9; John 15:3; 17:17; Eph. 5:25–26), counsels and guides (Ps. 119:24, 105), prevents sin (Ps. 119:11), revives (Ps. 119:50, 88, 93, 107, 149, 154, 156), strengthens (Ps. 119:28, 116), gives wisdom (Ps. 119:98, 130, 169), delivers (Ps. 119:170), and helps (Ps. 119:175).

The Scriptures are called a fire, to consume false teaching, and a hammer, to shatter man's hard heart (Jer. 23:29); food, to nourish man's soul (Ps. 119:103; Jer. 15:16; 1 Cor. 3:2; Heb. 5:13–14; 1 Peter 2:2); and a sword, for offense against Satan (Eph. 6:17; cf. Luke 4:4, 8, 12).

The psalmist, recognizing the life-related value of the Scriptures, used many words in Psalm 119 to describe his attitude toward them. Often those words are verbs, given variously in the indicative past, present, or future ("I delighted," "I delight," "I will delight") or in the imperative (e.g., "teach me Thy statutes," v. 12). Other times they are nouns (e.g., "Thy Law is my delight," v. 174). Sometimes those affirmations are given as a result of God's working in the psalmist's life; other times they are stated as means for obtaining God's blessing. These verbs include the following: *walk in* (v. 1); *observe* (vv. 2, 22, 33–34, 56, 69, 100, 115, 129, 145); *keep* (vv. 4–5, 8, 17, 34, 55, 57, 60, 63, 67, 88, 101, 106, 134, 146, 158, 167–168); *do* (v. 166); *trust in* (v. 42); *seek* (vv. 45, 94, 155); *delight* (vv. 16, 24, 35, 47, 70, 77, 92, 143, 174); *meditate* (vv. 15, 23, 48, 78, 97, 99, 148); *rejoice* (vv. 14, 111, 162); *behold* (v. 18); *understand* (vv. 27, 100, 104, 130, 169); *wait for* (vv. 74, 81, 114, 147); *teach* (and desire to *learn*) (vv. 7, 12, 64, 68, 71, 73, 108, 124, 135, 171); h*ope* (v. 49); speak of (v. 46); *remember* (and *not forget*) (vv. 16, 52, 61, 83, 93, 109, 141, 153, 176); *did not forsake* (or *turn aside, gone astray*) (vv. 87, 102, 110, 157); b*elieve* (v. 66); *consider* (v. 95); *esteem* (v. 128); *long for* (v. 40, 131); *love* (vv. 47–48, 97, 113, 119, 127, 140, 159, 163, 165, 167); *incline* (v. 112); *stand in awe* (and *afraid*) (vv. 120, 161); *sing* (v. 172); and *choose* (v. 173). Those verses make it abundantly clear that the instructions in the Scriptures (variously called in Ps. 119 God's commandments, judgments, law, precepts, statutes, testimonies, ways, and word) are given to man so that he may respond to them with commitment, delight, and obedience.

The New Testament makes it clear that the Old Testament has relevance for the present church age. In Matthew 15:7 Christ applied Isaiah 29:13 to the Pharisees when He said, "You hypocrites, rightly did Isaiah prophesy of you." And to the Sadducees Jesus said that the words of Exodus 3:6 were "spoken to you" (Matt. 22:31). Paul argues that the words, "He reckoned it to him [Abraham] as righteousness" (Gen. 15:6) were written not only for Abraham's sake "but for our sake also" (Rom. 4:23–24). And in Romans 15:4 Paul wrote, "For whatever was written in earlier times was written for our instruction [*didaskalia*, "teaching"], that . . . we might have hope." Certain events in Israel's wilderness wanderings "happened as examples [*tupoi*] for us" (1 Cor. 10:6), and "these things happened to them as an example [*tupikōs*, "in an examplary way"], and they were written for our instruction [*nouthesia*, "nurture"] . . ." (10:11).

It is evident that the purpose of the Bible is more than to give facts to satisfy one's curiosity. Its purpose is to change lives.

## The Efficacy of the Scriptures

Another reason for including application in Bible study and exposition is that the Bible—and the Bible alone—realistically and sufficiently meets man's deepest problems, longings, needs, and inadequacies. As Marshall puts it, "The Bible presents a picture of man and the human situation which rings true in the modern world and offers a diagnosis of our maladies which is profoundly true and relevant. Prescription for our maladies deserves equal respect."[23]

No other book provides the answers to man's need for deliverance from the penalty of sin, for spiritual progress, for daily victory over the power of sin, for guidance in personal relationships and conduct. "Scripture contains all the information which a man needs in order to set forth the way of salvation. Further, the Bible contains all the guidance which is needed for the continuous living of the Christian life."[24]

And the Bible speaks to people in all cultures, in all ages, and in all circumstances. As Schonkel wrote, "Holy Scripture is at once ancient and contemporary; incarnate in a particular time, it claims to speak to all generations; circumscribed in language and cultural perspective, it lays claim to universality."[25]

In all its pages the Bible shouts its relevance to man. How then can the Bible student or expositor neglect to relate the Scriptures and all their practicality to man's needs?

## The Nature of Learning

Application is necessary because without it true learning has not taken place. This writer has discussed this point elsewhere.

> Pupils have not necessarily learned if there is only a mental apprehension of truth without an actual experiencing of the truth, appropriated to their lives by the Holy Spirit. Facts not perceived. skills taught in

isolation, and verbalisms presented to passive, unmotivated pupils fall short of effecting genuine spiritual growth. Learning is the process in which a pupil modifies his behavior, through the Spirit's enabling, to conform more to the will of God and the image of Christ.[26]

## The Objective of Preaching and Teaching

Effective preaching and teaching has as its objective the changing of lives and the alteration of undesirable attitudes and behavior into desirable ones. This calls for proper attention to application.

Football teams do not play merely for the sake of throwing and catching the ball. They play in order to reach the goal line, to make touchdowns, to win the game. Likewise, effective Bible communicators drive toward a goal. Each message moves toward a climax, builds toward a verdict, calls for a "signing on the dotted line."

Educators commonly refer to three kinds of desirable behavioral changes: cognitive (knowledge), affective (feeling and attitude), and psychomotor (doing). Stated generally, teachers want three things to happen in their students: (1) that they will increase in what they know; (2) that they will improve in how they feel toward God, others, and themselves; and (3) that they will develop helpful skills, practices, and habits. Ford has divided the first of these three learning outcomes into two parts—"knowledge" and "understanding" (or "insight")—and calls the others "attitudes" and "skills."[27]

To enable the preacher or teacher to move toward a specific goal or learning outcome for his hearers or students, his sermon or lesson should state a purpose, written in terms of "what one expects to happen in the hearer."[28] That goal or purpose may be that the hearers/students will: (1) increase in knowledge (indicated by their ability to list, state, recite, write, identify, recall, describe, define, recognize, etc.); (2) gain insight (indicated by their ability to discuss, differentiate, analyze, compare, contrast, select, choose, examine, evaluate, think, discern, clarify, etc.); (3) improve in attitude (indicated by their desiring, determining, developing, planning, appreciating, being enthusiastic about, enjoying, committing, sympathizing, etc.); or (4) develop in skill or action (indicated by their ability to interpret, produce, make, use, solve, explain, assist, integrate, communicate, engage in, assist, etc.).

Because the ultimate objective of Bible exposition is to change lives by gaining an action/response from the hearers, preachers and teachers should state specific purposes for each sermon or lesson, and should focus their sermons or lessons toward those accomplishments, the climaxes of their messages.

## WHAT ARE SOME GUIDELINES FOR
## PROPER RELEVANCE-AND-RESPONSE APPLICATION?

### Application Must Stem from the Proper
### Understanding of the Passage

Correct interpretation of a passage is basic to proper application. If a text is interpreted inaccurately, then the application will be faulty as well. Unfortunately many people go to the Bible for a "blessing" or for guidance for the day, and therefore they either build an application on an invalid interpretation or ignore the interpretive process altogether. In their intense desire to find something devotional or practical, many Christians distort the original meaning of some passages of Scripture. "The first question of Bible study is not: "What is devotional here?' nor 'What is of practical importance here?' nor 'What is inspirational here?' but *What does this passage mean?*"[29]

The personal response to a passage should be based, as suggested earlier, on that passage's relevance, which in turn stems from the meaning of the text to its original audience in light of the purpose of the book. Sound exegesis, which may be defined as determining the meaning of a biblical text in its historical and literary contexts, is the only adequate basis for relevant application.

In exegesis one examines the meaning of a passage in its original setting, and in application he looks at the significance of that meaning for current situations. Using proper procedures of interpretation, exegesis seeks to answer the question, What did this text mean to its original audience? Application seeks to answer the question, How does that original meaning relate to present audiences? Only after the Bible student has accurately determined the meaning of the passage for the initial hearers in the "then and there" can he accurately apply that meaning to himself and others "now and here."

### Application Must Be Based on Principles

Principles, often stated in single sentences, serve as bridges between interpretation and application. Latent in the text, they summarize the essence of a Bible passage in terms that are applicable to a broad spectrum of readers and situations. Without such a bridge, a passage would simply remain as a recording of what God had done or said in the past. The principlizing bridge spans the gulf between the past and the present, with a truth that is relevant to both.

"To principlize is to discover in any narrative the basic spiritual, moral, or theological principles. These principles are latent in the text and it is the process of deduction which brings them to the surface. It is not an imposition on the text."[30]

A "principlizing bridge" is the same as the "relevance" of a passage discussed earlier. The relationship of this bridge to interpretation and application may be illustrated in this way:

| Determine the *meaning* of the passage to its original audience. | Write out the *principle*. | Decide on a specific *action/ response*. |
|---|---|---|
| *Interpretation* (Meaning) | | *Application* (Significance) |

The principle stems directly from the meaning and thus is inherent in the meaning. The principle also expresses the meaning's present relevance and thus is part of the application.

The principle is a generalized statement deduced from the specific original situation then and applicable to different though specific, similar situations now.

Principles are necessary because the emphasis of the Bible is on principles for moral and spiritual conduct more than it is a catalog of specific directions.[31] Sometimes the general principle underlies a concrete instruction. As Fisher illustrates, "When Jesus said, 'If anyone forces you to go one mile, go with him two miles' (Matt. 5:41), He was putting a general principle into concrete terms. The application goes far beyond the particular situation."[32]

Ramm gives several examples of principles drawn from biblical narratives:

> When David repeatedly refused to slay Saul we see the principle of obedience to powers that be. When Saul was not patient with God's prophet we see the principle of disobedience. When Isaiah prays for the shadow to retreat on the sundial we see the principle of great spiritual courage. In truth, Hebrews 11 is a magnificent example of principlizing. The great faith of a multitude of men is set before us as the true principle of their lives.[33]

The principle or general truth pertaining to Ramm's example of Saul and Samuel may be stated in this way: "Believers should be obedient to the Lord, for impatient disobedience results in punishment." Audiences or individuals may be challenged to respond to that principle in various specific ways, depending on their needs.

The words, "in everything give thanks" (1 Thess. 5:18), were addressed originally to the Thessalonian believers. The meaning of the passage in reference to that original audience could be stated this way: "Thessalonian believers should be thankful in every circumstance of life." The principle for all believers would be very similar in wording, because many commands in the epistolary literature of the Bible are obviously intended, by the inspiration of the Holy Spirit, for all believers. The principle may be worded, "All Christians should be thankful in every one of their circumstances." It can be seen that this is a universal statement that relates the truth of that verse to both the Thessalonian culture of Paul's day and to every generation of Christians in all cultures everywhere.

Numbers 15:32–36 instructs Israelites that if they gather wood on the Sabbath they will be stoned. The meaning may be stated, "If an Israelite does not follow God's commands explicitly, God will punish him." Since this is part of the Mosaic law and the Mosaic law has been abolished, that command is not directly relevant to Christians. But the underlying principle is relevant. Deduced from the passage and confirmed by other Scripture is the principle that "God punishes disobedience."

Mickelsen cites Paul's words to Euodia and Synteche to live in harmony in the Lord (Phil. 4:2), and adds these comments:

> Certainly, two Christians who are quarreling today . . . might well apply this statement about living in harmony to themselves. The principle, then, is that of believers living in harmony with one another. This is true even though today's Christians cannot—like those to whom Paul's statement first came—claim that they helped Paul the apostle in his ministry in Philippi. This obvious fact helps to make clear the confined or limited meaning in the passage as well as the universal possibilities of application in the principle of harmonious living.[34]

### Application Must Be Based on Elements the Reader Shares with the Original Audience

Sometimes the audience to which a passage of Scripture was initially addressed, such as the believers at Philippi, is similar to audiences today. For this reason the principle is similar in wording to the meaning of the text (meaning: "Euodia and Synteche should stop quarreling and should live harmoniously"; principle: "Christians who are quarreling should stop doing so and should live harmoniously").

Other times the audience to which a passage of Scripture was initially addressed, such as Israel in the wilderness, is rather dissimilar to present-day audiences. In this case the wording of the principle differs substantially from the summarized interpretation.

Applying to today the scriptural admonitions, commands, counsel, instructions, and truths given to those audiences requires finding a point in common between the original and the current audiences. The point in common between the Corinthians, for example, who were commanded to do all things to the glory of God (1 Cor. 10:31), and Christians today is that both groups are members of the church, the body of Christ. The instruction to the Corinthians is immediately relevant to today. The point in common, however, between Israel under the Law and believers today is that both are God's people. The first example of a point in common involves direct application and the second indirect application.

Situations between original and subsequent audiences are often diverse. For example, God's instruction to Noah to build an ark is hardly a directive for the twentieth century. And Paul's injunction to the Corinthians to refrain from eating meat sacrificed to idols in order to avoid causing other Christians difficulty (1 Cor. 8:7–13) is a situation that is not current now. Therefore application requires determining what aspects of those situations may be parallel to present circumstances. In the case of Noah and the ark, the parallel idea is not to build an ark, but to obey God when there is no visible evidence for doing so. In the case of the Corinthians, the parallel is to avoid involvement in any practice, innocent in itself, which may cause others to sin.[35]

This raises the hypothetical question of cultural relativity, that is, how to ascertain what in the Bible pertains only to those cultural situations and therefore has little direct relevance to the present, and what in the Bible pertains to present as well as past cultural environments. This involves ascertaining which Bible passages are "culturally conditioned" and which ones are "transcultural." It is evident that some commands in the Scriptures are a reflection of local custom. Jesus said, "Carry no purse, no bag, no shoes; and greet no one on the way" (Luke 10:4). As Sproul has observed, if this is transcultural, then evangelists should preach in their bare feet![36] He adds, "Obviously, the point of this text is not to set down a perennial requirement of barefooted evangelism."[37]

Space does not permit a full discussion of this involved issue,[38] but it may be helpful to point out four kinds of situations, with varying degrees of cultural transference.

1. Some situations, commands, or principles are repeatable, continuous, or not revoked, and/or pertain to more theological subjects, and/or are repeated elsewhere in Scripture, and therefore are transferable. Examples of those are Genesis 9:6; Proverbs 3:5–6; John 3:3; Romans 12:1–2; 1 Corinthians 12:13; Ephesians 6:10–19; Colossians 3:12–13; and 1 Peter 5:6.

2. Some situations, commands, or principles pertain to an individual's specific nonrepeatable circumstances, and/or nonmoral or nontheological subjects, and/or have been revoked, and are therefore not transferable. Examples of this are Leviticus 20:11 (cf. 1 Cor. 5:1–8); Matthew 21:2–3; 2 Timothy 4:11, 13; and Hebrews 7:12; 10:1.

3. Some situations or commands pertain to cultural settings that are only partially similar and in which only the principles are transferable. Examples are Deuteronomy 6:4–6; Romans 16:16; and 1 Corinthians 8.

4. Some situations or commands pertain to cultural settings with no similarities but in which the principles are transferable. Examples are Exodus 3:5 and Matthew 26:7.

The first category may be called "direct application" because the application is directly related without change to subsequent cultures.[39] Categories 3 and 4 may be called "indirect application" because the application does not arise in the immediate biblical context.[40]

In order for an expositor to determine the common elements shared by an original and a present audience, he must know something of the needs and characteristics of that present audience. Expositors often spend much time studying the biblical text and its historical background in order to know that original audience, to the neglect of studying their own contemporary hearers. Without knowledge of both audiences, the expositor may distort the shared part(s) and thus misconstrue the application.[41]

How do examples of Bible personalities relate to application? How does the Bible student determine which examples to follow and which ones not to follow? Several suggestions may be given.[42]

*Learn from poor examples what not to do.* "Certainly the rebellion of Saul, the immorality of David, the pride of Absalom, the treachery of Judas, the denials of Peter, and the lying of Ananias and Sapphira stand as examples of what not to do."[43] Studying examples such as these helps the Bible student see the serious consequences of wrongdoing.

*Learn from good examples what to do.* "The faith of Abraham, the obedience of Moses, the loyalty of Elijah, and the love of John the Apostle stand out as great examples to follow."[44] But are these and other worthy examples to be imitated today? Abraham is certainly to be commended for offering up his son Isaac in obedience to God, Solomon's building of the Temple is a praiseworthy accomplishment, and Paul's trip to Arabia is commendable. But are these to be heeded by all Christians today? No, for these were instructions to specific individuals, and thus are not universally applicable. This suggests another guideline.

*Follow the example if a transcultural biblical command or principle is related to it.*[45] Christian fathers are not to offer their sons as literal sacrifices as Abraham did because no such universal command is given to them. On the other hand, Elijah's fervency in prayer is an example for Christians to follow (James 5:17–18) for it illustrates the effectiveness of praying (5:16).[46]

Fee discusses this guideline. "For a biblical precedent to justify present action, the principle of the action must be taught elsewhere, where it is the primary intent so to teach."[47] He then develops this point further.

> Where there is ambiguity of models, or when a practice is reported but once, it is repeatable only if it appears to have divine approbation or is in harmony with what is taught elsewhere in Scripture. To illustrate: It would seem that some in what is often called the Jesus movement could justify their communal life and their having all things common on these grounds, since such life appears to have divine approval in Acts, and since there is no teaching elsewhere that would seem to prohibit such a practice. But one may well question the economic viability of the practice, since Paul eventually was raising money for the poor in Jerusalem.[48]

Wilson stresses the importance of determining the theological intent of the narrative passage (the principles) and its correlation to a current audience. "If we fail to discover the theological intent, we may make a good application from the wrong text. On the other hand, if we fail to ask the question of audience correlation, we may make a valid application, grounded in the theology of the text, but to the wrong audience."[49]

## Application Must Include Specific Action/Response

The goal toward which exposition and principlizing moves is a desired response on the part of the individuals in the congregation or class. As pointed out earlier, the communicator and the learner each has separate responsibilities.

*The expositor's responsibilities.* To encourage and motivate toward a proper response to the Word, the preacher or teacher may choose from several approaches.

1.  State during or at the end of the message or lesson one or more specific ways in which the truth can be implemented. Sometimes an illustration may be included on how others have applied the Word in one of those specific ways.
2.  In a class ask the students to list ways the truth can be carried out.

3. Have students individually write out ways they plan to put the truth into practice. This may be done at the end of one session (e.g., "How can I work out this scriptural principle in my life?") or at the conclusion of a series (e.g., "I plan to do these three things as a result of our study in the book of James").
4. Have the students share how they applied a biblical principle the previous week.
5. Lead the group in singing a hymn that expresses a practical response to the truth studied.
6. Encourage the students to keep a spiritual diary in which they (a) write out how they plan to personalize a verse or passage that week, and (b) write a report on how they succeeded or did not succeed in living out that biblical principle and what, if anything, remains to be done.
7. Suggest that the students ask themselves these six questions:
    - Is there any *example* for me to follow?
    - Is there any *command* for me to obey?
    - Is there any *error* for me to avoid?
    - Is there any *sin* for me to forsake?
    - Is there any *promise* for me to claim?
    - Is there any *new thought about God Himself?*[50]
8. Suggest that the hearers/students think of one response they can put into action in the coming week. (It is helpful to have a date for fulfilling the response.)
9. Distribute cards with the following formula, and ask the students to complete it: "Knowing that _____ (Scripture truth), I desire to _____ (overall objective), by _____ (specific attitude or action) by the date of _____." This formula puts together the intellectual, emotional, and volitional aspects of a learning response, and includes a time element.
10. Point out that some responses pertain to the improvement of one's actions whereas others pertain to attitudes or motives. Improper attitudes may take longer to correct than the carrying out of certain actions, and are often more difficult to deal with.

*The hearers'/students' responsibilities.* Application may be pointed out by a preacher or teacher (or counselor), but it must be carried out by the individual himself. Without this final step, application is aborted. An individual in personal study may see truths to apply, but it still remains his responsibility to carry them out, The following suggestions are offered to help individuals appropriate the Word in this crowning step in Bible study.
1. Have a receptive attitude toward the preaching and teaching of

294 Rightly Divided: Readings in Biblical Hermeneutics

the Word. Ask the Lord to give an openness to the Scriptures (cf. Acts 16:14, "The Lord opened [Lydia's] heart to respond to the things spoken by Paul," and Eph. 1:18, "I pray that the eyes of your heart may be enlightened").

2. During a message, lesson, or personal Bible study, be thinking of (and/or write down) one or more ways to apply the truth.

3. List areas of one's life where spiritual improvement is needed. Ask others to suggest (lovingly!) areas where one's life may be improved. Then as the Word is heard and studied, see if and how those passages relate to the area(s) of need.

4. Think of application in terms of relationships: one's relationship to God, to Satan, to others (at home, church, work, school), and to oneself.[51]

5. Choose one course of action or attitudinal response from the several possibilities.

6. Make a firm decision to carry out the response. Make this decision a firm commitment between the individual and the Lord. This will help motivate one toward the "doing."

7. Be personal. Use the first person singular pronouns ("I," "me," "my," "mine"), not plural pronouns ("we," "us," "our").[52] Application that remains in the "we" category is too general and impersonal.

8. Be specific. Application that is stated in general terms (such as "I should be more like Jesus" or "I should love my wife more") is inadequate and difficult to carry out. Complete the formula suggested in point 9 given earlier under *The expositor's responsibilities*. Or write a sentence beginning with the words "I will . . ." followed by one of the ninety action verbs (or others) from the accompanying list.

| | | |
|---|---|---|
| Accept | Commit | Encourage |
| Admit | Compliment | Enjoy |
| Analyze | Comply | Evaluate |
| Ask | Confess | Exemplify |
| Ask myself | Control | Experiment |
| Avoid | Count | Find |
| Be sensitive | Create | Follow |
| Be willing | Decide | Give |
| Build | Develop | Go |
| Buy | Direct | Guard |
| Choose | Discourse | Help |
| Claim | Do | Invite |
| Collect | Eliminate | Isolate |

| | | |
|---|---|---|
| Keep | Realize | Substitute |
| List | Record | Take |
| Listen | Rejoice | Talk with |
| Look for | Repair | Teach |
| Look up | Respond | Telephone |
| Love | Sacrifice | Thank |
| Meet with | Save | Think about |
| Memorize | Schedule | Value |
| Organize | Select | Visit |
| Plan out | Send | Wait |
| Praise | Share | Wake up |
| Pray about | Show | Walk |
| Pray to | Sing | Watch |
| Pray with | Spend time | Witness |
| Prefer | Stay away | Work on |
| Pursue | Stop | Write down |
| Read | Study | Write to |

Henrichsen illustrates this kind of specific action for applying meekness from the life of Moses:

> I will memorize Numbers 12:3 and review it daily throughout the year. I will write *meek* on a card and tape it to the mirror in the bathroom, so that daily I will be reminded of my need to work on this. Each morning I will review Numbers 12:3 and pray about its application in my life for *that* day.
>
> I will share this need with my spouse and with [a friend], who knows me well. Once a month I will talk over my progress with them and ask for a frank evaluation.[53]

9. Have a deadline for completing the application, and work toward it.
10. Review the progress. The day after the deadline for completing an action/response, evaluate the progress made and if necessary write the same, a revised, or an entirely different course of action for another date.
11. Pray for the enabling of the Holy Spirit to incarnate God's truth in one's life.

## CONCLUSION

A common reaction to many sermons and Bible lessons is the question, "So what?" People long to know how the Bible, written in ancient times, relates to them.

Indifference to the Bible often sets in after a prolonged exposure to applicationless preaching and teaching. But enjoyment of the Word comes as one not only observes its marvels (Ps. 119:18) and understands (interprets) what it says (cf. Acts 8:30–31), but also as he personalizes the Bible to himself. For after all, God has given His Word so that believers may "grow thereby" (1 Peter 2:2 KJV).

If you know these things, you are blessed if you do them (John 13:17).

# ENDNOTES

## Chapter 1

1. John F. MacArthur, *The Charismatics* (Grand Rapids: Zondervan, 1970), 57.
2. John Balchin, *Understanding Scripture* (Downers Grove, Ill.: InterVarsity, 1981), 8.
3. Milton S. Terry, *Biblical Hermeneutics*, 2d ed. (1883; reprint, Grand Rapids: Zondervan, n.d.), 20.
4. F. F. Bruce, "Interpretation of the Bible," in *Evangelical Dictionary of Theology*, ed. Walter A. Elwell (Grand Rapids: Baker, 1986), 505.
5. Also see Roy B. Zuck, *Teaching with Spiritual Power*, rev. ed. (Grand Rapids: Kregel, 1993), 62–63.
6. H. C. G. Moule, *Veni Creator: Thoughts on the Person and Work of the Holy Spirit* (London: Hodder & Stoughton, 1890), 63.
7. For more discussion of the role of the Holy Spirit in biblical interpretation, see *Teaching with Spiritual Power*, 58–66, 136–46.
8. Bernard Ramm, *Protestant Biblical Interpretation*, 3d rev. ed. (Grand Rapids: Baker, 1979), 14.
9. On the puzzling words, "You do not need anyone to teach you" (1 John 2:27), see *The Holy Spirit in Your Teaching*, 55–57.
10. For more on this subject see Moisés Silva, *Has the Church Misread the Bible?* (Grand Rapids: Zondervan, 1987), 77–97.

## Chapter 5

1. W. L. Lane, *Commentary on the Gospel of Mark* (Grand Rapids: Eerdmans, 1974), xii.
2. *John Wesley's Journal*, abridged by N. Curnock (London: Epworth, 1949), 51 (entry for May 14, 1738).
3. N. H. Snaith, *The Distinctive Ideas of the Old Testament* (Philadelphia: Westminster, 1946), 13.

## Chapter 6

1. As we have indicated at various points already, we position ourselves in the evangelical tradition, within the framework described, for example, by the Lausanne Covenant or the National Association of Evangelicals. Yet what follows need not be limited to "our circle" of Christians. The principles and methods we employ will yield significant understanding regardless of the

practitioner, though readers with differing presuppositions and preunderstandings will admit or reject our results in varying ways. To the extent that methods are neutral (and we insist most are), the results will be similar.

2. E. D. Hirsch, Jr., *Validity in Interpretation* (New Haven: Yale University Press, 1967), 75.

3. A. Richardson, *Christian Apologetics* (New York: Harper & Row, 1947), 105.

4. Is our concern to apply the Constitution in the way its original framers intended, or in some other manner?

5. B. Ramm, "Biblical Interpretation," in Ramm, et al., *Hermeneutics* (Grand Rapids: Baker, 1987).

6. Ramm's insights are worth consideration. The following discussion owes much to his presentation, "Biblical Interpretation," 18–28.

7. Ibid., 18.

8. Ibid.

9. Technically, of course, this text refers to the OT. But when the church canonized the NT, in effect it affirmed the same things for the NT.

10. Ramm, "Biblical Interpretation," 19.

11. G. D. Fee, *The First Epistle to the Corinthians*, NICNT (Grand Rapids: Eerdmans, 1987), 109. He goes on to assert Paul's point that only the person possessing God's Spirit is able to "'discern' in the sense of being able to make appropriate 'judgments' about what God is doing in the world" (ibid., 117). Finally, "the person who has the Spirit can discern God's ways. Not necessarily all things, of course, but all things that pertain to the work of salvation, matters formerly hidden in God but now revealed through the Spirit" (ibid., 118).

12. S. S. Smalley, *1, 2, 3 John*, WBC 51 (Waco, TX: Word, 1984), 125.

13. Ibid.

14. Ramm, "Biblical Interpretation," 20.

15. K. Snodgrass suggests: "At every point early Christians attempted to understand their Scripture [which, of course, was the Old Testament] in the new light of the ministry, death, and resurrection of Jesus Christ. They used the Old Testament to prove their Christian theology and to solve Christian problems. The Old Testament provided the substructure of New Testament theology. The Old Testament also provided the language and imagery for much of New Testament thought, although this is not always obvious to the casual reader. Therefore, New Testament concepts must be understood from Old Testament passages" ("The Use of the Old Testament in the New," in *New Testament Criticism and Interpretation*, ed. D. A. Black and D. S. Dockery [Grand Rapids: Zondervan, 1991], 409).

16. See D. L. Baker, *Two Testaments, One Bible* (Downers Grove, Ill.: InterVarsity, 1976) who provides a thorough survey of these issues and balanced conclusions. We provide further perspectives below in our section on Jesus and the Law.

17. We find an obvious example in the OT commands to sacrifice animals that are superseded and nullified in Christ (Heb. 9–10). The former was important and necessary, but in light of the new proves defective. Along the analogy of how old black-and-white movies are now "colorized" to make them more attractive, insights from the NT often help to cast new light or color on the OT. For further help see W. C. Kaiser, Jr., *Toward an Old Testament Theology* (Grand Rapids: Zondervan, 1978).

18. Ramm, "Biblical Interpretation," 23.
19. Ibid., 24.
20. Ibid., 25.
21. Ibid., 26.
22. Cf. Grant Osborne, *The Hermeneutical Spiral* (Downers Grove, Ill.: InterVarsity, 1991), 10, 324; W. J. Larkin, Jr., *Culture and Biblical Hermeneutics* (Grand Rapids: Baker, 1988), 302; and R. C. Padilla, "Hermeneutics and Culture: A Theological Perspective," in *Gospel and Culture*, ed. J. R. W. Stott and R. T. Coote (Pasadena, Calif.: William Carey Library, 1979), 63–78.
23. Larkin, *Culture and Biblical Hermeneutics*, 299.
24. Ibid., 300. However, as we will defend in detail below, we are on safer ground to set as a goal to detect the meaning of a given text rather than the meaning an author intended. Also, Larkin may be overly optimistic when he assures us, "interpreters who consciously set aside their cultural preunderstanding can be confident that the grammatical-historical-literary context will enable them to find the plain and definite meaning of the text" (ibid., 301). Whether we can set aside our cultural preunderstandings remains a huge question. A good starting point is simply to try to identify them and to assess their influence.
25. Ferguson, *Biblical Hermeneutics* (Atlanta: Knox, 1986), 17.

## Chapter 7

1. For applications of basic logic to the study of the Bible, see especially James W. Sire, *Scripture Twisting: Twenty Ways the Cults Misread the Bible* (Downers Grove, Ill.: InterVarsity, 1980); and D. A. Carson, *Exegetical Fallacies* (Grand Rapids: Baker, 1984).
 2. John Macquarrie, *Principles of Christian Theology*, 2d ed. (New York: Scribners, 1977), 109, 197.
 3. Umberto Cassuto, *A Commentary on the Book of Exodus* (Jerusalem: Magnes, 1967), 196.
 4. Elmer W. K. Mould, *Essentials of Bible History*, rev. ed. (New York: Ronald, 1951), 307. These words or comparable statements have been quoted favorably in recent books.
 5. C. A. Briggs, *General Introduction to the Study of Holy Scripture* (1900; reprint, Grand Rapids: Baker, 1970), 64, 65–67, 70–71. Cf. J. Barr's critique in *The Semantics of Biblical Language* (Oxford: Oxford University Press, 1961), 246ff.
 6. John Macquarrie, *Principles of Christian Theology* (New York: Scribner, 1966), 86, 333.
 7. The etymological relationships are taken from Robert Claiborne, *The Roots of English: A Reader's Handbook of Word Origins* (New York: Times Books, 1989), 119, 130–31, 184, 218–19.
 8. Gloria Neufeld Redekop, "Let the Women Learn: 1 Timothy 2:8–15 Reconsidered," *SR* 19 (1990): 242.
 9. William R. Newell, *Hebrews: Verse by Verse* (Grand Rapids: Kregel Publications, 1995), 3n.
10. R. C. H. Lenski, *The Interpretation of St. Paul's Epistles to the Galatians, to the Ephesians, and to the Philippians* (Minneapolis: Augsburg, 1961; orig. 1937), 802; *idem, The Interpretation of St. John's Revelation* (Minneapolis: Augsburg, 1961), 88.

## Chapter 8

1. For more extensive discussion of the sources of figures of speech, see E. W. Bullinger, *Figures of Speech in the Bible Explained and Illustrated* (reprint, Grand Rapids: Baker, 1968), *passim;* A. Berkeley Mickelsen, *Interpreting the Bible* (Grand Rapids: Eerdmans, 1963), 179–81; and G. B. Caird, *The Language and Imagery of the Bible* (Philadelphia: Westminster, 1980), 156–59.

2. Beekman and Callow, *Translating the Word of God* (Grand Rapids: Zondervan, 1974), 97–101.

3. Andrew Lincoln (*Paradise Now and Not Yet* [Cambridge: University Press], 139–68) has made an excellent and provocative case for the literal meaning of this term. I remain convinced that the figurative sense fits the context better.

4. Beekman and Callow, *Translating the Word of God,* 104–7.

5. In this section I am discussing only the positive side of Ricoeur's theory. For excellent discussions of Ricoeur's theory of metaphor, read Sandra W. Perpich, *A Hermeneutical Critic of Strucuralist Exegesis* (Lanham, Md: University of America Press, 1984), 130–33, and Kevin Vanhoozer, *Biblical Narrative in the Philosophy of Paul Ricouer* (New York: Cambridge University Press, 1990).

6. Paul Ricoeur, *Interpretation Theory: Discourse and the Surplus of Meaning* (Fort Worth: Texas Christian University Press, 1976), 50.

7. Ricoeur, *The Conflict of Interpretation* (Evanston, Ill.: Northwestern University Press, 1974), 83–84.

8. Beekman and Callow, *Translating the Word of God,* 124–26.

9. G. B. Caird, *The Language and Imagery of the Bible,* 145.

10. Barry J. Beitzel, "Exodus 3:14 and the Divine Name," *TJ* n.s. 1, 1980.

11. Mickelsen, *Interpreting the Bible,* 191.

12. Caird, *The Language and Imagery of the Bible,* 134.

13. Caird (*The Language and Imagery of the Bible,* 136–37) discusses this as a type of metonymy (above, 5a), but it has a different rhetorical function so we are considering it separately.

## Chapter 9

1. In a sign language, such as that of international road signs, there is also visual transparency.

2. Brown, Driver, and Briggs in their Hebrew lexicon use the sign "onomat" only rarely in their explanations of the origins of words.

3. There is also a secondary transparency between languages of a single family, e.g., the Romance languages. Some elements of English are transparent to those who know Greek and Latin.

4. *Israel,* 111. Cf. also G. A. Smith, "The Hebrew Genius," in *The Legacy of Israel,* Edwyn R. Bevans and Charles Singer, eds. (Oxford: Clarendon, 1928): "Hebrew may be called primarily a language of the senses" (10); "Few abstract terms exist in ancient Hebrew and no compound words. Abstraction and constructive power are almost as absent from the grammar and the syntax as from the vocabulary" (11).

5. Ibid., 30ff. For the distinction between general and abstract, see John Stewart Mill's attack on Locke ("A System of Logic," in *Utilitarianism and Other Essays,* ed. John Stuart Mills and Jeremy Bentham [Middlesex: n.p.], bk. 1 ch. ii. 4). Cf. S. Ullmann, *Words and Their Use* (New York: Philosophical Library, n.d.), 119; and on "primitive languages" see ibid., 120. Also A. O.

Barfield, "Poetic Diction," in *Essays Presented to Charles Williams* (1947; reprint, Eerdmans, 1966): "that luckless dustbin of pseudo-scientific fantasies, the mind of primitive man" (74).

6. *On Englishing the Bible* (London: Burns & Oates, 1949), 11.
7. Very occasionally they were confused by copyists (e.g., 2 Cor. 1:15; 3 John 4), but these are errors of sight or sound rather than of sense.
8. See J. Barr, *The Biblical Words for Time* (London: SCM, 1962).
9. Cf. Barfield, "Poetic Diction," "The service rendered by these latter [grammarians and philologists] both to speech and to thought is of the utmost importance; their error merely lay in supposing that life actually created language after the manner in which their logic reconstructed it," 82.
10. J. D. P. Bolton, *Glory, Jest and Riddle* (New York: Harcourt, Brace and World, 1963), 43.
11. S. I. Hayakawa, *Symbol, Status and Personality* (New York: Harcourt, Brace and World, 1963), 20.
12. C. S. Lewis, 86. A tactical definition is one in which a term is so defined as to guarantee the conclusion required.
13. *Mimesis*, 9.
14. For a structural analysis of this story, which tabulates all the missing features, see D. Patte, *What Is Structural Exegesis?* (Philadelphia: Fortress, 1986).
15. W. Empson in his *Seven Types of Ambiguity* includes some types from each class, along with that type of vagueness, here called indeterminacy.
16. *Iudaeos impulsore Chresto assidue tumultuantes Roma expulit.*
17. See F. Blass, A. DeBrunner and R. W. Funk, *A Grammar of New Testament Greek* (Chicago: University of Chicago Press, 1961), §§ 169–86.
18. For the evidence in favor of the appositive, see G. B. Caird, *Paul's Letters from Prison.* Rabbinic exegesis understood Psalm 68 to be about Moses' ascent of Sinai to receive the law and his descent to give it to Israel. The author of Ephesians (be he Paul or another) claims that the psalm is about Christ's ascent to heaven and His return "to earth below" at Pentecost to bestow spiritual gifts on the church.
19. Since two of these Old Testament passages are cited together in Romans 9:32–33, it is a plausible suggestion that both writers were using a common source, perhaps an early Christian hymn in which the quotations were already associated. See E. G. Selwyn, *The First Epistle of Peter* (Grand Rapids: Baker, 1981), 268–81.

## Chapter 10

1. *Gnomon of the New Testament* (Edinburgh: Clark, 1877), in loco.
2. Cf. Ewald Stier, *Words of the Lord* (New York: Tibbals, 1864), in loco.
3. Henry Alford, *The Greek Testament,* 4 vols. (London: Rivingtons, 1871), in loco.
4. Cf. J. B. Lightfoot, *Commentary on Galatians* (New York: Macmillan, 1890), on Galatians 4:11.
5. Charles Hodge, *An Exposition of the Second Epistle to the Corinthians* (New York: Armstrong and Son, 1891), in loco.
6. Arthur P. Stanley, *The Epistles of St. Paul to the Corinthians* (London: Murray, 1876), in loco.
7. Samuel Davidson, *Sacred Hermeneutics* (Edinburgh: Clark, 1843), 616.

8. On the history and character of all these ancient versions, see Harman's, Keil's, or Bleek's "Introduction"; also the various biblical dictionaries and cyclopaedias.
9. The commentaries of Theodoret and Theophylact are largely composed of extracts from Chrysostom. To the same class belong the commentaries of Euthymius, Zigabenus, Ecumenius, Andreas, and Arethas. The Catenae of the Greek Fathers by Procopius, Olympiodorus, and Nicephorus treat several books of the Old Testament. The celebrated Catena Aurea of Thomas Aquinas covers the Four Gospels, and was translated and published at Oxford in 1845 by J. H. Newman.

## Chapter 11

1. See E. D. Hirsch, *Validity in Interpretation* (New Haven: Yale University, 1961), chap. 1.
2. Second Timothy 3:16 refers to the *writings* (γραφή) as inspired. Paul spoke of "*words* taught by the Spirit" (1 Cor. 2:13). Over and over again the New Testament authors use the phrase "It is *written*" to describe the locus of divine authority (cf. Matt. 4:4, 7, 10).
3. This shift from the text to the author's intention behind the text is evident in Jack Rogers (who follows G. C. Berkouwer). See Rogers, *The Authority and Interpretation of the Bible* (New York: Harper & Row, 1979), 393, 430.
4. This is to say that language (i.e., a sentence) is not an instrumental cause of meaning; it is the formal cause. Individual words (symbols) are the instruments *through* which meaning is conveyed. But language (sentences) is that *in* which meaning resides. The failure to understand this distinction leads some wrongly to think of meaning as being *behind* language rather than being expressed *in* it.
5. Of course our understanding of any text depends on knowing the meaning of the words used. So in this sense all the "parts" (words) of the meaning are known apart from the text. However, the "whole" of the meaning itself stands alone and is independent of extratextual factors (see discussion on the hermeneutical circle below under "Context Determines Meaning").
6. Systematic theology is as meaningful as science is, for the theology is to the Bible (God's special revelation) what science is to nature (God's general revelation). Both are a systematic approach to the truths of God has revealed in a nonsystematic way. In each case God has given the truths and left it for man to organize them in an orderly way.
7. See Harold De Wolf, *A Theology of the Living Church* (New York: Harper & Brothers, 1953), 147; and Langdon Gilkey, *Maker of Heaven and Earth* (Garden City, N.Y.: Doubleday, 1959), 33.
8. See Letha Scanzoni and Virginia Mollenkott, *Is the Homosexual My Neighbor?* (New York: Harper & Row, 1978), 59–60; and Norman Pittenger, *Gay Life Styles* (Los Angeles: Universal Fellowship, 1977), 80–81.
9. See Rudolf Bultmann, "New Testament and Mythology," in Reginald H. Fuller, trans., *Kerygma and Myth: A Theological Debate*, ed. Hans Werner Bartsch (London: Billing and Sons, 1954), 1–8.
10. Rogers, *Authority and Interpretation*, 393, 428, and *Biblical Authority* (Waco, Tex.: Word, 1978), 17, 21, 42–43). Rogers wrote: "To keep to the thoughts and intentions of the biblical writers we must . . . remember that their purpose

was to bring us, not information in general, but the good news of salvation" (*Biblical Authority*, 21).

11.  In an interview in the *Wittenburg Door* (Feb.–March, 1980) Rogers said, "Let's get the record straight. I have never said verbally or in print, that the Bible has mistakes in it" (21). Kenneth Kantzer also cites Rogers's belief in "the complete truth of the Bible . . ." in *Christianity Today* (Sept. 4, 1981), 18.

12.  Rogers, *Authority and Interpretation*, 428–29.

13.  See Donald Glenn, "Psalm 8 and Hebrews 2: A Case Study in Biblical Hermeneutics and Biblical Theology," in *Walvoord: A Tribute*, ed. Donald K. Campbell (Chicago: Moody, 1982), 49.

14.  Ibid., 48.

15.  If only what the author is *concentrating on* is true but not everything he *affirms*, then two serious problems result. First, the classic statement of the inspiration of Scripture would not be true that "whatever the Bible says [affirms], God says [affirms]." This means that the Bible may be affirming some things that God is not affirming. If this is so then the Bible is not the Word of God; it simply *contains* the Word of God. Second, if truth is not centered in what the text is actually says (affirms), but only what the author is *concentrating on*, then hermeneutics is reduced to a guessing game about the state of the author's consciousness. In short, the focus has been shifted from the objective text to the subjective area of an author's intention behind the text.

16.  Ibid., 47.

17.  As cited by S. Lewis Johnson, *The Old Testament in the New: An Argument for Biblical Inspiration* (Grand Rapids: Zondervan, 1980), 64.

18.  Calvin may be interpreted another way than implied here. Calvin does not really say that by using the purpose (why) of the biblical author one can explain away a mistake the author makes. Rather, Calvin simply points out that the New Testament writers did not always use the *exact words* of the Old Testament writers they quoted, but they did remain faithful to the *meaning* of the Old Testament texts they quoted. In Calvin's own words, the biblical writers "have careful regard for the main object so as not to turn Scripture to a false *meaning*, but as far as *words* are concerned, as in other things which are not relevant to the present *purpose*, they allow themselves some indulgence" (*Calvin's New Testament Commentaries* [Grand Rapids: Eerdmans, 1979], 12.136; emphasis added).

19.  See Sidney Greidanus, *Sola Scriptura: Problems and Principles in Preaching Historical Texts* (Toronto: Wedge Publications Foundation), 70–71.

20.  The recent "Chicago Statement on Biblical Hermeneutics" by the International Council on Biblical Inerrancy (Nov. 1982) pointedly addresses this issue as follows: "WE DENY that Scripture may be interpreted in such a way as to suggest that one passage corrects or militates against another. We deny that later writers of Scripture misinterpreted earlier passages of Scripture when quoting from or referring to them" (Article XVII).

21.  Zechariah 12:10 ("They shall look on me whom they have pierced") is applied both to the first coming of Christ (John 19:37) and to His second coming (Rev. 1:7). Isaiah's teaching (chap. 53) about Jesus bearing our sickness is applied to both spiritual healing (1 Peter 2:24) and also to physical healing (Matt. 8:17).

22.  The end does not justify the means either in ethics or in hermeneutics. The

end manifests the means, but it does not *justify* it. The means must justify themselves. If there is no justification for the means, then they are unjustified. This applies to meaning as well as to values.

## Chapter 12

1.  *Expository Thoughts on the Gospel* II (Grand Rapids: Zondervan, 1953), 383.
2.  For example, Walter C. Kaiser, Jr., "The Eschatological Hermeneutics of Evangelicalism: Promise Theology," *Journal of Evangelical Theological Society* 13 (1970), 94–96.
3.  *A Grammar of the Greek New Testament in Light of Historical Research*, 4th ed. (1923), 735–36.
4.  F. Blass and A. DeBrunner, *A Greek Grammar of the New Testament*, rev. and trans. Robert W. Funk (Chicago: University of Chicago Press, 1961), 155.
5.  W. F. Arndt and F. W. Gingrich, *A Greek-English Lexicon of the New Testament* (Chicago: University of Chicago Press, 1957), 691.
6.  Briggs, *International Critical Commentary on 1 Peter* (Edinburgh: T & T Clark), 107–108; Selwyn, *The First Epistles of St. Peter* (London: Macmillan, 1955), 134–38.
7.  Blass, DeBrunner, Funk, *A Greek Grammar of the New Testament*, 155.
8.  For a discussion of this passage, see Moses Stuart's "On the Alleged Obscurity of Prophecy," *The Biblical Repository* 2 (1832), 239–40; "Remarks on Hahn's Definition of Interpretation and Some Topics Connected with It," *The Biblical Repository* 1 (1831): 146ff.; *Hints on the Interpretation of Prophecy*, 2d ed. (Andover: Allen, Morrill & Wardwell, 1842), 56–58.
9.  *Words of the Lord Jesus* VI (Edinburgh: Clark, 1865), 56.
10. As quoted in Edwyn C. Hoskyns, *The Fourth Gospel*, 2d ed. (London: Faber and Faber, 1947), 412; C. K. Barrett, *Gospel According to St. John* (London: SPCK, 1960), 339.
11. Stier, *Words of Lord Jesus*, 57.
12. B. F. Westcott, *Gospel According to St. John* (Grand Rapids: Eerdmans, 1967), 175. Other examples of John's use of irony are listed: John 7:41–42; 19:21.
13. Three interpretations are given to this "prophesying": (1) The accidental lots or circumstances of life were echoes by which the heavenly revelation was given to men; (2) Involuntary [?] prophecy like Balaam's words in Numbers 23–24; and (3) The high priest as bearer of divine revelation—usually through the Urim and Thummim.

    The second view is certainly wrong since Balaam and Scripture claimed divine authority for what he said. The first view is possible since Pharaoh, Saul, Nebuchadnezzar, and Pilate all were in act and word witnesses to the truth, but then "prophesied" would have a secondary sense in John's use. The third is likewise deficient in that the Urim and Thummim were used to obtain a yes or no answer. The office of prophet and apostle was God's channel of biblical revelation.
14. See, for example, Peter Richardson, "Spirit and Letter: A Foundation for Hermeneutics," *Evangelical Quarterly* 45 (1973): 208–18. He concludes (218) that while Paul based his argument on "what is written," Paul's method and results show a great deal of freedom so that there is "no final and authoritative interpretation, nor even, perhaps, a final and authoritative principle of interpretation"!

15. For further discussion on these texts, see Walter C. Kaiser, Jr., "The Weightier and Lighter Matters of the Law," in *Current Issues in Biblical and Patristic Interpretation*, ed. Gerald Hawthorne (Grand Rapids: Eerdmans, 1975), 187–88.

16. Once again E. D. Hirsch, Jr. has clarified this issue best in his *Aims of Interpretation* (Chicago: University of Chicago Press, 1976), 2–4: ". . . 'meaning' refers to the whole verbal meaning of a text and 'significance' to textual meaning in relation to a larger context—another mind, another era, a wider subject matter, an alien system of values. . . ."

17. "The Original Meaning of the Text and Other Legitimate Subject for Semantic Description," in *Questions Disputees d'ancien Testament*, ed. C. Brekemans (Leuven: Leuven University Press, 1974), 63–70.

18. For a sympathetic discussion, see John F. Johnson, "*Analogia Fidei* as Hermeneutical Principle," *Springfielder* 36 (1972–73): 249–59.

19. Kenneth Kantzer has wisely suggested that a better name for the phenomena described here would be something like the "Analogy of the Revelational Context," in other words, that part of Scripture which served as the context of revelation received prior to the writing of the immediate context under investigation. The "Analogy of Scripture" has been employed to designate various things in the history of the church. See my limited defense of this term in "The Present State of Old Testament Studies," *Journal of Evangelical Theological Society* 18 (1975): 73–74.

20. See the strong stand on this matter taken by George M. Landes, "Biblical Exegesis in Crisis: What Is the Exegetical Task in a Theological Context?" *Union Seminary Quarterly Review* 26 (1970): 275–77. "Any exegesis that refuses to expound the theological dimensions in these writings overlooks their *raison d'etre*."

## Chapter 13

1. Walter C. Kaiser, Jr., "The Single Intent of Scripture," in *Evangelical Roots*, ed. Kenneth C. Kantzer (Nashville: Nelson, 1978), 123–42.

2. Ibid., 138 (italics added).

3. Walter C. Kaiser, Jr., "A Response to Author's Intention and Biblical Interpretation," in *Hermeneutics, Inerrancy, and the Bible*, ed. Earl D. Radmacher and Robert D. Preus (Grand Rapids: Zondervan), 1984, 442 (italics his).

4. Ibid., 445–46.

5. Kaiser, "The Single Intent of Scripture," 126 (italics added).

6. "The Chicago Statement on Biblical Hermeneutics, Article XVIII," in *Hermeneutics, Inerrancy, and the Bible*, 889–900.

7. William Sanford LaSor, "The *Sensus Plenior* and Biblical Interpretation," in *Scripture, Tradition and Interpretation*, ed. W. Ward Gasque and William Sanford LaSor (Grand Rapids: Eerdmans, 1978), 260–77.

8. Ibid., 263.

9. Ibid., 266.

10. Ibid., 268.

11. Ibid. (italics added).

12. Walter C. Kaiser, Jr., *Toward and Exegetical Theology* (Grand Rapids: Baker, 1981).

13. Kaiser, "A Response to Author's Intention and Biblical Interpretation," 441–42.

14. I. Howard Marshall, "Introduction," in *New Testament Interpretation: Essays on Principles and Methods*, ed. I. Howard Marshall (Grand Rapids: Eerdmans, 1977), 11–14.

15. Kaiser, "A Response to Author's Intention," 442.

16. Ludwig Koehler and Walter Baumgartner, eds., *Lexicon in Veteris Testament Libros* (Leiden: E. J. Brill, 1958), 709.

17. *Theological Word Book of the Old Testament*, s.v. "עלמה," by Allan MacRae, 2:672.

18. Robert Dick Wilson, "The Meaning of 'ALMA (AV virgin) in Isaiah 7:14," *Princeton Theological Review* 24 (1926): 308.

19. Anthony A. Hoekema, *The Bible and the Future* (Grand Rapids: Eerdmans, 1979), 209.

20. *Theological Word Book of the Old Testament*, s.v. "אות," by Robert L. Alden, 1:19.

21. Willis J. Beecher, *The Prophets and the Promise* (1905; reprint, Grand Rapids: Baker, 1963).

22. *The New International Dictionary of New Testament Theology*, s.v. "σημειο ν," by O. Hofius, 2:627.

23. Edward J. Young, *The Book of Isaiah*, 3 vols. (Grand Rapids: Eerdmans, 1965, 1967, 1969), 1:291–92.

## Chapter 14

1. B. B. Warfield, *The Inspiration and Authority of the Bible* (Philadelphia: Presbyterian & Reformed, 1948), 143.

2. Ibid., 299ff.

3. Ibid., 240.

4. The material to be found under this heading has in substance been set forth with more detail in a paper presented to the sixth annual meeting of the Evangelical Theological Society, December 30, 1954, at Ringwood, New Jersey. This paper was published in Volume I of the *Gordon Review*, February and May, 1955. Further detail and discussion of the actual quotations in the New Testament, especially in Matthew, were presented in an S.T.M. thesis submitted by the present writer to the faculty of Gordon Divinity School in 1940 under the title: "The Old Testament Quotations in the New with special reference to the Doctrine of the Plenary Inspiration of the Bible."

5. Samuel Davidson, *Sacred Hermeneutics* (Edinburgh: Clark, 1843), 515.

6. If it be urged that these scholars were not inspired and that therefore their writings can scarcely be compared to Holy Writ, this point will be freely granted. What is significant here, however, is the fact that methods of quotation similar to those of the New Testament writers were used and are still now being used by men who can hardly be viewed as ignorant of the minor differences between the original text and the translations they adduce, and still less as intending to authenticate by their citation what they know to be divergent. These men's unquestioned competence, integrity, and attachment to truth prove, for themselves as well as for the inspired authors, that the methods in question do not connote an endorsement of error.

7. W. G. Campbell, *A Form Book for Thesis Writing* (New York: Houghton Mifflin, 1939), 15.

8. Franklin Johnson, *The Quotations of the New Testament from the Old*

*Considered in the Light of General Literature* (London: Baptist Tract and Book Society, 1896).

9. Patrick Fairbairn, *Hermeneutical Manual* (Edinburgh: Clark, 1858), 355.
10. C. H. Toy, *Quotations in the New Testament* (New York: Scribner's, 1884), xx.
11. Patrick Fairbairn, *Hermeneutical Manual* (Philadelphia: Smith, 1859), 413ff.
12. C. H. Dodd, *According to the Scriptures* (London: Nisbet, 1952), 130.
13. Ibid., 109.
14. Toy, *Quotations in the New Testament*, xxv.
15. Warfield, *The Inspiration and Authority of the Bible*, 218–20.
16. Ibid., 220.
17. Toy, *Quotations in the New Testament*, xxx.
18. R. Rothe, *Zur Dogmatik* (Gotha: Perthes, 1869), 177f.
19. E. Huehn, *Die Alttestamentlichen Citate . . . im Neuen Testament* (Tübingen: Mohr, 1900), 272.

## Chapter 15

1. Bright, *The Authority of the Old Testament* (Nashville: Abingdon, 1967), 202–3.
2. Cf. the examples given by B. F. C. Atkinson, "The Textual Background of the Use of the Old Testament by the New," *Journal of the Transactions of the Victoria Institute* 79 (1947): 49.
3. See NIV preface for further details.
4. R. E. Murphy, "The Relationship Between the Testaments," *Catholic Biblical Quarterly* 26 (July 1964): 356.
5. See NIV preface for further details; see also Atkinson, "The Textual Background of the Use of the Old Testament by the New," 39–41, 54–55; S. Lewis Johnson, Jr., *The Old Testament in the New* (Grand Rapids: Zondervan, 1980), 54; G. L. Archer, Jr., and G. Chirichigno, *Old Testament Quotations in the New Testament* (Chicago: Moody, 1983), ix, xi, xxv–xxvi; S. Davidson, *Sacred Hermeneutics* (Edinburgh: Clark; London: Hamilton Adams, 1843), 334–35; C. E. Armerding, *The Old Testament and Criticism* (Grand Rapids: Eerdmans, 1983), 106; R. Nicole, "New Testament Use of the Old Testament," in *Revelation and the Bible*, ed. C. F. H. Henry (Grand Rapids: Baker, 1958), 142.
6. See NIV footnotes at 2 Timothy 2:19; Hebrews 10:7.
7. Nicole, "New Testament Use of the Old Testament," 144.
8. See ibid., 144–45; R. T. France, *Jesus and the Old Testament* (Downers Grove, Ill.: InterVarsity, 1971), 27, 259; E. E. Ellis, *Paul's Use of the Old Testament* (Grand Rapids: Eerdmans, 1957), 11, 14–15; *Old Testament Quotations in the New Testament*, rev. ed., ed. by R. G. Bratcher (London: United Bible Societies, 1967), 103; Archer and Chirichigno, *Old Testament Quotations*, xxviii, xxxii; H. M. Shires, *Finding the Old Testament in the New* (Philadelphia: Westminster, 1974), 16–17; Atkinson, "The Textual Background of the Use of the Old Testament by the New," 39–41.
9. Nicole, "New Testament Use of the Old Testament," 137.
10. Shires, *Finding the Old Testament in the New*, 66.
11. Davidson, *Sacred Hermeneutics*, 446.
12. Nicole, "New Testament Use of the Old Testament," 137.
13. *Old Testament Quotations in the New Testament* (ed. Bratcher).

14. Nicole, "New Testament Use of the Old Testament," 138. Cf. also W. C. Kaiser, Jr., *The Use of the Old Testament in the New* (Chicago: Moody, 1985), 2.
15. Ellis, *Paul's Use of the Old Testament*, 11.
16. Johnson, *The Old Testament in the New*, 27.
17. Nicole, "New Testament Use of the Old Testament," 138.
18. Wenham, *Christ and the Bible*, 128.
19. See also the NIV footnote there for a discussion of textual variants in the verse.
20. Inexplicably the NIV reads "sin" in Deuteronomy 24:16 but "sins" in 2 Kings 14:6 and its parallel 2 Chronicles 25:4, though the Hebrew word is identical in all three passages.
21. Wenham, *Christ and the Bible*, 145; Davidson, *Sacred Hermeneutics*, 336–37; E. A. Blum, "Jude," in *The Expositor's Bible Commentary*, ed. F. E. Gaebelein (Grand Rapids: Zondervan, 1981), 12:393.
22. Atkinson, "The Textual Background of the Use of the Old Testament by the New," 45.
23. Ibid., 39.
24. C. H. Toy, *Quotations in the New Testament* (New York: Scribner's, 1884), xxxvii; R. V. G. Tasker, *The Old Testament in the New Testament* (Grand Rapids: Eerdmans, 1968), 146; Kaiser, *The Use of the Old Testament in the New*, 3.
25. Johnson, *The Old Testament in the New*, 17, agrees concerning Revelation that "there is not one formal citation from the Old Testament in the book" but immediately goes on to say—inexplicably and obfuscatingly—that "many of the allusions, however, are intended as citations."
26. Wenham, *Christ and the Bible*, 159.
27. Nicole, "New Testament Use of the Old Testament," 138.
28. Ibid.
29. For details see Atkinson, "The Textual Background of the Use of the Old Testament by the New," 52. Several of the volumes that deal extensively with quotations of the Old Testament in the New Testament include helpful indices that list, in canonical order, New Testament quotations as well as Old Testament passages cited (see, e.g., Toy, *Quotations in the New Testament*, 283–316; Shires, *Finding the Old Testament in the New*, 215–51).
30. "Interestingly the quotations from the Septuagint agree mainly with the characteristically Palestinian form of the LXX, represented by MSS A, Q and Lucian" (Wenham, *Christ and the Bible*, 95).
31. Archer and Chirichigno, *Old Testament Quotations in the New Testament*, ix. The situation with respect to the Book of Hebrews is not so clear as with Matthew, however; see, e.g., Atkinson, "The Textual Background of the Use of the Old Testament by the New," 39.
32. See, e.g., Toy, *Quotations in the New Testament*, xiv–xv; F. F. Bruce in Atkinson, "The Textual Background of the Use of the Old Testament by the New," 60–62.
33. See especially M. McNamara, *Targum and Testament* (Grand Rapids: Eerdmans, 1972).
34. J. R. Harris, *Testimonies*, 2 vols. (Cambridge: University Press, 1916, 1920).
35. See further Ellis, *Paul's Use of the Old Testament*, 98–113; D. M. Smith, Jr., "The Use of the Old Testament in the New," in *The Use of the Old Testament in the New and Other Essays*, ed. J. M. Efird (Durham: Duke University Press, 1972), 25–30.

36. See NIV footnotes at 2 Timothy 2:19; Hebrews 10:7; and Psalm 40:6.
37. Davidson, *Sacred Hermeneutics*, 335; Archer and Chirichigno, *Old Testament Quotations in the New Testament*, ix; Ellis, *Paul's Use of the Old Testament*, 12.
38. Johnson, *The Old Testament in the New*, 27; C. H. Dodd, *The Old Testament in the New* (Philadelphia: Fortress, 1963), 20; C. Westermann, *The Old Testament and Jesus Christ* (Minneapolis: Augsburg, n.d.), 12–14; S. L. Edgar, "Respect for Context in Quotations from the Old Testament," *New Testament Studies* 9 (1962–63): 55–62. Contrast R. T. Mead, "A Dissenting Opinion about Respect for Context in Old Testament Quotations," *NTS* 10 (1963–64): 279–89.
39. See, e.g., B. K. Waltke, "Is It Right to Read the New Testament into the Old?" *Christianity Today,* September 2, 1983, 77; Wenham, *Christ and the Bible*, 107.
40. Wenham, *Christ and the Bible*, 107.
41. France, *Jesus and the Old Testament*, 27.
42. Archer and Chirichigno, *Old Testament Quotations in the New Testament*, xxv.
43. Such free quotation need not distort the quoted author's intended meaning, of course; see, e.g., Johnson, *The Old Testament in the New*, 11; Wenham, *Christ and the Bible*, 93.
44. For further examples, see Ellis, *Paul's Use of the Old Testament*, 186.
45. Johnson, *The Old Testament in the New*, 76.
46. R. Youngblood, "A Response to 'Patrick Fairbairn and Biblical Hermeneutics as Related to the Quotations of the Old Testament in the New,'" in *Hermeneutics, Inerrancy, and the Bible*, edited by E. D. Radmacher and R. D. Preus (Grand Rapids: Zondervan, 1984), 779–88. See also R. R. Nicole in ibid., 767–76; S. L. Johnson in ibid., 791–99.
47. Murphy, "The Relationship Between the Testaments," 353.
48. See, e.g., Johnson, *The Old Testament in the New*, 76; A. B. Mickelsen, *Interpreting the Bible* (Grand Rapids: Eerdmans, 1963), 40; Wenham, *Christ and the Bible*, 99–107; W. M. Dunnett, *The Interpretation of Holy Scripture* (Nashville: Nelson, 1984), 49–54.
49. Murphy, "The Relationship Between the Testaments," 357.
50. London: Geoffrey Chapman, 1961.
51. See, e.g., Nicole, "New Testament Use of the Old Testament," 147–48.
52. B. B. Knopp in Atkinson, "The Textual Background of the Use of the Old Testament by the New," 66. See also similarly Nicole, "New Testament Use of the Old Testament," 148.

## Chapter 16

1. A survey of recent evangelical literature on this subject shows that at the technical monograph level, the evangelical societal level, and the level of more popular works, this issue is the subject of major concern. Article XIII of the Chicago Statement on Biblical Inerrancy dealt in its denial section with an issue raised by Old Testament in the New Testament phenomena. Also 2 of the 16 areas raised at the ICBI 1983 Summit Conference on Hermeneutics dealt directly with this subject, namely, "Author's Intention and Biblical Interpretation," and "Patrick Fairbairn and Biblical Hermeneutics as Related to

Quotations of the Old Testament in the New." These are chapters 7 and 14 of *Hermeneutics, Inerrancy and the Bible*, ed. Earl D. Radmacher and Robert D. Preus (Grand Rapids: Zondervan, 1984). At this conference, Article XVIII of the Affirmations and Denials dealt specifically with this subject. Article XVIII is presented in the Radmacher and Preus volume, page 885, while Article XIII can be found in *Inerrancy*, ed. Norman L. Geisler (Grand Rapids: Zondervan, 1979). 496. The last decade has produced a myriad of evangelical works in this area as this article will show.

2. The author hopes at a future date to write a follow-up work that sets forth a detailed consideration of the author's position on specific texts in relationship to the four schools referred to in this article. However, in fairness it should be stated that the author sees himself in most agreement with the second and third schools of the upcoming discussion: but as to which side among these two views he falls, even he cannot say at this time for reasons that this two-part series will show. The author's doctoral work at the University of Aberdeen was on this subject: see his *Proclamation from Prophecy and Pattern: Lucan Old Testament Christology* (Sheffield: *JSOT*, forthcoming), which examines all the major Christological Old Testament passages in Luke-Acts.

3. Walter C. Kaiser, Jr., *The Uses of the Old Testament in the New* (Chicago: Moody, forthcoming). Kaiser has kindly allowed the author access to proofs of his important new work. The references to it will be to sections of the book since it is not yet published. These remarks are made in his introduction to Part II: "The Prophetic Use of the Old Testament in the New." The book will be an important catalyst for discussion on this topic. [This book was published in 1985.—Editor's Note.]

4. See, for example, Kaiser's forthcoming work (see n. 3), Richard Longenecker, *Biblical Exegesis in the Apostolic Age* (Grand Rapids: Eerdmans, 1974); S. Lewis Johnson, *The Old Testament in the New* (Grand Rapids: Zondervan, 1980); and Bruce K. Waltke, "A Canonical Process Approach to the Psalms," in *Tradition and Testament*, ed. John S. Feinberg and Paul D. Feinberg (Chicago: Moody, 1981. However, these authors each represent a different approach to the issue.

5. Kaiser, *The Uses of the Old Testament in the New*, the chapter on the prophetic use of the Old Testament; and Walter C. Kaiser, Jr., "Legitimate Hermeneutics," in *Inerrancy*, esp. 133–38.

6. Kaiser. "Legitimate Hermeneutics," 137, citing Willis J. Beecher, *The Prophets and the Promise* (Grand Rapids: Baker, 1975), 130.

7. Beecher, *The Prophets and the Promise*, 130.

8. Kaiser, *The Uses of the Old Testament in the New*, in Part II on prophecy in the section on "Double or Generic Fulfillment" (italics his).

9. Ibid., Part II, section on "B.C. and A.D. Fulfillment?"

10. S. Lewis Johnson cites J. I. Packer with approval (*The Old Testament in the New*, 50). Elliott E. Johnson, "Author's Intention and Biblical Interpretation" in *Hermeneutics, Inerrancy and the Bible*, 409–29. One of the respondents to Elliott E. Johnson's paper was Kaiser (441–47).

11. More on this point will follow later in this section.

12. E. D. Hirsch, *Validity in Interpretation* (New Haven, Conn.: Yale University Press, 1967). Kaiser also appeals to Hirsch for support, but in the matter of human intention. The major difference between this school and Kaiser's view

is on the question of what the human author knew and the emphasis on full intention at different places: human author (Kaiser) versus divine author (Johnsons).

13. S. L. Johnson, *The Old Testament in the New*, 50.

14. Ibid.; and James I. Packer, "Biblical Authority, Hermeneutics, and Inerrancy," in *Jerusalem and Athens: Critical Discussion on the Theology and Apologetics of Cornelius Van Til*, ed. E. R. Geehan (Nutley, N.J.: Presbyterian & Reformed Publishing House, 1971), 147–48 (italics added, except for the words "sensus plenior").

15. E. E. Johnson, "Author's Intention and Biblical Interpretation," 416.

16. Semanticists suggest many levels at which the meaning of "meaning" may be discussed! They are: (1) meaning$^R$ (= referent or reference; identifies the specific person[s], things[s], or concept[s] named); (2) meaning$^S$ (= sense; describes the qualities of person[s], thing[s], event[s], or concept[s] named); (3) meaning$^V$ (= value, "this means more to me than to anyone else"); (4) meaning$^E$ (= entailment or implication, "this discussion means we are discussing the area of . . . or it involves including the following details of . . ."); (5) meaning$^I$ (= intention, what a speaker wishes to declare by his use of language); (6) meaning$^{EM}$ (= emotive meaning, the emotion which a speaker intends to convey); and (7) meaning$^{Sig.}$ (= significance, "this means that I must . . ."). In discussions on what an author "means," it is helpful to know what level of meaning one has in mind. Also with the issue of significance it is important to distinguish between "what it was intended to mean" (author's meaning) and "what it means to me" (significance) (see G. B. Caird, *The Language and Imagery of the Bible* [Philadelphia: Westminster, 1980], 37–40; and J. P. Louw, *Semantics of New Testament Greek* [Philadelphia: Fortress, 1982] 147–66).

17. E. E. Johnson, "Author's Intention and Biblical Interpretation," 427 (italics his).

18. An alternative way to view Psalm 16 in the same framework is to argue that David spoke of his own deliverance with such confidence that he knew "nothing would separate him from God," that is, God would not abandon him either in an early death (so some interpreters) or ultimately (so others). The sense of the passage is found in this expression of confidence; but the "how" of the passage, an aspect of the referent, depends on the subject fulfilling it. For David, the how of the referent is never historically revealed; but for Christ, the "how" is in resurrection. Therefore Peter, knowing that the fulfillment for David was never revealed and realizing that Christ did fulfill it, proclaimed Jesus as the Holy One who truly fulfills the Psalm 16 text in Acts 2:25–32. For details of this approach to the passage and alternative views, text in Acts 2:25–32. For details of this approach to the passage and alternate view, see Bock, *Proclamation from Prophecy and Pattern: Lucan Old Testament Christology*, the section on Acts 2:25.

19. The originator of this approach as it is grounded in Jewish methodology is Otto Michel, *Paulus und seine Bibel* (Gütersloh, 1929; reprint, Darmstadt: Wissenschaftliche Buchgesellschaft, 1972). The fundamental monograph study on Pauline Old Testament hermeneutics also comes from this school: Earle E. Ellis, *Paul's Use of the Old Testament* (Grand Rapids: Baker, 1957). For a brief introduction to Jewish hermeneutics, see Richard Longenecker, *Biblical Exegesis in the Apostolic Period* (Grand Rapids: Eerdmans, 1974), 19–50,

and the extremely well done but technical work by D. J. Moo, *The Old Testament in the Gospel Passion Narratives* (Sheffield: Almond, 1983), 5–78. This latter work is full of revelant historical data. Also see Earle E. Ellis, "How the New Testament Uses the Old," in *New Testament Interpretation*, ed. I. Howard Marshall (Grand Rapids: Eerdmans, 1977), 201–8.

20. Longenecker, *Biblical Exegesis in the Apostolic Period*, 205.
21. Ibid., 205–14. Walter M. Dunnett recognizes the tension such an approach creates and thus attempts to defend the concept of *sensus plenior* (*The Interpretation of Holy Scripture* [Nashville: Nelson, 1984], 39–64, esp. 57–64).
22. Dunnett, *The Interpretation of Scripture*. Another writer who defends *sensus plenior* and represents this viewpoint is Donald Hagner, "The Old Testament in the New Testament," in *Interpreting the Word of God: Festschrift in Honor of Steven-Barabas*, ed. Samuel J. Schultz and Morris Inch (Chicago: Moody, 1976), 78–104.
23. Ellis mentions their theological presuppositions, such as a salvation historical perspective that involves a two-stage consummation in Jesus' two comings, the use of typology, corporate solidarity, and the right to charismatic exegesis ("How the New Testament Uses the Old," 109–14).
24. The appeal to ideas of intertestamental Judaism need not be inherently a problem. The use of the term "the Messiah" as a technical term for the Davidic Descendant who will fulfill God's promise is an intertestamental term from the Psalms of Solomon 17–18. To cite such points of theology is not to make these works authoritative; rather it is to say that some developments in intertestamental Judaism were accurate reflections of divine realities based on the Old Testament. God is to be seen as working sovereignly in the conceptual world of the first century as much as He is seen to be working sovereignly in the sociopolitical world of the first century to prepare all the world for the message of Christ given in linguistic and conceptual terms to which they could relate. For an overview of intertestamental Jewish theology as expressed in its apocalyptic literature, see D. R. Russell, *The Message and Methods of Jewish Apocalyptic* (Philadelphia: Westminster, 1964).
25. Longenecker, *Biblical Exegesis in the Apostolic Period*, 207 (italics added).
26. Ibid., 207–8 (italics added).
27. The qualification "with greater detail" is important. The teaching of the Old Testament is not changed or overridden; rather it is either deepened, made more specific, or is given additional elements. For example, when God told the serpent that "his seed would bruise Adam's seed on the heel," but that Adam's "seed" would crush the head of the seed of the serpent (Gen. 3:15), what would Adam's or Moses' readers *at this point* in the narrative be able to understand about the promise? It would be something like this: *Adam's seed* will eventually *have victory* over the forces of evil as represented by the serpent. The statement is true enough but it lacks detail. What would New Testament readers or Christians today see in this promise? Nothing other than that the victory of *Jesus* over Satan at the *crucifixion and resurrection* with a view to His eventual total reign is what is in view. It is called, and rightly so, the *protoevangelium*. The progress of revelation has filled in the details of the meaning of the saying (or to use the language of the previous section, the "referents" of the passage). This process could be called the "principle of refraction" within revelation.

28. Bruce K. Waltke, "A Canonical Process Approach to the Psalms," 3–18, esp. 6–10. Also see Waltke, "Is It Right to Read the New Testament into the Old?" *Christianity Today*, September 2, 1983, 77. Waltke answers the question of this article with a resounding yes.

29. Waltke, "A Canonical Process Approach to the Psalms," 7.

30. Ibid., 8.

31. Ibid., 16.

32. Waltke, "Is It Right to Read the New Testament into the Old?" 77 (italics added except for the word "literal").

## Chapter 17

1. Darrell L. Bock, "Evangelicals and the Use of the Old Testament in the New, Part 1," *Bibliotheca Sacra* 142 (July–October 1985): 209–23.

2. This hesitation with regard to Waltke's position results from the fact that he claims to hold to the original author's intent; and yet in his example from Psalm 2:6–7 he moves from an "earthly" to a "heavenly" reference between the old dispensation and the new. Such a shift in understanding seems to leave the Old Testament prophetic intention somewhat unclear. So this writer places Waltke here with a question mark as to whether this description of his view is really an accurate one (Bruce K. Waltke, "Is It Right to Read the New Testament into the Old?" *Christianity Today*, September 2, 1983, 77.

3. Walter M. Dunnett, *The Interpretation of Holy Scripture* (Nashville: Nelson, 1984), 60.

4. Ibid., 62.

5. A full treatment of example texts is beyond the scope of this article. The description given of the relationship between the human and the divine author in these Old Testament-New Testament passages reflects studies by the present writer in Luke-Acts, his teaching of a doctoral seminar on the use of the Old Testament in the New, and teaching a course on the master's level jointly with Donald R. Glenn, whose aid in articulating these issues has been indispensable. The views stated here are the author's and not necessarily Glenn's.

   A sample listing of texts reflecting the author's views might be as follows: (a) in full consciousness (i.e., directly prophetic): Psalm 110; (b) in ideal language: Psalm 16 (where the psalmist is confident of deliverance but the details of the "how" of the deliverance are not entirely clear in light of the language of the whole psalm) and Isaiah 52:13–53:12: (c) in language capable of an expansion of reference and context (i.e., in the progress of revelation): Hosea 11:1, with use of the concept of the corporate solidarity of the Son with the nation; and (d) in language that involves a pattern of fulfillment (i.e., typological prophetic): Isaiah 7:14; Psalms 2; 16 (possibly if the above categorization is not correct); Psalms 22; 69; Exodus fulfillment language in the New Testament; Isaiah 52:13–53:12; and Deuteronomy 18. Often the difference between "ideal language" and "language capable of expansion" is slight and debatable. Other passages make use of both "ideal language" and "pattern of fulfillment" (e.g., Isa. 53 is classified as "ideal language" because by the point of Isa. 53, the servant figure is described in highly individualized language). The author sees "language capable of expansion" as drawing heavily on theological concepts outside the passage in question (the theological presuppositions or hermeneutical axioms of the New Testament author) to complete its fulfillment, while "ideal language" makes decisive use of only material in the cited text. If one prefers to think of "ideal language" as a subcategory that can operate either in the progress of revelation category or in the pattern category, such an approach could be defended. The author prefers the term "pattern" to typology for reasons he has defended elsewhere (Darrell L. Bock, *Proclamation from Prophecy and Pattern* [Sheffield: *JSOT*, forthcoming], chap. 1). [This book was published in 1987.—Editor's Note.]

6. This area needs more study by evangelicals in light of recent discussions and in light of issues raised in semantics and the history of hermeneutics.

7. Douglas Moo, *The Old Testament in the Gospel Passion Narratives* (Sheffield: Almond, 1983), 75–78, 387–97. Moo probably belongs in the historical school, but he is certainly aware of the semantic issues.

8. J. P. Louw, *Semantics of New Testament Greek* (Philadelphia: Fortress, 1982), 39–66. See Bock, "Evangelicals and the Use of the Old Testament in the New, Part 1," 222, n. 16.

9. The basic question is the one raised by Waltke's article in *Christianity Today*, especially when he calls the New Testament fulfillment a "literal" fulfillment. Dispensationalists have the best way to unify the Testaments on this issue, by arguing for a "both/and" fulfillment rather than an "either/or" approach.

10. Dunnett is sensitive to this distinction in referring to the importance of starting with the original context, while Waltke's approach seems less sensitive. Much teaching, exposition, and preaching can create a misimpression when it insensitively and without qualification reads back a teaching into an earlier text without making clear that that detailed teaching may not have been what the human author had in mind for his audience at the time. Rather it should be clear that this teaching is what God was ultimately pointing toward, as His whole revelation later clarified.

11. Some of these referential relationships do not deal directly with meaning but with significance, that is, they deal not with what the passage meant or declares (meaning) but why it is relevant to another situation (significance). Some of these relationships between sense and referent are unclear as to which side of the meaning/significance distinction they fall. More work by evangelicals is needed on this issue as well.

12. Bock, "Evangelicals and the Use of the Old Testament in the New, Part 1," 216–19.

13. It is remarkable how often in key fulfillment passages in Luke-Acts, the Jewish interpretation also had an eschatological strain that elevated either wisdom, the Torah, the Messiah, or the end time in general as the final fulfillment (Bock, *Proclamation from Prophecy and Pattern*, chaps. 2–5).

14. Bock, "Evangelicals and the Use of the Old Testament in the New, Part 1," 223, n. 24.

15. Corporate solidarity is seen in "the one and the many" concepts of the Old Testament. An example is the servant figure of Isaiah, who is seen as the nation or as an individual. The use of pattern is shown in the reuse of Exodus or creation motifs in the Old Testament prophets. These hermeneutical perspectives are part of Old Testament theology.

16. A term like "midrash" is variously used in scholarly literature to refer to "Jewish exposition in general," to "the application of the Scriptures to a new setting," or to "a specific type of literary genre of Jewish literature." A term like "pesher"

can refer to "any eschatologically focused exegesis that declares that this passage is that event" or it can refer to "a specific type of exegesis" that has a specific form, where a direct reference to the mystery revealed by the pesher interpretation is required. On midrash see Gary Porton, "Defining Midrash," in *The Study of Ancient Judaism*, ed. Jacob Neusner (New York: KTAV, 1981), 1:55–92. On pesher see M. Horgan, *Presharing: Qumran Interpretations of Biblical Books* (Washington, D. C.: Catholic Biblical Association of America, 1979).

17. By authenticity, reference is made to its technical meaning in New Testament studies, that is, that a passage is authentic if it comes out of the historical setting from which it claims to arise. Many critics argue that New Testament uses of the Old Testament that claim to emerge in a *Semitic* context from Jesus' life or from the Jerusalem church in Acts, but that use a peculiarly *Greek* wording from the LXX to make their point, cannot be authentic historically, since Jesus would have used a Semitic text with its Semitic wording, as the Jerusalem church would have done. The argument ignores the fact that it is inherently likely that a Greek text or tradition would use the Greek Old Testament to render Old Testament passages for the sake of the audience rather than engaging in retranslation. This latter point, however, simply pushes back the question to the level of the historical background of the passage's argument; it does not answer the charge. Jesus' authentic use of Psalm 110 is often rejected by the use of this argument. But see Bock, *Proclamation from Prophecy and Pattern*, on Luke 20:41–44; 22:69; and Acts 2:34–35.

18. The text-critical argument is complex because in the first century various versions of both the Greek and Hebrew Old Testament text were in existence. Therefore this argument in instances where only the Greek Old Testament text has the adopted reading, while none of the extant Hebrew manuscripts do—which is often the case. For a recent work comparing texts and often using this argument, see Gleason L. Archer and G. C. Chirichigno, *Old Testament Quotations in the New Testament: A Complete Survey* (Chicago: Moody, 1983).

19. Bock, *Proclamation from Prophecy and Pattern*, especially the treatments of Psalms 110; 16; and Isaiah 55. Of course, these examples do not deal with the situations where the wording of the Greek text is used in a Greek setting to make a point. For all such situations see points 4–10 in note 21.

20. Some say that this is what is occurring with Psalm 68 in Ephesians 4. The line cited is not so much a verbatim quotation as a summary citation drawing on the rest of the context of Psalm 68, which suggests God blesses those who fought with Him. However, some do not think Psalm 68 is cited at all in this passage, since the introductory formula need not be invoking Scripture. W. Hall Harris III, a colleague of this writer, has made this suggestion to the present writer. C. H. Dodd has championed the view that often New Testament writers refer to the larger context in citing a passage (*According to the Scriptures* [London: Collins, 1952]).

21. Moisés Silva in his article "The New Testament Use of the Old Testament," in *Scripture and Truth*, ed. D. A. Carson and John Woodbridge (Grand Rapids: Zondervan, 1983), 150–57, lists eight possible approaches to dealing with an Old Testament citation in the New to describe what might be occurring. To his list, the writer after dividing one category (nos. 4 and 5 are combined by Silva) adds one more (no. 8).

a.   Corruption in the transmission of the Hebrew text.

b.   Corruption in the transmission of the LXX.

c.   Corruption in the transmission of the New Testament text.

d.   The Masoretic understanding and pointing of the text are correct over that of the LXX.

e.   The LXX understanding and syntactical arrangement of the text are correct. (This is less commonly the case).

f.   Both the Masoretic text and the LXX are correct, that is, legitimate harmony exists.

g.   The New Testament quotation of the LXX has included an erroneous part of the LXX translation which the New Testament author is not affirming.

h.   The New Testament quotation of the LXX contains a figure different from that in the Masoretic text, but the point made from the figure is exactly the same as in the Masoretic (e.g., Ps. 40 in Heb. 10) or is close enough to the Masoretic text so as not to be a problem (perhaps Ps. 8 in Heb. 2 is an example).

i.   The difference is trivial (and the biblical author affirms it). Silva rightly rejects this category.

j.   The New Testament draws on an interpretive tradition about the passage from Judaism. This tradition draws on a context larger than the passage itself, including nonbiblical sources, and represents an interpretation of the text that the New Testament author supports. (This last category is how Silva solves the Heb. 11:21 problem he discusses, thus revealing his agreement with the Longenecker school.) This last category is much discussed, and more work needs to be done in evaluating its validity.

## Chapter 18

1.  This statement is not meant to imply that narrative portions never teach doctrine directly and explicitly. The Gospel accounts of Jesus' teaching ministry are examples of narrative portions of Scripture that contain significant amounts of direct, explicit, doctrinal teaching. Narrative accounts of men acting in a prophetic capacity as spokesmen for God also often contain doctrinal teaching.

2.  C. F. Keil and F. Delitzsch, *Commentary on the Old Testament* (Grand Rapids: Eerdmans, 1973), 1:351.

3.  Rom. 16:16; 1 Cor. 16:20; 2 Cor. 13:12; 1 Thess. 5:26; 1 Peter 5:14.

4.  For many other examples of behavior which has different meanings in different cultures, see Edwin Yamauchi, "Christianity and Cultural Differences," *Christianity Today*, June 23, 1972, 5–8.

5.  See Letha Scanzoni and Nancy Hardesty, *All We're Meant to Be* (Waco, Tex.: Word, 1975), 40, 64–67, for a discussion of the cultural significance of veiling among various Mediterranean cultures during biblical times.

6.  See Fred Wright, *Manners and Customs in Bible Lands* (Chicago: Moody, 1953), 74–75 for further discussion of this Oriental custom.

7.  The main ideas and some of the phraseology of these last two paragraphs were taken from R. C. Sproul, "Controversy at Culture Gap," *Eternity*, May 1976, 40. Sproul's discussion refers to a related but slightly different issue.

## Chapter 19

1. C. H. Kraft, *Theologizing in Culture* (Maryknoll, N.Y.: Orbis, 1978).
2. E. A. Nida, "Implications in Contemporary Linguistics for Biblical Scholarship," *JBL* 91 (1971) 73–89.
3. Cf. further Kraft, *Theologizing in Culture*.
4. See R. C. Sproul, "Controversy at Culture Gap," *Eternity* 27 (1976) 13–15, 40, for a useful discussion of this issue.
5. W. A. Smalley, "Culture and Superculture," *Practical Anthropology* 2 (1955) 58–71.
6. A. B. Mickelsen, *Interpreting the Bible* (Grand Rapids: Eerdmans, 1963), 353.

## Chapter 21

1. Cf. Paul Woolley, "The Relevance of Scripture," *The Infallible Word* (Philadelphia: Presbyterian & Reformed, 1946), 201–4.
2. "When we read of the failings, as well as the sinful actions of men, recorded in Scriptures, we may see what is in our own nature: for there are in us the seeds of the same sin, and similar tendencies to its commission, which would bring forth similar fruits, were it not for the preventing and renewing grace of God. And as many of the persons, whose faults are related in the volume of inspiration, we should learn from them, not only to 'be not high-minded, but fear' (Rom. 11:20); but further, to avoid being rash in censuring conduct of others" (Thomas Horne, *An Introduction to the Criticism of the Old Testament and to Biblical Interpretation* [London: Longman, Green, Longman, and Roberts, 1860], 1:427 [italics omitted]).
3. Herbert Sumner Miller, *General Biblical Introduction* (Houghton, N.Y.: Word-Bearer Press, 1937), 19.
4. Jephthah's cruel vow has been euphemized into a pledge of perpetual virginity, because it is felt that the Bible approved his act. Although the Bible nowhere condemns it, by the same token it nowhere approves it. The apology to be made at this point is not to distort the very clear meaning of the vow, but simply to indicate that in an inspired record, not all the deeds of even good men are approved by the mere token of being included in the inspired book.
5. "We should carefully distinguish between what the Scripture itself says, and what is only said in the Scripture, and, also, the times, places, and persons, when, where, and by whom anything is recorded as having been said" (Horne, 1:426 [italics omitted]).
6. "The only way of ascertaining the will of God . . . is to learn it by zealous application as students of the revelation of that will contained in the Scriptures. Short cuts such as pulling verses out of boxes, getting guidance by daily motto books, and letting the Bible fall open like a casting of dice are not only useless; they are deceptive" (Woolley, "The Relevance of Scripture," 195). His entire refutation of the magical use of the Bible is good.
7. John A. Broadus, *A Treatise on the Preparation and Delivery of Sermons,* 30th ed. (New York: Hodder and Stoughton, 1899), 33. Broadus has a learned and unusually wise discussion of the sermon and the interpretation of the text in Part I, Chapter II, "The Text–Interpretation."
8. Ibid., 47.
9. Ibid., 52 (italics his).

## Chapter 22

1. John R. W. Stott, *Understanding the Bible* (Glendale, Calif.: Gospel Light, Regal, 1972), 242.
2. T. Norton Sterrett, *How to Understand Your Bible*, rev. ed. (Downers Grove, Ill.: InterVarsity, 1974), 171.
3. Walter A. Elwell, "Belief and the Bible: A Crisis of Authority?" *Christianity Today*, March 21, 1980, 23.
4. David J. A. Clines, "Notes for an Old Testament Hermeneutic," *Theology, News and Notes*, March 1975, 10.
5. Ibid.
6. Ibid.
7. Ibid. (italics his).
8. Ibid.
9. Haddon W. Robinson, *Biblical Preaching* (Grand Rapids: Baker, 1980), 108.
10. Clines, "Notes for an Old Testament Hermeneutic," 10 (italics his).
11. Ibid.
12. Roy B. Zuck, *Teaching with Spiritual Power* (Grand Rapids: Kregel, 1993), 83–84.
13. Sidney Greidanus, *Sola Scriptura: Problems and Principles in Preaching Historical Texts* (Toronto: Wedge, 1970), 230.
14. C. Veenhof, cited by Greidanus, *Sola Scriptura*, 157.
15. Veenhof, cited by Greidanus, *Sola Scriptura*, 168 (italics Veenhof's).
16. Greidanus, *Sola Scriptura*, 172.
17. Ibid., 93,157.
18. Ibid.
19. Bernard Ramm, *Protestant Biblical Interpretation*, 3d ed. (Grand Rapids: Baker, 1970), 188.
20. Martin Luther, cited by A. Skevington Wood, *The Principles of Biblical Interpretation* (Grand Rapids: Zondervan, 1967), 80.
21. R. C. H. Lenski, *The Interpretation of St. Paul's Epistles to the Colossians, to the Thessalonians, to Timothy, to Titus and to Philemon* (Minneapolis: Augsburg, 1961), 847.
22. James Hope Moulton and George Milligan, *The Vocabulary of the Greek Testament Illustrated from the Papyri and Other Non-Literary Sources* (Grand Rapids: Eerdmans, 1930), 222.
23. I. Howard Marshall, "How Do We Interpret the Bible?" *Themelios* 5 (1980): 10.
24. Paul Woolley, "The Relevancy of Scripture," in *The Infallible Word* (Philadelphia: Presbyterian and Reformed, 1946), 199.
25. Luis Alonzo Schonkel, "Hermeneutics in the Light of Language and Literature," *Catholic Biblical Quarterly* 25 (1963): 382.
26. Zuck, *Teaching with Spiritual Power*, 122–23.
27. LeRoy Ford, "Developing Performance-Oriented Learning Purposes," *Search* 4 (Winter 1974): 31–40.
28. Robinson, *Biblical Preaching*, 108.
29. Bernard Ramm, "But It Isn't Bible Study," *Eternity*, February 1960, 22.
30. Ramm, *Protestant Biblical Interpretation*, 199–200.
31. Ibid., 186,
32. Fred L. Fisher, *How to Interpret the New Testament* (Philadelphia: Westminster, 1966), 167–68.

33. Ramm, *Protestant Biblical Interpretation*, 200.

34. A. Berkeley Mickelsen, *Interpreting the Bible* (Grand Rapids: Eerdmans, 1963), 357–58.

35. Fee suggests a distinction between what he calls "comparable contexts" and "extended application," illustrating this with 2 Corinthians 6:14–7:1, which prohibits Christians from being "unequally yoked" with unbelievers (v. 14, KJV). He says that, because no situation today is an exact equivalent of going with pagan friends to an idolatrous temple, using this passage against Christians marrying non-Christians may be called "extended application" (Gordon D. Fee, "Hermeneutics and Common Sense: An Exploratory Essay on the Hermeneutics of the Epistles," in *Inerrancy and Common Sense*, ed. Roger R. Nicole and J. Ramsey Michaels [Grand Rapids: Baker, 1980], 176–78).

36. R. C. Sproul, *Knowing Scripture* (Downers Grove, Ill.: InterVarsity, 1977), 106.

37. Ibid.

38. For more on the question of cultural relativity, see Alan Johnson, "History and Culture in New Testament Interpretation," in *Interpreting the Word of God*, ed. Samuel J. Schultz and Morris A. Inch (Chicago: Moody, 1976), 128–61; Charles H. Kraft, "Interpreting the Cultural Context," *Journal of the Evangelical Theological Society* 21 (December 1978): 357–67; Robert C. Sproul, "Controversy at Culture Gap," *Eternity*, May 1976, 12–15, 40; and Henry A. Virkler, *Hermeneutics: Principles and Practices of Biblical Interpretation* (Grand Rapids: Baker, 1981), 211–32.

39. The Scriptures are full of imperatives that are direct applications for Christians. Mickelsen refers to the many imperatives in 1 Thessalonians 5:13–22 (*Interpreting the Bible*, 361–62).

40. Elliott E. Johnson, "Application," class lecture notes in advanced hermeneutics, Dallas Theological Seminary, 1980, 4.

41. For more on the necessity of knowing the audience as an important step in applying Scripture, see Gregg Purviance, "An Application of Amos to Modern Society" (Th.M. thesis, Dallas Theological Seminary, 1980), 14–16, 19–20

42. For further discussion on the application of Old Testament historical narratives, see Dan R. Johnson, "Guidelines for the Application of Old Testament Narrative," *Trinity Journal* 7 (Spring 1978): 78–84; and Eugene A. Wilson, "The Homiletical Application of Old Testament Narrative Passages," *Trinity Journal* n. s. 1 (Spring 1980): 85–91.

43. Ramm, *Protestant Biblical Interpretation*, 191.

44. Ibid.

45. Walter A. Henrichsen, *A Layman's Guide to Interpreting the Bible*, rev. ed. (Grand Rapids: Zondervan, 1978), 31.

46. Related to the problem of applying examples is the applying of commands and promises. Helpful principles are given by Henrichsen (*A Laymen's Guide to Interpreting the Bible*, 42–48), Ramm (*Protestant Biblical Interpretation*, 189–90, 192–95), and Sterrett (*How to Understand Your Bible*, 172–76).

47. Gordon D. Fee, "The Genre of New Testament Literature and Biblical Hermeneutics," in *Interpreting the Word of God*, 118.

48. Ibid.

49. Wilson, "Homiletical Application," 87.

50. Frank Houghton, *Quiet Time* (Downers Grove, Ill: InterVarsity, 1945), 20 (italics his).
51. Irving L. Jensen, *Enjoy Your Bible* (Chicago: Moody, 1969), 120–21.
52. Henrichsen, *A Laymen's Guide to Interpreting the Bible*, 218.
53. Ibid., 219.